Cooperation under Fire

A volume in the series

CORNELL STUDIES IN SECURITY AFFAIRS

edited by Robert J. Art, Robert Jervis,
and Stephen M. Walt

A full list of titles in the series appears at the end of the book.

Cooperation under Fire

ANGLO-GERMAN RESTRAINT
DURING WORLD WAR II

Jeffrey W. Legro

Cornell University Press

ITHACA AND LONDON

First published 1995 by Cornell University Press.

Printed in the United States of America

The Naval Institute Press has generously given permission to reprint the poem
"Battleships Are Title B," by Lt. Cdr. Richard G. Voge, USN, from Theodore Roscoe,
United States Submarine Operations in World War II. Copyright © 1949 by the U.S. Naval
Institute, Annapolis, Maryland.

∞ The paper in this book meets the minimum requirements
of the American National Standard for Information Sciences—
Permanence of Paper for Printed Library Materials, ANSI Z39.48-1984.

Library of Congress Cataloging-in-Publication Data

Legro, Jeffrey.
Cooperation under fire : Anglo-German restraint during World War II /
Jeffrey W. Legro
p.   cm.
Includes bibliographical references.
ISBN 0-8014-2938-2
1. World War, 1939–1945—Germany.   2. World War, 1939–1945—Great
Britain.   3. Great Britain—Military relations—Germany.
4. Germany—Military relations—Great Britain.   5. Cooperation—
Germany—History—20th century.   6. Cooperation—Great Britain—
History—20th century.   7. International cooperation.   8. Limited war.   I. Title.
D757.L39   1995
940.53\43—dc20   94-35482

For my parents
Janet Wenner Legro and
Robert "Jess" W. Legro, 1926–1977

Contents

Preface

Why do nations cooperate, even as they try to destroy each other? I address this question in the context of the Second World War, where states attempted to sustain agreements limiting the use of force in three forms of combat considered heinous and unthinkable—commerce raiding by submarines, strategic bombing of civilian targets, and chemical warfare. In some instances, cooperation endured, yet in others it failed. Why this was so, is important for two reasons. First, understanding past attempts can make future efforts to limit warfare more effective. Second, determining why collaboration succeeded or failed in such extreme circumstances can provide a range of insights into the general phenomenon of international cooperation.

Collaboration among enemies in war may seem a curious subject, but, in fact, classic analyses of cooperation—including Thomas Schelling's *Strategy of Conflict,* Robert Jervis's "Cooperation under the Security Dilemma," and Robert Axelrod's *Evolution of Cooperation*—have considered exactly that combination. As with most other work in international relations, these studies focus on the interaction between parties to account for cooperation. In this book, however, I emphasize the importance of the *preference formation*—that is, what nations seek and why they seek it—that undergirds interaction. I compare three broad approaches—realism, institutionalism, and organizational culture. These perspectives differ on what forces will be most important in shaping the perceptions, analysis, planning, and actions of nations. All offer a priori explanations of restraint in war. And it should not be surprising to learn that all capture some part of what occurred in World War II. I want to determine which of the three provides the best overall account and in what ways that perspective might be joined with the stronger aspects of the other two.

In broad terms, I argue that organizational culture—the beliefs and customs that dominated the military services of states—determined when cooperation succeeded or failed. The organizational-culture perspective details how informal beliefs interact with formal bureaucratic structure to shape the identity and cognition of groups. Furthermore, I explain why some bureaucracies matter more than others, or even political leaders, in national choices. In World War II, the various military services favored some modes of warfare over others, evaluated the strategic environment and enemy activity, and developed plans and capabilities to meet anticipated threats according to their various cultural predispositions. Thus, directly and indirectly, the organizational cultures of these militaries shaped the preferences and actions of states in ways that often defied both balance-of-power considerations and international norms.

This book makes several contributions to the literature on international relations. First, it illustrates the significant role that preference formation and change play in international cooperation. This influence has been overlooked by the dominant paradigms of international relations, which take state interests as fixed (and therefore analytically uninteresting). Second, it argues that preferences are formed at the domestic level. Domestic explanations, particularly sociological ones based on collective beliefs and customs, have been relatively neglected in the study of international cooperation, particularly in security affairs. Third, it illustrates the power and utility of cultural analysis in politics and suggests ways culture can illuminate other problems in international relations. The findings also have implications for practical statecraft, suggesting the need for new strategies in the contemporary management of conflict and cooperation.

Finally, this study is the first systematic comparison of the three central means of warfare states attempted to control in World War II. In search of answers to my questions, I dug in the archives of several nations to find documents that shed light on American, British, German, and even Soviet decisions. I hope that the results add to our understanding of the monumental events leading to and culminating in the Second World War.

In writing this book, I was under, and on, fire at many times. Fortunately, mentors, colleagues, friends, and supporters were always there to silence the guns and douse the flames. My largest intellectual debt is to Arthur Stein and Richard Rosecrance. They have been unfailingly encouraging, always on call, and unnervingly incisive in their criticism and suggestions. Whether as scholars, teachers, or advisers, Stein and Rosecrance represent the best of academia.

This project had its origins in the hallways of Harvard's Center for Science and International Affairs, then under Joseph Nye's leadership. William Jarosz initially piqued my curiosity about restraint in war by pointing out the anomaly of the refusal to use gas in World War II. Kurt Campbell was quick to encourage me to pursue the topic. Along the way many have contributed, and I am indebted to Deborah Avant, Douglas Blum, Horst Boog, Scott Bruckner, Robert Dallek, David D'Lugo, Peter Feaver, Karen Gohdes, Donna Gold, Arnold Horelick, Iain Johnston, Peter Katzenstein, Elizabeth Kier, Janet M. Manson, Lisa Martin, Stephen Meyer, John Ellis van Courtland Moon, Williamson Murray, Richard Price, Lars Skalnes, and Adam Stulberg. At the University of Minnesota, my colleagues have offered help whenever it was needed, and I am grateful to Lawrence Jacobs, Daniel Kelliher, Ido Oren, Diana Richards, Kathryn Sikkink, and particularly Raymond Duvall and John Freeman. Robert Jervis deserves special mention for reading two entire drafts and providing a gold mine of helpful suggestions. On the editing and publishing end, Andrew Lewis, Roger Haydon, and Elizabeth Holmes provided excellent guidance on the final product. Many of the arguments on inadvertent escalation first appeared in "Military Culture and Inadvertent Escalation in World War II," *International Security* 18 (spring 1994): 108–42.

The extensive research needed for this study was possible only thanks to generous funding from the Ford Foundation, the Rand-UCLA Center for Soviet Studies, Harvard's Center for Science and International Affairs, a Peace Scholar Award from the Jennings Randolph Program for International Peace of the United States Institute of Peace, the Institute for the Study of World Politics, the Institute on Global Conflict and Cooperation, UCLA's Graham Fellowship, and the Department of Political Science at the University of Minnesota. I have also benefited enormously from the expertise of the specialists who guided my pursuit of history at the National Archives, the Naval Historical Center, the Library of Congress, the Public Record Office, the Admiralty Naval Historical Branch, and the Bundesarchiv-Militärarchiv. While I visited some of those places, friends such as Joe Higdon and Ellen Sudow, Shawn and Janice Smeallie, Tom Powers, and Adam Elstein offered lodging and much more.

Finally, I thank the one other person who has lived this book from

beginning to end and in doing so made the largest contribution—
the Reverend Janet Hatfield Legro, extraordinary minister, counselor,
friend, spouse, and new parent.

JEFFREY W. LEGRO

Minneapolis, Minnesota

Cooperation under Fire

[1]

Theories of Cooperation

Even enemies can cooperate. Churchill and Hitler were bitter opponents, and their countries fought an unforgiving fight. Nonetheless, Britain and Germany reached accords on the use of force, and some of those agreements endured the bloodshed of the Second World War. This cooperation involved three means of warfare—submarine attacks against merchant ships, aerial bombing of nonmilitary targets, and use of poison gas—that in the interwar years were denigrated as especially inhumane, illegitimate, and "unthinkable."[1] At the start of World War II, countries explicitly wanted a firebreak between restraint and escalation in each of these three militarily significant means of warfare. Shortly after fighting broke out, however, submarine warfare escalated beyond restrictions. Strategic bombing was restrained for only a year and then employed extensively. Yet chemical weapons, despite expectations and preparations, were never used. How can we explain this variation? Why do states cooperate in some areas but not in others? And, more generally, how can we best understand international cooperation?[2]

Much of the literature of the social sciences, particularly on international relations, provides unsatisfactory answers. Cooperation is gener-

[1] "Unthinkable" refers to the stigma attached to the use of certain instruments of warfare by public opinion and the international community. It does *not* mean that states, and especially their military organizations, do not think about, and plan for, their use in war. See Herman Kahn's *Thinking about the Unthinkable* (New York: Horizon Press, 1962), which discusses "unthinkability" and nuclear war.

[2] Restraint in war is a form of international cooperation—defined as governments adopting policies regarded by their partners as facilitating realization of their own objectives, as the result of a process of policy coordination. See Robert Keohane, *After Hegemony: Cooperation and Discord in the World Political Economy* (Princeton: Princeton University Press, 1984), pp. 51–52.

ally conceptualized as the product of a two-step process: first, actors form their preferences; second, they interact until they reach an outcome. As Gordon Tullock has argued, this model suggests that both a science of preferences and a science of interaction are necessary for understanding results.[3] Yet frequently cooperation—whether the parties are legislators, business firms, or sovereign states—is explained primarily in terms of the second step, the characteristics of interaction, which include the number of players, whether contracts are enforceable, time horizons, communication and information asymmetries. The first step, preference formation, is typically not the focus: preferences are posited and assumed to be stable. This is a problem when preference formation or change is central to understanding outcomes. Still another problem is that many studies examine only events ending in cooperation and disregard instances when cooperation does not occur. I argue that preference formation and change are central to cooperation—and its absence—even in war where strategic interaction would seem likely to play the decisive role in policy choices. In World War II, interaction between states was similar across the cases of submarine, aerial, and chemical warfare. But mutual restraint in the use of these three types of warfare varied because of changes in preferences.

What, then, shapes preferences? In this book I develop and test an alternative explanation of state preferences that is unorthodox in the study of international cooperation. The *organizational-culture* approach, an important variation on traditional organization theory, asserts that the beliefs and customs of national bureaucracies determine state desires for collaboration. I argue that organizational culture most convincingly explains why states did, and *did not,* cooperate in war even while trying to eliminate one another. Within military bureaucracies, collective philosophies of war fighting—a type of culture—shaped how soldiers thought about themselves, perceived the world, formulated plans, advised leaders, and went into action. Despite international constraints, and the desire of top civilian leaders for change, military cultures often endured. Culture decisively defined organizational preferences on the use of the different types of unthinkable weapons. And

[3] Gordon Tullock, "Economic Imperialism," in James M. Buchanon and Robert D. Tollison, eds., *The Theory of Public Choice* (Ann Arbor: University of Michigan, 1962), pp. 324–25. Also see Duncan Snidal, "The Game Theory of International Politics," in Kenneth Oye, ed., *Cooperation under Anarchy* (Princeton: Princeton University Press, 1986), pp. 40–44; James D. Morrow, "Social Choice and System Structure in World Politics," *World Politics* 41 (1988): 77; Robert Jervis, "Realism, Game Theory, and Cooperation," *World Politics* 40 (April 1988): 322–29; and Andrew Moravcsik, "Liberalism and International Relations Theory," Center for International Affairs Working Paper 92-6 (Cambridge: Harvard University, 1992), pp. 11–12.

these preferences, with surprising frequency, guided nations' preferences on the use of force during World War II.

The organizational-culture approach does more than simply clear up insignificant variance that other explanations miss. I have found that in a head-to-head test with the two dominant approaches in contemporary international relations theory—realism and liberal institutionalism—organizational culture explains cooperation better and more comprehensively. Realism contends that state actions are a product of calculations shaped by the power asymmetries of a particular international situation. Yet in World War II the decisions of states usually did not match realism's predictions because states either misinterpreted the situation, chose to ignore the evidence that was available, or were limited in their choices by existing capabilities that made little strategic sense. Institutionalism argues that the rules, norms, and conventions that characterize the international system are crucial to cooperation. But states did not make decisions in line with the varying power of the different norms as institutionalism would predict. Given the involvement of force and international norms, both realism and institutionalism should provide reasonable accounts of restraint in World War II. Yet although each illuminates key elements, neither school explains the variation in cooperation as well as organizational culture does.

This argument is important for theory and policy. In terms of theory the implications are threefold. First, the centrality of preference formation indicates the need to rethink the existing foci in the study of cooperation. Although strategic interaction is certainly not to be ignored, I argue that preference formation is more consequential than has generally been recognized. The most important advances in understanding cooperation might well be realized by supplementing the existing focus on interaction with more attention to the "science" of preferences.

Second, my thesis corrects the prevailing view that systemic forces will shape the preferences and/or behavior of states, particularly when national security is threatened.[4] In World War II, when international pressures should have dominated, I demonstrate that organizational

[4] Barry Posen, *The Sources of Military Doctrine* (Ithaca: Cornell University Press, 1984), pp. 59–79, 228–36; Sidney Verba, "Assumptions of Rationality and Non-rationality in Models of the International System," *World Politics* 14 (October 1961): 115; Arnold Wolfers, *Discord and Collaboration* (Baltimore: Johns Hopkins University Press, 1962), pp. 13–16; Theodore Lowi, *The End of Liberalism: Ideology, Policy, and the Crisis of Public Authority* (New York: Norton, 1969), pp. 158–60; Matthew Evangelista, "Issue-Area and Foreign Policy Revisited," *International Organization* 43 (winter 1989): 148–51; Benjamin Miller, "Explaining Great Power Cooperation in Conflict Management," *World Politics* 45 (October 1992): 17–26.

culture, an internal force, was most influential in shaping how states perceived, anticipated, and reacted to their circumstances. The traditional distinction that internal considerations drive economic affairs, but external factors drive security matters, is put in doubt. Clearly, we need a better understanding of the domestic development of state desires and how international factors affect or supersede that process. In the conclusion, I offer a conceptual synthesis to address this need.

Third, my results strongly assert the relevance of a much denigrated variable in political analysis: culture.[5] To the extent accounts of international politics based on variations within states exist, they emphasize *formal* structures such as constitutional arrangement (democracy vs. authoritarianism), policy networks (the strength or weakness of the state), and bureaucratic organization.[6] I maintain, however, that formal structure is inadequate, that one must also take account of *culture*, the hierarchy of beliefs, that characterize structures. For example, based as it is on the notion that similar bureaucratic structures will lead to similar behavior, traditional organization theory cannot explain the different outcomes of World War II.[7] It is only by bringing in a well-specified notion of culture that we are able to see why states choose escalation in some circumstances and not in others. This conclusion suggests an explanatory role for culture in a range of subject-matter areas studied primarily in terms of formal structure, be it organizational design, constitutional type, or the distribution of international power.

Finally, the argument also has practical relevance for policy and policy making. Restraint will be a central concern of states in future conflicts in which there is a risk that "illegitimate" means of warfare will be resorted to. How should nations ensure such restraint? In the past, countries seeking limitations on force have tended to pay great attention to their own capabilities, deterrence dynamics, and even the pur-

[5] For critiques of cultural approaches, especially those based on political culture, see Ronald Rogowski, *Rational Legitimacy* (Princeton: Princeton University Press, 1974), or Carole Pateman, "Political Culture, Political Structure, Political Change," *British Journal of Sociology* 1 (1971): 291–306. The dominant systemic and rational-choice interaction models found in the international-relations literature usually ignore culture.

[6] Michael Doyle, "Liberalism and World Politics," *American Political Science Review* 80 (1986): 1151–69; Peter Katzenstein, "Conclusion: Domestic Structures and Strategies of Foreign Economic Policy," in Peter Katzenstein, ed., *Between Power and Plenty* (Madison: University of Wisconsin Press, 1978), pp. 295–336; Graham T. Allison, *Essence of Decision* (Boston: Little, Brown, 1971).

[7] Whereas a cultural approach predicts that militaries can either foster or inhibit escalation, the traditional school—as explicated in Allison, *Essence of Decision;* Posen, *Sources of Military Doctrine;* and Richard Betts, *Soldiers, Statesmen, and Cold War Crises* (Cambridge: Harvard University Press, 1977)—anticipates that militaries will favor offense and foster escalation in war.

[4]

suit of international agreements and principles. I suggest that leaders desiring limitation must also look inward. The cultures of bureaucracies can lead to policies ill-suited to strategic aims or international conditions. In formulating strategy, states must understand and influence, not only the opponent and the environment, but also the idiosyncratic beliefs of their internal strategy-making community. In military policy this suggests the need for a new system of civil-military relations, one that is about not formal control but the very ideas and customs that guide national policy.

In the rest of this chapter I develop the theoretical foundations of the study. Three tasks are involved. First, in a brief overview of the existing literature on international cooperation I indicate its shortcomings for the task at hand and the need for an understanding of preference formation. Second to address this need, I develop propositions on cooperation in war based on three broad perspectives: realism, institutionalism, and organizational culture. Finally, I discuss the logic of testing these perspectives against cases from World War II.

A necessary starting point for generating propositions on cooperation is the extant literature. These writings contain powerful insights into international collaboration, but they are limited by two traits that have inherently biased our understanding of that phenomenon.

First, cooperation among states is evaluated mainly as a problem of strategic interaction.[8] These studies, based largely on a type of game-theory analysis that takes states as unitary actors, emphasize characteristics of strategic interaction such as the number of players, the discount rate, strategy selection, and a variety of transactions concerns (such as signaling, information, and commitment).[9] This focus follows

---

[8] Strategic interaction refers to the dependence of outcomes on the interaction of strategies of at least two parties. In practice it is the bargaining, negotiation, and coercion that takes place among states. For a good discussion of this topic and of strategic interaction as a level of analysis, see Arthur A. Stein, *Why Nations Cooperate* (Ithaca: Cornell University Press, 1990), pp. 13–20, 175–84.

[9] Some of the dominant and most recent works on cooperation are based on game-theory or strategic-interaction logic. For example, Thomas C. Schelling, *The Strategy of Conflict* (Cambridge: Harvard University Press, 1960), sees the ability of actors to make credible commitments to one another as central to cooperation. Robert Jervis, "Cooperation under the Security Dilemma," *World Politics* 30 (1978), points to the technological traits of interaction. Robert Axelrod, *The Evolution of Cooperation* (New York: Basic Books, 1984), features the discount rate, and he and Steve Weber, *Cooperation and Discord: U.S.-Soviet Arms Control* (Princeton: Princeton University Press, 1991), underscore the importance of strategy selection. Robert Axelrod and Robert Keohane, "Achieving Cooperation under Anarchy: Strategies and Institutions," in *Cooperation under Anarchy*, pp. 226–54, adds to this the number of players, and along with Lisa L. Martin, *Coercive Cooperation: Explaining Multilateral Economic Sanctions* (Princeton: Princeton University Press, 1992), singles out the institutional context of bargaining. Some theorists using game theory logic have relaxed the unitary-actor assumption in an effort to incorporate domestic

the classic game-theory model in which preferences are taken as given (and stable). Of course, few would assert preferences are irrelevant or even unimportant. Preferences produce the payoff matrix that decides what "game" is being played and whether the "players" have compatible interests. The nature of the model, however, tacitly pushes preferences to the background by assuming them.[10] The prevalence of this methodological tendency contains an orientation toward international politics: variations in cooperation are seen as a function of variations in strategic interaction. The possibility that they might also be caused by changing preferences is rarely considered.[11]

An analysis of restraint and escalation in World War II that focuses exclusively on interaction while assuming stable preferences is limited. In that conflict, the most prominent conditioning elements of state relations were consistent across the three types of warfare, yet outcomes varied. For example, the number of players, the "shadow of the future," and the ability to make commitments and signal intentions were uniform for all three types of warfare.[12] On the brink of conflict states were in agreement in each of the three areas that cooperation was desirable. Thus the question of interest is *why* preferences changed, leading to escalation, or persisted, maintaining restraint.

---

politics. See Robert Putnam, "Diplomacy and Domestic Politics: The Logic of Two-Level Games," *International Organization* 42 (summer 1988): 427–59; Bruce Bueno de Mesquita and David Lalman, *War and Reason: Domestic and International Imperatives* (New Haven: Yale University Press, 1992); Helen Miller and B. Peter Rosendorff, "Dividend Government, Domestic Politics, American and International Cooperation: A Signaling Model," paper prepared for the 1993 American Political Science Association Convention in Washington, D.C., Sept. 2–5, 1993; and James D. Fearon, "Domestic Political Audiences and the Escalation of International Disputes," *American Political Science Review* 88 (September 1994): 577–92.

[10] A desire for parsimony entices many to assume preferences—particularly for collective entities such as states, where preference formation can be a messy business. Even in economics, however, the orthodox view of preferences is subject to criticism—see, for example, Robert R. Keller, John R. McKean, and Rodney D. Peterson, "Preference and Value Formation: A Convergence of Enlightened Orthodox and Institutional Analysis?" *Journal of Economic Issues* 16 (1982). An effort to deal with preference change is Michael D. Cohen and Robert Axelrod, "Coping with Complexity: The Adaptive Value of Changing Utility," *American Economic Review* 74 (1984): 30–42.

[11] As Robert Powell points out in "Anarchy in International Relations Theory: The Neorealist-Neoliberal Debate," *International Organization* 48 (spring 1994): 320, the importance of assuming preferences depends on the model and the problem for which it is constructed. He suggests theories are needed for preferences in situations where it is not obvious what to assume about state preferences. The use of stigmatized means of warfare is an area where state preferences over outcomes (not strategies) such as mutual restraint, unilateral use, or mutual use are not obvious.

[12] Axelrod and Keohane, "Achieving Cooperation under Anarchy: Strategies and Institutions," esp. pp. 232–38.

A second bias in studies of international cooperation is that if preference formation is considered, it is typically seen as a product of the international system.[13] Factors internal to states are generally ignored or played down. Systemic causes are thought to be particularly dominant in issues involving security; that is, when a nation's existence is at stake, domestic politics, class disputes, and interest-group politics are likely to be put on hold as countries unite to protect their well-being. Deviations from the national interest produced by dissident organizations or other such forces will be corrected by the intervention of statesmen responding to the unavoidable external challenge. The central theme is that states will behave more like unitary actors when responding to international circumstances. The largest body of literature that addresses restraint directly—the "classical" limited-war studies of the 1950s and 1960s—reflects this bias. In this literature it is assumed that nations show restraint in order to avoid nuclear war.[14] Of course, because we have not had a nuclear war, this answer seems unassailable, but it is also unsupported, and these theorists rarely examined their ideas against other historical cases.[15] Like the cooperation literature overall, the limited-war studies give less attention to factors within countries.

More recently, several authors have questioned the systemic bias of

[13] This is true across a range of schools. Kenneth N. Waltz, *Theory of International Politics* (Reading, Mass.: Addison Wesley, 1979), for example, stresses systemic power and advantage; Keohane, *After Hegemony*, emphasizes systemic institutions; Alexander Wendt, "Anarchy Is What States Make of It: The Social Construction of Power Politics," *International Organization* 46 (spring 1992): 391–425, highlights the social knowledge and meanings that are collectively held internationally; Kenneth A. Oye, *Economic Discrimination and Political Exchange: World Economy in the 1930s and 1980s* (Princeton: Princeton University Press, 1992), pp. 50–57, suggests that interaction itself conditions state desires. In general, scholars of international political economy have been more attentive to the domestic sources of preferences than scholars focusing on security affairs.

[14] Driven by the U.S. and Soviet discovery of the thermonuclear bomb and the precedent set in Korea, such studies (especially the early ones) focus on *how* nuclear weapons can be used to serve national aims without unleashing a general war that might destroy both countries. Lawrence Freedman, *The Evolution of Nuclear Strategy* (New York: St. Martin's, 1981), pp. 91–117, provides an overview.

[15] Morton Halperin's *Limited War in the Nuclear Age* (New York: John Wiley & Sons, 1963) tries to link propositions on limited war to an empirical base of "local" wars (such as Korea, the Taiwan straits, and so on). More recent efforts to correct this ahistorical bent include Richard Smoke's *War: Controlling Escalation* (Cambridge: Harvard University Press, 1979), which is notable as a study that approaches restraint from a psychological perspective and investigates propositions through comparative historical cases (mainly from the nineteenth century) of major-power war, and Michael Howard, ed., *Restraints on War: Studies in the Limitation of Armed Conflict* (Oxford: Oxford University Press, 1979), which links restraint to history in a less systematic fashion.

the study of international cooperation. They argue that domestic factors may be critical to understanding outcomes, particularly in terms of influence on preference formation.[16] Raising the question, however, hardly proves the point that domestic factors are important and systemic ones are not. Nor should it suggest that only domestic-level approaches speak to preference formation and strategy selection. Many systemic-level theories do this too. What raising the question does do is highlight the potential of domestic-level analyses as a significant alternative (or necessary complement) to the dominant systemic explanations. But what is clearly required is a test of the ability of different approaches to account for cooperation and its absence.

THREE PERSPECTIVES

Three broad perspectives—realism, institutionalism, and organizational culture—offer a good starting point for exploring cooperation. Each is a major approach to state behavior; each represents a different type of analysis; and each speaks to the issue of restraint in stigmatized warfare.[17] I summarize at Table 1 the distinctive views of the three.

Realism

Realism focuses on the need of groups of people for security in a world that is inherently competitive and violent. It paints a bleak picture of prospects for cooperation, but nonetheless attempts to account for it. States are assumed to be identical, rational units of the international system that value their survival above all else. Since there is no sovereign in the world arena, there is no authority to resolve disputes. Each state must protect itself as well as it can, but in doing so, may threaten the security of other states. Nations must always worry about their position relative to their global neighbors: friends can become

---

[16] See Joanne Gowa, "Anarchy, Egoism, and Third Images: The Evolution of Cooperation and International Relations," *International Organization* 40 (1986): 180–82; Stephan Haggard and Beth A. Simmons, "Theories of International Regimes," *International Organization* 41 (summer 1987): esp. 513–17; Jervis, "Realism, Game Theory, and Cooperation," pp. 324–29; Morrow, "Social Choice," pp. 96–97; Helen Milner, "International Theories of Cooperation among Nations: Strengths and Weaknesses," *World Politics* 44 (April 1992): 466–96; and Putnam, "Diplomacy and Domestic Politics," pp. 427–59.

[17] I use the terms "school," "approach," "perspective," but avoid "theory" because of the plurality of views within each. As categories, however, they are analytically distinct and provide useful competing propositions.

Table 1. Perspectives on international cooperation

Theory	Sources of preferences	Level of analysis	View of the state	Expectations of cooperation
Realism	Distribution of capabilities	Systemic	Unitary	When the situation offers no advantage to either side for escalation.
Institutionalism	Strength of international norms	Systemic	Unitary	When institutions are robust and norms are specific, durable, and widely accepted.
Organizational Culture	Beliefs of key subnational bureaucracies	Nation	Decentralized	When the war-fighting creeds of militaries are compatible with the given cooperative action.

enemies in short time. In such a world, cooperation is rare, especially during war when the latent threats of international anarchy have become overt. Yet with its focus on security and survival, realism should be well-positioned to explain state decisions concerning the use of force. Issues of national security are, after all, the bread and butter of realism. Certainly in matters involving choices over which strategy—restraint or escalation—best serves the survival of a state at imminent risk, realism should have something to say.

At the most general level, realism explains cooperation with balance-of-power logic. It argues that the tendency of nations toward conflict is only contained by the penalties that might be incurred by taking on a stronger opponent or coalition of opponents. The primary incentive for states to cooperate is to counter, or "balance" against, a state aspiring to hegemony. Nations must always weigh the possible reactions of third parties in cases in which outside support could tip the balance either for or against their own interests. Ultimately, how nations manage the challenge of survival in anarchy depends fundamentally on relative power and capabilities.[18]

---

[18] See the discussion in Joseph M. Grieco, *Cooperation among Nations: Europe, America, and Non-tariff Barriers to Trade* (Ithaca: Cornell University Press, 1990), pp. 36–40; Posen, *Sources of Military Doctrine*, pp. 233–36; Waltz, *Theory of International Politics*, esp. chap. 6. Like Posen's and Grieco's, my portrayal of realism relies on neorealism but pulls it in the direction of classical realism.

What would realism anticipate about the preferences on restraint of states that are engaged in mutual destruction?[19] Realists assume that states are concerned with survival and security and will pursue whatever outcome best serves those interests. Thus states will desire restraint as long as and only as long as they see it as being to their relative advantage. Realism, however, is more than a generic rational-actor approach because it is quite specific on how a nation perceives "advantage."[20] According to realism national preferences are the product of constraints and opportunities shaped by the international balance of power.[21] For example, states are thought to be more sensitive to changes in relative capabilities to use force, rather than to changes in international law or norms. The former can threaten survival whereas the latter are scarcely relevant, according to realism's core principles. Factors internal to the state, such as ideology, political structure, interest groups, national culture, and organizational influence are considered peripheral. A state's preferences concerning restraint are formed and changed by the systemic balance of capabilities, tempered by geography and technology.[22] Overall then, we can deduce the following proposition from realist logic: *States will desire mutual restraint when the balance of power implies relative disadvantage to first use (of a particular mode) of force. They will prefer escalation when the balance indicates relative advantage can be gained by first use.*

A peculiarity of realism is its emphasis on survival at the expense of all other objectives. According to realism a state whose existence is threatened will adopt any means that prolongs its life. The question

[19] Realism's logic is certainly applicable to other issues than the machinations of alliances. For example, Posen, *Sources of Military Doctrine*, wields realist reasoning to explain the military doctrines of states. And in a study specifically addressing cooperation, Grieco, *Cooperation among Nations*, utilizes realism to account for why states do and do not adopt non-tariff barriers to trading. Both authors argue that states focus their efforts on protecting their relative positions within the context of external constraints and opportunities.

[20] A generic rational-choice approach has nothing to say about where preferences come from. It simply assumes that states will weigh costs and benefits, no matter how they are derived, and select the option that yields the largest net gain.

[21] Kenneth N. Waltz, "The Emerging Structure of International Politics," *International Security* 18 (fall 1993): 61–70, explicitly discusses how relative power shapes national preferences.

[22] Robert Gilpin, *War and Change in World Politics* (Cambridge: Cambridge University Press, 1981), pp. 87–88, and he notes (p. 200) that in a "hegemonic war" such as World War II, "the limitations on violence and treachery tend to be only those necessarily imposed by the state of technology, the available resources, and the fear of retaliation"; Posen, *Sources of Military Doctrine*, pp. 36, 61–62; Grieco, *Cooperation among Nations*, pp. 39–40; Waltz, *Theory of International Politics*, pp. 97–99, 183–92.

is no longer whether a state will benefit more than the opponent by escalating, but instead, whether escalation will help it to delay political extinction.[23] A modern example of this perspective is the fear of many analysts that nuclear war is likely if the homeland of a state with nuclear weapons is attacked and/or if its defeat is imminent.[24] From a realist perspective, escalation should be particularly likely as a state faces a limited future.

Realists also recognize the possibility of inadvertent escalation. Leaders sometimes misperceive and miscalculate. As Clausewitz has noted, unintended events just happen. His term for this is "friction"; others have called it fog of war. A variety of unforeseeable factors impose themselves unexpectedly between plans and actual outcomes. Communication and control breaks down. Frightened or exhausted soldiers make mistakes. Amidst the chaos of combat, intelligence confuses or misleads. Clausewitz writes, "This tremendous friction which cannot, as in mechanics, be reduced to a few points, is everywhere in contact with chance, and brings about effects that cannot be measured, just because they are largely due to chance."[25] Clausewitz suggests that accidents are particularly likely when force deployment is complex, the battle is intense, and communication and intelligence gathering are uncertain and unreliable.[26]

Another idea on inadvertence compatible with the systemic focus of realism is the "security dilemma," which describes how the structure and technology of a conflict situation influence the possibility of misperception and inadvertence. This dilemma is produced by the anarchic nature of international relations: one nation's effort to improve its security can make other nations feel less secure. A response in kind can result in "spirals of hostility" or escalation. It is easy to grasp how

---

[23] Waltz, *Theory of International Politics*, pp. 91–92. For a thorough explanation of this idea and detailed discussion of extinction and national survival, see A. Stein, *Why Nations Cooperate*, pp. 87–112.

[24] A number of the studies from the limited-war literature also assume this to be the case. For example, Halperin, *Limited War in the Nuclear Age*, p. 99.

[25] Carl von Clausewitz, *On War*, ed. and trans. Michael Howard and Peter Paret (Princeton: Princeton University Press, 1984), p. 120, also see pp. 113–22.

[26] Modern-day accident theorists echo Clausewitz's thesis by positing that unwanted incidents will be more likely in areas of technical and organizational complexity. Charles Perrow, *Normal Accidents: Living with High-Risk Technology* (New York: Basic Books, 1984), pp. 3–4, 330–35. Perrow's argument is that complex organizations using high-risk technologies will have accidents. An application of this thesis in the military realm is Chris C. Demchak, *Military Organizations, Complex Machines* (Ithaca: Cornell University Press, 1991). For an application of this thesis to the nuclear weapons accidents of the United States, see Scott D. Sagan, *The Limits of Safety* (Princeton: Princeton University Press, 1993).

the insecurity and uncertainty characteristic of ongoing armed conflict could make each side fear that the other might abrogate a pledge of nonuse to gain an advantage. The security dilemma is magnified and escalation is made likelier when defensive capabilities cannot be distinguished from offensive ones and offense has the advantage. This structural circumstance seems particularly likely to lead to first use in two ways. First, when a state's doctrines or weapons depend on surprise for effectiveness, that country has an incentive to undertake a first strike. An opponent who is aware of this incentive is likely to be particularly ready to launch counterstrikes.[27] Second, leaders may decide that their own security is endangered if they do not act first, thus inviting preemptive escalation.

If the realist perspective is correct, several dynamics appear likely. Restraint will result when neither side can see a clear advantage in unrestricted warfare. When one side can gain relatively by initiating use, escalation is likely. Leaders in charge of the state apparatus will weigh the international situation and assess the costs and benefits of particular courses of action. Especially as threats to security grow they can be expected to concentrate national efforts on meeting the external challenge. Preferences on withholding or using force will change when the balance of power indicates a different relative advantage. When national survival is at risk, however, nations will be tempted to use any weapon that might delay extinction. When state choices or outcomes are contrary to systemic conditions, realism blames random miscalculation or accident. Similarly, when inadvertent escalation results, realism blames chance or the particular characteristics of the situation or means of warfare involved.

Institutionalism

Liberal institutionalism focuses on how the development of norms and rules can mitigate the competitive nature of the international system and foster cooperation. Like realism, institutionalism considers states to be unitary rational actors and focuses its analysis on the systemic level. Despite these similarities, realism and institutionalism differ on the nature of world politics.[28] Institutionalists do not believe that the system is only conflict-ridden and disorderly. They emphasize the existence of a variety of regulatory mechanisms that circumscribe state

---

[27] Jervis, "Cooperation under the Security Dilemma," pp. 187–205.
[28] See David A. Baldwin, ed., *Neorealism and Neoliberalism: The Contemporary Debate* (New York: Columbia University Press, 1993).

behavior and permit significant community and collaboration. According to institutionalists, important obstructions to cooperation are found in misunderstandings, the lack of trust, and divergent interpretations and expectations that plague collective action. The main claim is that international institutions help to alleviate these problems and, by doing so, promote cooperation.[29] The applicability of such institutions in the heat of war is obviously a hard test for this perspective. Nonetheless, even in time of war, when stigmatized means of warfare and the problem of restraint are at issue, institutionalist logic anticipates a connection between the international norms involved and the likelihood of escalation.

Institutions are defined as "persistent and connected sets of rules (formal and informal) that prescribe behavioral roles."[30] In this meaning, institutions are clearly more than buildings with plaques on them. Formal organizations such as the United Nations are institutions, but so are explicit arrangements such as "international regimes" like the General Agreement on Tariffs and Trade (GATT) and the often informal norms and conventions that have traditionally governed diplomatic procedures, various trade mechanisms, and the immunity of national leaders from assassination.[31]

Institutions are important because they encourage cooperation where there are incentives for actors to act unilaterally even when effective mutual action is more desirable. There are three ways institutions inhibit opportunism and encourage cooperation.[32] The first is by raising the costs of violating rules, conventions, and norms. Violating

[29] Works in this tradition include a range of studies on regimes. For an introduction, see Stephen D. Krasner, ed., *International Regimes* (Ithaca: Cornell University Press, 1983). Here I rely mainly on Robert O. Keohane, *International Institutions and State Power* (Boulder, Colo.: Westview Press, 1989). For other versions of this school, see Walter Powell and Paul DiMaggio, eds., *The New Institutionalism in Organizational Analysis* (University of Chicago Press, 1991), pp. 1–40.

[30] This is based on Keohane, *International Institutions*, p. 3, who defines "institutions" as "persistent and connected sets of rules (formal and informal) that prescribe behavioral rules, constrain activity, and shape expectations." Keohane's definition is problematic if we are concerned with the question of whether institutions affect behavior, because his wording assumes that they do.

[31] Regimes are defined in Krasner, *International Regimes*, p. 2, as "principles, norms, rules and decision making procedures around which actors' expectations converge in a given area of international relations." As Oran Young, "International Regimes: Toward a New Theory of Institutions," *World Politics* 39 (October 1986): 7, notes, many of terms in the institutionalist literature are imprecise. Here I use such terms as "rules" and "norms" interchangeably. I generally use "institution" to refer to international institutions and organizations and "organization" to refer to domestic bureaucracies.

[32] Haggard and Simmons, "Theories of International Regimes," pp. 513–14; Joseph S. Nye, "Nuclear Learning and U.S.-Soviet Security Regimes," *International Organization* 41 (summer 1987): 399–400.

the rules of institutions can lead to immediate penalties—such as sanctions, political ostracism, and domestic political damage—that leaders must add to the costs of certain decisions. For example, by violating norms against the use of nonstate force, Libya has been shunned and penalized by potential allies and trading partners who oppose terrorism.

A second way institutions encourage cooperation is by decreasing transactions costs—the expense of making and maintaining agreements. This appears to be the case in certain arms control agreements and accords that delineate property rights. In this latter category we can include such economic pacts as the International Coffee Agreement. Institutions may augment enforcement by facilitating linkage to other issues, enhancing the effectiveness of side payments and punishments. They can also offer a way to separate a particular issue from the swings of an overall relationship. Joseph Nye asserts that the Non-Proliferation Treaty insulated U.S.-Soviet cooperation in that area from the decline in overall relations in the early 1980s.[33]

A third and more subtle form of influence is exerted when institutions shape how states see themselves and their opponents, over time transforming the very perception of self-interest. This can happen in several ways. Institutions may facilitate the flow of information, which can alter the way states view issues, opponents, and even their own preferences. States can ultimately begin to think differently about their interests in cooperation and conflict. For example, new knowledge about disease paved the way for international accord on quarantine rules.[34] Some theorists see institutions as the structures of meaning

[33] Elinor Ostrom, *Governing the Commons: The Evolution of Institutions for Collective Action* (Cambridge: Cambridge University Press, 1991), details how institutions can alleviate the transaction and monitoring costs in self-governing common-pool resource problems. On arms control, see Janice Gross Stein, "Detection and Defection: Security 'Regimes' and the Management of International Conflict," *International Journal* (autumn 1985): 599–627. On the coffee regime, see Bart S. Fisher, *The International Coffee Agreement: A Study in Coffee Diplomacy* (New York: Praeger, 1972), as cited in A. Stein, *Why Nations Cooperate*, pp. 40–41. On linkage, see Martin, *Coercive Cooperation*. Nye, "Nuclear Learning," p. 39.
[34] On information, ideas, and self interest, see the special issue of *International Organization* 46 (winter 1992) edited by Peter M. Haas, especially his article, "Introduction: Epistemic Communities and International Policy Coordination," pp. 1–35; Ernst Haas, *When Knowledge Is Power* (Berkeley and Los Angeles: University of California Press, 1990); and Judith Goldstein and Robert O. Keohane, eds., *Ideas and Foreign Policy: Beliefs, Institutions, and Political Change* (Ithaca: Cornell University Press, 1993). On quarantine rules, see Charles O. Panneberg, *A New Health Order: An Inquiry into the International Relations of World Health and Medical Care* (Germantown, Md.: Sigthoff & Noordhoff, 1979), pp. 179–80, as cited in A. Stein, *Why Nations Cooperate*, pp. 49–50.

that provide the fundamental context of interaction for states.[35] Institutions also affect the nature of the state by facilitating change in the standard operation procedures of national-level procedures. For example, the GATT regime has affected U.S. lawmaking. As a subset of U.S.-Soviet efforts to avoid nuclear war, bureaucracies of the two nations elaborated a set of rules that altered naval actions. Abram Chayes asserts that arms control treaties actually lead to bureaucratic behavior that enhances compliance. Finally, institutions also provide possibilities for new intrastate coalitions. Peter Haas argues that the Mediterranean Action Plan, a regime for the control of ocean pollution, helped to shift coalitions within governments, leading to compliance with international rules.[36]

Institutions are generally viewed as continuous, rather than dichotomous, variables: they are not simply present or absent, but exist in varying strengths. A number of criteria have been suggested for gauging institutionalism.[37] For examining and comparing the norms and rules of behavior relevant to restraint in the Second World War, the degree of institutionalization can be measured by three criteria: specificity, durability, and concordance. *Specificity* refers to how well the

---

[35] Constructivists focus on structures and social interaction that shape actor roles and identities, considerations that are unquestioned assumptions in mainstream liberal institutionalism. See Friedrich Kratochwil and John G. Ruggie, "International Organization: A State of the Art on an Art of the State," *International Organization* 40 (autumn 1986): 753–75; Alexander Wendt and Raymond Duvall, "Institutions and International Order," in Ernst-Otto Czempiel and James N. Rosenau, eds., *Global Changes and Theoretical Challenges* (Lexington, Mass.: Lexington Books, 1989), pp. 51–73; Wendt, "Anarchy," pp. 391–425.

[36] On GATT, see Charles Lipson, "The Transformation of Trade: The Sources and Effects of Regime Change," in Krasner, *International Regimes*, pp. 262–64. On the rules of naval action, see Sean M. Lynn-Jones, "The Incidents at Sea Agreement," in Alexander George, Philip J. Farley, and Alexander Dallin, eds., *U.S.-Soviet Security Cooperation* (New York: Oxford University Press, 1988), pp. 482–509. Abram Chayes, "An Inquiry into the Workings of Arms Control Agreements," *Harvard Law Review* 85 (March 1972): 935–42. Peter M. Haas, "Do Regimes Matter? Epistemic Communities and Mediterranean Pollution Control," *International Organization* 43 (summer 1989): 377–403, and his book *Saving the Mediterranean: The Politics of International Environmental Protection* (New York: Columbia University Press, 1990).

[37] This is a standard idea of regime theory. Keohane, *International Institutions*, pp. 2, 6, is somewhat ambiguous on this point. For different criteria for institutionalization, compare Keohane, *International Institutions*, pp. 4–5; Nye, "Nuclear Learning," p. 375; Roger Smith, "Institutionalization as a Measure of Regime Stability: Insights for International Regime Analysis from the Study of Domestic Politics," *Millennium: Journal of International Studies* 18 (1989): 234–36; and Oran Young, *International Cooperation: Building Regimes for Natural Resources and the Environment* (Ithaca: Cornell University Press, 1989), p. 23. In comparative politics, see Samuel P. Huntington, *Political Order in Changing Societies* (New Haven: Yale University Press, 1968).

guidelines for restraint and use are defined. *Durability* covers how long the rules have been in effect and how well they have weathered challenges to their authority. *Concordance* means how widely accepted the rules are in diplomatic discussions and treaties. The general assumption is that if a principle is clearly stated, firmly established, and widely endorsed, it will have a greater impact on the behavior of states than if it is not. These three traits are, in principle, as pertinent to *informal* institutions as they are to formal ones: they are *not* simply a measure of physical or legal properties. The issue for assessing restraint in World War II is the degree to which prewar norms, negotiations, and agreements affected decisions on restraint. Based on institutionalism I would predict: *States are most likely to prefer mutual restraint in areas of warfare where institutions of restraint are most robust in terms of specificity, durability, and concordance. Conversely, states are likely to favor escalation where institutions are least developed.*

Institutionalists expect the *inadvertent* demise of cooperation in war to vary with institutional strength just as the deliberate choice not to cooperate tends to vary. In areas where principles and norms are developed, communication and cooperation make accidents, misinterpretation, and misunderstanding less probable, and the level of trust is higher, which makes states more willing to exercise restraint. In areas where norms are weak, suspicion and doubt intensify concerns about security and make escalation more likely—*even if no one wants it.*

If institutionalism is right, we can anticipate restraint in those areas where the degree of institutionalization is greatest. Once a norm, a negotiation, or agreement is accepted, expectations of future restraint should shift as it becomes more deeply ingrained in international society. National and bureaucratic procedures will be adjusted so that they are in line with it. Leaders will refer to it when making decisions and will recognize the penalties of violating it—indeed, they may even take the norm for granted and not even consider violating it. But in those areas where agreements have not been concluded or are thinly developed, restraint is more likely to break down. Costs of violation will be seen as acceptable. Leaders will attempt to cut corners on restrictions. The related norms will not be identified with self-interest, nor will they be integrated with bureaucratic procedures. The effect of prohibitions on decision making will be minimal. Finally, institutionalism does not usually predict short-term changes in state attitudes toward escalation and restraint. Instead, according to this view, the preferences of nations, in proportion to the stability of the norms, are relatively stable.

Organizational Culture

The organizational-culture perspective on cooperation asserts that the preferences of state bureaucracies shape national preferences and actions in ways not anticipated by either realism or institutionalism.[38] First, according to this approach, state interests originate not in the international system or in strategic interaction but instead within the nation itself. Outcomes are driven not by external conditions but by the internal differences of states. Second, states are not considered simply as unitary actors but as collectives of entities. Still, the type of organizational approach I use here does consider states as rational actors. Nations do indeed weigh alternatives, seek information, and generally choose options that yield the greatest net benefits. The organizational-culture view simply argues that the alternatives considered, the information sought, and the costs and benefits compared are shaped by internal beliefs and customs rather than by considerations of external power or principle. To explain the organizational-culture approach, one must examine its differences from traditional organization theory, how culture affects organizational preferences, and how organizational preferences shape national preferences and policy.

Organization theory itself is a broad and eclectic literature about how structured groups of people form, make decisions, behave, and change. It has largely centered on economic subjects such as industries and firms, but has also been applied to international politics.[39] Despite the breadth of the literature, the ideas applied to understanding foreign policy have been relatively narrow. This "traditional" approach was popularized by the work of Graham Allison and extended elsewhere.[40] The variant of organization theory I develop here builds on this tradition, but with two major differences.

First, traditional organization theory relies on the assumption that similar units within the context of similar structures should exhibit

---

[38] David Welch, "The Organizational Process and Bureaucratic Politics Paradigms: Retrospect and Prospect," *International Security* 17 (fall 1992): 114, notes that analysts of international relations have largely failed to develop and test theories rooted in the intragovernmental level of analysis.

[39] An overview of this literature is provided by Charles Perrow, *Complex Organizations,* 3d ed. (New York: Random House, 1986), and Gareth Morgan, *Images of Organization* (Newbury Park, Calif.: Sage Publications, 1986). The classic application to foreign policy is Allison, *Essence of Decision.* For a more recent discussion, see Robert L. Kahn and Mayer N. Zald, eds., *Organizations and Nation-States* (San Francisco: Jossey-Bass, 1990).

[40] Allison, *Essence of Decision.* For recent critiques of Allison's organizational model, see Welch, "Paradigms," pp. 112–46, and Jonathan Bendor and Thomas H. Hammond, "Rethinking Allison's Models," *American Political Science Review* 85 (June 1992): 301–22.

similar behavior.[41] This, of course, is the central paradigm that the organizational-culture approach aims to correct by stressing that despite similar structures, beliefs and behavior can differ.[42] Traditional organization theory anticipates that militaries, as similar organizations seeking to maximize autonomy and size and reduce uncertainty, will display common characteristics. They will prefer offensive strategies and doctrines and resist civilian intervention in operational planning and implementation because restraint conflicts with the very nature of autonomy-seeking, offense-oriented, war-winning military organizations.[43] Research has indicated that although soldiers do not always desire war, after the decision for war has been made, professional soldiers do demand operational autonomy. Once a war is underway, militaries are inclined to use all means at their disposal. Gradualism and restraint can cost lives and are inconsistent with such hallowed principles as concentration of force and the goal of total victory.[44] The proposition that follows from this logic is that militaries are likely to foster escalation in any usable means of warfare. From a traditional organizational perspective, there is little reason to expect military organizations to prefer restraint.[45] But restraint—aided by organizational complicity—did occur in the Second World War.

The second difference relates to the aggregation of organizational preferences. How does organizational culture come to shape state pref-

---

[41] Posen, *Sources of Military Doctrine*, p. 37, states this explicitly.

[42] As one author noted, "Evidence is mounting that firms with apparently identical formal contracts, organizational structures, and incentive schemes may perform quite differently, depending on the nature of individual expectations and beliefs, social norms and leadership." Gary J. Miller, *Managerial Dilemmas: The Political Economy of Hierarchy* (Cambridge: Cambridge University Press, 1992), p. 12.

[43] Building on Allison's work, this is the interpretation given by Posen, *Sources of Military Doctrine*, pp. 41–59; Jack Snyder, *The Ideology of the Offensive* (Ithaca: Cornell University Press, 1984), pp. 24–25; Stephen Van Evera, "Why Cooperation Failed in 1914," in Oye, *Cooperation under Anarchy*, p. 97, and "Causes of War" (Ph.D. diss., University of California, Berkeley, 1984), esp. chap. 7; and Leon Sigal, *Fighting to a Finish: The Politics of War Termination in the United States and Japan, 1945* (Ithaca: Cornell University Press, 1988), pp. 19–25. Although they emphasize the structural tendencies toward similarities among organizations (for example, militaries are offense-oriented), Snyder and Van Evera seem to allow for the possibility of a defensive policy depending on "organizational essence." The latter view is more compatible with the notion of organizational culture. On organizational essence, see Morton H. Halperin, *Bureaucratic Politics and Foreign Policy* (Washington, D.C.: Brookings Institution, 1974), p. 28.

[44] Betts, *Soldiers, Statesmen, and Cold War Crises*.

[45] Van Evera, "Causes of War," chap. 7, presents a detailed case on how the organizational dynamics of militaries favor escalation. Attesting to this expectation are the discussion and examples on organization theory given in Barry Posen, *Inadvertent Escalation: Conventional War and Nuclear Risks* (Ithaca: Cornell University Press, 1992), pp. 16–19.

erences? Allison's answer to this question is that organizational routines simply become foreign policy.[46] This is hardly complete. What is needed is a systematic conceptualization of how organizational influence accrues, of how subnational organizations become important, and of when and how they shape outcomes. What remains to be explained, therefore, are the cultural origins of organizational preferences and how they join to determine national policy.

In the last decade, culture has emerged as a central concept in organizational research. Analysts in the field of management became dissatisfied with the structural approach. Part of this discontent grew out of an empirical problem. Observers of Japanese firms could not understand why these companies performed so much better than their Western counterparts when their formal structures were so similar to those of Western corporations. Many believe the answer rests in organizational culture—defined as a pattern of assumptions, ideas, and beliefs that proscribe how a group should adapt to its external environment and manage its internal affairs.[47] It should be noted that this use of culture is quite different from broader notions found elsewhere that emphasize "way of life" or fundamental values.[48] The problem with such general conceptualizations is that they are often ambiguously connected to the actual thinking and behavior of actors and therefore risk circularity. But the notion of culture used here—a pattern of beliefs prescribing action—avoids circular reasoning by offering specific propositions concerning decision making and behavior.[49] As I demon-

---

[46] In some ways—such as organizational impact on implementation of policy—this idea is reasonably accurate. But Allison's *Essence of Decision* does not convincingly demonstrate how organizations shaped the higher-level decisions and outcomes during the Cuban Missile Crisis. See Robert J. Art, "Bureaucratic Politics and American Foreign Policy: A Critique," *Policy Sciences* 4 (1973): 478–80; Stephen D. Krasner, "Are Bureaucracies Important? (Or Allison Wonderland)," *Foreign Policy* 7 (summer 1972): 159–79; and Welch, "Paradigms," pp. 122–25.

[47] This definition is loosely based on Edward Schein, *Organizational Culture and Leadership* (San Francisco: Jossey-Bass, 1985), p. 9. For an overview of the early evolution of the concept of organizational culture, see William G. Ouchi and Alan L. Wilkins, "Organizational Culture," *Annual Review of Sociology* 11 (1985): 457–83; for a more recent treatment, see Peter J. Frost et al., eds., *Reframing Organizational Culture* (Newbury Park, Calif.: Sage Publications, 1991).

[48] For the distinctions between these different versions of culture, see Ann Swidler, "Culture in Action: Symbols and Strategies," *American Sociological Review* 51 (April 1986): 273–86. I differ with Swidler's position on key notions discussed later.

[49] Although differences in analysis exist, other studies that have used terms similar to culture include Philip Selznick, *TVA and the Grass Roots: A Study of Politics and Organization* (Berkeley and Los Angeles: University of California Press, 1980), p. 181, and *Leadership in Administration: A Sociological Interpretation* (Evanston, Ill.: Row, Peterson, 1957), pp. 14–16, 38–42, on "character"; Herbert A. Simon, Donald W. Smithburg, and Victor A. Thomp-

strate with the case of U.S. submarine warfare, the predictions made by the organizational-culture approach are disprovable.

The impact of culture on organizational behavior is distinct from *individual* influence and *environmental* change. Organizational beliefs are neither a product of nor equivalent to the desires of individuals. Culture is a collectively held phenomenon.[50] It neither reflects one person's beliefs nor is it some simple mathematical aggregation of many people's beliefs. This is not to say all individuals accept a dominant culture. Many organizations, in fact, are characterized by several cultures that compete for dominance or cooperate, which gives the organization a multifaceted character.[51] Nor should the influence of particular individuals at certain times be excluded. The point is that cultures are generally not reducible to individuals. This is especially true because even though individuals can change cultures, the reverse is more likely the case. People are socialized by the beliefs that dominate organizations. One theorist has noted that a person "does not live for months or years in a particular position in an organization, exposed to some streams of communication, shielded from others, without the most profound effects upon what he knows, believes, attempts to, hopes, wishes, emphasizes, fears, and proposes."[52] Those

---

son, *Public Administration* (New York: Knopf, 1950), pp. 543–44, on "philosophy" or "ideology"; Michel Crozier, *The Bureaucratic Phenomenon* (Chicago: University of Chicago Press, 1964), p. 198, on "personality"; and Halperin, *Bureaucratic Politics and Foreign Policy*, p. 28, on "essence."

[50] The effects are sometimes akin to cognitive and motivational biases discussed in Robert Jervis, *Perception and Misperception in International Politics* (Princeton: Princeton University Press, 1976), and Robert Jervis, Richard Ned Lebow, and Janice Gross Stein, *Psychology and Deterrence* (Baltimore: Johns Hopkins University Press, 1985). The difference is that cultural biases are not only based in the information processing capacity of individuals or their emotions, but also in collective understandings. A collective ideational emphasis is also found in studies on operational codes, ideology, and ideas. See Alexander George, "The 'Operational Code': A Neglected Approach to the Study of Political Leaders and Decision-making," *International Studies Quarterly* 13 (June 1969): 190–222; Peter Hall, ed., *The Political Power of Economic Ideas* (Princeton: Princeton University Press, 1989); Kathryn Sikkink, *Ideas and Institutions: Developmentalism in Brazil and Argentina* (Ithaca: Cornell University Press, 1991); Goldstein and Keohane, *Ideas and Foreign Policy*; Judith Goldstein, *Ideas, Interests, and American Trade Policy* (Ithaca: Cornell University Press, 1993).

[51] As Sonja A. Sackmann, "Culture and Subcultures: An Analysis of Organizational Knowledge," *Administrative Quarterly* 37 (1992): 140–61, demonstrates, detailed work on organizational culture will inevitably unveil subcultures, even in "strong culture" organizations. This does not preclude, however, a unifying or dominant set of collective beliefs.

[52] Herbert A. Simon, *Administrative Behavior*, 3d ed. (New York: Free Press, 1976), p. xvi.

who heed the prevailing customs are rewarded and promoted.[53] Those who do not are given little authority or they are fired. For many years, failure to wear a white shirt and dark suit at IBM was hazardous for the health of an employee's career. The company had no written policy on attire, but according to one former executive, there was "an unwritten dress code that's as effective as if it were engraved in steel—or as if it had a loaded gun behind it."[54] Individuals come and go, but organizations often show little change, even when formal structures are altered.

The influence of organizational culture is also distinct from "objective rationality" or environmental pressures. What may seem completely irrational to an outsider may make perfect sense to those within a certain community. Buddhist monks setting themselves on fire or World War II Japanese pilots carrying out massive kamikaze attacks are difficult to understand unless seen through the lens of the particular cultural milieu in which those actions originated.[55] And when external circumstances change, culture and behavior may not. Even functional demands to make corrections in order to survive go unheeded. The number of large companies that have failed to adapt to changing market conditions are legion.[56] This occurs because cultures help define organizational interests and maintain them in ways that may be contrary to environmental demands.[57] In bureaucracies, culture is not simply a weather vane of the winds of international or domestic politics. Militaries, for example, do not consistently adopt war-fighting strategies suited to a given circumstance.[58] Nor is culture a strict reflec-

---

[53] Thus even individuals who superficially accept a culture in order to rise in it may become "captured" by their own instrumental use of it. On a similar effect in domestic politics, see Jack Snyder, *Myths of Empire* (Ithaca: Cornell University Press, 1991), pp. 41–42. For a thoughtful discussion on the instrumental uses of culture, see Alastair I. Johnston, "An Inquiry into Strategic Culture: Chinese Strategic Thought, the Parabellum Paradigm, and Grand Strategic Choice in Ming China" (Ph.D. diss., University of Michigan, 1993).

[54] F. G. "Buck" Rodgers, *The IBM Way* (New York: Harper & Row, 1986).

[55] On "irrationality" in the Japanese government, see Chihiro Hosoya, "Characteristics of Foreign Policy Decision-Making in Japan," *World Politics* 26 (April 1974): 353–69.

[56] Many are trying to change their culture by making large-scale personnel changes at the top. See Thomas C. Hayes, "Faltering Companies Seek Outsiders," *New York Times*, 18 January 1993, C1 and C4.

[57] When existing methods come up short, goals, instead of means, are often altered. Crozier, *Bureaucratic Phenomenon*, p. 187; Barbara Levitt and James G. March, "Organizational Learning," *Annual Review of Sociology* 14 (1988): 325.

[58] One well-known case of this was the endurance of the horse cavalry in the twentieth century despite the clear demands of the modern battlefield. Edward L. Katzenbach Jr., "The Horse Cavalry in the Twentieth Century," *Public Policy* (1958): 120–49.

tion of the political structure of the state. As we will see, organizational cultures are influential in both strong and weak states.[59] This is not to say that cultures never change. Of course they do. The point is that this change is much less automatic and efficient than functional theories based on environmental forces would suggest.

Culture plays a pivotal role in defining organizational priorities and behavior. The ideal organization is one in which an executive (committee) establishes specific and concrete goals, which in turn determine programs and SOPs. For example, in most business firms, profits, revenues, or sales are the desired end. Other organizations, particularly bureaucracies, often have less tangible goals, which become concrete only in specific situations or interpretations. James Q. Wilson cites several examples from the *United States Government Manual:*

- Department of State: "Promote the long-range security and well-being of the United States."
- Department of Labor: "Foster, promote, and develop the welfare of the wage earners of the United States."
- Bureau of Indian Affairs: "Facilitate the full development of the human and natural resource potential of Indian and Alaskan Native people."[60]

This uncertainty adds to the likelihood that these organizations will focus their efforts around modes or methods of output, rather than actual goals, particularly when there is no market to adjudicate results. In effect, means become ends.[61]

Cultures, once established, tend to persist. Those individual members of a culture who adhere to its creed tend to advance in an organization and become the dominant culture's new protectors. The State Department, for example, values diplomacy and open communication above all else. Security specialists, however, favor rigid rules of access and compartmentalized communication. Not surprisingly, security

[59] On strong and weak states, see Katzenstein, "Conclusion: Domestic Structures," pp. 306–23. In security studies, political structure is seen as crucial variable in Matthew Evangelista, *Innovation and the Arms Race* (Ithaca: Cornell University Press, 1988), pp. 22–25, and Snyder, *Myths of Empire*, pp. 14–19, 308–11. Elizabeth Kier, *Imagining War: France and Britain between the Wars* (Princeton: forthcoming), argues that domestic politics and culture influence the propensity of civilians to intervene and influence organizational culture.

[60] James Q. Wilson, *Bureaucracy* (New York: Basic Books, 1989), p. 32.

[61] See Selznick, *TVA*, pp. 69–70, 250–59; Selznick, *Leadership*, p. 16; Halperin, *Bureaucratic Politics and Foreign Policy*, p. 28; and Swidler, "Culture in Action," pp. 276–77. This is not to suggest that mission certainly eliminates the role of culture. Even organizations with specified missions and suitable environments to test them (such as firms in markets) can become means (or culture) oriented rather than ends oriented.

specialists have difficulty advancing in the State Department's hierarchy, and lapses in embassy security seem to be a constant problem.[62]

Cultures also tend to live on because they act as templates for organizational development, much the same way a theoretical paradigm can shape intellectual thought. Cultures necessarily influence the perceptions of their members. Environmental data and facts that contradict cultural (pre)conceptions will be discounted as deviant. Tasks or "hypotheses" not compatible with the dominant creed will be relatively ignored.[63] Within military organizations, the use of exercises or maneuvers often reflects this type of learning. Realists expect exercises to ensure that doctrine is optimally suited to the given strategic circumstances. Institutionalists, meanwhile, anticipate that exercises will reflect the dominant international principles and norms. Organizational-culture theorists, however, predict that exercises will reflect and reaffirm internal beliefs and customs.

In a material sense, culture shapes organizations through resource allocation in capabilities. Collective beliefs dictate which enterprises are inherently better and should get support. Organizations will channel resources to methods suited to culture, which subsequently appear more feasible than those that have been deprived of funding and attention because they are incompatible.[64] Thus culture is a determinant of resource decisions that in later periods tend to reinforce the viability of cultural assumptions regardless of their fit with situational "strategic" circumstances.

Finally, cultures persist for utilitarian reasons. It is difficult and expensive to reorient operational philosophy in an organization, especially a large, complex one. David Kreps asserts that corporate cultures, even inefficient ones, facilitate communication and coordination.[65] Stephen Krasner has argued that organizational procedures that seem to be illogical in a situational context may make sense given the overall

---

[62] Wilson, *Bureaucracy*, pp. 90–91, 93–94. For other organizational peculiarities of the State Department, see James Gibney writing as Harry Crosby, "Too at Home Abroad," *Washington Monthly* 23 (September 1991): 16–20.

[63] Ashley Schiff, *Fire and Water: Scientific Heresy in the Forest Service* (Cambridge: Harvard University Press, 1962), details the subordination of "objective science" to the organizational doctrine of the early forest service. On theoretical paradigms, see Thomas S. Kuhn, *The Structure of Scientific Revolutions*, 2d ed. (Chicago: University of Chicago Press, 1970).

[64] This is the "competency trap." Certain technologies or means in which a great deal of time and resources have been invested seem better even if others are actually superior. See Levitt and March, "Organizational Learning," p. 322.

[65] David M. Kreps, "Corporate Cultures and Economic Theory," in James E. Alt and Kenneth A. Schepsle, eds., *Perspectives on Positive Political Economy* (New York: Cambridge University Press, 1990), pp. 90–143.

costs of search procedures and change.[66] This is not to suggest, however, that the organizational-culture approach relies on an environmen-
tally optimal cost-benefit analysis. Even when the strategic setting
requires functional adaptation—and the costs are not insurmountable—cultures and creeds often maintain their inertia. For example,
the U.S. Army had prepared for two decades before the Viet Nam war
to carry out the "Army Concept," which focused on the conventional
deployment of massive mechanized formations that relied on firepower
to avoid casualties. This it proceeded to do—unsuccessfully—in the
jungles of Southeast Asia, against an unconventional enemy, in the
face of evidence that other methods, such as the Marine Corp's Combined Action Platoons, would be more effective.[67]

Cultural birth and change are large topics that generally lie outside
the scope of this study.[68] A few points are, however, in order. In the
origins of cultures, many factors can be significant that will not be as
consequential in later periods. For example, individuals and the external environment might be much more important. "Founding fathers"
are thought to leave a definitive legacy.[69] And organizations are often
created to provide a certain function that responds to a particular environmental demand. Nonetheless, even at birth, cultures are frequently
not clean slates. For instance, the Central Intelligence Agency (CIA)
was founded in 1946 to act as a coordinator of foreign intelligence
received by a variety of other governmental departments. Yet many of
its prominent employees had served in the Office of Strategic Services
(OSS), which managed covert operations during World War II. The
CIA inherited the OSS creed of clandestine intelligence collection and
operations, which was soon competing with the original mission to
coordinate and evaluate intelligence for attention and resources.[70]

Once established, cultures can also change. The sources of such
change are myriad and include such factors as technology, domestic
and international environments, individuals, and accident. What is

---

[66] Krasner, "Are Bureaucracies Important?" p. 164.

[67] See Andrew F. Krepinevich Jr., *The Army in Viet Nam* (Baltimore: Johns Hopkins
University press, 1986), esp. pp. 4–7, 172–77, 258–68. A similar case of how a culture
can inhibit adaption is seen in Tim Travers, *The Killing Ground: The British Army, the
Western Front, and the Emergence of Modern Warfare, 1900–1918* (London: Allen & Unwin, 1987).

[68] The main exception is the analysis of whether culture results from either realist or
institutionalist forces.

[69] Selznick, *TVA*, p. 182; Selznick, *Leadership*, pp. 62, 151. Also Edgar H. Schein, "The
Role of the Founder in Creating Organizational Culture," *Organizational Dynamics* 12
(summer 1983).

[70] Wilson, *Bureaucracy*, pp. 56–58.

central to the process of change, however, is that core precepts of culture must be discredited or made obsolete. The dynamics of cultural change resemble a paradigm shift in science. Evidence gradually accumulates that weakens and discredits the dominant culture paradigm. Sometimes a single critical case or crisis causes the collapse. Indeed, the actual change can look like a political battle for control of how the organization/state/firm defines "truth."[71]

But cultural change cannot be explained simply by reference to the culture undergoing the change. External factors must also play a role. Theories that emphasize culture generally highlight the forces of stability; they cannot explain change as well. The problem here is that a notion of "culture" that can explain any variations in behavior may be either empty or spurious.[72] Despite the possibility of change and the associated difficulties with explaining it, however, I return to the basic contention of the organizational-culture approach: culture often persists, even when environmental circumstances or individual preferences seem to indicate it should change.

Left to be untangled is how attributes at the level of a subnational organization can determine national preferences and choices. As Robert Art and Stephen Kraser have pointed out, there are important limitations to the influence of government organizations.[73] It is recognized that bureaucracies are not always the central force in national decisions: in fact, it is widely believed that in periods of crisis the role of bureaucracies—including the military—will be weakened.[74] Nonetheless, I argue that bureaucratic influence should not be quickly dis-

[71] See Allen W. Immershein, "Organizational Change as a Paradigm Shift," *Sociological Quarterly* 18 (winter 1977): 33–43. Some theorists emphasize the notion that crisis is integral to change. By definition, a challenge to an organization's central beliefs would be a crisis. See Crozier, *Bureaucratic Phenomenon*, pp. 195–96. In the case of military doctrine, Stephen Peter Rosen, *Winning the Next War: Innovation and the Modern Military* (Ithaca: Cornell University Press, 1991), argues that innovation is like a political battle over the ideology that will govern a service community.

[72] Swidler, "Culture in Action," esp. p. 280, argues that culture explains inertia and transformation, but "culture" in her framework seems largely spurious: environmental forces explain which "strategy of action" is selected.

[73] Art, "Bureaucratic Politics," pp. 467–90; Krasner, "Are Bureaucracies Important?" pp. 159–79.

[74] Posen, *Sources of Military Doctrine*, pp. 74–78, 233–35; Ole R. Holsti, "Crisis Decision Making," in Philip E. Tetlock et al., eds., *Behavior, Society, and Nuclear War* (New York: Oxford University Press, 1989), 1: 16–18; B. Miller, "Explaining Great Power Cooperation," pp. 20–22. Art, "Bureaucratic Politics," p. 486, holds out the possibility that the bureaucratic paradigm may work better in some issue areas (such as institutional issues) than others (such as military intervention or major policy shifts). It would be difficult, however, to classify restraint in war as an "institutional issue."

[25]

counted. The question then is which bureaucracies will matter and when? What is needed is an *organizational-salience* model that provides a framework for thinking about the relative influence of bureaucratic culture on national preferences and actions. I propose one that varies along four dimensions: (1) the nature of the organization; (2) the extent to which it has monopoly power on expertise; (3) the complexity of the issue: and (4) the time available for action.

First, the nature of the organization must be taken into account. The utility of the concept of culture may be most useful in particular organizational settings. In hierarchical organizations characterized by a uniform set of beliefs and customs, where criteria for assessing the effectiveness of the dominant philosophy are complex or absent, culture is likely to be an especially useful tool for analysis.[75] Militaries are highly structured communities with rigid hierarchical orders. Each service has its own culture, which is distinct from those of the other services, but is especially distinct from that of society as a whole. Life is very routinized and the role of procedures is large. Militaries generally have loosely defined goals (for example, "provide security") and the flexibility to determine the methods they will use to achieve these goals.[76]

Second, when one organization has a monopoly on expertise, there is less pressure to change and organizational biases receive little outside correction.[77] Organizations are thought to learn best in a "community."[78] Militaries generally lack such a community. The armed forces of states are granted the sole license on the international use of large-scale violence. Especially in war, governments have few, if any, alternative sources of knowledge, advice, or options.

Third, the complexity of an issue must be considered, for that will

[75] In security studies, the concept of culture has been applied in different ways. See, for example, Ken Booth, *Strategy and Ethnocentrism* (New York: Holmes & Meier, 1979); Jack L. Snyder, *The Soviet Strategic Culture* (Santa Monica, Calif.: RAND, 1977); Colin Gray, *Nuclear Strategy and National Style* (Lanham, Md.: Hamilton Press, 1986); and Carl H. Builder, *The Masks of War Analysis* (Baltimore: Johns Hopkins University Press, 1989). Three notable recent studies are Kier, *Imagining War*; Thomas U. Berger, "America's Reluctant Allies: The Genesis of the Political Military Cultures of Japan and West Germany" (Ph.D. diss., M.I.T., 1992); and Johnston, "Inquiry."

[76] For example, as Wilson, *Bureaucracy*, p. 32, notes, the U.S. Army is guided by the vague injunction to "organize, train, and equip active duty and reserve forces for the preservation of peace, security, and the defense of our nation." To deal with this void, the Army must develop principles that govern in detail how this is to be accomplished.

[77] In such situations there is a greater possibility that organizational interests will transcend national ones. See Francis E. Rourke, *Bureaucracy and Foreign Policy* (Baltimore: Johns Hopkins Press, 1972), p. 47.

[78] Levitt and March, "Organizational Learning," pp. 331–32.

affect the degree to which specialist knowledge is required for decisions. The more complex the issue, the less that senior authorities can oversee the operations, the more organizational preferences will be felt. For example, Mao Zedong's oversight of the disastrous "Great Leap Forward" program was limited by his ignorance of economic affairs, which forced him to rely on bureaucratic economic specialists.[79] And some of the problems that troubled the Cuban Missile Crisis occurred because President Kennedy lacked the military expertise to ask the right questions.[80] The business of war fighting is very complex. The technologies and techniques involved demand expert knowledge. It is not surprising that it is exactly in times of conflict that national command structures often change, elevating professional military authorities to influential decision-making positions.

Fourth, the time available for decision making can also affect bureaucratic effect. When there are no particular time constraints, executives can rearrange organizations to ensure that procedures match desires.[81] But when decision-making cycles are short there is little time for such maneuvers. In war this is often the case because years are required to develop military strategies and capabilities, yet decisions must be made immediately.

An organizational-culture perspective leads to predictions on restraint that are often at odds with those of traditional organizational theory. Where the traditional approach expects similar interests and behavior from similarly structured organizations with similar functions, the cultural approach allows for differences in interests and behavior based on variations in beliefs and customs.[82] For example, the traditional perspective cannot easily explain the defensive orientation of the French army in the interwar period, but the cultural approach does not claim that military organizations will inevitably turn to offensive strategies or the unrestrained use of force within war.[83] An organizational-culture perspective posits that state preferences on restraint originate in the fit between a particular means of warfare and the collective beliefs of the military services that deploy the means in

---

[79] David Bachman, *Bureaucracy, Economy, and Leadership in China: The Institutional Origins of the Great Leap Forward* (Cambridge: Cambridge University Press, 1991), pp. x, 237–40.

[80] Even though he had served notably in the military. Welch, "Paradigms," p. 139.

[81] There are, of course, limits in this area. Sometimes leaders are not able to act because of resource constraints, insufficient power, or lack of information.

[82] I do not mean to deny that organizational tendencies toward autonomy, resource hoarding, and uncertainty reduction are important. I argue that even these processes are shaped by the culture of an organization.

[83] For an excellent analysis of this issue, see Kier, *Imagining War*. Also see D. C. Watt, *Too Serious a Business* (Berkeley and Los Angeles: University of California Press, 1975).

question. Faced with choices about how, where, and when to employ violence, each service develops a culture to guide war fighting. These "paradigms" either advocate or ignore specific means of warfare. Those means compatible with the dominant war-fighting culture will be adopted and advocated by the military, those means not compatible will suffer benign neglect. Because of the central role of the armed forces in international conflict, their preferences and biases have a significant influence on state decisions. Change in state preferences in war is expected to result from organizational pressures—through direct advice, estimates of the situation, and the capabilities developed—coming to the fore. Thus, this view would predict: *States will prefer mutual restraint in a particular mode of force if it is antithetical to the war-fighting culture of their military bureaucracy. States will favor escalation when the organizational cultures of their military bureaucracies are compatible with use.*

In addition to its role in choosing between restraint and escalation, organizational culture can also subtly inhibit or fuel inadvertent escalation. The organizational-culture perspective predicts that accidents and escalation will be particularly likely in those means congruous with a military's beliefs about the "right way" to fight wars.[84] In areas compatible with culture, organizational thinking, tools, and activities will be geared toward use, not restraint. With such a predilection, accidents that favor escalation become more likely. Yet in those types of warfare that are incongruous with culture the emphasis will be on restraint. More attention will be given to avoiding inadvertent use of stigmatized means of warfare.

Overall, the organizational-culture view asserts that restraint will occur where a particular means of warfare does not correspond with the military's dominant war-fighting culture. There should be weak planning and little advocacy by the top military leadership for escalation. Exercises will attest to the limited utility of that means and intelligence findings and advice will be biased against use. Enemy accidents that occur will be accepted as such and not allowed to escalate into a spiral of use. On the other hand, escalation is likely where a means of warfare is central to the war-fighting philosophy that governs a military's thinking. In this case, we can expect energetic advocacy, well-developed plans, strategies, and capabilities, and optimistic intelligence reports both on the need and expected impact of weapons that

---

[84] In contrast, the traditional organizational approach expects all organizational activities to be equally likely to end in inadvertent escalation. See, for example, Posen, *Inadvertent Escalation*, pp. 16–19.

complement the dominant way of war making. Any enemy accidents that occur in these areas will be seized on as intentional or as evidence of an inevitable intensification of the war that must be met with a response in kind.

THE METHOD

The three perspectives detailed above offer competing accounts of, and prescriptions for, cooperation. Which proposition gives the best explanation of the cooperation of restraint has important implications for both the study and practice of international relations. Therefore, how these propositions will be assessed deserves a few words.

Cooperation in war is a systemic phenomenon: it is the product of two or more states opting for restraint. To understand that choice, the unit of analysis is national decision making because escalation occurs by the decision of a single country and because a national level focus is useful for examining preference formation in choices that determined cooperation. The preferences of states are assessed primarily by the record of the internal discussions of governments regarding their desired outcomes and there is every reason to believe these discussions reflect actual preferences. Thus preferences are not simply "revealed" by behavior. In practice, there was a close correspondence between preferences and action with two exceptions. First, in some cases states actually used a certain weapon, even though they preferred restraint, as a response to the other side's first use. A second source of divergence between preferences and action were accidents and inadvertent behavior that led to escalation when restraint was preferred or restraint when escalation was desired.

Operational measures of the causal variables represented in the three competing propositions are also required. The realist approach is gauged by the opportunities and constraints that confronted states, particularly with regard to relative advantage in escalation. In view of national aims, did the balance of capabilities in a situation offer a country relative gains or losses in escalating? This is sometimes a counterfactual exercise in that it identifies an objective situation to which a state may not have "correctly" adapted. In those instances, I show that by standards of reasonable judgment, states should have had different preferences given the situation (if realist predictions are accurate).

I judge variation in institutionalization according to the three criteria—specificity, durability, and concordance. Specificity is assessed by examining how simple the prohibitions are. Is there a laborious code that is complex and detailed? Do countries argue about what the restraints mean or entail? Durability is measured by the age of the norm and whether sanctions were levied when violations occurred, which speaks to the continuing legitimacy of a prohibition. Finally, concordance can be assessed by reviewing the records of national and international discussions that involved the norms. States sometimes put special conditions on their acceptance of prohibitions, a tendency that diminishes concordance.

Organizational culture is measured according to the ideas and beliefs about how to wage war that characterized a particular military bureaucracy.[85] A portrait of this culture is developed by reviewing available internal correspondence, planning documents, regulations, exercises and the memoirs of individual members. These multiple sources provide a composite picture of the hierarchy of legitimate beliefs within an organization. Cultural explanations are often accused of post-hoc tautological explanation: a certain cultural belief can always be found after the fact that explains a given action. Obviously it is necessary to avoid defining culture by the behavior I am attempting to show was influenced by culture. However, organizational cultures—especially military ones—are often quite tangible and can be assessed independent of outcomes.[86]

Choices on the use of force in war represent a hard test for my argument. Within the category of war there have been few modern clashes as encompassing or intense as World War II. All of the major powers were engaged. No outside power could act as a referee to control the scale of fighting. The stakes involved "unconditional surrender": defeat would entail the political, if not literal, extinction of the state. To avoid such an outcome, entire industrialized societies devoted themselves to war-making. The cast of characters also did not bode well for limitation. One of the central decision makers, Hitler, seemed psychotic and not capable of respecting any limitation on force. The cooperation of restraint in such a conflict is inherently peculiar.

Within World War II, submarines, strategic bombing, and chemical warfare deserve the spotlight because they were the three main candidates—quite distinct from others—that states considered for limita-

---

[85] For an example of empirical research on organizational culture in business firms, see Geert Hofstede et al., "Measuring Organizational Cultures: A Qualitative and Quantitative Study across Twenty Cases," *Administrative Science Quarterly* 35 (June 1990): 286–316.

[86] For example, the U.S. Navy's organizational culture favored restraint in submarine warfare. This bias was incompatible with subsequent behavior—the Navy escalated on the first day of war.

tion. These three also make sense in light of the aim of assessing the different causal explanations represented by realism, institutionalism, and organizational culture. In terms of realism, the relative balance of advantage changes within and between cases. With regard to the institutionalist perspective, all three means of warfare were subjects of extensive "convention-building" discussions concerning arms limitation and rules of conflict in the interwar period. The degree of formal and tacit accord reached varied among the three types of warfare. Finally, in relation to organization theory, military cultures differed on the desirability of restraint and escalation among the three types of warfare.[87]

The choice of cases from the same war has the strong advantage of permitting controls for a number of variables. For example, the personalities, the causes of the conflict, the stakes at risk, and the general international setting—are the same for all three types of warfare. Thus these considerations cannot explain the differences in outcomes. Some might argue that this cooperation is a product of a particular historical period. This point, however, begs the question of why restraint occurred in a period of "total war."[88]

The countries selected for case studies deserve attention for various reasons. In submarine warfare, Germany and Britain were the main opponents in the Atlantic sea war. When Hitler invaded Poland, the last thing he wanted was a clash with Britain. Because he knew that unrestricted warfare would provoke the British, he gave his U-boats strict orders to obey the rules of submarine warfare. Yet in short time— even though Hitler still wanted peace with Britain and the German navy had far too few U-boats to achieve decisive results—Germany allowed its captains total freedom in the offensive against British merchant ships. Britain had the most to lose from an unrestricted submarine war with its many exposed trade routes, yet it took measures,

[87] There were, of course, other instances of restraint and escalation that may seem relevant, ranging from the temporary limitation in the use of metal strips to hinder radar devices to the dropping of the atom bomb. But none allow a fair consideration of the three independent variables. None carried the same international moral stigma or the same relative advantage dynamics as the main three. For example, the atom bomb was employed for the first time in World War II, unlike submarine warfare, strategic bombing, and gas, which saw their main first use in World War I. And the Americans never had to fear that Japan might retaliate in kind. Among other accounts, see Robert C. Batchelder, *The Irreversible Decision, 1939–1950* (New York: Macmillan, 1961).

[88] Hew Strachan, *European Armies and the Conduct of War* (London: George Allen & Unwin), p. 3, argues that there have been three periods of limited war in modern times, 1648–1792, 1815–1914, and 1945 to the present. "Total war" is a common description of World War II. See, for example, Peter Calvoressi, Guy Wint, and John Pritchard, *Total War: The Causes and Courses of the Second World War* (New York: Pantheon Books, 1989).

[31]

such as arming its merchants, that provoked unrestricted attacks. Furthermore, even after Germany had "broken" the rules, Britain continued to limit its submarine attacks even though military gains were sacrificed by doing so. The United States was one of the most ardent supporters of the rules of submarine warfare and appeared to comply completely with the mandated restrictions in the interwar period. Yet within five hours of the attack on Pearl Harbor, U.S. submarines were ordered to conduct unrestricted attacks on Japanese ships, a mission they were ill suited to carry out.

In strategic bombing, Britain and Germany were the central participants. Britain's decision to initiate unrestricted bombing is puzzling in light of its deep fear of air attacks, its vulnerable position, and its perceived inferiority in air power. Germany, on the other hand, led by an unscrupulous dictator and possessing an enviable position in occupied France for attacking the United Kingdom desired restraint.[89]

In chemical warfare, Britain, Germany, and the Soviet Union are the central countries of interest because they were the three main European combatants and all were facing direct challenges to survival.[90] Britain was believed to be one of the nations most opposed to the use of gas. Yet despite an acknowledged inferiority in chemical warfare, Britain appeared to be ready to use gas against a Nazi invasion of the British Isles. Later in the war when England had superior chemical-warfare capabilities, Churchill pushed to initiate chemical warfare, but Britain maintained restraint. Germany was viewed as having inherent industrial and societal advantages for chemical warfare, but despite imminent political extinction, Hitler's "mad dog" reputation, and suitable opportunities for using gas, the Third Reich never used chemical warfare. Finally, the Soviet case is intriguing because the survival of the USSR, world communism, and Stalin's regime all hung in the balance, but restraint endured even though chemical weapons were be-

---

[89] I did not examine strategic bombing in the Pacific war because Japan did not have the ability to retaliate against the United States, which prevents a good relative test of the three theories. By the time the United States had entered the European war, restraints had already been abandoned. Among other studies, see Ronald Schaffer, *Wings of Judgment: American Bombing in World War II* (New York: Oxford University Press, 1985), and Conrad C. Crane, *Bombs, Cities, and Civilians: American Airpower Strategy in World War II* (Lawrence: University Press of Kansas, 1993).

[90] I did not review the U.S. decision not to use gas strategically at the end of World War II because of the inability of the Japanese to retaliate against the U.S. homeland. On U.S. chemical-warfare policy in the Pacific, see John Ellis van Courtland Moon, "Project SPHINX: The Question of the Use of Gas in the Planned Invasion of Japan," *Journal of Strategic Studies* 12 (1989): 303–23, and Barton J. Bernstein, "Why We Didn't Use Gas in World War II," *American Heritage*, August/September 1985, pp. 40–45.

lieved to be especially useful on the defensive, and the Red Army had adopted a "scorched earth" strategy. How can these perplexing outcomes be assessed?

To answer this question, I rely on the comparative case method. Two types of comparisons are most relevant: why some means of warfare were restricted whereas others were not and why some countries initiated a specific type of combat whereas others did not. This approach is especially suited for complex phenomena such as limited war where theories are neither well articulated nor substantiated and where the number of cases is small.[91] In order to assess which perspective best explains restraint I examined which of the approaches most accurately captures the shaping of choices on limitation and escalation. Differentiating the impact of the three propositions is possible because of the fluctuations evident in both causes and outcomes.[92] In many instances the three perspectives offer competing explanations.

The broad strokes of comparing the three types of warfare are given content by "process-tracing."[93] This procedure goes beyond merely trying to confirm the presence or absence of a variable. Its purpose is to determine whether an observed correlation between hypothesized cause (reflected in the three different approaches) and actual outcome (preferences) is real or spurious and to provide an explanatory account of that relationship. Do events happen according to the mechanisms that the perspectives suggest take place?

The historical evidence for making judgments has been gathered from two types of sources. First, given the broad nature of the enterprise, I have relied on a range of excellent secondary works on the countries and matters of concern. Despite this wealth of material, some of the phenomena—particularly the role of international norms and organizational culture—have not been adequately covered in the ex-

[91] Charles Tilly, *Big Structures, Large Processes, Huge Comparisons* (New York: Russell Sage Foundation, 1984). Alexander George and Timothy McKeown, "Case Studies and Theories of Organizational Decision Making," in Robert Coulam and Richard Smith, eds., *Advances in Information Processing in Organizations* (Greenwich, Conn.: JAI Press, 1985), 2: 21–58.

[92] The philosophy of science underlying this study comes from Imre Lakatos. No theory can be proven conclusively. Therefore we assess the power of an idea by how well it explains a given phenomenon not only in absolute terms but also relative to other ideas which also claim to offer explanations. See Imre Lakatos, "Falsification and the Methodology of Scientific Research Programmes," in Imre Lakatos and Alan Musgrave, eds., *Criticism and the Growth of Knowledge* (Cambridge: Cambridge University Press, 1970).

[93] Process-tracing "is intended to investigate and explain the decision process by which various initial conditions are translated into outcomes." George and McKeown, "Case Studies," p. 35.

isting literature. Therefore, I have also done considerable archival research in Germany, Great Britain, and the United States. Despite this effort, gaps remain. Either evidence has been destroyed, or it did not exist, or I have not found it. The most substantial shortfall is that Soviet documents on chemical-warfare policy remain largely unavailable, despite recent political changes. Nonetheless, a good deal of material has been uncovered in the German, British, and U.S. archives on Soviet policy. And because of the intrinsic interest of that history, the case merits attention.

In international relations and national affairs, the ability of actors to accommodate one another significantly affects human welfare in a number of areas, including economic growth, environmental preservation, and the prevention of conflict. Therefore, the phenomenon of cooperation has attracted attention from across the social sciences. Many analysts have studied cooperation by emphasizing strategic interaction and neglecting preference formation. In this book I highlight the role of, and give an explanation for, preferences in cooperation. I develop an organizational-culture approach and test its plausibility in an area where its influence is generally not expected. In problems of mutual restraint on the use of force, analysts have generally relied on strategic-interaction or systemic explanations. Not only does organizational culture—a domestic-level perspective—offer powerful explanatory leverage, but it also accounts for the variations in cooperation in World War II better than two of the dominant systemic schools of international politics, realism and institutionalism.

The proof of this argument is in the chapters that follow, and these have a parallel structure. A brief introduction giving an overview of that means of warfare is followed by case studies of national policies on restraint and use. The history of each case is structured by the three perspectives. I marshal the evidence available to highlight supporting data and/or contradictions among the three propositions. The central question is always the same: Which perspective in that case best explains restraint and/or escalation?

[2]

Submarine Warfare

The submarine today is accepted along with tanks, airplanes, and artillery as a standard item in the armed forces of the world. Yet the underwater boat has an infamous history. In the 1920s and 1930s, the submarine—known as the "viper of the sea"— was viewed as one of the more heinous tools of combat.[1] It was a favorite target of proposals for abolition or limitation in the interwar years, yet was one of the first means used in the ensuing clash. It was not so much the weapon itself that was stigmatized but its employment against civilian ships and personnel. Nations acknowledged that submarines could sink warships and other combatants. What they considered illegitimate was the destruction of civilian ships without attention to the safety of their crews—a practice that came to be known as unrestricted submarine warfare.

The origins of the distinction between warships and merchant or passenger vessels are found at the start of the twentieth century. In the years leading up to the Great War, several international conferences convened to discuss the laws of war. The First and Second Hague Conferences (1899 and 1907) and the London Naval Conference (1909) produced a number of conventions on the regulation of conflict. Although many of these provisions had to do with sea warfare, none applied specifically to the submarine, for the underwater boat had never played a major role. What was clearly established in international law and practice, however, was that in cases where it was legitimate to sink a merchant ship, because it was either an enemy vessel or carrying contraband that would aid the war effort, the attacker was required to

---

[1] "To Rob the 'Sea Viper' of Its Venom," *Literary Digest*, 22 February 1930, pp. 9–10.

provide for the safety of the ship's passengers and papers. The only exception was a merchant ship that tried to escape or resist.[2] As we will see, these rules designed for surface ships sometimes posed difficulties for submarines.

In the course of World War I, submarine warfare saw varying degrees of restraint, from complete adherence to the norms of sea warfare to the no-holds-barred sinking of noncombatants. Germany set the trend, and it officially turned to unrestricted warfare on 1 February 1917. Although all sides viewed the submarine as a warship bound by the laws of the sea, Germany justified its attacks as reprisals for Allied transgressions of international law, primarily England's blockade. Other nations, however, were outraged. Civilians were being killed. One of the more dramatic episodes was the destruction of the passenger liner *Lusitania*, which resulted in the deaths of twelve hundred men, women, and children. Britain even faced the possibility of having to sue for peace for lack of food and materials to supply its war effort.[3] And, of course, the neutral trading states, such as the United States, were losing wealth, ships, and citizens. It was, in fact, Germany's blatant violation of the norms of submarine warfare that brought the United States into the war, a crucial step toward Germany's ultimate defeat.[4]

The notion that the victor writes the rules is especially appropriate to submarine warfare. Of those countries, Britain and the United States emerged as the dominant powers in the postwar period. They had a good deal to say about what would and would not be considered legitimate and they opposed the unrestricted use of the submarine. This was reflected as early as the Treaty of Versailles and as late as the Spanish civil war. By the beginning of World War II all the major powers had explicitly accepted that unrestricted attacks on noncombatant merchant ships were an illegitimate means of combat. This principle served as the basis of the interwar regime in submarine warfare.

The rules of submarine warfare were debated at the entire gamut of the international conferences on disarmament and conflict management from 1919 to 1939. Starting with the Treaty of Versailles, the submarine became the focus of special attention. The first provision of the naval terms of the Versailles treaty demanded the destruction of all German submarines and related equipment.

[2] See James Wilford Garner, *International Law and the World War* (London: Longmans, Green, 1920), pp. 355–65.

[3] Admiral J.R. Jellico, *The Submarine Peril* (London: Cassell, 1934), pp. 1–2.

[4] Ernest R. May, *The World War and American Isolation, 1914–1917* (Cambridge: Harvard University Press, 1959), esp. pp. 416–37.

Submarines were soon discussed again at the 1921–22 Washington Conference on the Limitation of Armaments. Britain pressed hard for total abolition, but was rebuffed by countries that saw the underwater boat as crucial to their security. First and foremost was France, which favored the cheaper submarine as a counter to the more numerous surface ships of the Royal Navy. The French could not afford a large battle fleet so they planned on using the submarine to interdict British trade in the event of war with their island neighbor. The submarine was seen as the "weapon of the weak" that France and other smaller naval powers felt they could not do without.

The submarine issue threatened to block the Washington Conference until the deadlock was broken by a set of proposals offered by Elihu Root of the U. S. delegation. The Root resolutions, which prohibited attacks on noncombatant vessels, amounted to a code of warfare for the submarine. The provisions mandated that merchant ships could not be attacked unless they fled or resisted, they had to be searched before they were seized or sunk, and the safety of passenger and crew had be secured (see the Appendix). Although all the powers signed the treaty, it never legally went into effect because France refused to ratify it.

The rules of submarine warfare were next discussed at the London Naval Conference of 1930. Again the issue of abolition was raised and rejected; however, some limits on tonnage and armaments were accepted. In addition, the signatories decided to reaffirm the acceptable provisions of the Washington Treaty Relating to the Use of Submarines and Noxious Gases in Warfare. The final agreement included the following:

(1) In their action with regard to merchant ships, submarines must conform to the rules of International Law to which surface ships are subject.
(2) In particular, except in the case of persistent refusal to stop on being duly summoned, or of active resistance to visit or search, a warship, whether surface vessel or submarine, may not sink or render incapable of navigation a merchant vessel without having first placed passengers, crew, and ship's papers in a place of safety. For this purpose, the ship's boats are not regarded as a place of safety unless the safety of the passengers and crew is assured, in the existing sea and weather conditions, by the proximity of land, or the presence of another vessel which is in the position to take them aboard.

The main difference between this treaty and the 1930 London Naval Treaty was that the latter dropped provisions of the former (articles 3 and 4) concerning piracy and the implication that the rules prohibited any kind of attack on commerce by submarines.

The resiliency of the submarine rule is seen in how even as the interwar dialogue on disarmament was unraveling, the agreement on limiting submarine warfare endured. When Japan withdrew from the Second London Naval Conference of 1935–36, the nations that had attended the first London Naval Conference—Britain, France, the United States, Japan, and Italy—decided to renew their commitment to the submarine rules anyway, although the original agreement was still valid.[5] In addition, all other major powers, including Germany, signed this *Procès-Verbal Relating to the Rules of Submarine Warfare.*[6] There appeared to be a clear consensus that submarine attacks against merchant ships were unacceptable.

The first test of the rules actually came before World War II. In the midst of the events surrounding the Spanish civil war in August 1937, a number of indiscriminate submarine attacks on merchant ships (conducted covertly by Italian submarines in support of the Spanish Nationalists) took place in the Mediterranean. Several countries gathered at Nyon, France, to "ensure that the rules of international law be strictly enforced." They settled on special "collective measures taken against piratical acts perpetrated by submarines." They agreed that naval forces (primarily Britain's and France's) would counterattack against submarines that harassed merchants. The pact was not a universal sanction because Germany and Italy did not participate for political reasons connected to the war in Spain. Nonetheless, the pact showed a willingness on the part of the powers involved to react to transgressions of the London Protocol and was seen as largely effective in ending the attacks.[7]

The rules of submarine warfare can be assessed in terms of the three

[5] Richard Dean Burns, "Regulating Submarine Warfare, 1921–1941: A Case Study in Arms Control and Limited War," *Military Affairs* 35 (April 1971): 58.

[6] I refer to this agreement as the London Protocol or simply the Protocol. It restates the submarine provisions of the 1930 London Naval Treaty. See Leon Freidman, ed., *The Law of War: A Documentary History*, Vol. 1 (New York: Random House, 1982).

[7] Italy did, however, soon join, despite its actions that violated the rules, to avoid conflict with Britain in the Mediterranean. In effect, Italy joined the hunt for its own submarines! German submarines also played a brief secret part in the civil war, but did not successfully sink Republican and Soviet merchant ships they had been ordered to attack. For an overview of the agreement, see Arnold J. Toynbee, *Survey of International Affairs, 1937*, Vol. 2, *The International Repercussions of the War in Spain (1936–37)* (London: Oxford University Press, 1938), pp. 339–49. For an account of the role of German and Italian submarines in the war, see William C. Frank, "Politico-Military Deception at Sea in the Spanish Civil War, 1936–39," *Intelligence and National Security* 5 (July 1990): 84–112.

criteria discussed in Chapter 1—durability, specificity, and concordance. These rules had proven extremely durable. Over the course of some twenty-years, they had been repeatedly discussed and approved. Even when other international agreements were crumbling in the wake of rising international tension in the late 1930s, countries literally went out of their way to reaffirm that it was illegal for underwater boats to attack merchant ships. When the London Protocol was violated in 1937, countries took action to punish any further violations.

Although one prominent historian has noted that "nothing could be more explicit and legally binding" than the London Protocol,[8] the rules of submarine warfare did present some problems in specificity. For example, it was not exactly clear what constituted a "merchant ship." Whether arming a vessel, even if for defensive purposes, made it an actual combatant was hotly disputed. Britain was adamant about retaining the right to arm its merchants and denied this altered their civilian status.[9] Nonetheless, even defensive armaments were a threat to submarines that were highly vulnerable on the surface while conducting the search and seizure required by the Protocol. The rules were also vague on what it meant to provide for the safety of passengers and crews when sinking merchant vessels. Because underwater boats had small crews, they could not spare personnel to sail the captured ship to a friendly port. Furthermore, they could not generally take the noncombatant's crew and passengers aboard because of the lack of space. These people could be put in their lifeboats, but not all the countries involved considered this safe.

Finally, in terms of concordance, the regime received widespread support. The submarine rules were ratified by all the major powers—a total of forty-eight states in all—before the war. And in a period when other agreements were repudiated, countries once again avowed support for limitations in the London Protocol. Overall, the submarine rules represented the most robust institution of the three I examine in this book.

All nations believed that the submarine had a valid military role, but it was generally ignored or slighted in the reigning naval theories of

[8] Samuel F. Bemis, "Submarine Warfare in the Strategy of American Defense and Diplomacy, 1915–1945," pp. 15–16, 15 December 1961, Manuscripts and Archives Box 1603A, Yale University Library. Samuel Eliot Morison, the U. S. Navy's historian for World War II, called the rules "perfectly explicit." See Samuel Eliot Morison, *History of United States Naval Operations in World War II*, Vol. 1, *The Battle of the Atlantic, September 1939–May 1943* (Boston: Little, Brown, 1951), p. 8. I thank Dr. J. E. Talbott for providing me a copy of Bemis's "Submarine Warfare."

[9] Burns, "Regulating Submarine Warfare," p. 58.

the day. According to the philosophy of Alfred Mahan, the battleship and its complements would be the arbiters of naval sea power by all who could afford them. Writing at the turn of the century, Mahan asserted that the key to national power was "command of the sea," which ensured the safety of trade routes and lines of communication to colonies. He preached that sea wars would be decided by decisive fleet engagements, which nowadays are reminiscent of medieval knights charging at each other with lances.

In this strategic vision, the submarine played a strictly ancillary role. In the early 1900s, technical limitations prevented the submarine from participating in the grand engagement of the fleets. And Mahan explicitly denounced attacks on commerce as unworthy of naval effort.[10] As World War II approached, the aircraft carrier also became more important, but the submarine remained a weapon for navies on tight budgets. In many navies the underwater boat in and of itself had little status among warships. It could contribute little to fleet engagements, and worse, combatting submarines took up considerable resources that would have been otherwise employed. At the end of World War I the Royal Navy was using some three thousand antisubmarine vessels to contain the handful of remaining U-boats that plied the seas.[11]

There were, however, a number of acceptable roles for submarines. They could conduct reconnaissance in areas closed or inaccessible to surface ships or airpower. The submarine could also attack enemy fleets directly, usually by means of lying in wait by the opponent's routes. In addition, the underwater boat was a stealthy vehicle for laying mines. But the problem was that submarines could also be used to strike directly at the enemy's population by attacking merchant ships. Civilian passengers and crews would be drowned, and the goods to feed a country and sustain its war economy would be destroyed. This strategy would be most effective against nations that were dependent on trade. Britain and Japan, for example, relied on the sea for the transport of their livelihood. Naturally, unrestricted submarine warfare made attacking merchants easier, but it was not inevitable; even Germany had shown restraint for the first two years of World War I.

Clearly, restricted submarine warfare was not a symmetrical good in

---

[10] Alfred Thayer Mahan, *The Influence of Sea Power upon History* (1889; reprint, New York: Hill & Wang, 1940), esp. pp. 119, 481.

[11] Janet M. Manson, "Regulating Submarine Warfare," in Richard Dean Burns, ed., *Encyclopedia of Arms Control and Disarmament* (New York: Charles Scribner's Sons, 1993), p. 739.

the sense of having the same worth for all. Some countries valued it more than others due to their dependency on ocean trade. Britain, for example, favored restricting submarine warfare but France did not because if the two were ever to go to war, Britain could blockade France with its surface fleet but France would only be able to retaliate under water.

The existence of these asymmetries should not suggest that nations agreed on the objective uses of submarines and acted accordingly. In fact, the different countries and their militaries viewed the qualities of submarines in ways that did not necessarily correspond to strategic circumstances. This is seen in Japanese submarine policy. Naval policy in Japan favored the battleship and relegated the submarine to combatting warships and scouting. Merchant vessels were seen as secondary targets. Despite the vulnerability of U. S. supply lines and the ineffectiveness of Japanese submarines against U. S. warships, Japan never effectively adopted an antimerchant strategy.[12] Robert Kuenne has called this "the most shameful avoidable waste of a military resource in World War II."[13] The United States expected such a campaign and diverted extensive resources to convoying, but when the threat never materialized, was able to put the forces to other uses.[14] Japan both misperceived and failed to adapt to external circumstances.

Thus although states did weigh the relative benefits of submarines in making strategic choices on the use of force, how they perceived the value of the underwater boat and its restricted use may have been equally decisive in how they employed the submarine in time of war. All countries, however, even ones that planned anticommerce strategies, had signed the submarine protocol and agreed to abide by the search and seizure procedure. Why did some states in World War II adhere to restricted submarine warfare but others did not? The calcula-

[12] Not surprisingly, there were relatively few reports of Japanese violations of the submarine protocol in World War II. See Mochitsura Hashimoto, *Sunk: The Story of the Japanese Submarine, 1941–1945* (London: Cassell, 1954), p. 62; Burns, "Regulating Submarine Warfare," p. 60; and Manson, "Regulating Submarine Warfare," p. 744.

[13] Robert Kuenne, *The Attack Submarine: A Study in Strategy* (New Haven: Yale University Press, 1965), pp. 4–5.

[14] When Japan finally did attempt to attack military sea lines of communication in the South Pacific after the campaign in the Solomons, it sank only twenty merchants and lost seven submarines. Arthur Hezlet, *The Submarine and Seapower* (New York: Stein & Day, 1967), p. 123. Samuel Eliot Morison, *History of the United States Naval Operations in World War II*, Vol. 4, *Coral Sea, Midway and Submarine Actions, May 1942–August 1942* (Boston: Little, Brown, 1951), p. 198.

tions and decisions of Germany, Britain, and the United States help to answer this question.

THE UNLEASHING OF THE U-BOAT

On 1 September 1939, German soldiers dressed in Polish uniforms fired across the German-Polish border, providing a pretext for Hitler's invasion of Poland. Honoring treaty commitments to Poland, Britain declared war on Germany two days later. This was the outcome that Hitler feared most. He had planned a series of limited wars aimed at gaining hegemony of continental Europe, but he had hoped to avoid war with England. In fact, he preferred a division of labor: Britain could have its empire, and Germany would control the Continent.[15] Accordingly, when German submarines were sent to sea in August, they were given strict orders to obey "prize rules" limiting submarine attacks against civilian and merchant ships.[16] Germany knew that violating international rules in submarine warfare would infuriate England and offend important neutrals, especially the United States, which would lead to an escalation of hostilities. Given that Germany had only twenty-six oceangoing U-boats, restraint seems to have made strategic sense. After all, the head of the U-boat force, Captain (later Admiral) Karl Dönitz, argued that three hundred would be needed to defeat Britain.[17] What is surprising, however, is that within a month (see Table 2), even though Hitler had few U-boats and still hoped that England could be pacified, unrestricted German submarine warfare against Britain was under way.[18]

The three propositions provide explanations of varying persua-

[15] F. H. Hinsley, *Hitler's Strategy* (Cambridge: Cambridge University Press, 1951), pp. 4–9.

[16] Prize rules are those provisions of international law regulating the capture and seizure of enemy merchant ships. See Peter Padfield, *Dönitz: The Last Führer* (London: Gallanz, 1984), p. 191.

[17] Memorandum, Dönitz to OKM, "Gedanken über den Aufbau der U-Bootswaffe," 3 September 1939, RM 7/891, Bundesarchiv-Miltärarchiv, Freiburg, Germany (hereafter BA-MA). Dönitz discussed this memo with Raeder, the CINC of the Navy, in late August and submitted it officially in early September. See Karl Dönitz, *Memoirs: Ten Years and Twenty Days* (New York: World Publishing, 1959), pp. 42–45.

[18] Germany did not drop restrictions on attacking neutrals until the United States declared a zone around the British Isles in November in which it prohibited American ships or citizens to sail. In that area, Germany allowed unrestricted attacks against all ships (except Irish vessels). The overall restrictions against U. S. ships were maintained until December 1941.

Table 2. German submarine warfare: a brief escalation chronology, fall 1939

1 September	Germany invades Poland.
3 September	Britain declares war. *Athenia* sunk.
23 September	Hitler gives approval to sink enemy merchants that use their radio to signal their (and the U-boat's) position.
2 October	German U-boats receive permission to attack unlit ships in an area around the British Isles without warning.
4 October	German U-boats receive permission to attack British merchants that can be identified without warning.
6 October	Hitler makes his "last" peace overture to Britain.
9 October	Hitler realizes Britain cannot be pacified.
12 October	Chamberlain rejects the peace offer.
16 October	German U-boats receive permission to sink British passenger ships in convoys or without lights.
10 November	British passenger ships become unrestricted targets.
24 November	Germany announces an operational zone around the British Isles where unrestricted warfare against all ships will occur. The area of the zone matched the area in which the United States prohibited its ships to operate as of 4 November.

siveness for this escalation. Institutionalism has the most difficult time accounting for the rapid turn to unlimited attacks in an area where norms of restraint were fairly well developed. Germany did pay attention to the submarine regime in making its decision, but ultimately the prohibitions were not decisive. Realism would explain escalation by arguing that Hitler concluded that Britain could not be placated but it could be beaten by unrestricted submarine warfare. Yet as events indicated, and the Führer himself recognized at times, neither of these arguments captures the central dynamic. Germany's escalation cannot be fully understood outside the context of organizational preference and influence. The U-boat force developed an antitrade creed that was largely incompatible with restrictions on submarine attacks. In both explicit decisions and inadvertent actions, this culture molded national preferences and was a significant part of the story of German U-boat warfare.

Rules and U-Boats

When Hitler learned of England's decision to fight, he went into a rage and vowed revenge, "I will build U-boats, U-boats, U-boats . . . !"[19] Yet in calmer moments, he reasoned that Britain and France might yet be pacified. Above all, Hitler did not want to provoke neutral powers,

---

[19] Padfield, *Dönitz,* p. 186.

especially the United States. In World War I, unrestricted submarine attacks had brought the United States into the war. In accordance with international agreements signed before the war, restraint was actively pursued. When a German U-boat sank the passenger liner *Athenia* on 3 September and escalation threatened, Hitler was quick to reissue the command to the captains that restrictions must be respected. In fact, he put additional limitations on the submarines by prohibiting attacks on convoys and French warships.[20] This temporary action seems to suggest the influence of the rules in German calculations. Several of the Nazi wartime leaders claim that Germans did not violate the submarine protocol. They were simply responding to British transgressions. Retaliation was the implicit sanction in the existing regime.[21] Although this position provides a neat justification for Nazi behavior, the story was more varied and complex than the former Third Reich officials maintain. British actions, although relevant to Germany's decisions, were often less a cause of, than a cover for, escalation. This story begins at the close of World War I.

As part of the Versailles treaty, Germany was stripped of its submarines and prohibited from building more. Germany played no direct role in the international talks on the submarine at Washington in 1922 and London in 1930. Domestically, submarine warfare was simply not an issue of concern as it was, for instance, in the United States. German citizens had not been the victims of the U-boat. The German submarine openly returned to the world scene after the Anglo-German naval negotiations of 1935. The subsequent treaty from those talks shattered the Versailles limits on naval rearmament. Germany would be allowed to expand to 35 percent of the British fleet, and submarines could increase to 45 percent with the possibility of future parity after "friendly discussions." The Third Reich also agreed to become a signa-

---

[20] "Kriegstagbuch 1939 für Völker-and Seekriegerecht, Politik and Propaganda," RM 7/198, BA-MA; "Reflections of the Chief, Naval Staff, on Atlantic Warfare, 20 September 1939," in *Führer Conferences on Matters Dealing with the German Navy, 1939* (Washington, D. C.: Office of Naval Intelligence, 1947), p. 5. Germany's propaganda chief Goebbels alleged that Britain itself had sunk the *Athenia* to incite hostility against the Third Reich.

[21] See Dönitz, *Memoirs:*, pp. 55–59; Kurt Assmann, "Why U-Boat Warfare Failed," *Foreign Affairs* 28 (July 1950): 660–61; Eric Raeder, *My Life* (Annapolis, Md.: United States Naval Institute, 1960), pp. 294–95; Judge Admiral Dr. Curt Eckhardt, "International Law and Germany's Economic Warfare at Sea," in Donald S. Detwiler, ed., *World War II German Military Studies* (New York: Garland Publishing, 1979) 20:9. On the laws of war and reprisals, see W. T. Mallison Jr., *Studies in the Law of Naval Warfare: Submarines in General and Limited Wars*, Naval War College International Law Studies 1966, 58 (Washington, D. C.: U. S. GPO, 1968), pp. 19–20.

tory of the London Protocol, which prohibited unrestricted submarine attacks on noncombat vessels.

Germany's motives for joining the submarine regime, however, gave no reason to hope that they would adhere to it. The Third Reich accepted the 1936 London Protocol almost as an afterthought to the Anglo-German Naval Treaty. For the same reasons it made sense for Germany to sign the treaty limiting the size of its own navy, so too was it reasonable to adopt the submarine accord. The central aim was to come to an understanding with Britain. Agreeing to the submarine rules contributed to that goal. Dönitz, the head of U-boats, claims he was never consulted in the decision. He noted that Germany signed the Protocol and agreed to its restrictions because it fulfilled British desires. At the time, a debate was raging in the House of Commons over whether to accept the Anglo-German naval pact, particularly given the number of submarines the pact would permit the Third Reich. The German acceptance of the Protocol helped to swing the debate in favor of British ratification of the treaty.[22]

Germany apparently did translate the rules into official navy instructions. After Germany signed the London Protocol, a committee of representatives from the High Command of the Navy, the Foreign Ministry, the Ministry of Justice and a group of scientific experts revised regulations held over from the last war to conform to the new agreement. These regulations were published in 1938 as an internal ordinance of the Navy. At his Nuremburg trial, Dönitz claimed to have prepared the U-boatmen to fight the war in accordance with the prize regulations.[23] During the 1938 fall maneuvers, a number of exercises were arranged allegedly to acquaint officers with the new regulations. These exercises were apparently not extensive, and the captains seemed not to learn the lessons very well. At the outset of war the Navy felt it necessary to distribute to the U-boat commanders a disc-shaped slide rule to look up the correct procedure.[24]

Unlike the United States or Britain, Germany made targeting merchant ships a central focus of operations and exercises. Commerce

---

[22] *Trial of the Major War Criminals before the International Military Tribunal, Nuremburg* Vol. 13, *Proceedings 3 May 1946–15 May 1946* (New York: AMS Press, 1971), p. 358 (hereafter cited as IMT by volume and page number). Dönitz, *Memoirs* p. 34. Raider, *My Life,* p. 190. Stephen Roskill, *Naval Policy between the Wars,* Vol. 2, *The Period of Reluctant Rearmament, 1930–1939* (Annapolis, Md.: United States Naval Institute Press, 1976), p. 306.

[23] IMT 13:248. Herbert Sohler, *U-Bootkrieg and Völkerecht,* Beiheft 1, *Marine Rundschau,* September 1956, pp. 13–14.

[24] See Fregatten-Kapitän Hessler's testimony in *IMT* 13:528. Hessler was Dönitz's son in law.

warfare was considered a powerful tool, and German military leaders expected that as it had in World War I, Britain would take a number of actions, such as arming merchants and convoying, that would make the rules difficult to implement and law-abiding submarines ineffective. Dönitz conducted sea maneuvers in the belief that Britain would convoy.[25] In German eyes, to convoy meant providing defensive measures that nullified the restrictions. The Navy had a saying, "Whoever travels with armed help must face armed combat."[26] Ships sailing with military escort could be sunk as if they were military vessels themselves. The German U-boats practiced attacking convoys, which in wartime would include merchant ships. Allegedly, even the acoustical detection arrays in the German boats were designed for an antishipping role.[27]

The rules did have an influence, but mainly by reinforcing preexisting tendencies. Undoubtedly, they increased the stigma of submarine attacks on merchant ships. For example, the London Protocol may have marginally reinforced Germany's calculation that transgressing the rules would give England resolve to continue with its declaration to fight, add to its morale and spirit, or provoke U. S. participation in the war.[28]

What is not clear is whether the submarine treaties affected the fundamental decision for escalation. The roots of the Protocol appear to be largely realist in nature. British and American opposition to the submarine originated with Germany's unrestricted assault on British and U. S. sea trade during World War I. As the victors they were able to brand unrestricted submarine warfare as illegal and immoral.[29] It is

[25] Memorandum from Erich Albrecht (deputy director of the legal department of the foreign office) to State Secretary Weizsäcker, D-851, in *Nazi Conspiracy and Aggression: Supplement A* (Washington, D. C.: U. S. GPO, 1947), pp. 971–72 (hereafter *NCA*). Janet M. Manson, *Diplomatic Ramifications of Unrestricted Submarine Warfare, 1939–1941* (Westport, Conn.: Greenwood Press, 1990), pp. 97–98. Dönitz, *Memoirs*, pp. 34–35.

[26] "Wer Waffenhilfe in Anspruch nimmt, muß Waffeneinsatz gewärtigen." Sohler, *U-Bootkrieg und Völkerecht*, pp. 14–15. The Protocol did not speak explicitly to the legality of convoys. The British denied that merchants in convoys were legal targets.

[27] Padfield, *Dönitz*, pp. 171–75. Rear Admiral G. W. G. Simpson, *Periscope View* (London: Macmillan, 1972), p. 61.

[28] For example, one German document mentions increasing British morale as an undesirable consequence of violating the agreement. See staff study by Korvettekapitän Roll, "Die (Welt)propaganda als Mittel zur Auswertung militärischer Erfolge als Mittel zur Abschwächung der Wirkung militärischer Mißerfolge," Winterarbeit 1937/8, T-1022, Roll 1970, National Archives of the United States (hereafter NA).

[29] Had Germany won the First World War, the submarine would have probably not been discussed. Undoubtedly, blockades would have been branded as illegal and immoral.

not clear that the increased institutionalization in the interwar period significantly strengthened the norms of limitation. Even without the more robust consensus and durability of the rules, similar considerations on use would have been evident. The precedent of World War I would have been sufficient to make Hitler worry about the United States entering the war in response to unrestricted submarine attacks that transgressed its interests. And British and American citizens would still have been outraged to see their livelihood and fellow country men perish at sea.

The nature of the submarine regime's imprint is apparent in the dynamics of German decision making. The issue was not how to remain with the regime, but how to circumvent it in the least costly fashion. In fact this was a matter that had been contemplated, at least at the staff level, as early as 1937. Lieutenant-Commander Roll of the naval propaganda arm argued that unrestricted submarine warfare must be implemented if restrained warfare was not successful. He recommended that world opinion be informed that "those that go into dangerous areas get hurt."[30]

During the war, the Third Reich chose its words carefully to avoid reminding others how Germany created new enemies in World War I through its unrestricted use of the U-boat. The terms "submarine warfare" and "unrestricted submarine warfare" were prohibited. The authorized reference was "war against merchant ships." Eric Raeder, the commander in chief (CINC) of the Navy, proposed that when the timing was right Germany should declare a "siege of England" because "such a military system would free" Germany from its promises under the Protocol. Raeder believed if a weapon is effective, then the law must be restricted, not the weapon.[31]

The Protocol also affected the pace of escalation. Germany recognized that world opinion viewed unrestricted submarine warfare as tantamount to piracy. Thus even though it was militarily desirable to shirk the Protocol, it was not possible without a political justification for doing so.[32] British attempts to protect its merchant trade were used as grounds for escalation. Even though Germany appeared to recognize that defensive arming of merchants was not technically contrary

---

[30] "Wer sich in Gefahr begibt, kommt darin um." "(Welt)propaganda."

[31] "Conference between the Chief, Naval Staff, and the Führer on 23 September 1939 in Zoppot," *Führer Conferences,* p. 9. "Denkschrift: den verschäftigten Seekrieg gegen England," in Michael Salewski, *Die deutsche Seekriegsleitung 1935–1945* (Frankfurt am Main: Bernard & Graefe, 1970), 3:73.

[32] Salewski *Die deutsche Seekriegsleitung* 1:120. Albrecht to Weizsäcker, in *NCA,* pp. 971–72.

to the submarine rules, it was felt that British actions would make U-boat escalation more acceptable to world sentiment.[33] For example, Germany delayed implement of one step in its plan to escalate the submarine war until the submarine could be made more acceptable to international opinion, particularly in the Untied States. On 23 September 1939, Hitler agreed that ships traveling without lights in the English Channel could be fired on without warning, but the command was not implemented immediately. The Foreign Ministry appealed for a four-day propaganda campaign to influence international opinion before an intensification of the submarine campaign.[34] Germany used the British order to its merchant ships to ram U-boats as an opportunity to enact its own violation of the London treaty on 2 October 1939. Two days later, the U-boats were allowed to attack without warning any British merchant that could be positively identified.[35] Thus although retaliation was involved in German decisions, it was often the pretext for, not the cause of, escalation in the U-boat war.

That the submarine regime had an effect on German decision making is indisputable. How important this influence was on policy outcomes, however, is arguable. Germany made decisions in a different manner and took actions at different time than it would have in the absence of a convention against attacking merchant ships. Yet escalation became the clear choice, despite the injunctions of the submarine regime. The only question for Nazi leaders was which approach would be the most effective: the decision was not whether, but how, to violate the submarine protocol.

The External Calculus

Realism gives an uneasy account of Germany's submarine escalation. Although Hitler's strategic aims toward Britain varied during the war, in the initial weeks so crucial to decisions on restricted warfare, he was clearly intent on pacifying Britain. Germany's U-boat force was

---

[33] A naval staff paper noted that the Protocol leaves the status of armed merchants open and the Washington and London negotiations resulted in the opinion that merchants armed for defense would remain noncombatants. The paper argued that the point was still debatable. See "Gedanken über den Einsatz der deutschen U-bootswaffe bei der Lage, wie sie am 1 September 1939 vormittags vorhanden war," RM 8/1247, BA-MA.
[34] See "Kurze Aufzeichnung über das Ergebnis der Besprechung in der Seekriegsleitung am 27.9.39," RM7/200, BA-MA.
[35] Manson, *Diplomatic Ramifications*, pp. 104–6. This move was justified by the British arming of its merchants.

not very large. This suggests that restraint was in the Third Reich's interests. Yet Germany quickly turned to escalation. Some might say that Germany initiated unrestricted submarine warfare simply because it was militarily advantageous, or because the High Command considered it inevitable and decided not to wait, or merely to respond to British actions. Although each of these interpretations offers an element of the story, none captures the central cause of what transpired.

German U-boat policy had a rich history involving balance-of-power dynamics prior to World War II that provides a necessary backdrop to the wartime decisions. In World War I Germany waited two years before launching unrestricted attacks on merchant ships even though it had not prepared for a U-boat war. The CINC of the Germany navy, Alfred von Tirpitz, would have preferred a surface engagement, yet when the Royal Navy succeeded in bottling up the High Seas Fleet, Tirpitz turned to his U-boats because "if we come to the end . . . without the fleet having bled and worked, we shall get nothing more for the fleet and all the scant money there may be will be spent on the army."[36] The results were devastating for Britain but fatal to Germany. The latter's unrestrained attacks, which also affected neutral merchant ships, precipitated U. S. entry into the war. The balance of power was irreparably altered, and Germany was defeated.

Hitler's strategy at the beginning of World War II was to avoid provoking France and Britain to allow for a settlement short of war. He figured that since they were not actively fighting back, they might be willing to end hostilities.[37] Hitting their merchant ships might push them into a corner where bloodshed was the only option.

Equally important, Hitler wished to avoid antagonizing neutral countries whose merchant ships traded with England. Having Britain as an enemy was bad enough. Provoking the United States would be a first-class disaster. Germany did not want to once again inflame U. S. animosity and opposition. When the *Athenia* was sunk in September 1939, Germany realized Britain would try to draw comparisons with the *Lusitania* incident, and Hitler responded by tightening restrictions on German U-boats.[38]

Against such formidable potential costs, Germany had to weigh the possible advantages of unrestricted submarine warfare. These resided

---

[36] May, *World War*, p. 114.

[37] See *Führer Conferences*, pp. 3–5.

[38] See "Summary of U-Boat Trade War for September 1939," RM 8/1247, BA-MA. H. L. Trefousse, *Germany and American Neutrality, 1939–1941* (New York: Octagon Books, 1969), pp. 35–42.

mainly in the number of additional sinkings that would result from being released of the burden of search and seizure rules. Germany had a geostrategic advantage in that it was not as dependent on sea trade as Britain. Britain was relatively more vulnerable to unrestricted submarine warfare. To the extent that the Third Reich could be hurt by having its sea lines of communication imperiled, Britain could and would do so largely without the help of submarines. Thus the British threat of "retaliation in kind" would impose few additional penalties on Germany.

But this argument ignores the limited potential of the U-boat force at the time. Since only one-third of the Reich's small fleet of ocean-going U-boats at the start of war could normally be on station at any one time, significant results could not be expected if Germany were to violate the submarine restrictions in the fall of 1939.[39] Even the "maximum damage" to trade that Germany could inflict would fall far short of defeating Britain, and the costs of provoking neutrals were seen as outweighing the benefits of destroying additional British ships. Furthermore, some believed that the U-boats were vulnerable to Great Britain's new submarine detection system "asdic."[40] Thus as a naval staff paper argued on the day Poland was invaded, restraint—for the time being—was the correct policy, given these tactical and strategic considerations. But this did not mean the Navy wanted to forgo escalation. It simply wanted to wait for a more opportune time—namely, when Britain began to implement its countermeasures—to drop the restrictions.[41]

In fact, during the crucial decision period, German leaders may not have explicitly weighed the costs against the projected gains. It was certainly not self-evident that escalation was the strategy of choice. For example, the State Secretary of the Foreign Ministry Ernst von Weizsäcker doubted whether the additional military damage that would come from the unrestricted warfare Raeder was pushing for— even in light of British measures—was worth the potential political negatives. The Foreign Ministry asked the Navy to provide statistics

[39] Remember that Dönitz, after all, had argued that three hundred U-boats would be needed to get the job done. See his memo to the OKM, "Gedanken über den Aufbau der U-Bootswaffe."

[40] See Dönitz, *Memoirs*, p. 12; Werner Fürbringer, "Denkschrift: Welche Entwicklungsaufgaben und welche operativen Vorbereitungen müssen heute zur Führung eines U-Boots-Handelskreises gegen England in aller erste Lini gestellt werden?" 17 May 1939, T-1022, Roll 2138, NA. Concerning asdic, see note 92.

[41] See "Gedanken über den Einsatz der deutschen U-bootswaffe." Albrecht to Weizsäcker, in *NCA*, pp. 971–72.

on this calculation and to talk further, but there is no record that the meetings took place.[42]

A second realist explanation relies on the same balance-of-power logic used to explain Germany's initial restraint. Hitler supposedly turned to unrestricted warfare against Britain only when he realized on 9 October 1939 that Britain could not be pacified and conflict was inevitable. But this interpretation does not jibe completely with Hitler's aims and strategy or with the sequence of decisions on submarine warfare during the fall of 1939. As noted, the Führer desired a settlement with Britain, a hope that resurfaced at various times throughout the war. That Hitler's choice of escalation in early October 1940 was driven by his dashed hopes for accommodation with the Allies is put in doubt by the sequence of decisions. On 6 October, Germany made a "last" peace overture to the Western democracies. By 9 October, Hitler was already planning what to do in case of a negative response, and by 12 October, Chamberlain had officially rejected the offer. Thus according to the "pacify the West" argument, before 6 October, Hitler should have desired restraint in the submarine war against Britain and France, and after 12 October restrictions should have been lifted. But this was not the case. For example, on 4 October, the U-boat arm received permission to ignore prize rules in attacks on British merchants.[43] This occurred despite an appeal by the Foreign Ministry on the previous day that an order to attack all enemy merchant vessels not be given "in consideration of the peace efforts now in progress."[44] And yet after 12 October not all restrictions were removed. It was not

[42] Memorandum, Weizsäcker to the Foreign Minister, 14 October 1939, no. 256, and memorandum, Weizsäcker, 17 October, 1939, no. 270, in *Documents on German Foreign Policy Series D (1937–1945)*, vol. 8, *The War Years, September 4, 1939–March 18, 1940* (Washington, D. C.: U. S. GPO 1954). Weizsäcker's 17 October memo notes that a scheduled meeting on this issue between the High Command of the Wehrmacht, the Foreign Ministry, and the offices related to economic warfare does not appear to have taken place, or if it did, no records of it were kept.

[43] Manson, *Diplomatic Ramifications*, pp. 98–99, 107; Anthony Martienssen, *Hitler and His Admirals* (New York: E. P. Dutton, 1949), pp. 22–24. Hinsley, *Hitler's Strategy*, pp. 34–35 and 42, says Hitler foresaw on 9 October Chamberlain's reply in the negative on 12 October 1939. Herwig, for instance, contends Hitler sought accommodation as late as June 1940 and notes that West German historian Andreas Hillgruber saw Hitler seeking accommodation as late as the Ardennes offensive in December 1944. See Holger H. Herwig, *Politics of Frustration: The United States in German Naval Planning, 1889–1941* (Boston: Little, Brown, 1976), p. 205. Hinsley, *Hitler's Strategy*, pp. 35–42. Gunther Hessler, *The U-Boat War in the Atlantic* (British Admiralty, 1950), 1:42, ADM 186/802, Public Record Office, Kew, England (hereafter PRO).

[44] Memorandum, Woermann, the director of the Political Department of the German Foreign Office, to Admiral Schniewind, chief of the Naval War Staff, 3 October 1939, no. 187, in *Documents on German Foreign Policy*, 8:203–4.

until 10 November that British passenger ships could be sunk without warning.[45]

The final explanation from the realist perspective is that Germany was merely responding to British violations. Strategic interaction is central to this analysis; however, it seems that England's operations were more a pretext for than a cause of Germany's escalation. Undoubtedly, British actions made the Navy's argument for unrestricted attacks stronger, but Raeder and Dönitz were pressing their case before the British counter measures were even enacted, which raises the question, would Germany have escalated if the Royal Navy had not ordered merchant vessels to ram U-boats? I think so. It is likely that some excuse would have always been found—the British blockade is illegal, air attacks on submarines are too dangerous, and so on—to allow the U-boats to carry out the tasks they had learned. Furthermore, given Germany's strategic aim of pacifying Britain and the limited U-boat forces available (insufficient to halt British trade or troop movements to France), responding in a tit-for-tat fashion to British attempts to protect its merchant force lacked strategic sense. To understand this escalation, we must look at the beliefs and actions of the Navy.

Organizational Culture

The power of the organizational culture of the German navy to influence Germany's decision to initiate unlimited submarine warfare appears limited for two reasons. Both reasons are incorrect. First, Hitler is generally believed to have dominated military decision making, allowing little room for the preferences of the armed forces. Unlike other leaders he did not set grand policy goals and leave military affairs to generals and admirals. He often took an interest in, and maintained control of, day-to-day operations.[46] Perhaps, yet rarely does one individual's preferences and idiosyncracies determine *all* state behavior, even in a dictatorship. If this were the case, we would be acutely interested in such personality traits as Hitler's inability to swim and his "panicky fear" of water and sailing. We might even suspect that such a person might intuitively sympathize with the plight of unarmed civilians being drowned by a surprise submarine attack. Yet Hitler ap-

[45] "Report of the Commander in Chief, Navy, to the Führer on 10 November 1939," in *Führer Conferences*, p. 37.
[46] This, of course, was much less true in naval affairs than for the Army's plans and operations.

proved such attacks.[47] Despite the Führer's unquestionable power, the Navy was able to influence substantially choices concerning submarine rules.

Second, the U-boat arm did not officially exist from 1919 to 1935, and thus its culture could not have been that important. Indeed, for most of the 1920s and 1930s the submarine played a minor role in naval debates. Thus the U-boat force's organizational creed should have been, in effect, a clean slate. But as we will see, it was not. Given the experience in World War I, the strategic situation, and the leadership of Karl Dönitz, commerce raiding became a pillar of the U-boat doctrine by the start of war and allowed Dönitz's aggressive U-boat men to play an important role.[48] A brief overview of this evolution is in order.

The official doctrine of the Navy in the interwar period up to the mid-1930s was that of Admiral Tirpitz. Tirpitz was the founder of the modern German navy and developed a considerable fleet in the late nineteenth and early twentieth century. Influenced by Mahan, he favored a battleship force, one that could take on the hegemon of the sea, the Royal Navy, in a decisive engagement. Although Tirpitz retired after World War I, his philosophy persisted. When Eric Raeder was appointed to CINC of the Navy in 1928, he quickly adopted Tirpitz's outlook. Although Raeder may have been a personal follower of Tirpitz, his main reason for doing so appears to be instrumental. He needed an ideology around which the postwar Navy could be unified and strengthened. Tirpitz's emphasis on a world-class battleship fleet that would make Germany a world power was exactly the right kind of theme for institutional empire building; however, this worldview allowed the U-boat only a secondary role. Raeder discouraged an open assessment of the U-boat in World War I and its potential in the future

[47] Herwig, *Politics of Frustration*, p. 188. This case provides an interesting contrast with German chemical warfare policy. Some maintain that because Hitler was gassed in World War I, he (and Germany) did not use poison chemicals in World War II. Obviously this type of individual-level analysis, based on Hitler's personal experience and fears, cannot account for both outcomes.

[48] Carl-Axel Gemzell, *Organization, Conflict, and Innovation: A Study of German Naval Strategic Planning, 1888–1940*, Lund Studies in International History 4 (Stockholm: Scandinavian University Books, 1973), p. 289; and Michael Salewski, "The Submarine War: A Historical Essay," in Lothar Gunther Buchheim, *The U-Boat War* (New York: Knopf, 1978). Allison W. Saville, "The Development of the German U-Boat Arm, 1919–1935" (Ph.D. diss., University of Washington, 1963), chronicles the covert development of the submarine arm from 1919–1935.

to bolster the Tirpitzian creed in order to foster the Navy's cohesion and sense of purpose.[49]

Nonetheless, the submarine society of the German navy was a vibrant one. Forced underground by the Versailles treaty, the U-boat arm endured and even developed in the interwar years to a degree not seen in the "legal" submarine forces of either Britain or the United States. Germany's success against British trade in World War I had created a cult of believers in the undersea boat. Some writers openly criticized the Tirpitzian philosophy and Germany's hesitant conduct of its submarine campaign in World War I. As early as 1921, torpedo-boat exercises may have been used to work on U-boat tactics. In 1926–27, eight out of ten of the annual winter studies were on the U-boat. German sailors and technicians developed technical aspects of submarine production covertly, often in other countries. The building plan of 1932 included sixteen boats, a number enlarged to seventy-two by 1934.[50]

Despite the Versailles treaty, the submarine arm maintained a unique and distinct character. It attracted many ambitious and talented officers. The leadership of the reborn force came from the ranks of World War I submariners, thus insuring institutional memory of the prior unrestricted war. Dönitz himself claims to have stuck with the submarine forces in its dark years because he was captivated by its distinct camaraderie. As commander of U-boats, he purposely fostered a belief in the effectiveness of submarines. He told his men that the Navy was the cream of the armed forces and U-boats the cream of the Navy.[51]

German thinking on submarine warfare was also influenced by the external world that realism would emphasize. Particularly relevant was the nature of the expected opponent. In the first part of the interwar period, France and Russia were considered the most likely adversaries. This presented the Navy with a strategic situation different from that of World War I—these two countries were not dependent on sea trade

[49] And, of course, U-Boats were outlawed by the Versailles treaty and therefore were very controversial. Holger H. Herwig, "The Failure of German Sea Power, 1914–1945: Mahan, Tirpitz, and Raeder Reconsidered," *International History Review* 10 (February 1988): 70–73. Keith W. Bird, "The Origins and Role of German Naval History in the Inter-War Period 1918–1939," *Naval War College Review* 32 (March–April, 1979): 42–58.

[50] See Phillip K. Lundeberg, "The German Naval Critique of the U-Boat Campaign, 1915–1918," *Military Affairs* 27 (fall 1963): esp. 113 and note 51. Padfield, *Dönitz*, p. 101. Saville, "Development," pp. 230–40. Eberhard Rössler, *The U-boat: The Evolution and Technical History of German Submarines* (Annapolis, Md.: Naval Institute Press, 1981), and "U-Boat Construction, 1920–1935," D-851, in *NCA*, pp. 977–978. Gemzell, *Organization, Conflict, and Innovation*, p. 289.

[51] Terrence Robertson, *Night Raider of the Atlantic* (New York: E. P. Dutton, 1956), p. 16. Dönitz, *Ten Years*, pp. 5, 12–13.

and thus less vulnerable to unrestricted warfare against merchants. The best use of the submarine, especially given its slower speed, was believed to be reconnaissance, mining, and attacks on the enemy outside his harbor.[52] The switch in German strategy from direct engagement to commerce raiding came with a change in the anticipated foe. After planning for a war against Poland, France, and/or Russia for most of the interwar period, Hitler announced to his top command in November 1937 that Britain would ultimately have to be confronted, although probably not until 1944 or 1945.[53] Although Dönitz may have been unaware of this meeting, two weeks later, on 23 November, he issued a report that favored the strategy of commerce raiding. Citing the example of World War I, Dönitz concluded that the U-boat was suitable for threatening enemy trade. He further postulated that attacking enemy sea line-of-communication was the best means of offense and under certain conditions could be "war decisive."[54]

Although the shift in external opponents did allow the U-boat to move to center stage earlier, this change alone is not enough to account for the large role it played in German decisions. The balance of power does not exclusively define internal culture. The preexisting orientation of the U-boatmen was a necessary condition: had the antitrade submarine culture not existed, Germany likely would not have pursued escalation, or at least not as early as it did. One can speculate about what would have happened had the U-boats been a standard battleship-support force. The Reichsmarine may well have lacked the plans, skills, and equipment—not to mention the conceptual horizons—to make an unrestricted trade war a worthwhile option. Any transition to an antitrade strategy under such conditions would have taken considerable effort and time, if it had even been seen as feasible.

In Germany, the full transition to an antitrade strategy was marked by the Navy's strategic review of 1938, chaired by Vice Admiral Günther Guse and authored by Captain Hellmuth Heye, which provided the basis in 1939 for the Reich's five-year building plan also known as the "Z-plan." The odd part of the plan was that even though British commerce was to be the main target, the German surface fleet was to continue to be the primary means of attack. More submarines would be built (some 249), but Heye mistakenly believed that the U-boat—

---

[52] Memorandum, Dönitz, "Vergleicher Bericht über das 712t und 500t U-Boot," 1936, RM 6/32, BA-MA. Memorandum "Grundsätze für den Einsatz U-Boote," October 26, 1936, RM 6/32, BA-MA.

[53] Martienssen, *Hitler and His Admirals*, p. 11.

[54] Padfield, *Dönitz*, pp. 158–60.

especially in light of Britain's asdic and treaty restrictions—would have a fairly limited impact. Instead, battleships would punch holes in the British blockade and cruisers and airpower would knock out the British merchants. The assumption of this strategy was that Britain would have to be confronted as the enemy, but not for five years.[55]

Although some were pessimistic about the U-boat's potential, Karl Dönitz was not. He argued that asdic would not make the submarine obsolete and that his "wolf-pack" tactics of sending groups of submarines after targets, especially merchants in convoys, would be lethal. Dönitz's enthusiasm to establish the worth of his U-boats biased the very exercises intended to test U-boat utility. He established conditions unrealistically favorable to the U-boat and drew positive conclusions from ambiguous results. Dönitz later used these exercises to argue that the submarine should be the backbone of the Navy's trade war against Britain.[56]

The U-boat chief sought to infuse his sailors with a sense of confidence that their task was not insurmountable. He did this by building discipline and offensive spirit.[57] After receiving a report that three U-boats were on the tail of a convoy of ships Dönitz wrote in his diary on 15 September 1939, "They may have luck. I have hammered it into Commanders again and again they must not let such chances pass."[58] The U-boat culture, confident in an offensive antitrade strategy, would affect both inadvertent outcomes and intentional decisions during the war.

At the start of hostilities, Germany's oceangoing U-boats had already taken up action stations around the British Isles. In case Britain entered the war, the submarines were posed to strike. Nonetheless, they had gone to sea with strict directions to adhere to the rules of prize warfare and on the afternoon of 3 September 1939 Dönitz reminded his captains via wire of that order.[59] One of the submarines was Joseph Lemp's U-30 on patrol 250 miles northwest of Ireland. On the evening of 3 September, the day Britain declared war, Lemp located a potential tar-

---

[55] Draft memorandum by Captain Hellmuth Heye, "Seekriegführung gegen England," 25 October 1938, RM 29/884, BA-MA. Also see Cajus Bekker, *Hitler's Naval War* (Garden City, N. Y.: Doubleday, 1974), pp. 28–34; Herwig, *Politics of Frustration*, pp. 192–93; Gemzill, *Organization, Conflict, and Innovation*, p. 284; and Padfield, *Dönitz*, pp. 166–69.

[56] Memorandum, Dönitz to Konteradmiral Schneiwind, 23 May 1939, T-1022, Roll 2138, NA; Dönitz to OKM, "Gedanken über den Aufbau der U-Bootswaffe." Padfield, *Dönitz*, pp. 176–80.

[57] Dönitz, *Memoirs*, p. 13.

[58] Dönitz, Kriegstagebuch, 15 September 1939, RM 87/3, BA-MA.

[59] Oberkommando des Kriegsmarine, "Chronik des Seekriegs: Heft I (1939 and 1940)," Berlin, PG 32610B, Roll 4078, NA.

get and identified it as enemy. The vessel was indeed British, but it was the passenger linear *Athenia*. The crew aboard the *Athenia* knew that the war had begun, but they did not worry about U-boat attack because they believed the ship was protected by the London Protocol.[60] Lemp's U-30, however, spit out two torpedoes that burst the vessel; 1088 passengers reached the lifeboats, but 112 drowned. The sinking of the *Athenia* started off a spiral of mistrust and retaliation that contributed to the unraveling of the interwar submarine regime.[61]

How can this incident be explained? No doubt some of the blame can be attributed to the "fog of war." The young captain Lemp was probably tense in the face of possible enemy contact and not thinking as clearly as he might have been. It is unlikely that he purposely blasted the passenger liner. Since accidents are inherently undesired and more likely in times of tension and confusion, it is difficult to "falsify" Clausewitz's friction thesis. Maybe Lemp just made a mistake. But simply to blame "operator error" is to mistake human presence with human fault.[62] We must ask if there was evidence to suggest that factors other than pure chance under complexity were at work, whether certain predilections tended to push randomness in regular directions.

The environment of combat that evening was not particularly suited to "friction" in the form of Lemp's misidentification. Although Clausewitz had much more in mind than the weather, the analogy of "fog" does not fit.[63] That particular night was clear, making misidentification unlikely. Nonetheless, Lemp claimed that he thought the *Athenia* was an auxiliary cruiser because it was zig-zagging and showing no lights. Neither of these observations was true. Furthermore, Lemp's U-boat closed to such a short distance that it could not have easily missed the outline of the lifeboats and the lack of guns that marked the ship as a passenger liner.[64] Nor did Lemp misunderstand his orders. Hitler's strong interest in restraint was clearly communi-

[60] Edwin P. Hoyt, *Death of the U-Boats* (New York: McGraw-Hill, 1988), pp. 15–16.

[61] Britain, claiming that Germany had broken the submarine restraints, began to convoy her merchant ships. At Dönitz's Nuremburg trial, his lawyer claimed that Britain falsely disseminated through Reuters on 9 September 1939 that Germany had begun unrestricted submarine warfare. IMT 18:322.

[62] On the problems of attributing accidents to individuals, see Perrow, *Normal Accidents*, pp. 9, 23–30, 330–31, 339 (see Chap. 1, n. 26).

[63] Clausewitz, *On War*, p. 120, writes, "One [source of friction], for example, is the weather. Fog can prevent the enemy from being seen in time, a gun from firing when it should, a report from reaching the commanding officer. Rain can prevent a battalion from arriving, make another late by keeping it not three, but eight hours on the march, ruin a cavalry charge by bogging the horses down in mud, etc." (see Chap. 1, n. 25).

[64] Manson, *Diplomatic Ramifications*, pp. 64–66 and note 44. Padfield, *Dönitz*, p. 191.

cated to the U-boat commanders both when they went to sea and at the beginning of the war.[65]

Finally, there were no incentives to escalate. The Nazi submarines were not at risk by avoiding attacks on noncombatants (which they were ordered to do by the highest authorities) and would still be able to disrupt British trade if they decided to do so at a later time.[66] In Lemp's particular case there is no evidence that he thought the *Athenia* had detected his U-boat. In short, the incident cannot be explained from the realist perspective.

From an organizational-culture perspective, however, the *Athenia* incident is less puzzling. Lemp simply was zealously implementing his training.[67] Germany's "sea wolves" were first and foremost taught to let no opportunity to attack pass. U-boat mariners were not well-trained to differentiate one target from another.[68] Lemp had no reason to attack except the cultural preference for unrestricted commerce warfare that distinguished the U-boat force. This incident might be considered unforeseeable and unintentional. Although the episode certainly has an inadvertent element, it cannot be deemed entirely accidental in light of the creed of the U-boatmen.

When news of the *Athenia's* destruction reached Germany on the day that war was declared, Hitler and Raeder were convinced that it could not have been caused by a German U-boat. After all, German submarines had strict orders to operate under prize rules. Only Dön-

[65] The orders were laid out to the commanders as they put to sea in August, and Dönitz reminded his captains of that order by wire 3 September 1939. See note 16.

[66] They were however more vulnerable by following the rules than by not doing so, but restraint was central to Hitler's grand strategy. And certainly with immediate unrestricted warfare, the U-boats could have scored a few easier kills right at the beginning before Britain could organize its convoys and defensive measures. But no significant strategic advantage was expected from such action.

[67] Later in September one naval staff member advocated giving submarines permission to sink darkened ships without any warning. Due to the "political situation"—that is, the possibility of another *Athenia* or *Lusitania* incident—this could not be approved. The suggestion was made that the Navy leadership give its "silent approval" to attack freely darkened ships in areas where only British vessels operated. The one condition was that the submarines had to claim in their war diaries that any sunken merchants had been mistaken for warships! This is what Lemp claimed and what Padfield, *Dönitz*, p. 193, says was official Navy policy in such situations. See "Forderungen des B. d. U. und militärische Möglichkeiten der Durchführung," 22 September 1939, RM 7/844, BA-MA. Dönitz and Wagner testified at Nuremburg that this memo was written by a staff officer and the Navy never forwarded such an order.

[68] Which is why U-boat captains had to be given special instructions summarized on circular slide-rules explaining the procedures they were to follow in order to avoid violating the rules of submarine warfare. See Fregattenkapitan Hessler's testimony in *IMT*, 13:528. Padfield, *Dönitz*, p. 196.

itz, the trainer of the "sea wolves" realized that it may very well have been one of his captains that destroyed the passenger liner.[69] The creed of the U-boat force had made such an "accident" likely.

Germany's explicit decision to disregard the restrictions of the use of submarines also originated in the Navy's preferences and influence. From the beginning, the Reichsmarine had pushed for a decisive war with Britain. This strategic agenda was quite different from Hitler's initial plan, which favored accommodation. With the outbreak of war in September, Raeder became an enthusiastic supporter of the U-boat.[70] No civilian intervened to force Raeder to see the light. Hitler, in fact, favored battleships at this time, but surface ships took a long time to build and the blockade by the powerful British fleet restricted their effectiveness. The submarine appeared to provide the most promising vehicle for action against Britain. Pressure from *within* the Navy— Dönitz's advocacy of his U-boats in an antitrade role—made sure this option was appreciated. In almost every meeting Raeder had with Hitler in the fall of 1939, he pushed him both to build U-boats and to loosen war-fighting restraints.[71]

Raeder made his case on two grounds. First, the British had armed their merchant vessels and ordered them to report submarine sightings and ram surfaced U-boats, measures which threatened the U-boat fleet. Second, and perhaps more important, Dönitz's submarines were returning to port brimming with news of successful missions, while at the same time complaining that the prize laws limited their effectiveness. As it turned out, the successes were exaggerated—not as many ships had been sunk as claimed—but Dönitz used the figures uncritically to bolster his case.[72] He told Hitler in person on 28 September that "in the U-boat we have, and always have had, a weapon capable of dealing Britain a mortal blow at her most vulnerable spot"—but

[69] Martienssen, *Hitler and His Admirals*, p. 23.

[70] In 1936 Raeder also urged the construction of U-boats noting, "The military and political situation urgently demands that the extension of our U-boat fleet should be taken in hand immediately and completed with the greatest energy and dispatch, as it is a particularly valuable part of our armament at sea and possesses special striking powers." See memorandum, Raeder, "U-Boat Construction," 11 November 1936, D-806 in *NCA*, p. 954.

[71] Dönitz to OKM, "Gedänken über den Aufbau der U-Bootswaffe." "Conference in Zoppot," in *Führer Conferences*, p. 10.

[72] See Kapitänleutnant von Dresky, "Kriegstagebuch des Unterseebootes 'U33'," 19.8.1939–28.9.1939, NA, and Kapitänleutnant Rollman, "Kriegstagebuch des Unterseebootes 'U34'," 19.8.1939–26.9.1939, NA; Hoyt, *Death of the U-Boats*, p. 24; Assmann, "Why U-Boat Warfare Failed," p. 665.

more boats would be needed.[73] The naval leaders were quick to support their case with their own successes, even if overstated, while at the same time pointing out British transgressions of the rules. Raeder was able to convince Hitler bit-by-bit to rescind the submarine restrictions.

One example of this phenomenon comes from the daring raid by Gunther Prien—"The Bull of Scapa Flow." Prien slipped his U-boat into one of the Royal Navy's safe home harbors and sank the battleship Royal Oak. Raeder flew Prien to Berlin on his return to be decorated by Hitler personally on 16 October. It was at that time that Hitler gave Raeder permission to escalate the U-boat war. Any passenger vessels in convoys or without lights could now be torpedoed without warning. Prien's raid in terms of enemy losses was psychologically important, but operationally only a moderate success. It certainly did not demonstrate that U-boats could win the war at sea, but the short-term surge of promise it provided helped Raeder to persuade Hitler to remove restrictions.[74]

Even before permission had been granted by Germany's political leadership, the Navy readied itself for unrestricted submarine warfare. On 20 September 1939, without discussing the matter with Hitler, Raeder directed his staff to consider and "mentally" prepare for unrestricted U-boat attacks.[75]

Hitler only partially fulfilled Raeder's requests. The Führer could not provide the U-boats the Navy wanted because of resource constraints. He was obsessed by the land campaign and the army was given priority in terms of raw materials and labor. Still, given his uncertainty concerning Britain, and the Navy's pressure, Hitler could and did drop one or two restrictions at a time.[76]

Conclusion: A Short-Lived Cooperation

The German decision for restraint was fleeting. To the extent the Protocol was heeded, the Nazis did so largely out of broader balance-of-power considerations. Hitler prohibited unrestricted U-boat attacks in order to avoid provoking France, England, and the United States. He hoped that a peace settlement could be reached, especially with

---

[73] Dönitz, *Memoirs*, p. 123.

[74] Salewski, *Die Deutsche Seekriegsleitung*, pp. 123–24; Padfield, *Dönitz*, p. 202.

[75] Summary of U-Boot trade war for September [1939], RM 8/1247, BA-MA. Also see note 67.

[76] Rössler, *U-boat*, pp. 124–25. Gemzell, *Organization, Conflict, and Innovation*, p. 368.

Britain. This choice recognized the linkage between the tactical and strategic levels of conflict. Germany's tactical use of the submarine had much broader implications than merely triggering reciprocal British use. It also affected how Britain (and it allies) viewed Germany's intentions and Germany's threat to British (and Allied) national interests. For example, the Germans hoped that restraining their submarine attacks would send a signal to the British that a settlement was desired. Hitler wanted to avoid pushing the British populace into demanding German blood. Hitler also wanted to avoid threatening a declared U.S. interest in "freedom of the seas." Balance-of-power considerations largely explain why orders forbidding attacks on American merchant shipping remained in effect outside of war zones until the United States joined the war in December 1941. In the case of U-boat warfare, lower-level naval operations were integrally linked to higher-level political-strategic considerations.

In the war against Britain, however, the organizational culture of the Reichsmarine turned Clausewitz on his head: tactical military considerations shaped strategic political goals. Assmann claimed after the war that the Navy always recognized the primacy of policy.[77] But the Navy's influence at all levels of decision making in sea warfare undermined this primacy. The Reichmarine's focus on proving its worth, narrowly calculating the relative *naval* advantage to be derived through unrestricted submarine warfare, replaced the overriding aim not to incite the potential enemies of the Reich. The Navy argued that the restrictions robbed them of victories.[78] In terms of the number of enemy ships sunk this was certainly true; however, in terms of the number of countries that Germany expected to face as enemies, it was not. In the fall of 1939, Raeder went so far as to contend that Germany's U-boats must sink American ships without heeding the submarine rules even though it would risk war with the United States. The Naval Staff actually welcomed U.S. entry into the war because it meant more targets and fewer restrictions.[79] Organizational culture was not overly

---

[77] Assmann, "Why U-Boat Warfare Failed," p. 659.

[78] Submariners returned from patrols protesting restraints as inhibiting and dangerous. See von Dresky, "Kriegstagebuch des Unterseebootes 'U33'," and Rollman, "Kriegstagebuch des Unterseebootes 'U34'"; Hoyt, *Death of the U-Boats*, p. 24.

[79] Herwig, *Politics of Frustration*, p. 197. Herwig also notes that, "Hitler and his admirals from the very beginning found themselves committed to diametrically opposed concepts of the war in the West" (198). Manson, *Diplomatic Ramifications*, p. 124.

sensitive to balance-of-power considerations. That is why, in the fall of 1939, the unrestricted U-boat offensive against Britain was unleashed.

The Restraint of His Majesty's Submarines

Britain's approach to submarine warfare was single-minded in one respect; the existence of the underwater boat was considered detrimental to British interests. As an island national dependent on trade and defended by a large surface fleet, submarines could only be injurious to the United Kingdom. Therefore, throughout the interwar period, British statesmen energetically promoted prohibition of, or restrictions on, submarines. Although relentless in its diplomatic opposition to the submarine, Britain was decidedly equivocal in its policy on the uses of, and defense against, the underwater boat. Employment policy faithfully respected restraint, whereas defensive policy favored escalation. Offensively, the Navy saw very limited possibilities for employing the submarine and adopted a meticulous policy of restricted submarine warfare.[80] Even when the strategic situation in the 1920s and 1930s suggested that the submarine could play a significant role, this contribution was overlooked. And in war, after Germany had already transgressed the submarine rules, Britain continued to maintain restraint, despite the sacrifice of military gains.

Britain's planned defense against the enemy's underwater offensive, however, was not consistent with a policy of restraint. The United Kingdom implemented a variety of measures aimed at protecting its merchant ships against German attacks—whether they were legal or not. Even though Britain's leaders realized that the result could be unrestricted war, the defensive measures were adopted anyway. Why did Britain intentionally choose a policy that could lead to the type of unrestricted warfare it most wanted to avoid? And when Germany did violate the submarine rules, why did Britain then continue to forego possible military gains by exercising restraint?

Realism offers a reasonable explanation for why Britain adopted defensive measures that risked escalation of submarine warfare. Britain calculated that it had the capability to withstand even unrestricted German U-boat attacks. Where realism falls short is that this calculation itself was fundamentally unrealistic. Furthermore, there was no shortage of information indicating the problems of the plans. Institu-

---

[80] The Royal Navy did not consider using the submarine to blockade Germany because it fully expected to assume command of the seas with its surface fleet.

tionalism helps to account for why Britain initially showed restraint. England wanted to avoid offending neutrals that valued the rules. Neither realism nor institutionalism can explain, however, why Britain maintained restraint even after Germany had violated the rules and when military gains could have been achieved by unrestricted attacks. In this case, then, organizational culture provides the decisive link: it explains why Britain both overestimated its defensive capabilities and underestimated the gains to be had from retaliating in kind.

A Realist Account

If realism is to clarify Britain's submarine policy, it must answer why Britain exercised offensive restraint but pursued an active defense that created escalation pressures. How could both policies, given their contradictory consequences, be considered a rational reaction to external circumstances?

The British calculation was not so much one of relative capabilities, but one of relative vulnerabilities.[81] The submarine threatened British power two ways. First, the underwater boat was a challenge to the Royal Navy's strong surface fleet. In the early nineteenth century, Prime Minister William Pitt had supported the idea of the submarine. When inventor Robert Fulton demonstrated the effect of an underwater charge to the First Lord of the Admiralty Lord St. Vincent in 1805, the latter commented, "Pitt was the greatest fool that ever existed to encourage a mode of war which those who commanded the seas did not want, and which if successful, would deprive them of it."[82] Britain's leaders felt the same way in the interwar period and they wanted to return to the days when the submarine was not a threat.

Second, as an island-centered empire, Britain's sea lines of communication were put at risk. These lines supplied vital materials to the economy and food to the population. The submarine could attack those lifelines and threaten national existence. Many of Britain's immediate potential opponents—Germany, the United States, and France—

---

[81] In fact, the United Kingdom could have been a submarine hegemon. At the end of World War I, Britain had the largest submarine fleet, totaling 138 boats. Yet a mere two years later, this fleet had already shrunk to 51 boats. In 1939 Britain had rough parity with Germany in underwater forces, thus indicating no strong incentive either for or against restraint. Naval Staff History, Second World War, *Submarines*, vol. 1, *Operations in Home, Northern, and Atlantic Waters* (Historical Section Admiralty, 1953), pp. 3–4, BR1736(52)1, Admiralty Naval Historical Branch, London.

[82] Quoted in John Terraine, *Business in Great Waters: The U-Boat Wars, 1916–1945* (London: Leo Cooper, 1989), p. 145.

were not as vexed by this problem. Britain was asymmetrically vulnerable to the underwater boat. As early as 1918, the British naval staff had concluded that the submarine was antithetical to Britain's interests.[83] It is not surprising that Britain consistently advocated abolishing the submarine outright. Having failed to ban the submarine, Britain did what it could to restrict its use against trading vessels.

The focus of the United Kingdom on vulnerabilities and not capabilities manifested itself in several areas. First and foremost, this tendency was evident in the development of submarines. Although overall naval policy was guided by the "one-power standard," intended to ensure a fleet as large as that of any other single country, few efforts were made to match the submarine-building programs of other states. Britain was especially reluctant to build the cruiser submarines suited for attacking commercial vessels. The Royal Navy believed that submarine attacks on trade were only necessary in areas where the enemy had surface control of the ocean. Since the Admiralty expected to retain its traditional command of the seas, it saw little sense in a commerce raider, particularly in light of economic constraints. Furthermore, the Royal Navy wanted to avoid implicitly advocating a weapon they saw as disadvantageous by procuring it. As Britain was a leading power, it was especially likely that other countries might emulate its armaments program.[84]

This logic, taken in the context of World War II and hostilities with Germany, is clear and rational. But it seems less clear and less rational, however, when we recall that during much of the interwar period the Royal Navy expected that it would eventually have to fight not Germany but Japan. Like Britain, Japan was an island nation, largely dependent on trade. As Germany had demonstrated during World War I, such countries were vulnerable to antitrade submarine warfare. Britain

---

[83] "The condition which would most surely guard our naval security in the future would be the surrender of the whole of Germany's submarine fleet and an international agreement that no power was to build that class of vessel in the future." "Discussion of Draft Terms of Peace with Germany," Naval Staff, 10 November 1918, ADM 116/1861, as cited in David Henry, "British Submarine Development and Policy, 1918–1939" (Ph.D. diss., War Studies, Kings College, University of London, 1976). (All documents cited as ADM are found in the Admiralty Files located at the PRO.)

[84] Henry, "British Submarine Development," pp. 99, 334–35. A 1924 Admiralty report noted that the number of submarines needed did not depend on the number the enemy had, because fleet submarines did not fight fleet submarines and the number of cruiser and reconnaissance types depended on the number of enemy bases and distance to patrol areas. "Construction Program 1924," ADM 1/8672/230; "Functions of a Cruiser Submarine or Submersible," February 1925, ADM 1/8403/158.

realized it would have a difficult time gaining command of the sea in the Pacific, at least until its main fleet arrived. And if an opponent had to be faced at the same time in home waters, Hong Kong and Singapore could expect little help against possible Japanese aggression. According to its own logic, the Royal Navy should have acquired submarines for this mission. In fact, Britain did keep one flotilla of submarines constantly on station in Asia. But these boats were to function only as a "strategic holding force" until the fleet arrived. The British gave very little attention to using submarines against commerce and never developed an underwater vessel with sufficient range to conduct effective commerce raiding in the Pacific.[85]

Realism seems particularly well suited for accounting for Britain's plans to defend its shipping against German submarine attack even though the plans were recognized as likely to provoke escalation. The British believed that the Royal Navy had the advantage over the German U-boat. As discussed below, opinions varied on whether, and how long, Germany would show restraint. Amidst this uncertainty, there was a stronger faith that unilateral defensive measures—even if they provoked escalation—would stem an unrestricted U-boat onslaught. From this viewpoint, the decision was simply one of relative advantage.

British confidence that it could largely master a German submarine challenge with unilateral measures is evident in its prewar planning. In 1937 the Shipping Defence Advisory Committee was formed to manage preparations for the protection of Britain's merchant vessels. At the very first meeting, First Sea Lord Admiral Chatfield announced that the submarine menace, "will never be, in my opinion and the opinion of the Navy, what it was before. We have means of countering a submarine which are effective and which will reduce our losses from that weapon. It will never to my mind be a fatal menace again as it was in the last war."[86] The measures Chatfield was referring to included the defensive arming of merchants, a policy of active resistance, and enhanced protection for convoys of trading vessels.[87]

---

[85] Henry, "British Submarine Development," pp. 190, 319, 357–58, 422–23. In the run-up to the 1935 naval talks, the Navy's director of plans argued that smaller submarine limits should be accepted to protect British trade, even though larger boats would be useful against Japan. "Proposed Submarine Policy for 1935 Naval Conference," Director of Plans, 23 February 1934, ADM 1/9728.

[86] "Shipping Defence Advisory Committee—1st Meeting," 10 March 1937, ADM 116/3635.

[87] Among other activities related to wartime policy for commercial shipping, the Shipping Defence Advisory Committee produced a guidebook *The Defence of Merchant Shipping* for shipowners. This manual indicated that British merchants would be required

One big issue for Britain was the point at which it would arm its merchants. Traditional policy was to wait until the enemy's tactics were evident. This would avoid providing Germany a justification for disobeying international law. But in 1938 it was decided to begin defensive arming at the start of war. Britain's leaders reasoned that an enemy could wage unrestricted warfare immediately, but arming merchants would take six to twelve months. Thus even though escalation might not occur immediately, Britain opted for readiness. In essence, the United Kingdom weighed the costs of not being prepared as greater than the advantages of avoiding provoking escalation. In fact, as a clash with Germany appeared more likely in June and July 1939, the Admiralty approved the immediate arming of vessels on certain routes (such as to South America). It was decided that the "defensive" arming of ships was within the bounds of international law.[88]

Perhaps more important than arming the ships, the Government also commanded that they should resist attack or capture whether legal or not, if there was opportunity of escape. The First Lord of the Admiralty—Winston Churchill—acknowledged that this policy might give Germany an excuse to turn to unrestricted warfare.[89] The London Protocol itself allowed merchant ships to be sunk if they persistently refused to stop or resisted search and seizure. The Navy considered announcing that the merchants would not use their weapons unless the Germans ignored the rules. But in the end the First Lord recommended, and the Cabinet accepted, a policy of resistance. The leaders did not want to face the political consequences that might result should tonnage or lives be lost because the Government had ordered a ship not to resist. On 1 October, Britain escalated its defensive measures by ordering its commercial vessels to ram German U-boats if necessary. Britain also ordered its merchants to report the position of any U-boat encountered. Under the Protocol, however, the use of radio for the

---

to arm, radio their positions, and fight if attacked. See Martin Doughty, *Merchant Shipping and War: A Study in Defence Planning in Twentieth Century Britain* (London: Royal Historical Society, 1982).

[88] Doughty, *Merchant Shipping*, p. 53–60; Committee for Imperial Defence (CID), 1466–B, "Defence of Merchant Shipping," 27 July 1938, CAB 4/28. (All documents referred to as CAB can be found in the Cabinet Records located at the PRO.) Stephen W. Roskill, *The War at Sea, 1939–1945*, vol. 1, *The Defensive* (London: HMSO, 1954), pp. 21, 45.

[89] Despite willingness to fight, it is not clear whether Britain adopted the policy that merchants should use their guns before late November. The decision was made not to use defensive armaments until at least 75 percent of the trade vessels were armed and only 20 percent were at the time. See the correspondence in ADM 1/10584.

purposes of military intelligence revoked a merchant's protected status. Britain had earlier acknowledged the legitimacy of this revocation.[90]

A final aspect of defensive policy was to convoy merchants with armed protection. At the outbreak of war, the Admiralty assumed control of all British merchant shipping, and the plans put together by the Shipping Defence Advisory Committee were implemented. Official naval policy was that convoys would only be organized if Germany conducted unrestricted submarine warfare. Thus the initiation of convoys is commonly portrayed as a reaction to the sinking of the *Athenia* on 3 September 1939; however, the first convoy sailed from Gibraltar to Cape Town on 2 September, the day *before* Britain declared war and the *Athenia* was sunk.[91] Apparently convoying was likely regardless of how Germany employed the submarine.

Undergirding the entire defensive effort was an exaggerated faith in the device for detecting submarines known as "asdic."[92] Although it was not developed in time for use in World War I, asdic significantly affected British thinking on the submarine in the interwar period by ameliorating the perceived threat. Admiral Chatfield wrote in 1936 that the Navy's antisubmarine warfare techniques would be 80 percent successful.[93] The British Naval staff declared in 1937 that "the submarine should never again be able to present us with the problem we faced in 1917."[94] And in March 1939, Churchill assured the prime minister, Neville Chamberlain, that "the submarine has been mastered."[95]

The irony of the British faith in asdic was that the device had notable shortcomings which were dramatically exposed by the successes of the U-boats in World War II. It had a range of only 1500 yards and could not detect submarines on the surface. Since a popular U-boat tactic in

---

[90] *IMT*, 18:322. "Report of the Committee on International Law Questions Which Particularly Concern Naval Officers Afloat," 6 August 1928, ADM 116/2585.

[91] J. R. M. Butler, *Grand Strategy*, vol. 2, *September 1939–June 1941* (London: HMSO, 1957), p. 83; Morison, *History of the United States Naval Operations in World War II*, vol. 1, pp. 9–10; Henry, "British Submarine Development," p. 380. British officials recognized that the *Athenia* might be an isolated incident. See memorandum, William Malkin, Foreign Office, to Lord Seal at the Admiralty, 5 September 1939, ADM 1/10584. Terraine, *Business in Great Waters*, p. 244.

[92] During the First World War a group was formed to look into new technologies that might be applied in the war against the U-boat. This Anti-Submarine Detection Investigation Committee developed a device that could detect submarines even while the hunting ship was on the move. Known as sonar today, it was named after the committee's acronym—asdic.

[93] Roskill, *Naval Policy between the Wars*, 2:227.

[94] Stephen W. Roskill, *Naval Policy between the Wars*, vol. 1, *The Period of Anglo-American Antagonism, 1919–1929* (London: Collins, 1968), p. 34.

[95] Roskill, *Naval Policy between the Wars*, 2:456.

World War I was the night surface attack, this was a significant drawback. Furthermore, ships using asdic to search for U-boats could sweep at a maximum of ten knots under the best of weather conditions. This was clearly inadequate since submarines could use their higher surface speed to change positions before submerging to attack. The problems of asdic were revealed in exercises but never officially recognized.[96]

It is obvious from the foregoing that Britain was willing to risk escalation with its defensive actions because of its estimate of the relative effectiveness of its own capabilities. This choice is congruous with realism. What is perplexing, however, is why Britain *over*estimated its ability to defend against submarines. In fact, German submarines did inflict heavy damage on the United Kingdom with a relatively small force. Britain's flawed estimate is important because it was the cornerstone of Britain's choice on defensive measures.

Another question realism cannot convincingly answer is why British submarines continued to show restraint even after the end of October 1939, when it was fairly clear that Germany had turned to unrestricted submarine warfare.[97] There was no longer any reason for Britain to restrict it own activities. Germany was beyond being contained by the threat of retaliation in kind. Yet Britain showed restraint, despite military advantages that would have accrued otherwise. In this same period the Third Reich was shipping iron ore—a raw material critical to Germany's war industry—from Sweden and Norway. But the underwater boats were limited to observing this traffic until April 1940—some five months after Germany abandoned its observance of the Protocol.

One of the key aspects of Britain's choice of restraint was the low strategic value assigned to the submarine. The deputy chief of the Naval Staff commented in October of 1939 that "if it could be shown that it was essential for us to take full advantage of the latitude allowed by the Submarine Protocol in order to achieve some war aim, then I would say that we should have to do so but, at the present moment, I do not think this is the case."[98] Others, however, have argued that British submarines could have made a significant difference in hindering the ore shipments, in defeating the invasion of Norway, and later in the Mediterranean, in thwarting Italy's efforts in Africa and in the

[96] Roskill, *War at Sea*, 1:355; Terraine, *Business in Great Waters*, p. 178. Henry, "British Submarine Development," pp. 320–21. Simpson, *Periscope View*, pp. 49, 57–58, 75.

[97] "Monthly Anti-Submarine Report," Trade Division, October 1939, ADM 199/878, notes, "The method of the U-boat has in this month had a radical change. No longer are courtesy and chivalry being shown to merchant vessels."

[98] Minute 08070/39, Deputy Chief of the Naval Staff, 25 October 1939, ADM 199/878.

war in general.[99] In fact, if the British had appreciated the military value of the submarine, Britain's policy toward Japan and decisions on defensive measures might also have been different. But the submarine's potential was consistently overlooked. In light of the information available concerning the effectiveness of trade warfare and the short-comings of asdic, realism cannot explain this systematic error. Institutionalism and organizational culture offer different rationales for this oversight.

Sea Lords and Sea Laws

As I have shown, neither the London Protocol nor related aspects of international law kept Britain from taking defensive measures that were illegal in spirit and often letter. But the submarines of the Royal Navy did show restraint in the offense, which raises the question, Did the submarine conventions influence this outcome? The answer to this question seems to be that the submarine rules *did* play a role, albeit a circumscribed one, in both Britain's interwar policy and its wartime decisions.

If Britain had had its way at Versailles—or for that matter, at any of the interwar naval negotiations—not only Germany, but all powers would have surrendered their underwater fleets for good. Unfortunately for Britain, other countries with less capable surface fleets were not inclined to give up the underwater boat. At the Washington Conference, Britain established a pattern that it repeated for the next twenty years. It pressed for the abolition of the submarine, failed, and accepted rules restricting submarine attacks against merchants. Britain also tried to establish rules against any possibility of commerce raiding by submarines. France, Japan, Italy, and others successfully objected to this at the 1930 London Naval Conference.[100]

The effect of the rules restricting submarine warfare on a seemingly supportive Britain can be judged by their impact on national proce-

[99] See Roskill, *War at Sea*, 1:334–35; William King, *The Stick and the Stars* (New York: Norton, 1958), pp. 55–56; Hezlet, *Submarine and Seapower*, pp. 138–40; and Simpson, *Periscope View*, pp. 87–89.

[100] On Versailles, see "Discussion of Draft Terms of Peace with Germany," 18 November 1918, ADM 116/1861, as cited in Henry, "British Submarine Development," p. 191. On the Washington Conference, where Britain also proposed qualitative and quantitative limits on submarine building, see "Limitation of Naval Armaments," Naval Staff Paper, 9 October 1925, ADM 1/8683/131; "Reduction and Limitation of Armaments Policy Committee," Cabinet, 6 July 1931, ADM 116/2611; "Proposed Submarine Policy for the 1935 Naval Conference," Director of Plans, 23 February 1934, ADM 1/9728; and Henry, "British Submarine Development," p. 297.

dures, expectations, and actions. Concerning procedures, we can look to operations of the British submarine force itself. Never interested in a strategy of commerce raiding, the Royal Navy took few extra efforts to ensure that the Protocol would be followed. This was not because Britain's *Naval Prize Manual* did not record the rules—it did. In fact, the British version was even stricter than required by the London Protocol. And the Navy was certainly expected to heed the restrictions. But because commerce warfare was not even considered, it was almost taken for granted that the rules would be followed. The implementation of the prohibitions was hardly considered before mid-November 1939 when it was suggested that officers taking part in operations against merchants should be supplied with Prize manuals so that they could acquaint themselves with the rules they would have to observe. Before that time, submarines were not assigned extra sailors to act as prize crews on ships. Prize manuals were not even distributed until the end of 1939.[101] Submariners were told at the beginning of war not to attack merchants and they obeyed. But as we will see, this obedience was more a product of the Royal Navy's lack of interest in commerce raiding as a means of waging war than it was adherence to international conventions.

Concerning expectations, it seems that Britain's view of future conflict was not dramatically affected by the establishment of the submarine regime. As early as July 1922, the Admiralty concluded that the Root resolutions could not be relied on for the defense of commerce.[102] In 1938, Churchill called the rules the "acme of gullibility" and later explained that one could not expect the U-boats to sit and wait as women and children starved.[103] Aneurin Bevan attacked his Government's support of the London Protocol in Parliament by questioning whether a nation on the edge of defeat, with victory possible by violating a convention, would hesitate to violate it.[104] Many did expect, however, that Germany might delay adopting unrestricted warfare not because Germany had signed the Protocol, but because Germany lost using unrestricted submarine warfare in the First World War. Still another opinion, also based on the World War I experience, was that

[101] His Majesty's submarines could not put crews from prize ships in lifeboats at sea, it had to put them on board a ship. Memorandum, Admiralty Lords to Rear Admiral (submarines), 13 November 1939, ADM 199/878. Naval Staff History, *Submarines*, 1:8–9.

[102] "Root Resolutions in Regard to Submarine Warfare," Naval Staff, July 1922, ADM 116/3165.

[103] Winston S. Churchill, *The Second World War: The Gathering Storm* (Boston: Houghton Mifflin, 1948), p. 140.

[104] Roskill, *Naval Policy between the Wars*, 2:306–7.

Germany might escalate right away in hopes of quick victory. Even though the Third Reich had relatively few U-boats, only a small number had been needed during World War I to cause a great deal of damage.[105]

The British were less open about calculations that we might consider as compatible with realism as with institutionalism. They concluded that even if their own defensive actions provoked German escalation, Germany would probably be blamed. The rules could be made into a tool of relative advantage. As in World War I, the result might be a loss of critical neutral support for the German cause. That Britain did in fact hope for this outcome can be seen in certain decisions made just before and at the beginning of World War II.

In the summer of 1939, the commander of the submarine force, Rear Admiral B. C. Watson wanted Britain to announce danger zones around British overseas possessions where submarines could defend against invasion by attacking convoys without restrictions. The Admiralty vetoed the proposal. It was feared that if Britain initiated action, it would not be able to shift blame onto the Germans for escalation and thus would not be able to retaliate with "other measures besides a strict tit-for-tat."[106] Thus, the rules of submarine warfare—and the *appearance* of restraint—were to be used as weapons against the foe.

This dynamic was again evident in the early months of war. On 19 September, Churchill, as First Lord of the Admiralty, expressed concern over the Swedish iron ore that was being shipped to Germany from either Sweden or (in the winter) Norway.[107] Total German imports of iron ore in 1938 had been 22 million tons. The British blockade had already cut that number by nine million tons. It was estimated that another nine million were coming from Sweden.[108] In October, proposals began to circulate that submarines should be used to intercept the iron ore trade. In the winter—due to icebound Baltic ports—the iron ore was sent to Narvik and shipped through Norwegian coastal waters and across the Skagerrak and Kattegat.[109]

At the time it was becoming increasingly clear that Germany was violating the rules of submarine warfare, and Britain considered how

[105] "The Protection of Shipping at Sea," September 1936, ADM 199/2365; "Naval Appreciation (1937) of War with Germany, 1939," ADM 199/2365.

[106] Memorandum, RA(S) to Secretary of the Admiralty, "Remarks on the Use of Submarines in Defence of Territory," 3 August 1939, ADM 1/10360. Minute 07295/39, Head of the Military Branch, 21 August 1939, ADM 1/10360.

[107] Memorandum, First Lord, 19 September 1939, ADM 199/892.

[108] Roskill, *War at Sea*, 1:156.

[109] British surface ships were less useful for the task because they were too vulnerable in the Kattegat and Skagerrak and would more visibly violate Norwegian waters.

to respond.[110] Several ideas were forwarded, ranging from a looser interpretation of the London Protocol to permitting unrestricted warfare in the Baltic.[111] Churchill called the idea of unrestricted attacks on the ore traffic "of the highest importance, at the same time delicacy." He believed that reprisals should be made against Germany to a similar extent that the U-boats were making unrestricted attacks.[112] But other officials would not agree to this plan or even to relax Britain's strict interpretation of the Protocol's search and seizure rules. The central reason for this decision was concern that the goodwill that Britain was attempting to build among neutral countries would be dissipated—indicating a link to realist balance-of-power concerns. If Britain adopted measures similar to Germany's, it could no longer claim the moral high ground. The officials sensibly feared that some accident would result that would antagonize important countries such as Norway and Sweden.[113] England wanted to avoid antagonizing neutrals on one issue especially, the control of German exports. Britain had already instituted a "contraband" system to limit imports to the Third Reich. Now it wanted to do the same to the Reich's outgoing trade. To accomplish this, however, the Royal Navy had to tread lightly on the interest of neutrals because their support would be needed. Therefore, the British plan was to forego replying to Germany's breaches of the London Protocol with tit-for-tat, but to let the illegalities accumulate and respond with controls on exports.[114]

The Protocol, therefore, was an instrument of leverage, but its leverage was never exerted. Britain implemented export controls in December in response to Germany's "illegal" mining activity, not its submarine violations. Furthermore, Britain put plans (Operation Wil-

[110] Memorandum, William Malkin, Foreign Office, 24 October 1939, ADM 1/10584, notes that as of 5 October 1939, nine of thirty-one cases related to the submarine rules were violations. He called it a "formidable list of illegalities" although he was not completely sure that it indicated unrestricted submarine warfare. By the end of October, the Navy had concluded Germany was making illegal attacks. See Minute, Head of the Military Branch, October 1939, ADM 199/892.

[111] Such as allowing submarines to put the crews of enemy vessels in lifeboats instead of on other ships. Minute, Deputy Chief of the Naval Staff, P. D. 08070/39, 25 October 1939, ADM 199/878; Minute, Head of Military Branch, October 1939, ADM 199/892; Minute, Director of Plans, 3 November 1939, ADM 199/892.

[112] Memorandum, First Lord, "Home Fleet Memo about Fleet Bases, Policy as Regards Northern Patrol and Unrestricted Use of Submarines," 31 October 1939, ADM 199/892.

[113] Minute, Head of Military Branch, October 1939, ADM 199/892; Minute, Director of Plans, 3 November 1939, ADM 199/892, which was approved by the First Lord, the First Sea Lord, and the deputy chief of the Naval Staff.

[114] Minute, Deputy Chief of the Naval Staff, P. D. 08070/39, 25 October 1939, ADM 199/878; Minute, Head of Military Branch, October 1939, ADM 199/892.

fred) into motion in early April 1940 that violated Norwegian waters, but restraints on submarines were maintained.[115] Thus even though Germany conducted unrestricted warfare and neutral reaction became less of a concern, Britain did not permit escalation of submarine warfare, although it was allowed to do so according to the Protocol. The Royal Navy maintained this restraint for five months beyond the onset of German escalation—while ore shipments continued and even into the first days of the Nazi invasion of Norway in April 1940. Why did Britain continue to show restraint in the face of German transgressions and the sacrifice of military gains? To answer this question we must turn to the organization culture of the Royal Navy.

A Battleship-Bound Culture

The Royal Navy, perhaps more than any other sea power of that day, was shaped by an organizational culture dominated by the battleship. A strong surface fleet, led by the battleship, was considered requisite to world power. Even when Britain's strategic situation changed, the battleship culture did not. Within that culture, the submarine was accorded little respect. It was considered a tool of weaker powers, not of mighty Britain. Sight unseen, the submarine could strike without warning at undefended merchants and even the proud warships. Not only was it a threat to the war fleet, but the existence of the submarine demanded that warships be engaged in less dashing tasks, such as providing convoy escort, when they would otherwise be seeking battle. Submariners found little welcome in the battleship world of the Royal Navy. The chasm between the dominant battleship culture and the marginal world of submarines affected official perception of the strategic value of the submarine, the effectiveness of antisubmarine measures, the desirability of restrictions on submarines, and ultimately British decisions on restraint and escalation.

In the eyes of the Royal Navy, the surface fleet, particularly the battleship, was the touchstone of strategic thought. Victory at sea was decided first and foremost by a decisive clash of opposing battle fleets. Certainly the U-boat in World War I had caused significant (perhaps exaggerated) concerns and forced the Royal Navy to alter its Grand Fleet strategy. But despite the U-boat successes, the British were quick to reestablish the importance of the battleship in the postwar period. A "Lessons of War" committee concluded that in combat on the high seas, "the capital ship is the final arbiter, in other words, the battleship

[115] Roskill, *War at Sea*, 1:102, 156–58.

retains her old predominant position."[116] This conclusion, however, was highly subjective. As Captain (later Sir Admiral) Herbert Richmond noted in his diary, the committee "had merely made statements, assertions: had not examined the war to find out what the influence of the big ship was, or whether she was still in the position she used to be [in]. The thing i.e. the future of the battleship must be approached in a far more scientific manner."[117] But Britain's devotion to the battleship would endure through the next two decades.

It is no surprise that within such a navy, the submarine was ignored if not scorned. The reigning attitude toward the underwater boat seems not altogether different from that of the turn-of-the-century admiral who described it as "underhand, unfair, and damned unEnglish."[118] Senior officers found it difficult to accept a warship that could not take part in fleet actions. The lack of attention to submarine development was particularly acute in the area of commerce warfare. To the extent the Royal Navy saw the submarine as playing a role, it was to be an adjunct to the surface fleet by fulfilling such needs as reconnaissance and, when the expected rare opportunity presented itself, attacking warships. The Royal Navy was loath to develop a means of warfare that would just present problems for the fleet. Naval officers especially resented the substantial actions and resources needed to combat submarines, when they could have been applied to offensive tasks elsewhere. The very existence of the submarine was an inconvenience.[119]

The bias against the submarine within the Royal Navy is particularly evident in the conduct of exercises, the perception of German strategy, and evaluations of the submarine threat. Exercises are important because they are supposed to be the objective means of judging the utility of different means and methods of warfare. These exercises, however, gave submarines little chance to prove their worth. For most of the 1920s and 1930s submarines were used mainly as practice targets in

---

[116] "Final Report of the Post-War Questions Committee," 27 March 1920, ADM 1/8586, as cited in Roskill, *Naval Policy between the Wars*, 1:115. Also Terraine, *Business in Great Waters*, pp. 117–18.

[117] Diary entry for 10 November 1919, as cited in Roskill, *Naval Policy between the Wars*, 1:115–16.

[118] Ibid., 2:231.

[119] In the words of Admiral Sir Frederick L. Field, First Sea Lord, it "hampers enormously every operation in any area in which it may be found." See "Reduction and Limitation of Armaments Policy Committee," Cabinet, 6 July 1931, ADM 116/2611. Henry, "British Submarine Development," p. 416. "Construction Program 1924," ADM 1/8672/230; Hezlet, *Submarine and Seapower*, pp. 122–23; Roskill, *War at Sea*, 1:355. Roskill, *Naval Policy between the Wars*, 1:536.

antisubmarine warfare drills. To the extent the submarines took part in an offensive maneuver, warships were always the target. And even these exercises were prejudiced against the underwater boat. Sometimes the submarines were put at unfair disadvantage; when victorious, their victories were simply denied. The Navy assumed that submarines were relatively ineffective, structured exercises accordingly, and rejected results that suggested otherwise. At the end of an exercise in 1939, a submarine officer accurately reported to a hall of one thousand officers that torpedoes hit their targets 22 percent of the time. Instead of asking any questions, Admiral Sir Charles Forbes, the commander of the Home Fleet, stood up, declared that the officer was clearly wrong, that 3 percent was correct, and ended the session.[120]

The culture of the battleship and its corollary inattention to the submarine also affected how the British viewed German strategy. The British tended to project their own views onto their opponent. They believed that the Germans would act as they themselves were acting. Thus the British discounted the U-boat threat because they thought little of the submarine. They never expected, for example, German surface night attacks because they had little experience with this tactic. To the extent that the British anticipated a challenge to their commerce, they saw it as coming from the German surface fleet, not submarines. In fact, the British did not conduct a single exercise in protection of a slow convoy against the submarine between 1919 and 1939.[121]

Finally, Britain's view of its own capabilities vis-à-vis the submarine threat was also sculpted by the culture of the Royal Navy. The foreign submarine challenge was never taken as seriously as it should have been because the Royal Navy did not consider the underwater boat to be of much value. As noted above, Britain's faith in its own antisubmarine warfare capabilities, especially asdic, was crucial in its calculations and decisions. But what the organizational-culture perspective emphasizes is the prejudice of this conviction. The implicit trust in the surface fleet over the submarine has much to do with why antisubmarine-warfare measures such as asdic were not evaluated more critically.

Did Britain's emphasis on the battleship make sense, given the international circumstances Britain faced? Might culture simply be a product of underlying realist considerations? After all, as many argued, an

[120] See Simpson, *Periscope View*, pp. 48–49, 57–58, 74–76; Hezlet; *Submarine and Seapower,* p. 119; Alastair Mars, *British Submarines at War, 1939–1945* (London: William Kinder, 1971), p. 33; Roskill, *Naval Policy between the Wars,* 2:230, 430–31.
[121] Henry, "British Submarine Development," pp. 381–82. Roskill, *Naval Policy between the Wars,* 2:336–37, 477; Roskill, *War at Sea,* 1:45, 355, 536.

underwater fleet aimed at trade was only a good idea where the enemy had local command of the sea.[122] Yet Britain's main opponent during most of the interwar period was Japan, an island national that had local command of the sea and was dependent on trade. The British fleet could not remain on station in Asia and in a two-front war might not arrive there at all. Despite the obvious role for submarines in such a situation, Britain did not adapt. As John Terraine has noted, the only difference having Japan as an enemy made in the mind of the Royal Navy was a change of location for the great battleship clashes: "The Trafalgars and Jutlands of the future would be fought east of Singapore."[123]

In this situation, to hope for innovation from within the Royal Navy, especially from Britain's own submarine force, was to ask too much from too little. The submariners represented less than 4 percent of the naval manpower at the beginning of World War II. The officers of the underwater boats were hardly in a position to make their case. They were relatively junior and had few opportunities for advancement.[124] A standard practice was for submarine officers to do two years service in capital ships after one year in submarines. It is almost comic that one of the main activities of the senior submarine officer (Rear Admiral Submarines) from 1935 to 1939 seems to have been trying to find a location for his headquarters near that of the CINC of the Home Fleet. The Rear Admiral (Submarines) did not succeed in moving to London and gaining closer contact with the decision makers in the Admiralty until March 1940.[125] This episode symbolized the gulf between submarines and the Royal Navy at large.

Britain's attitude in submarine warfare contrasts sharply with that of Germany. This disparity, highlighting the impact of organizational culture, is evident in doctrine, accidents, and the evaluations made of the submarine in key instances. In terms of doctrine at the beginning of war, the primary mission of the Royal Navy's underwater boats was to report on movements of enemy warships. The warships could also be attacked, if possible, but only if it would not delay the transmission

[122] "Functions of a Cruiser Submarine or Submersible," February 1925, ADM 1/8403/158.

[123] Terraine, *Business in Great Waters*, p. 158.

[124] This contrasts with the experience of another "new" weapon—the Fleet Air Arm—that fared better in the hierarchy in part because it was represented on the Board of Admiralty by a Fifth Sea Lord. Henry, "British Submarine Development," p. 7; Nigel John Gilbert, "British Submarine Operations in World War II," *United States Naval Institute Proceedings* 89 (March 1963): 73.

[125] That, of course, was about the time that submarine rules were relaxed. Naval Staff History, *Submarines*, 1:7 and 25.

of intelligence.[126] The head of submarines, Rear Admiral Watson, did request both "defensive" free attack zones and a looser interpretation of the Protocol, but made little headway.[127]

As with Germany and the *Athenia* incident, the first submarine attack by Britain was also an accident. On 10 September 1939 the *Triton* torpedoed another British submarine, the *Oxely*, by mistake.[128] Both the *U-30* and *Triton* were acting in accordance with their organizational culture. Each inadvertently destroyed a ship, but it was the type of vessel each had been trained to attack. British submarines had a legacy of successful antisubmarine warfare in World War I.[129] German strategy was based on commerce raiding. This difference appears to have been reflected even in the physical structure of the submarines. The acoustical detection array in German U-boats was designed for an antishipping role, whereas in British submarines, it was for attacking other underwater boats.[130] From an organizational-culture viewpoint it is not surprising that the first "accident" of the war for a British ship was the destruction of a friendly submarine, whereas Lemp's error was the destruction of a passenger liner.

The difference between Britain and Germany is just as evident in what did not happen, as in what did. When the British submarine *Salmon* sighted the German passenger liner *Bremen* 2000 yards away on 12 December 1939, a repeat of the *Athenia* incident seemed likely. Yet the *Salmon* surfaced and ordered the ship to stop for search and seizure according to the Protocol. A Luftwaffe plane appeared and frightened the *Salmon* off. Ironically, the *Bremen* was being used as a troopship at the time and had been a legitimate target all along.[131]

---

[126] See "Submarine War Orders: Orders for Heligoland Bight Patrol," 29 August 1939, ADM 199/311; "War Memorandum RA(S) Number Five," 18 August 1938, ADM 1/9540.

[127] RA(S) to Secretary of the Admiralty, "Remarks on the Use of Submarines in Defence of Territory"; Minute 08070/39, Deputy Chief of the Naval Staff, 25 October 1939, ADM 199/878.

[128] See A. S. Evans, *Beneath the Waves: A History of H. M. Submarine Losses* (London: William Kinder, 1986), pp. 195–99.

[129] The day before the *Oxely* was destroyed, Admiral Watson, the commander of the submarine force, requested that his boats be used more in an antisubmarine role. Memorandum, RA(S) to Secretary of the Admiralty, "The Use of Submarines in Defence of Our Trade in the Atlantic," 9 September 1939, ADM 199/1920.

[130] Simpson, *Periscope View*, p. 61.

[131] The captain of the *Salmon* noted, "I had no special instructions with reference to intercepting *Bremen* and considered myself bound by international law, a rigid adherence to which had been specifically stressed to submarine commanding officers at the beginning of war." See Memorandum, Commanding Officer HMS *Salmon* to Captain(S) Third Submarine Flotilla, "HMS *Salmon* Patrol Report December 2–16, 1939," ADM 199/288. Gilbert, "British Submarine Operations," p. 73.

Britain missed several opportunities to disrupt the German war effort because it discounted the potential contribution of the submarine. For example, Germany imported iron ore from Scandinavia unimpeded. On 10 October the first submarine intelligence summary pointed out the importance of the iron-ore trade and suggested interdicting it at the Rhine,[132] but no action was taken. The Admiralty simply did not appreciate the anticommerce potential of the submarine. If the Admiralty had loosened the submarine regulations, the underwater boats might have been used with considerable effectiveness both off the coast of Norway and in the sea channel between Germany and Sweden and Norway. British restraint prevailed even into the early stages of Germany's invasion of Norway. The crews of the Royal Navy submarines stationed in the Kattegat sat and watched in April 1940 while German shipping delivered invasion troops to Norway, even though the gray uniforms of the Wehrmacht had been spotted on board. Britain had twenty submarines in the waters through which Germany's invasion ships sailed, but restraint obtained a crucial forty-eight hours until 9 April—a considerable "missed opportunity."[133]

A final instance of puzzling restraint occurred in the early summer of 1940, at the beginning of hostilities with Italy in Africa. On 10 June Italy declared war and announced a sink-on-sight policy within twelve miles of the coasts of Italy and Italian East Africa. Italy's campaign in Africa was dependent on sea trade. The CINC of the Mediterranean naval forces saw submarine action as his only recourse, given Italian surface and air control. Thinking that Italian actions would free his hands, he requested that British boats be allowed to attack at will. It was considered "vital" to stop the transport of troops and supplies to Africa and he repeated the request on 20 June. But because of unspecified "political considerations," submarines did not receive permission to attack the Italian ships without restrictions (in a limited area) until 18 July—a critical month after Italy's entry into the war.[134]

Driven by a battleship creed, the main objective of Britain's submarine force remained destruction of the enemy's warships, and not seaborne trade, until 1943.[135] Britain's failure to recognize the utility of the submarine despite German actions and strategic needs illustrates how

[132] "Submarine Intelligence Summary #1," 10 October 1939, ADM 199/311.

[133] Hezlet, *Submarine and Seapower*, p. 125. Simpson, *Periscope View*, p. 89.

[134] Butler, *Grand Strategy*, 2:296. Naval Staff History, 2:1–4. Restraints in the Mediterranean were not totally removed until 5 February 1941. See Roskill, *War at Sea*, 1:439.

[135] Roskill, *War at Sea*, 1:306; Gilbert, "British Submarine Operations," p. 77.

resilient organizational culture can be in the face of external incentives and demands.

Conclusion: The Two Faces of British Submarine Policy

British policy toward submarine warfare had two faces. The one central to this study was the policy of restraint in the employment of the submarine against merchant ships. The second was a plan for defensive measures that encouraged unrestricted warfare. These two often worked at cross-purposes, one favoring cooperation, the other escalation.

Each of the three perspectives offers insights on this apparent confusion, but organizational culture provides the decisive connecting thread. Institutionalism's logic helps to clarify why Britain did not immediately adopt unrestricted warfare in October of 1939. It wanted to avoid offending neutral countries by breaking international conventions that neutral countries valued. The calculation was that more benefits—particularly help from neutrals in controlling Germany's exports—would follow from restraint than from allowing free attacks on German trade.[136] Realism seems to explain why Britain took actions to protect its trade even though it recognized that they would likely lead to unrestricted submarine warfare. Because Britain believed (inaccurately) that its defenses were more than equal to the German submarine threat, it was deterred from taking actions that might end in escalation.

Yet behind the decisions of both offensive restraint and defensive escalation was a fundamental judgment on the utility of the submarine and submarine defenses. This judgment—against the value of the submarine and in favor of the might of defense—was fundamentally a product of organizational culture. It evolved not in accord with external circumstances or conventions, but according to the internal beliefs of the Royal Navy. For example, had the submarine's value as a commerce raider and strategic tool been more appreciated, the calculus of restraint might have been quite different. Similarly, had Britain recognized the inadequacies of its plans to take on the U-boat, it may well have been more cautious in its defensive measures related to the London Protocol.

The battleship culture of the Royal Navy systematically devalued

---

[136] This may appear to be realist reasoning; however, the key element that makes it institutionalist is the assertion that rules affected the calculations, and hence the decisions, of states. Such rules are minimized in realism.

submarine warfare. The origins of this bias were neither realist nor institutionalist. After all, external circumstances vis-à-vis Japan in the interwar period suggested the need to pay attention to underwater commerce warfare, but Britain ignored it. Likewise, there is little evidence to indicate that international norms shaped organizational culture. The battleship culture predated the rules and did not change in response to them. The British preferences that ultimately decided choices on cooperation in submarine warfare were the product of neither international society nor anarchy, but instead, of internal bureaucratic preference.

AMERICAN ESCALATION UNDER THE PACIFIC

In the Washington twilight of 7 December 1941—approximately five hours after the Japanese had attacked Pearl Harbor—the United States's chief of naval operations (CNO) Admiral Harold Stark issued a command to U.S. forces: "Execute unrestricted submarine and air warfare against Japan."[137] Historians of submarine policy contend that this order was unexpected. Naval leaders realized the directive was a violation of existing treaties. In fact, the first submarines to sea following the Pearl Harbor fiasco carried a letter from Rear Admiral Thomas Withers Jr., the commander of Pacific Fleet submarines, authorizing attacks on merchant ships. The aim of this note was to protect the captain and crew from being hanged as pirates if they were captured sinking merchant vessels in violation of the London Protocol.[138]

For those familiar with the history of the nasty and brutish Pacific war, the order for unrestricted warfare is, in hindsight, unsurprising. Yet in the interwar period, the United States consistently advocated restrictions on submarine warfare. Up to the eve of conflict, an unrestricted offensive on enemy sea commerce was neither prepared nor anticipated. Why were the submarine rules discarded on the first day of the war?

[137] Copies of this order can be found in the Map Room Papers in the Franklin D. Roosevelt Library in Hyde Park, New York; as cited in Manson, *Diplomatic Ramifications*, p. 158.
[138] Clay Blair, Jr., *Silent Victory: The U.S. Submarine War against Japan*, vol. 1 (Philadelphia: J. B. Lippincott, 1975), pp. 84, 88; Ernest Andrade, Jr., "Submarine Policy in the United States Navy, 1919–1941," *Military Affairs*, April 1971, p. 55; Commander of Submarines, Pacific Fleet, "Submarine Operational History World War II," Navy Department, Office of the CNO, 1947, p. 1, World War II Command File, Submarines Pacific Fleet, Box 357, Operational Archives, Naval Historical Center, Washington, D. C. (hereafter OA).

A second puzzle of the U.S. policy was why the United States ever supported the rules of restraint, particularly given its position in the Pacific. As early as 1919, U.S. naval officers had recognized that Japan, the expected main opponent of a future war, was an island nation dependent on trade and particularly vulnerable to attacks against its sea lines of communication. Based on the World War I record, it was clear that submarines were the most effective weapons against merchant shipping and that the rules that governed attacks on such ships were not easy to apply.[139] Why did the United States adopt restrictions so contrary to its strategic opportunities?

In this case, neither the institutionalist nor organizational-culture approach predicts escalation, yet that is what occurred. In light of the well-formulated rules and America's ardent support of them, the logic of institutionalism is unable to account for escalation. Likewise, the U.S. Navy had a culture that shunned unrestricted submarine warfare, yet policy choices seemingly turned that culture on its head. Realism provides the most convincing answer for escalation by anticipating that the United States would adjust its policy to take advantage of the strategic opportunities offered. Nonetheless, the adjustment was long delayed and almost thwarted. An exsubmariner calls it "an accident of history" that the underwater boat developed in the interwar period for use against enemy warships also "proved ideal against merchant ships."[140] The time it would have taken to develop, manufacture, and launch a new class of submarines would have further set back the anticommerce offensive that contributed so significantly to the U.S. victory in the Pacific.[141] Culture (and to a lesser extent the submarine rules) were responsible for this delay. Thus the collapse of the tenability of the Navy's battleship philosophy in the Pacific may have been a

[139] Memorandum, Captains W. Evans, H. E. Yarnell, and T. C. Hart to the CNO 18 January 1919, File 420-15, 1919, Box 108, DepNav, RG 80, National Archives, Washington, D. C. (hereafter NA). On the difficulty of applying the rules, see F. T. P. 68 Tentative Submarine Tactical Instructions, 1926, p. 76, CNO Fleet Tactical Publications Series, World War II Command File, Box 107, OA. Yarnell and Hart had advocated unrestricted warfare at several points during the interwar years.

[140] Blair, *Silent Victory*, p. xvi. That the United Sates was lucky is evident when we consider the British case. Britain never developed a long-range submarine suitable for an anti-commerce role in the Pacific. A "Pearl Harbor" at the British bases at Singapore or Hong Kong would not have provoked the Royal Navy to adopt unrestricted warfare because it lacked the means to make such a policy effective.

[141] One Navy report maintained that submariners constituted 1 percent of U. S. forces in the Pacific, but they sank 60 percent of total Japanese shipping. See Manson, *Diplomatic Ramifications*, p. 159.

necessary condition of the last-minute strategic adjustment in submarine warfare to circumstances in the Second World War.

Righteous on Rules

In the United States, the legal regulation of submarine warfare had a long history of support stretching from World War I to Pearl Harbor and encompassing at least four diplomatic conferences.[142] Woodrow Wilson, president during the First World War, would have considered the World War II decision to wage unrestricted submarine warfare immoral. Wilson considered submarines "utterly incompatible with the principles of humanity."[143] Unrestricted German submarine attacks in the Great War had brought the United States into that war.[144] A decade later, Ridley McLean, Commander Submarine Division, Battle Fleet, wrote to Curtis D. Wilbur, the Secretary of the Navy, "it is inconceivable that submarines of our service would ever be used against merchant ships as was done during the World War."[145]

Indeed, U.S. policy was consistent from World War I to the attack on Pearl Harbor. During the First World War, President Wilson, with a great deal of public support, castigated Germany for attacking merchant ships without respecting the rules of search, seizure, and safe passage for noncombatants. The U.S. Navy was prohibited from such "inhumane" attacks by its official "Instructions for the Navy of the United States Governing Maritime Warfare, 1917,"[146] however, these instructions were never put to the test for the Royal Navy had cleared

[142] These were the Washington Conference, the Havana Convention of 1928 on the Rights and Duties of Neutrals in Time of War, the London Conference of 1930, and the London Conference of 1935–36.

[143] Wilson was reportedly so powerfully affected by the sinking of the *Lusitania* by a German U-boat that he went into seclusion for two days after the tragedy. Arthur S. Link, *Wilson, the Struggle for Neutrality, 1914–1915* (Princeton: Princeton University Press, 1960), pp. 379–81, as cited in Manson, *Diplomatic Ramifications,* pp. 33–34. J. E. Talbott, "Weapons Development, War Planning and Policy: The U.S. Navy and the Submarine, 1917–1941," *Naval War College Review* (May–June 1984): 53–54.

[144] May, *World War,* pp. 416–37.

[145] Memorandum, Ridley McLean, Commander Submarine Division, Battle Fleet, to the Secretary of the Navy, 18 July 1928, File 420-15, 1925–28, Box 109, DepNav, RG 80, NA. Similar comments can be found elsewhere in these records. For example, one lieutenant commander notes, "the 'laws of humanity' must, however, be observed in such [commerce] warfare, despite the increased risks entailed upon the submarine." Memorandum, Lt. Commander E. L. Cochrane to the Secretary of the Navy, 20 January 1931, File 420-15, 1931–33, Box 111, DepNav. RG 80, NA.

[146] Bemis, "Submarine Warfare," p. 4.

the seas of German merchant ships by the time the United States joined the conflict in 1917.

At the Washington Conference the United States was the first advocate of restrictions on submarine warfare. This posture was the result of a political squeeze. The Wilson administration had loudly trumpeted the immorality of unrestricted submarine attacks in World War I. The German submarine assault on the passenger liner Lusitania with its 1,198 passengers and crew (including 128 Americans) crystallized abhorrence of the underwater weapon in the public mind.[147] When efforts to abolish the submarine at the Versailles Peace Conference and the Washington Conference had failed, U.S. leaders were caught in a bind. The Harding administration wanted a naval agreement, but the submarine issue stood in the way. It could not be ignored because of public interest. The newspapers were following the talks closely, and they were against the submarine. The U.S. delegation received 400,000 responses urging abolition or drastic limitation of the underwater boat, and only 4,000 favoring retention.[148] Popular opinion, influenced by the U.S. leadership of World War I, helped convince the United States to favor a treaty that only restrained submarine use.

The U.S. Navy had no strong views on submarine warfare and little influence on U.S. negotiating positions in the interwar period. The General Board, the Navy's main advisory body on policy, generally opposed abolition of the submarine, contending that it was a legitimate weapon of war. Nonetheless, it also argued that unrestricted warfare should not be allowed, a sentiment that seems to have been more a nod to public opinion than a hard strategic judgment. It was recognized at the Versailles peace talks of 1919 that the U.S. public—and politicians—might not allow the use of the submarine in its most effective role of commerce killer. The General Board opposed the Root resolutions, but its advice was ignored. The rules were accepted by the Navy, without relish, but also without any significant opposition. There appears to have been little resistance on the part of naval authorities to the rules for most of the interwar years.[149]

---

[147] May, *World War*, p. 136. Manson, *Diplomatic Ramifications*, p. 33 n. 1, notes that the *Lusitania* sinking dominated the news in the *New York Times* for more than a week, often filling the entire front page and the six to seven following it.

[148] Harold Sprout and Margaret Sprout, *Toward a New Order of Sea Power: American Naval Policy and the World Scene, 1918–1922* (Princeton: Princeton University Press, 1940), pp. 192–93.

[149] Lester H. Brune, *The Origins of American National Security Policy: Sea Power, Air Power, and Foreign Policy, 1900–1941* (Manhattan, Kans.: MA/AH Publishing, 1981), pp. 56–58. Roskill, *Naval Policy between the Wars*, 1:307–9, 325. Warner R. Schilling, "Weapons, Doctrine, and Arms Control: A Case from the Good Old Days," *Journal of Conflict Resolution*

Judging by the Navy's organizational routines, the treaties appear to have had some influence. The Navy's official "Rules of War Governing Maritime and Aerial Warfare" prohibited unrestricted attacks on merchant ships. Submarine commanders were taught to "commit to memory" the provisions of the London Protocol. During the interwar years U.S. submarines never practiced attacking merchant ships.[150]

Yet one must not mistake correlation for causation. Just because official policy was compatible with the norms against unlimited trade warfare that does not mean that either produced the other. Wilson's support of the antisubmarine regime in World War I was fully compatible with a realist view; U.S. trade and citizens were threatened by unrestricted warfare. The U.S. Navy's big-ship culture was as important as Wilsonian idealism as source of restraint both in World War I and the interwar period.[151] Indeed, the restrictions on submarine warfare may have been obeyed only because they reinforced preexisting tendencies in their favor.

There is, however, at least one instance of institutional effect where concerns about negative political consequences appear to have constrained U.S. leaders on the very brink of war. At that time some officials in the Navy began to acknowledge the possible benefits of using submarines against shipping. When the General Board considered the matter, however, it advised that the United States not change the rules because it would be "contrary to international law and U.S. policy" and instead recommended maintaining a traditional posture until circumstances rendered modification advisable.[152] The Japanese attack on Pearl Harbor, though not in violation of the London Protocol, provided an excuse for U.S. leaders to violate the existing rules.[153] But

---

(1963), reprinted in Robert J. Art and Kenneth N. Waltz, eds., *The Use of Force: International Politics and Foreign Policy* (Boston: Little, Brown, 1971), p. 463. Bemis, "Submarine Warfare," p. 16.

[150] Commander of Submarines, Pacific Fleet, "Submarine Operational History World War II," DepNav, Office of the CNO 1947, p. 2, World War II Command File, Submarines Pacific Fleet, Box 357, OA.

[151] One U. S. naval officer, Thomas Hart, wrote shortly after World War I that the Navy supported abolition "due to a big ship conservatism and reluctance to deal with a thing that may upset the old order." Quoted in Schilling, "Weapons, Doctrine, and Arms Control," p. 475. There were, of course, officers such as Hart and Yarnell in the Navy that supported submarines. Hart commanded U. S. submarines in Europe in World War I.

[152] General Board Study No. 425, 15 May 1941, Amendment of rules of Maritime Commerce, Box 133, DepNav, RG 80, NA; Bemis, "Submarine Warfare," pp. 26–27.

[153] Bemis, "Submarine Warfare," pp. 36–37, recounts what appears to be an unrestricted Japanese attack on a merchant ship several hundred miles northeast of Honolulu just after the Pearl Harbor attack, but the United States could not have known of the

the reason for doing so is intimately connected to the collapse of the Navy's preferred strategy.

The Collapse of Culture

Naval strategic thought deserves attention because it provided the overall framework within which thinking about the submarine was deeply embedded. The U.S. Navy of the 1920s and 1930s was largely dominated by Mahan's concept of the battleship as the key to naval power. To the extent the battleship paradigm in the U.S. Navy had a challenger, this role was played by the aircraft carrier.[154] The surface fleet dominated strategic vision, the submarine was a second-class citizen. A poem by a submarine captain during World War II reflects this idea while gloating over the actual results.

> Battleships are title B,
> That's Lesson One in Strategy.
> They are the backbone of the Fleet,
> Their fighting power can't be beat.
> They dominate the raging Main,
> While swinging round the anchor chain
> And bravely guard your home and mine,
> While anchored out there all in line.
> They fill the Japs with fear and hate,
> From well inside the Golden Gate.
>
> Now Lesson Two in strategy—
> Our subs and planes are title C.
> Just send them out on any mission,
> and win your battles by attrition.
> Where'er you send the subs or planes,
> You're bound to chalk up lots of gains—
> And losses, too, but what the hell,
> Who cares about their personnel?
> For planes are chauffeured by young studs,
> Lieutenant Commanders run the subs.[155]

---

action at the time it turned to unrestricted warfare. In short, the U. S. decision was not retaliation for Japanese violation of the London Protocol.

[154] Mahan, *Influence of Sea Power*. The aircraft carrier initially gained support as an adjunct to the battleship: it would act as the "eyes' of the battle fleet. During the interwar period, the carrier gained an increasing prominence and came into its own in World War II. See Rosen, *Winning the Next War*, pp. 68–70 (see Chap. 1, n. 71).

[155] Lt. Commander Richard G. Voge, "Naval War College 1942," or "Old Fuds, Young Studs and Lieutenant Commanders," as found in Theodore Roscoe, *United States Submarine Operations in World War II* (Annapolis, Md.: U. S. Naval Institute, 1949).

The strong influence of this battleship creed is apparent in submarine procurement, doctrine, and training.

The cult of Mahan mandated the type of force the United States would buy. The standard by which the Navy judged its power was the capital ship. In 1928 the General Board called the battleship "the ultimate measure of the strength of the Navy."[156] Victory in clashes between fleets was viewed as the decisive measure of naval power. Accordingly, a priority in U.S. construction was that newer boats be able to keep pace with, and take part in, fleet battles.[157]

U.S. doctrine going into the First World War allocated two missions to the submarine: coastal defense and, to the extent improvements in speed and durability made it possible, fleet support. Despite the lessons evident in Germany's nearly successful anticommerce strategy against England, the United States went into the interwar years with this doctrine unchanged.[158]

The odd part of this strategy was that a nation vulnerable to commerce raiding was the main perceived adversary. From the end of the First World War throughout the interwar period, it was clear to the U. S. Navy that Japan was the primary threat. Between 1919 and 1941, at least 136 campaign war games were played and recorded at the Naval War College. Of that number, 127 were conducted against Japan and only 9 against Germany and Italy combined (and all of these took place *after* 1939). The fleet assignment for submarines was also odd because maneuvers in the late 1920s and early 1930s showed that this role was unfeasible. Submarines did not have the speed to keep up with the fleet, were often ineffective, and were perceived as very vulnerable to antisubmarine warfare. The General Board recommended that the Navy abandon the idea of incorporating the submarine into the fleet.[159]

Here was the perfect opportunity to make the case for a commerce-raiding strategy against the exposed Japanese sea lines. Submarines could operate individually in such a mission and would not have to

[156] Roskill, *Naval Policy between the Wars*, 2:23.

[157] "Record of the Control Force Conferences Held at the Submarine Base, New London, Connecticut from 16 May 1930–19 December 1930 for the Study of Submarine Warfare Under the Direction of Rear Admiral T. C. Hart, USN, Commander Control Force," File 420–15, 1931–33, Box 111, RG 80, NA.

[158] Andrade, "Submarine Policy," p. 50.

[159] Michael Vlahos, "Wargaming, An Enforcer of Strategic Realism: 1919–1942," *Naval War College Review* (March–April 1986): 17; Andrade, "Submarine Policy," p. 53; Blair, *Silent Victory*, pp. 28–36.

keep up with the fleet. Yet even submariners did not advocate this crucial role. Instead they were concerned with developing an underwater boat that could keep pace with the surface ships and take part in fleet-on-fleet battles. They responded to the General Board's finding by advocating a new fleet-support mission—long-range scouting and intelligence. Submarines would lie outside enemy harbors to report on the opposing fleet and if lucky would attack any battleships that presented themselves as targets. Accordingly, boats were designed to stay at sea for a long time.[160]

The dominance of the surface fleet was more than mere planning. In training exercises, the underwater boats practiced antifleet tactics only. Submarine commanders, under threat of demotion, were forced to act with extreme care, lest they be destroyed by enemy warships assumed to be effective at antisubmarine warfare. No periscope attacks were allowed. Instead sonar attacks at depths greater than one hundred meters were encouraged to avoid enemy detection. Raids on merchant craft were not practiced. This regimen reduced the initial effectiveness of the U.S. offensive against Japanese shipping. After Pearl Harbor, new methods of submarine warfare were developed within the U.S. Navy and nearly a third of the submarine commanders had to be relieved before the new strategy yielded any returns. The old captains were overly cautions when attacking the slower, poorly armed merchants ships and missed many an easy kill. In addition, prewar targeting formulas were based on mast sizes of enemy fleet ships, all of which were known. The masts of the merchant fleet, however, were unfamiliar, and it took time to develop new methods.[161]

The culture of the U.S. Navy dictated that the battleship would be the star of the team. The value of the submarine as a commerce raider was overlooked. This oversight, largely a product of the Navy's organizational culture, would persist to the very onset of hostilities. The aversion to unrestricted submarine warfare, however, crumbled once

[160] Charles A. Lockwood, *Down to the Sea in Submarines* (New York: Norton, 1967), pp. 167–209; John D. Alden, *The Fleet Submarine in the U. S. Navy: A Design and Construction History* (Annapolis, Md.: Naval Institute Press, 1979), p. 5; Blair, *Silent Victory*, pp. 36–37; Andrade, "Submarine Policy," p. 53.

[161] Of course, there were also other problems that plagued the submariners, the most important of which was faulty firing mechanisms on torpedoes. Blair, *Silent Victory*, pp. xvi–xviii, 45, 88–89, 97; Rosen, *Winning the Next War*, pp. 131–42; Holmes *Undersea Victory: The Influence of Submarine Operations on the War in the Pacific* (Garden City, N. Y.: Doubleday, 1966), pp. 47–48; Montgomery C. Meigs, *Slide Rules and Submarines* (Washington, D. C.: National Defense University Press, 1990), pp. 155–56.

the war began. To understand why this was so, we turn to considerations that fit best with the logic of the realist perspective.

Sensible Adaptation to Circumstance

The underpinnings of realism—strategic adaptation to the international situation—is key to understanding U.S. decisions on submarine policy. Driven by a creeping realization that it would not have the tools to implement its battleship strategy in the Far East, the Navy made last-minute preparations for a backup plan based on the submarine. The attack on the U.S. surface fleet at Pearl Harbor was the final blow to the viability of an already questionable battleship creed. Consequently, Admiral Stark ordered unrestricted underwater warfare. If we are to understand this dramatic change, we must review the evolution of U.S. naval policy in Asia.

Dating back to 1904, the Army-Navy Joint Board developed a series of plans requiring the cooperation of the two services. These plans were classified according to the color assigned to the primary enemy. Japan was "ORANGE." The basic tenets of naval policy were to build a navy second to none, uphold the Monroe doctrine, and keep the "door open" to Chinese trade. The ORANGE plans, which concerned the last part of this policy, remained basically unchanged from 1919 to 1938. Any war was expected to be primarily naval. At the beginning of a conflict, the United States hoped to seize the offensive against Japan's fleet and economic life. The aim was to win by command of the seas—particularly the vital sea lanes of communication. The key to this plan would be to secure a forward base, designated as Manilla, from which the surface fleet offensive against Japan could be launched; however, because the 1922 Washington treaty prohibited the United States from fortifying its forward bases in peacetime, the fleet would be required to advance across the Pacific in stages before assuming offensive operations.[162] The linchpin of these offensive operations would, of course, be the battleship.

In the late 1930s, however, the credibility of the battleship strategy in the Pacific eroded. The U.S. Navy began to shift uneasily away from the assumptions and biases that had dictated doctrine since the end of the First World War. The first signs of strategic uncertainty were evident in a 1935-36 split between the Army and Navy over their joint

---

[162] Roskill, *Naval Policy between the Wars*, 2:23; Louis Morton, *The War in the Pacific: Strategy and Command: The First Two Years in the U. S. Army in World War II* (Washington, D. C.: Office of the Chief of Military History, Department of the Army, 1962), pp. 22–72.

war plans against Japan. The Army saw the difficulty of trying to reinforce the forward outpost of Manilla and favored a defensive strategy
based on holding the Panama-Hawaii-Alaska triangle. The Navy, however, wanted to stick to its offensive strategy. At the end of 1937, Admiral Harry Yarnell, the CINC of the Asiatic Fleet, sent Admiral William
Leahy, the CNO, a plan for a sea war against Japan that did not require
the deployment of land forces (or the help of the Army). He believed
Japan could be strangled by economic pressure and blockade, and he
challenged the battle-fleet concept.[163]

Training scenarios in the 1935-41 period began to deemphasize destruction of the Japanese fleet in favor of eliminating the enemy capacity to wage war. The reason for this shift was the growing recognition
that taking the offensive against Japan would be difficult and holding
Manilla would probably not be possible. Not only was Japan growing
more powerful, but the Depression had hurt the readiness of the fleet.
Nonetheless, up to 1939, the basic naval-fleet offensive strategy remained intact.[164]

The beginning of the end for the U.S. Navy's battleship culture—
and the policy of restraint—however, was the rising threat of Axis
aggression in the Atlantic with the outbreak of World War II. In 1939,
the official ORANGE plans for war with Japan were replaced by a new
scheme known as RAINBOW. This plan (of which there would be
five versions) was based on a two-ocean war and gave priority to the
protection of the Panama Canal, the Caribbean sea lanes, and the
South Atlantic. As the threat in the Atlantic grew, so did the Navy's
attention to that theater. In a "Europe-first" policy, operations in the
Pacific would be held to a minimum while the offensive was conducted
in the Atlantic. Forces were redistributed accordingly, and battleships
earmarked for a Pacific war were transferred to the Atlantic.[165]

Eventually, the war in Europe also forced the Navy to reappraise the
use of the submarine in war. With the declining prospects for a battle-
fleet strategy in the Pacific, some naval leaders began to consider the
use of submarines. In light of the need to contain Japan and the lack
of alternative forces, the idea of using submarines as commerce destroyers—even in violation of the rules—began to circulate.[166]

---

[163] Roosevelt, a naval enthusiast saw the plan and commented, "Yarnell talks a lot of sense." Roskill, *Naval Policy between the Wars*, 2:365; Morton, *War in the Pacific*, pp. 37–41.

[164] Vlahos, "Wargaming," pp. 13–14; Morton, *War in the Pacific*, pp. 22–72.

[165] Morton, *War in the Pacific*, pp. 69–75.

[166] Despite the evolution in naval strategy, official submarine policy remained fairly stable. The last version of RAINBOW before Pearl Harbor (RAINBOW 5) assigned subma-

Meanwhile, when the European war broke out in 1939, the Navy decided to update its rules of warfare (for the first time since 1917) to prepare for the possibility of conflict. A draft of the Instructions, which included the rules limiting submarine attacks on merchant ships, was circulated to top officials in February 1941. In response, the president of the Naval War College sent a memorandum to the CNO (who passed it on to the secretary of the navy) recommending that the naval regulations be altered to permit unrestricted warfare. The War College had done a study that assumed that existing rules would limit action and that given the surface forces available, a blockade was not possible. It recommended announcing "strategic areas"—large zones allowing unrestricted warfare designed to cut off Japan's trade.[167]

The idea was sent to the General Board for consideration. Despite the collapse of the rules between Britain and Germany in the Atlantic theater, the Board advised that the United States should maintain its traditional position until circumstances allowed for change. The General Board did not reject the idea of unrestricted warfare; however, it felt that in light of the long-standing commitment to the submarine restrictions—with which the strategic zones were not compatible—it was better to wait. The "Tentative Instructions" issued in May 1941 repeated the legitimacy of the submarine restrictions although the cover letter noted the possibility of additional instructions in response to future circumstances.[168]

Clearly, many were leaning toward escalation. Frank Knox, the secretary of the navy, asked Cordell Hull, the secretary of state, in the summer of 1941 for permission to conduct unrestricted warfare in the event

---

rines to scouting and patrolling. In procurement policy, the ratio of expenditures on submarines (relative to other components of the fleet) was steady throughout the 1930s. Yet behind the facade of official policy, some officials were reconsidering the submarine's role and rules. Not surprisingly, Hart in a January 1941 memo was at the forefront. See Manson, *Diplomatic Ramifications*, p. 150.

[167] Memorandum, President, Naval War College, to the CNO, 20 March 1941, in "G. B. Study No. 425–May 15, 1941: Amendment of Rules for Maritime Warfare," Box 133, RG 80, NA.

[168] Memorandum, Chairman, General Board (Sexton), to Secretary of the Navy (Knox), 15 May 1941, File 425, January–June 1941, Box 134, DepNav, RG 80, NA. Bemis, "Submarine Warfare," pp. 19–27. The notion of strategic areas, however, was not forgotten. Both the RAINBOW 3 (December 1940) and RAINBOW 5 (26 May 1941) allowed commanders of the fleets to declare "strategic areas" where merchant shipping would not be protected. At the same time, however, the plans required that the submarine rules be respected for the time being. See "United Nations in the Pacific Theater and Navy Basin, Plan RAINBOW 5," WPL-46, Box 147F, Strategic Plans Division Records, OA; "WPL-46 (and WPL-44, Navy Basic War Plan, RAINBOW 3) Letters and Dispatches, 12/40–12/41," Box 147J, Strategic Plans Division Records, OA. Bemis, "Submarine Warfare," p. 19.

of war with Japan. He maintained that the precedent (of escalation) that Germany and Britain had set would pave the way for unlimited U.S. operations. Especially since Japan would be a member of the Axis, it was equally responsible for Germany's unrestricted warfare, which would permit the United States to ignore the Protocol.[169]

Perhaps more consequential were the plans taking shape at the operational level. Communications between the CNO (Admiral Stark) and the CINC of the Asiatic Fleet (Admiral Thomas Hart), based in Manilla, indicated that intentions were leaning heavily toward escalation. Hart, asking for clarification on the rules, wanted to conduct unrestricted submarine attacks. Stark cabled him back that in the event of formal war, unrestricted warfare could be initiated in the Far East.[170] Stark apparently drafted the contingent order without talking with the State Department or legal advisors, but he claims to have consulted President Roosevelt on "an oral basis."[171]

Stark's command after Pearl Harbor to conduct unrestricted submarine attacks was neither a simple reprisal nor total surprise. Orders for unrestricted warfare had been prepared before the Japanese attack. In fact, it appears that Hart was so sure the United States would escalate, he commanded his Asiatic Fleet submarines to attack merchant ships without restraint even before authorization from Washington arrived.[172]

The surprise attack at Pearl Harbor removed any doubt about whether Hart had overstepped his authority or what the U.S. Navy would do. The European war had already led to a decline in the strength of the U.S. naval power in the Orient. The Japanese attack added to the perceived limitations of the U.S. surface fleet in the Pacific. Six of the nine Pacific Fleet battleships were either sunk or severely damaged.[173] America's leaders and populace wanted immediate

---

[169] Manson, *Diplomatic Ramifications*, p. 154.

[170] This included that part of the Pacific Ocean lying south and west of a line joining 30° N, 122° E, and 7° N, 140° E. In the event of hostilities without formal declaration, Hart was to await orders. See CNO, H. R. Stark, to CINC, Asiatic Fleet, Dispatch 271442, 26 November 1941, Dispatch File, Naval History Division, cited in Bemis, "Submarine Warfare," p. 31.

[171] Bemis, "Submarine Warfare," pp. 29–32. Hart also received information through a Commander Fife from Washington who had visited Manila. See *U. S. Naval Administration in World War II: Submarine Commands* (Office of Naval History, Submarine Commands, 1946), 1:113–14, boxes 354 and 355, OA.

[172] *U. S. Naval Administration in World War II: Submarine Commands*, 1:114, boxes 354 and 355, OA.

[173] John Mueller, "Pearl Harbor: Military Inconvenience, Political Disaster," *International Security* 16 (winter 1991–92): 175–79. Mueller argues that the military damage at Pearl Harbor was relatively insignificant. Yet he also recognizes that it further diminished an

action. With the disintegration of any plans based on the battleship, the Navy quickly deployed the only offensive tool ready for action and commenced unrestricted submarine warfare.

Conclusion: The Rapid Turn

Realism provides the best account for America's about-face on submarine restrictions. Japan was dependent on sea-borne trade, the United States was not. Japan could retaliate against American escalation by unleashing its own antimerchant war, but it simply could not hurt the United States as much—or so the Naval leaders thought.[174] Thus, the United States secured a relative advantage by violating the restrictions on submarine policy once the war had begun.

The puzzling aspect of this history is why the United States did not abandon its policy of restraint until the eve of war. In 1919, naval officers recognized the advantages of a submarine campaign against Japan. And in the early 1930s, Roosevelt himself acknowledged that if a war with Japan should come, it would ultimately lose because of economic weakness.[175] Furthermore, there were costs to respecting the London Protocol. By adhering to a policy of restricted warfare, the Navy was caught unprepared for its anticommerce campaign and was relatively ineffective in the first part of the conflict. Why did the United States not act earlier to prepare itself to seize this strategic opportunity?

To a certain degree, the international rules constrained the official turn to a policy of unrestricted submarine attacks on the brink of war. The General Board did not want to allow premeditated violation of the law but recommended waiting for some sort of justifying circumstances. But the more fundamental basis of America's interwar posture is found in organizational culture. The Navy hierarchy in the interwar years lauded the Mahanian surface fleet and ignored the advantages of the underwater boat. In fact, the United States turned to the submarine only when the feasibility of its prevailing surface-fleet culture collapsed. This was not so much the result of a threat from Japan, or a simple calculation of relative advantage in submarine warfare. It was

---

already hobbled force (p. 186) and that part of the reason the damage was seen as so significant was because of the misguided emphasis put on battleships (p. 188).

[174] Japanese submarines could have been used to dislocate the Allied supply effort in Asia. Germany encouraged Japan to strike at U. S. merchants. But Japanese submarines were also governed by a fleet philosophy and largely ignored the anticommerce role. See Morison, *History of United States Naval Operations in World War II*, vol. 1, pp. 196–98; Hashimoto, *Sunk*, p. 62.

[175] Roskill, *Naval Policy between the Wars*, 2:159.

the disintegration of the Navy's preferred strategy that opened the way to a realistic appraisal of the most effective U.S. use of the submarine. If the United States had faced only Japan, the surface fleet strategy would have retained credibility, and the Navy may well have abided by the restrictions on submarines despite the strategic advantages of unrestricted warfare.

[3]

Strategic Bombing

From 20,000 feet the familiar surroundings of life—buildings, homes, cars—appear unnaturally small. "The people look like ants!" is a commonly heard refrain among first-time airline passengers. Perhaps it was this perspective which made it easier for the young aviators of World War II to flatten the homes of enemy civilians hundreds of miles behind the front lines, much as one might squash a nest of pesky insects. Although this practice became commonplace during the war, in the 1920s and 1930s it was considered barbaric and potentially avoidable.

Statesmen made considerable efforts in the interwar years both to reduce air armaments and to regulate conflict by agreeing on rules and restrictions. The main distinction they hoped to enforce was between civilians and combatants. Those participating directly in the war effort were generally seen as legitimate targets of airpower. All others were to be considered illegitimate victims, on whom only the inhumane and criminal would drop bombs.[1]

Air warfare can be divided into two categories—"tactical" and "strategic"—which correspond roughly to the conventions that classified bombing objectives as legal or illegal.[2] Tactical air operations, designed

---

[1] J. M. Spaight, *Air Power and War Rights*, 3d ed. (London: Longmans, Green, 1947), p. 43.

[2] My use of "tactical" and "strategic" differs from that of classical military terminology, but is generally consistent with Anglo-American terminology in the war. For a discussion of this distinction and its analytical impact, see Williamson Murray, "The Influence of Pre-War Anglo-American Doctrine on the Air Campaigns of the Second World War," in Horst Boog, ed., *The Conduct of the Air War in the Second World War: An International Comparison* (New York: Berg Publishers, 1992), pp. 241–43. Although the terms may vary, the general contrasts, are relatively consistent among authors. See, for example, Charles

to aid ongoing military campaigns, are generally directed at the enemy's forces or immediate rear area and supply chain. Strategic air operations, on the other hand, are directed at the sources of the enemy's power—the factories, the utilities, the food-supply system, and, most importantly, the morale and even the lives of the nation's citizens. Of the two categories, tactical bombing was considered legitimate, whereas strategic bombing challenged and often transgressed any notion of humane air war.

Strategic air operations can be further defined. Such bombing can be either discriminating or indiscriminate, precision-or area-oriented. Discriminating and precision bombing are intended to destroy a discrete target but leave the surrounding area relatively untouched. Indiscriminate and area bombing attack a wide group of targets or a geographic region where accuracy is not as important. As the terms might suggest, "discriminating" or "precision" strategic attacks could be legitimate as long as the target was military-related. Indiscriminate or area bombing behind the lines, however, would have been deemed illegal by many interwar jurists because no attempt would have been made to distinguish between civilians and other more acceptable targets. In fact, once the World War II air conflict escalated, the target of indiscriminate and area attacks was often intentionally those civilians whose ability to support and endure conflict was considered central to national resolve. The background of this story is the history of employment of, limitations on, and usefulness of air warfare before World War II.

Even before the Wright Brothers made their historic flight with a winged aircraft in 1903 at Kitty Hawk, North Carolina, international efforts were made to regulate the use of air power in war. The origins of this movement date back to efforts to control land warfare. At the Brussels Conference of 1874 countries agreed that undefended "open" cities could not be attacked or shelled and that only fortified cities could be bombarded. This provision helped establish the distinction between combatant and noncombatant that characterized efforts to limit bombing. At the Hague Conference of 1899 participants reaffirmed the principle of the open city, and the countries attending (with the exception of Britain) approved a declaration that forbade the dropping of weapons from balloons or "other new methods of a similar nature" for five years. In 1907 representatives again gathered at the Hague to consider the control of warfare. This time, however, the major

---

Webster and Noble Frankland, *The Strategic Air Offensive against Germany, 1939–1945* (London: HMSO, 1961), 1: 6–16.

powers did not renew the 1899 declaration. France and Germany had enough of an interest in the new air weapon to prevent any measures outlawing its use. What they did approve, however, was article 25 of the 1907 Hague Convention concerning land warfare: "The attack or bombardment, *by whatever means*, of towns, villages, dwellings, or buildings which are undefended is prohibited." The qualification "by whatever means" is noteworthy because the discussions of the conference indicate that it was inserted with air bombing in mind.[3]

At the beginning of World War I, strategic bombing did not exist. During the first three years of the war, the use of airpower (German zeppelins and early-model Allied planes) was mainly limited to tactical operations near the front lines. The exceptions to this rule were British strikes on the zeppelin bases and German airship raids against Britain itself. The Zeppelin attacks on London, which began on 31 May 1915, were the first of the war to cross this threshold. The aim of the German air assault was to break British morale by striking at factories, armories, and docks. British defensive efforts soon curtailed this offensive, but it was not without effect. Despite the relatively minor damage, the English public was stunned by the loss of its traditional insulation from continental conflicts. Light Allied raids on German industrial targets were generally rebuffed by German defenses or were ineffective, and most air attacks were directed at tactical targets by 1917.[4]

A second phase of the World War I air war began in May 1917. Germany renewed its strategic campaign against Britain in May and June of 1917 with the deployment of a new fleet of Gotha bombers. The Gotha raids were relatively light, numbering some twenty-seven in 1917 and 1918. In all of World War I air attacks killed only 1,413 and injured only 3,407.[5] Yet despite the low number of casualties (in comparison to the carnage on the Continent), the air attacks shook

[3] M. W. Royse, *Aerial Bombardment and the International Regulation of Warfare* (New York: Harold Vinal, 1928) pp. 147–73. Geoffrey Best, *Humanity in Warfare* (New York: Columbia University Press, 1980), p. 262. Hamilton DeSaussure, "The Laws of Air Warfare: Are There Any?" *Naval War College Review* 23 (February 1971): 37. W. Hays Parks, "Air War and the Laws of War," in Boog, *Conduct of the Air War*, pp. 324–30.

[4] Francis K. Mason, *Battle over Britain* (Garden City, N.Y.: Doubleday, 1969), pp. 17–18. George Quester, *Deterrence before Hiroshima: The Airpower Background of Modern Strategy* (New Brunswick, N.J.: Transaction Books, 1986), pp. 24–30. Also see H. A. Jones, *The War in the Air* (Oxford: Clarendon Press, 1935).

[5] Mason, *Battle over Britain*, pp. 19–22. John Terraine, *The Right of the Line: The Royal Air Force in the European War, 1934–1945* (London: Hodder & Stroughton, 1985), pp. 9–10.

Britain's civilian morale on several occasions, causing public panics.[6] The British did not respond immediately to these attacks either with new defenses or with offensive reprisals because of internal disagreement over the efficacy of diverting airpower from tactical to strategic missions. Nonetheless, two squadrons were temporarily assigned to homeland air defense, and by October deep-penetration raids were being launched at Germany. As the war progressed, plans for bombing the opponent's cities and civilians became more and more destructive. The Germans prepared incendiary raids intended to raze London and Paris. These were ultimately ruled out as futile as the overall German military situation grew increasingly hopeless. The British planned massive air attacks, some involving poison gas, against Germany for the spring of 1919, but the war ended first. The aim of the British raids would have been to destroy German morale.[7]

The aftermath of World War I witnessed the reduction of air forces along with initial efforts to limit airpower development and use. The Versailles treaty forced Germany to surrender, destroy, or dismantle military aircraft, engines, airships, and even hangars. Military planes, equipment, and training were forbidden to the newly scaled-down German armed forces. For a short time, even the production of air equipment was prohibited.[8]

The statesmen of the major powers discussed restrictions next at the Washington Conference. The attending states decided that meetings should be held to draw up new rules of aerial warfare. From December 1922 to February 1923, legal experts from the United States, Britain, France, Italy, Japan, and the Netherlands gathered at the Hague to consider the issue. In three months they put together a code that charted a middle course between the "necessities of war and the requirements of the standards of civilization."[9]

The thrust of the Hague rules was to prohibit attacks on nonmilitary objectives. Legitimate military targets would include "military forces, military works, military establishments or depots, factories constitut-

---

[6] Uri Bialer, *The Shadow of the Bomber: The Fear of Air Attack and British Politics, 1932–1939* (London: Royal Historical Society, 1980); Richard J. Overy, "Air Power and the Origins of Deterrence Theory before 1939," *Journal of Strategic Studies* 15 (1992): 78.

[7] Quester, *Deterrence before Hiroshima*, pp. 32–39, 44–45, 48.

[8] Edward L. Homze, *Arming the Luftwaffe: The Reich Air Ministry and the German Aircraft Industry, 1919–1939* (Lincoln: University of Nebraska Press, 1976), p. 2.

[9] See DeSaussure, "Laws of Air Warfare," p. 37; John Basset Moore, *International Law and Some Current Illustrations* (New York: Macmillan, 1924). Moore was the U. S. delegate at the Hague talks.

ing important and well-known centers engaged in the manufacture of arms, ammunition or distinctively military supplies, lines of communication or transportation used for military purposes." Bombing these would not be allowed, however, if doing so would cause destruction to the surrounding population, *except* in situations where the military concentration was significant enough to risk the danger to civilians. Although an important landmark in air disarmament efforts, these rules were never ratified because of disagreements over the definitions of important terms, such as "military target," and France's objection to the entire enterprise.[10]

The World Disarmament Conference of 1932 also addressed the limitation of air warfare. A number of proposals were considered, including the complete abolition of bombing and bombers. The aim of the talks was to identify "qualitatively" aggressive weapons and outlaw them. The commission covering air matters, though, could not agree on which types of aircraft to declare unquestionably offensive. The long-range bomber was considered particularly dangerous, but smaller aircraft and especially civilian planes could also be used to attack targets in heavily populated areas. When no agreement could be reached on which aircraft to ban or limit, the General Commission proposed to focus instead on drawing up rules for air war. The first rule, "Air attack against the civilian population shall be absolutely prohibited," was agreed to readily, but the second, "All bombardment from the air shall be abolished," depended on an agreement to limit military and civilian aircraft. This never happened. Thus no progress was made by the time the conference broke up in 1934 in the wake of Germany's rearmament.[11]

No further multilateral conferences on war in the air convened in the remaining years of the interwar period. But there were efforts to control the threat of strategic bombing. In February 1935 the British and French foreign ministers proposed that the signatories of Locarno treaties join in a similar effort to prevent air attack by pledging to assist any victim of an aggressor with their air forces. Hitler, however, desired an accord pertaining only to Germany's western border. The other countries would not go along with this. In the summer of 1935, the Führer himself suggested prohibiting bombing outside the actual battle zone, but the idea was thwarted by smaller powers, which had—cor-

---

[10] The French contended that existing land and naval regulations in international law covered air warfare. Spaight, *Air Power and War Rights*, p. 244, Bialer, *Shadow of the Bomber*, pp. 109–10.

[11] Marion William Boggs, "Attempts to Define and Limit 'Aggressive' Armaments in Diplomacy and Strategy," *University of Missouri Studies* 16, no. 1 (1941): 56–59.

rectly—realized that their territories might fall *inside* the zone Hitler was referring to.[12]

When war broke out in 1939, the only formal international agreements then in effect were the 1907 Hague Land War Conventions prohibiting the bombing of undefended places, which could not have been very reassuring, given the events of World War I. Yet even without a formal treaty, there did appear to be a consensus that nonmilitary, civilian targets should be spared in any future bombing campaign.[13] Shortly after the outbreak of war on 1 September 1939, President Roosevelt made a plea, "I am addressing this urgent appeal to every Government which may be engaged in hostilities publicly to affirm its determination that its armed forces shall in no event and under no circumstances undertake bombardment from the air of civilian populations or unfortified cities, upon the understanding that the same rules of warfare shall be scrupulously observed by all their opponents."[14] The British and French sent a formal acceptance to this appeal to the Germans on 3 September 1939, promising to bomb only "strictly military objectives in the narrowest sense of the word."[15] Hitler responded, "It is a precept of humanity in all circumstances to avoid bombing non-military objectives. . . . [T]he German Air Force has received the command to confine itself to military objectives." Both sides declared that their restraint was contingent on similar behavior by the other side.[16]

The nature of the rules of the air warfare can be summarized in terms of the three criteria of the institutional perspective: concordance, specificity, and duration. Concordance was nearly nonexistent. No agreement on aerial bombing had been accepted between World War I and World War II. At the start of the Second World War, Britain and Germany did agree verbally to restraint. But this last-minute accord raised, at a minimum, questions of sincerity. Specificity cannot be judged because no formal agreement existed. We can, however, use the rules drawn up at the Hague in 1923 as a benchmark. These rules were the most detailed of the interwar years, but they were troubled

[12] Spaight, *Air Power and War Rights*, pp. 248–49.

[13] This conclusion is based on the views of military and disarmament experts found in the Inter-Parliamentary Union, *What Would be the Character of a New War?* (London: Victor Gollanz, 1933), and Spaight, *Air Power and War Rights*, p. 43.

[14] As quoted in Spaight, *Air Power and War Rights*, p. 259. Roosevelt's plea was not that ingenuous. He expected Britain, France, and Poland to accept and Germany to refuse and thus be castigated by international opinion. See Crane, *Bombs, Cities, and Civilians*, pp. 31–33 (see Chap. 1, n. 89).

[15] *Documents on German Foreign Policy*, 7: 537 (see Chap. 2, n. 42).

[16] Spaight, *Air Power and War Rights*, pp. 259–60.

by disagreement. The main point of contention was the precise definition of a military objective. Was a factory with civilians producing parts for airplanes a legitimate target? Was it acceptable to bomb troop barracks surrounded by hospitals and schools? Each state seemed to have a different way of differentiating civilian from combatant, safe zone from battle area, legitimate from illegitimate.[17] Duration was also negligible. The ad hoc last-minute appeal by Roosevelt was the only vestige of official authority restricting bombing. To the extent that the Hague rules were an institution, they were not very well enforced in the alleged infractions that occurred during the 1930s in places such as Spain and China. Overall, the norms of air warfare were less developed than those relating to either submarine or chemical warfare.[18]

The military utility of airpower in strategic operations, particularly against enemy "morale" (i.e., civilians), was a matter of argument among experts in the interwar period. It was generally accepted that airpower would be important in future war, but its proper role was debated in each country. In World War I, strategic preference and technological limitations kept airpower primarily in a tactical support role; however, in the 1920s, a school of theorists emerged that strongly advocated the strategic use of airpower and even promoted it as a "decisive" means of warfare.

One of the leading strategic bombing enthusiasts was the Italian Giulio Douhet.[19] In his classic 1921 book *Command of the Air*, Douhet stressed the importance of an autonomous, ever-ready aerial force as the key to victory in future conflict. He expected that the conquering countries in a projected war would be those which had achieved "command of the air"—defined as preventing the enemy air force from flying. The airplane was considered the "offensive weapon par excellence." Douhet believed that bombing could be used directly against the enemy's peacetime industry, commerce sites, transportation, and civil population. He predicted the cumulative result would be the rupture of morale and possibly the country's social structure.[20]

---

[17] Moore, *International Law*, pp. 194–202; Spaight, *Air Power and War Rights*, pp. 43–47.

[18] Parks, "Air War and the Laws of War," pp. 310–72, argues that the rules were largely illegitimate.

[19] Although it is unclear how familiar Douhet's ideas were, advocates of strategic airpower in other countries included Marshal of the RAF Lord Hugh Trenchard (Britain), General Dr. Robert Knauss (Germany), and General William "Billy" Mitchell (United States).

[20] Giulio Douhet, *Command of the Air*, trans. Dino Ferrari (New York: Coward-McCann, 1942).

What was uncertain in the interwar years was whether Douhet's notion of strategic bombing was the best strategy. Several important questions existed. One was the effect that bombing would actually have on civilian morale. Some argued that hitting cities would stiffen resistance, not weaken it. The strategic position of each country should have affected its assessment of the utility of bombing. Airpower offered either advantages or disadvantages to states depending on their geography, demography, and industrial concentration. Those nations with vital centers far removed from their coasts and frontiers or possessing widely dispersed industries, shipping, and population were relatively less vulnerable. Another issue was whether strategic bombing was an intelligent use of resources. Effort and materiel invested in striking at cities behind the lines would inevitably detract from immediately advantageous tactical bombing against military targets.[21] Thus, like chemical warfare and submarine warfare, the military value of strategic bombing was interpreted by states in a variety of ways.

Little practical experience was available to resolve the uncertainties of the value of strategic bombing. World War I air offensives were limited by fleet size and aircraft capabilities. During the 1920s and 30s bombing operations were carried out by Italy in Ethiopia, Japan in China, and in the Spanish civil war. These confrontations, however, did not provide clear-cut lessons. In the first two, one side had overwhelming airpower (Italy and Japan), thus few insights were offered regarding the effectiveness of air defenses. In the Spanish civil war, airpower was primarily used in tactical missions. The strategic bombing of Barcelona and Madrid was mostly small scale and indecisive. The exception was the air campaign against Barcelona on 16–18 March 1938, which reportedly did shake morale considerably.[22] Yet as Richard P. Hallion has noted, overall "critics took away from the Spanish Civil War what they wished to believe, and they searched its lessons carefully to selectively acquire supporting data for their own particular viewpoint."[23] These viewpoints subsequently had much to do with

---

[21] For a general overview, see R. Ernest DuPuy and George Fielding Eliot, *If War Comes* (New York: Macmillan, 1937), pp. 60–61. George Fielding Eliot, *Bombs Bursting in Air: The Influence of Air Power on International Relations* (New York: Reynal & Hitchcock, 1939), p. 53.

[22] Eliot, *Bombs Bursting in Air*, pp. 28 and 56–57.

[23] Richard P. Hallion, *Strike from the Sky: The History of Battlefield Air Attack, 1911–1945* (Washington, D.C.: Smithsonian Institution Press, 1989), p. 110.

different decisions Germany and Britain made in air warfare in the Second World War.

THE AIR ARTILLERY OF THE THIRD REICH

Hitler was very specific on one aspect of the Luftwaffe's operations. He personally would make the decision on when restrictions on bombing raids would be lifted, particularly when terror was the object and London was the target.[24] Despite the unrestricted nature of the sea war, the limitation on Luftwaffe bombing remained in place for almost a year. On the night of 24 August 1940, twelve German bombers overshot their intended targets consisting of aircraft factories and oil refineries located at Rochester and Thameshaven, twenty miles east of London. Instead, they dropped their loads on the British capital, setting off a chain of reprisals that ended any hope for restraint in strategic bombing in the Second World War.[25] The Führer was enraged that his orders had been disregarded, even accidentally. The bomber crews responsible were sent to the infantry.[26]

The irony of this incident is that it may have made sense for Germany to wage an unlimited bombing campaign. The Third Reich had the advantage in airpower in the summer of 1940.[27] Even more important, Germany was in a uniquely favorable geostrategic position. Having conquered Scandinavia, the Low Countries, and France, Germany could easily reach Britain, but British bombers would have to fly over these areas to strike at German cities. And as the Luftwaffe

---

[24] See Führer War Directives no. 1, "Plan of Attack on Poland," 31 August 1939; no. 9, "Instructions for Warfare against the Economy of the Enemy," 29 November 1939; and no. 17, "For the Conduct of Air and Sea Warfare against England," 1 August 1940. These, and all directives cited below, are reprinted in H. R. Trevor-Roper, ed., *Blitzkrieg to Defeat: Hitler's War Directives, 1939–1945* (New York: Holt, Rinehart & Winston, 1964).
[25] Jerome Klinkowitz, *Their Finest Hours: Narratives of the R.A.F. and the Luftwaffe in WWII* (Ames: Iowa State University Press, 1989), pp. 101–2.
[26] Cajus Bekker, *The Luftwaffe War Diaries* (New York: Doubleday, 1968), p. 172. This punishment contrasts sharply with the minimal rebuke that Lemp received for violating the submarine rules by sinking the *Athenia*.
[27] Britain had some 900 bombers and 1150 fighters. Germany had 980 bombers and 1480 fighters, *facing England* (2100 bombers and 1700 fighters overall). The German forces were 69 percent ready following the campaign in France. See British Air Ministry, *The Rise and Fall of the German Air Force, 1933–1945* (New York: St. Martin's, 1983), p. 76. Both categories for the RAF were considered 75 percent serviceable. See Operations Staff IC, Oberkommando der Luftwaffe, "German Intelligence Appreciation of the R.A.F. and Comparison with Current Luftwaffe Strength," 16 July 1940, as reprinted in Mason, *Battle over Britain*, pp. 507–8.

recognized in 1939, Britain was more vulnerable to terror attacks than Germany was because of the greater density of its large cities.[28] Why did the Nazis show restraint?

The three perspectives point to different answers to this question. Institutionalism, given the weak conventions on aerial bombing and the rogue nature of Nazi Germany, would not have predicted restraint in this instance, but that was the chosen policy. Realism is also inadequate. Given the relative advantages the strategic situation offered Germany, the Luftwaffe should have pursued strategic bombing more aggressively, but it did not. Restraint was chosen because the organizational culture of the Luftwaffe considered strategic bombing less valuable militarily than those uses of airpower more closely tied to the Army's land campaign. Thus organizational culture most accurately accounts for Germany's unexpected restraint in the air war.

The Third Reich and Bombing Mores

Germany had a rather abrupt encounter with efforts to outlaw aerial bombing in the wake of World War I. The Versailles treaty mandated the elimination of the German Air Force. In all, some 15,000 aircraft and 27,000 engines were destroyed, the manufacture or import of aircraft and engines was prohibited for six months, restrictions on civilian aircraft were not lifted until the Paris Air Agreement of 1926, and limitations on military aircraft were never officially removed. Hitler rejected them over a decade later.[29]

Instead of halting German military air activity, the Versailles agreement pushed it underground. Germany pursued secret rearmament with the Soviet Union. General Hans von Seekt, head of the Truppenamt (the successor to the outlawed General Staff), positioned a small group of officers in the various sections of the Army dealing with aviation. These officers, who included Walter Wever, Albert Kesselring, and Hans-Jürgen Stumpff, were to serve as the seed of the future Luftwaffe. Sports flying clubs were established and supported by the Reichswehr (the army) for the purpose of developing aviation skills.

---

[28] Excerpts from intelligence report "Studie Blau" completed in the summer of 1939 found in General J. Schmid, "Beitrag zur Operationsstudie: 'Die Luftschlacht um England,' August 1940 bis April 1941," ZA 3/73, BA-MA. "Die Luftlage in Europa, Frühjar 1939," 2 May 1939, BA-MA. Chef. 1. Abt., "Luftkriegführung gegen England," 22 November 1939, RL 2 II/24, BA-MA.

[29] British Air Ministry, *Rise and Fall*, p. 1; Homze, *Arming the Luftwaffe*, pp. 1–4.

These ventures provided the basis for the rapid expansion of the Luftwaffe under the Nazi regime.[30]

Efforts to establish international rules on aerial warfare and armaments also occupied the 1920s. Germany, however, would not participate in these negotiations until after 1926 when it joined the League of Nations. Still officially constrained by the Versailles treaty, Germany's position was one based on strategic interests: it wanted equality in airpower with Britain and France. At the World Disarmament Conference at Geneva of 1931–32, the Germans pressed for either immediate disarmament or the creation of an interim German air force, while the Western powers made gradual reductions. The British and French were unwilling to make such a deal.[31] Germany's withdrawal from the conference appeared to put an end to any efforts at disarmament. In February 1935, Hitler officially unveiled the existence of an independent air arm—the Luftwaffe.

From 1935 to 1939, a number of proposals for limiting air warfare were circulated. On 21 July 1935 Hitler proposed in the Reichstag that Germany was ready to prohibit dropping bombs outside the battle zone. A more specific plan sent to the British in April of 1936 would have banned bombing within the range from the front of medium heavy artillery. Hitler had also advocated, like his Weimar predecessors, a complete prohibition on bombing.[32] Ultimately, of course, the Führer's plans for aggression ruled out any hopes for air disarmament.

This is not to suggest that Germany necessarily planned to violate any limitations. The Luftwaffe's doctrinal regulations issued in 1935 and 1940 maintained that attacks intended to terrorize the civilian population were to be avoided except in retaliation. And internal ordinances on international law reaffirmed the relevance of the Hague Rules of 1923, despite the failure of the international community to adopt them formally.[33]

---

[30] See F. L. Carsten, *The Reichswehr and Politics, 1918–1939* (Oxford: Clarendon Press, 1966). Homze, *Arming the Luftwaffe*, chaps. 1 and 2.

[31] Quester, *Deterrence before Hiroshima*, pp. 76, 80–81.

[32] Combat zone limitations were rejected by smaller powers, who foresaw their countries being quickly overrun and their cities exposed. Spaight, *Air Power and War Rights*, pp. 248–50. On this offer, skepticism is in order. Germany may have had ulterior motives in disarmament proposals. Weizäcker, the Foreign Ministry State Secretary, cynically urged his colleagues not to talk down disarmament, "since this is the only cheap coin in which we can pay." See *Documents on German Foreign Policy*, 1: 175; also see pp. 89–90, 174, 237, 242, 245, 248, 258.

[33] It was noted that the rules were not legally binding but were indicative of the future direction of international law. Horst Boog, "The Luftwaffe and Indiscriminate Bombing up to 1942," in Boog, *Conduct of the Air War*, pp. 377–78.

Furthermore, the underlying norm against bombing noncombatants—even if not cemented in treaties—did figure in Germany's intrawar signaling to the British concerning its intentions. Once again, the crucial link was the relationship of the norm to the balance of power. As with the submarine campaign, the Führer wanted to avoid provoking England by damaging cherished cities and killing civilians—particularly before Germany felt capable of dealing a decisive blow. Abandoning restraint would indicate war to the bitter end, and Hitler would have gladly settled the conflict short of that—at least in the early summer of 1940. In the Führer's racially-warped perspective, the English were a "Germanic" people and worthy of keeping around—unlike Jews and Slavs. Following the fall of France, Hitler seemed ready to concede world-power status to Britain in order to reach a peace in the West. He wanted to turn his forces toward Russia.[34] Any decision to terror bomb would be an implicit acknowledgment of total war and that was a choice that Hitler did not want to have to face.

The rules of air warfare and their link to the balance of power, however, cannot adequately account for what occurred. First, the lack of institutional robustness in the rules of air warfare indicated escalation was likely, but Germany practiced restraint. Still, there is little evidence that the Third Reich practiced restraint out of respect for the rules. Germany certainly did not choose restraint in order to keep its promise to Roosevelt. Hitler had already issued orders *not* to attack the British homeland from the air before the Polish campaign even began, but in a secret speech of October 1939, the Führer declared that he had no intention of adhering to the rules and would attack undefended cities.[35] Yet even after the Führer decided that a peace was not possible—that Germany must invade England—restraint was still maintained. There was apparently more to German restraint than international prohibitions—or the Führer's preferences.

External Opportunities

George Quester, in *Deterrence before Hiroshima*, argues that restraints in war are determined through a bargaining process between states,

---

[34] See Führer War Directives no. 1, "Plan of Attack on Poland," 31 August 1939; no. 2, "Hostilities in the West"; and no. 13, "Next Object in the West." Albrecht Kesselring, *The Memoirs of Field-Marshall Kesselring* (London: Greenhill Books, 1988), p. 48. Norman Rich, *Hitler's War Aims*, vol. 1, *Ideology, the Nazi State, and the Course of Expansion* (New York: Norton, 1973), p. 157.

[35] See Führer War Directive no. 1, "Plan of Attack on Poland," 31 August 1939. The 1923 Hague rules, although never ratified, appear to have been respected in the planning in the spring and summer of 1939. See "Planstudie 39, Heft I," RL 2/II/4, BA-MA,

not by the calculations of individual nations.[36] This is true to a point; Germany moved away from limited bombing against the British when it perceived that Britain had already done the same. It would not be accurate, however, to claim that the bargaining aspect implicit in deterrent logic was the central impetus behind Germany's original decision for restraint. After all, the Third Reich limited its air war when it had superiority in the ability to inflict pain. This was especially notable following the conquest of the Low Countries and France and continued into the first stages of the Battle of Britain. From a realist standpoint, this advantage should have led to escalation. But Germany chose restraint.

The British certainly expected Germany to attack English cities with the outbreak of war in September 1939. His Majesty's subjects widely believed that the Nazis had overwhelming airpower and they braced themselves for the onslaught.[37] Germany itself recognized that it had the strongest air force in Europe. In late November 1939 following the defeat of Poland, the head of Luftwaffe Intelligence even suggested that Germany should launch an air campaign targeting only British imports and docks. If Britain were to retaliate with terror attacks against civilians, they would be at a disadvantage in the war that would follow because of the greater density of London and other big industrial centers.[38]

But other factors were more compelling. First, Germany's strategy was oriented toward land warfare. The intention was to capture territory in the Low Countries and France, from which future air and sea raids would be launched against England. As one staff study noted, fuel and ammunition used in an air campaign would limit ground operations.[39] The other problem that stood in the way of launching an extensive bombing campaign against Britain was the lack of a long-range bomber. As Hitler had noted in his first War Directive, "Inconclu-

and "Luftkriegsrecht," Juli 1939, RL 4/82, BA-MA. Boog, "Luftwaffe and Indiscriminate Bombing," p. 375.

[36] Also see George Quester, "Bargaining and Bombing in World War II in Europe," *World Politics* 15 (April 1963): 417–37.

[37] Bialer, *Shadow of the Bomber*, pp. 159–60.

[38] "Die Luftlage in Europa, Frühjahr 1939," 2 Mai 1939, RL 2 II/464, BA-MA. "Proposal for the Conduct of Air Warfare against Britain," 22 November 1939, AHB Translation VII/30, as cited in Williamson Murray, "The Luftwaffe before the Second World War: A Mission, A Strategy?" *Journal of Strategic Studies* 4 (September 1981): 267. Also see Chef. 1. Abt., "Luftkriegführung gegen England," 22 November 1939, RL 2 II/24, BA-MA.

[39] Chef. 1. Abt., "Luftkriegführung gegen England," 22 November 1939, RL 2 II/24, BA-MA.

sive results with insufficient forces are to be avoided in all circumstances."[40] The choice in this instance appeared to be whether Germany should make use of its advantage immediately, or to delay to make use of an even better geographical advantage after conquering the Low Countries. The choice was not clear. The Luftwaffe also expected its air superiority to wane in the future since British production would likely increase faster than that of Germany.[41] Nonetheless, expectations were high as indicated by a note attached to Hitler's War Directive no. 6 in October 1939, "If we were in possession of Holland, Belgium, or even the straits of Dover as jumping off bases for German aircraft, then, without a doubt, Great Britain could be struck a mortal blow, even if the strongest reprisals were attempted."[42]

With the fall of France, any question of Germany's superior position for waging an unrestricted air campaign was erased. Luftwaffe Intelligence concluded, "The Luftwaffe is clearly superior to the RAF as regards strength, equipment, training, command, and location of bases. In the event of an intensification of air warfare, the Luftwaffe, unlike the RAF will be in a position in every respect to achieve a decisive effect this year."[43] On 24 May 1940 Hitler announced that as soon as the units could be mustered, the Luftwaffe would embark on its independent mission against England—but the targets would be ports, shipping, and military industry, not terror raids against civilians. Hitler had again hoped for some kind of accommodation with the British in June 1940, but getting no positive responses, he began to draw up other plans.[44]

On 16 July Hitler ordered his armed forces to prepare for Operation Sealion—the invasion of Britain. The Luftwaffe was to forego its independent campaign. Its task was to defeat the RAF so it would not interfere with the German invasion. After that the Luftwaffe would act as a kind of "airborne artillery" in support of the land forces. Some Luftwaffe leaders were anxious to attack London, not to wage an unre-

[40] On Hitler's plans, see Führer War Directive no. 6, "Plans for Offensive in the West," 9 October 1939; Führer Directive no. 1, "Plan of Attack on Poland," 31 August 1939.

[41] Excerpts from intelligence report "Studie Blau" completed in the summer of 1939, in General J. Schmid, "Beitrag zur Operationsstudie: 'Die Luftschlacht um England,' August 1940 bis April 1941," ZA 3/73, BA-MA.

[42] Hitler, "Memorandum and Directives for the Conduct of the War in the West," 9 October 1939, Doc. L-52, in *NCA*, 7: 806 (see Chap. 2, n. 25).

[43] Operations Staff IC, Oberkommando der Luftwaffe, "German Intelligence Appreciation of the R.A.F. and Comparison with Current Luftwaffe Strength," 16 July 1940, as reprinted in Mason, *Battle over Britain*, pp. 507–8.

[44] Führer War Directive no. 13, "Next Object in the West," 24 May 1940. Rich, *Hitler's War Aims*, pp. 157–59.

stricted bombing campaign aimed at breaking civilian morale, but to achieve air superiority by destroying RAF fighters seeking to defend the capital which had otherwise refused to expose themselves. Others, including Hitler, considered whether indiscriminate bombings might cause an uprising among disgruntled workers. Nonetheless, Hitler still maintained restraint on attacks on London, despite the incentives for escalation.[45] It was not until the British attack on Berlin, allegedly in reprisal for the accidental German raid on London, that Hitler allowed his forces to abandon restraint in the air.

Those who would want to rescue realism in this case would argue that Hitler chose restraint because he was concerned about German vulnerability to air attack—thus he was "deterred." It is alleged that he worried that the support of the German people for his regime might wane if the British began to bomb cities wantonly.[46] But the evidence for this argument is sparse. There is little to indicate that the Führer believed then that Germany would crack before Britain. In fact, in the summer of 1940, following the defeat of France, German confidence was relatively high.[47] There were even reports of public impatience over the delay in finishing England.[48] This, of course, is not to say that there was no concern on the part of the Nazi leadership in this area (what leader would not care?), but instead the point is that this problem cannot explain why Hitler did not pursue an unrestricted campaign at this time.

The answer to this puzzle comes in an understanding of Hitler's— and, indeed, the Luftwaffe's—expectations of the success of an unrestricted strategic bombing campaign. In the initial stages of the war, the goal was to defeat Britain by cutting off its air and sea trade, to shut down the British economy by attacking it at decisive points.[49] But

[45]Führer War Directive no. 16, "On Preparations for a Landing Operation against England," 16 July 1940. Karl Klee, "The Battle of Britain," in H. A. Jacobsen and J. Rohwer, eds., *Decisive Battles of World War II: The German View* (New York: G. P. Putnam & Sons, 1965), pp. 81, 88; Bekker, *Luftwaffe War Diaries*, p. 172; David Irving, *The Rise and Fall of the Luftwaffe: The Life of Luftwaffe Marshal Erhard Milch* (London: Weidenfeld & Nicolson, 1973), pp. 97, 105; Boog, "Luftwaffe and Indiscriminate Bombing," pp. 389–90.
[46]Quester, *Deterrence before Hiroshima*, p. 100; Richard J. Overy, "Hitler and Air Strategy," *Journal of Contemporary History* 15 (July 1980): 411.
[47]See the reports on popular mood in Heinz Boberach, *Meldungen aus dem Reich* (Neuwied: Herman Luchterhard, 1965), pp. 79–97.
[48]John Lukacs, *The Duel: 10 May–31 July 1940, The Eighty-Day Struggle between Churchill and Hitler* (New York: Ticknor & Fields, 1991), pp. 173–74.
[49]See Führer War Directives no. 6, "Plans for Offensive in the West," 9 October 1939, and no. 9, "Instructions for Warfare against the Economy of the Enemy," 29 November 1939.

this did not include morale bombing. A July 1939 Luftwaffe Intelligence report pointed out that the British were known for their toughness and it was not certain that an air campaign alone would bring their defeat.[50] Already in May of 1939, Hitler had told his service chiefs that Britain could not be defeated by air attack alone.[51] In July 1940, Reich Marshal Hermann Göring, Luftwaffe CINC, challenged the assumption that an independent Luftwaffe campaign would destroy the British will to fight when no one believed that the Germans would stop fighting if Berlin were bombed.[52] Hitler also lacked faith in a terror campaign. When his impatience grew with the air and sea blockade strategy, he began to plan the invasion of England, not a massive bombing campaign. Even the Luftwaffe bomber pilots at times appeared in the camp of the skeptics.[53] A lack of expectation of success in morale bombing, reinforced by such obvious drawbacks as possible retaliation against German cities, produced a preference for restraint.

Was an unrestricted, independent strategic bombing campaign likely to fail? The standard argument claims that it was, that Germany erred when in the fall of 1940 it switched to bombing cities instead of sticking with its attacks on Fighter Command installations. Given the specific evolution of the Battle of Britain, this view has merit, but it also overlooks what might have been, had Germany's plans and capabilities been different. Several historians, along with actual participants (for example, Field Marshal Erhard Milch, Director General of Luftwaffe Air Armament), have maintained that if Germany had possessed heavy bombers and plans for their deployment earlier in the war, the course, and perhaps the outcome, of the war may have been different. The Luftwaffe could have attacked Britain's navy and merchant ships more effectively, which would have made it much more difficult for Britain to keep its vital sea lines open. Germany also would have been able to firebomb English cities before Britain could retaliate in kind. Furthermore, British air defenses, effective against medium bombers, would have been sorely tested by the larger, more powerful heavy bombers.[54]

---

[50] Excerpts from "Studie Blau," in Schmid, "Beitrag zur Operatiionsstudie," ZA 3/73, BA-MA.

[51] "Minutes of a Conference on 23 May 1939," in Doc. L-74, in *NCA*, 7: 852–53.

[52] Matthew Cooper, *The German Air Force, 1933–1945: An Anatomy of Failure* (London: Jane's, 1981), p. 127.

[53] General Werner Baumbach, ex-bomber ace, believed that air alone was not enough to defeat Britain in 1940 and cooperation between all arms of the military was necessary. See his memoirs, *Broken Swastika: The Defeat of the Luftwaffe* (London: Robert Hale, 1960), p. 77.

[54] The heavy bomber also might have proved useful in the Mediterranean and for attacking industrial targets in the East. Oberst Hans Heming Freiherr von Beust, Beitrag

Of course, given the limitations of strategic bombing revealed not only in World War II but also in Korea and Vietnam, these claims must be treated with care. Nonetheless, they suggest how the availability of different capabilities and strategic views could have made a significant difference in Germany's conduct of the war.

Why the Germans lacked faith in an independent air campaign, particularly one directed against enemy morale, is the real puzzle of German airpower policy in World War II. Why did the Germans not pursue the apparent benefits of the strategic air offensive?

The Culture of Land Power

The answer to this question lies in the body of beliefs that resulted from the organizational evolution of the Luftwaffe, and more generally, the armed forces as a whole. Having only come into existence as an independent service (Germany's third after the Army and Navy) in 1935, the Luftwaffe's culture was relatively unsettled. What happened thereafter is a matter of debate. Was the Luftwaffe a "handmaiden" of the Army or was it guided by the same type of enthusiasm for strategic bombing found in other air forces?[55] Neither of these extremes stands up to scrutiny. The schools of thought at the command level spanned a conceptual range from strategic bombing to supporting army operations. By the beginning of the war, however, the Luftwaffe had become increasingly dominated by a philosophy of airpower attached to land operations. It was certainly an independent arm of the Wehrmacht, and some of its leaders did at times advocate strategic bombing. But strategic bombing was rarely associated with the type of morale bombing thinking that emerged in the Royal Air Force. This departure from

---

zur Studie 1, "Die deutsche Luftwaffe im spanischen Krieg," 18 August 1955, ZA 3/14, BA-MA. See Richard J. Overy, "From 'Uralbomber' to 'Amerikabomber': The Luftwaffe and Strategic Bombing," *Journal of Strategic Studies* (September 1978): 174–75; Richard Suchenwirth, *Historical Turning Points in the German Air Force Effort*, USAF Historical Study no. 189 (Maxwell Air Force Base, Ala.: USAF Historical Division, 1959), pp. 43–44; Andreas Nielson, *The German Air Force General Staff*, USAF Historical Study no. 173 (Maxwell Air Force Base, Ala.: USAF Historical Division, 1959), pp. 172–73.

[55] See Williamson Murray, *Luftwaffe*, (Baltimore, Md.: Nautical and Aviation, (1985), p. 1 and note 1. Murray criticizes the "handmaiden" notion for giving short shrift to the substantial support for strategic bombing within the Luftwaffe. Also Klaus A. Maier, "Total War and German Air Doctrine before the Second World War," in Wilhelm Diest, ed., *The German Military in an Age of Total War* (Warwickshire, U.K.: Berg, 1985), p. 212. In "Luftwaffe and Indiscriminate Bombing," and in *Die deutsche Luftwaffenführung, 1935–1945* (Stuttgart: Deutsche Verlags-Anstalt, 1982), Horst Boog presents a more composite approach, though his emphases differ from Murray's.

a morale offensive creed was a significant determinant of Germany's restraint in air warfare. The story of this influence can be seen in the origins, capabilities, and policies of the Luftwaffe.

The roots of the Luftwaffe were firmly planted in Army tradition. At the end of World War I, the Luftstreitkräfte or Air Service analyzed that conflict's lessons and found little value in strategic bombing. This perspective largely characterized the work of the shadow air staff that covertly studied and developed airpower for Germany until the early 1930s.[56]

Between 1933 and World War II, three rough categories of airpower theory—which over time moved away from morale bombing—are evident in the Luftwaffe's development. The first category, and the one closest to British thinking, maintained that air forces are capable of producing victory on their own by attacks on the opponent's morale (via the bombing of civilians, food supply, utilities, and so on). In Nazi Germany, this argument was made in 1933 by Dr. Robert Knauss, a Lufthansa executive and future director of the Air War Academy. Using a deterrence-type logic, he contended that a large bomber force would scare off interference by outside powers in Germany's rearmament. Knauss recommended a four-hundred bomber "risk fleet," which would threaten enemy industry and population centers and make adversaries think twice about interfering in the Reich affairs; however, due to Army resistance, resource constraints, and technical shortcomings, this risk fleet was never built.[57]

A second school of airpower that emerged in the mid-1930s was championed by General Wever, the first chief of the Air Staff. Wever did not believe that the Luftwaffe would win a war on its own. Instead, he argued that cooperation between the services was the key to victory. Since the Army was the largest, the Luftwaffe would support it first by gaining air superiority and destroying the enemy air force, then by interdiction—the disruption of enemy troops, supplies, and communications—and then by direct support of surface operations. Behind these came the strategic bombing role that targeted the enemy's sources of military power such as industry. Destroying the morale of the enemy was the goal, but Wever argued that this could be done best by crushing the enemy's armed forces. Terror attacks on civilians were specifically ruled out except in reprisal. Nonetheless, if ground

[56] James S. Corum, *The Roots of Blitzkrieg: Hans von Seekt and German Military Reform* (Lawrence: University Press of Kansas, 1992), pp. 144–68. Corum also notes exceptions to this thinking.

[57] Murray, *Luftwaffe*, p. 8; Homze, *Arming the Luftwaffe*, pp. 54–56.

operations did reach a stalemate, the door was left open for a turn to full-fledged independent strategic air actions.[58]

The third school evident in the Luftwaffe was tied to support for the Army. It emerged most fully in the course of Germany's intervention in the Spanish civil war in 1936–39.[59] In response to a plea for help from General Franco and the Nationalists, the Nazis sent the Condor Legion. Göring welcomed the intervention as a chance to test his pilots. Under the advocacy of Baron Wolfram von Richtofen (a cousin of Manfred von Richtofen), Germany developed the tactics of close air support of army operations. Forward controllers would call in air strikes in support of the land battle in progress. In the words of one participant, the Condor Legion was used as a "long arm of the artillery."[60] Richtofen's emphasis on close air support spread through the Luftwaffe and had a significant influence on overall doctrine.[61] The Germans did not generally use strategic city bombing in Spain, despite well-publicized attacks on cities. Guernica, for example, popularly known as the site of the test case for Nazi terror bombing, was according to Richtofen's personal diary a tactical target: it was an important center of communications for the retreating Basque forces.[62] Overall, the German experience in Spain helped to push Douhetian conceptions in the Luftwaffe to the background.[63]

[58] These were articulated in his speech at the opening of the Air Warfare Academy, 1 November 1935, reprinted in Boog, *Die deutsche Luftwaffenführung,* pp. 631–35, and Eugene J. Emme, ed., *The Impact of Airpower: National Security and World Politics* (Princeton, N.J.: Von Nostrand, 1959), pp. 181–85, and the Luftwaffe's statement of doctrine (L.DV. 16—"Luftkriegführung"), which first appeared in 1935 and is reprinted in Karl-Heinz Wölker, *Dokumente und Dokumentarfotos zur Geschichte der deutschen Luftwaffe* (Stuttgart: Deutsche Verlags Anstalt, 1968), pp. 466–86. For a similar view of Wever's ideas, see K. H. Völker, *Die deutsche Luftwaffe, 1933–1939: Aufbau, Führung und Rüstung der Luftwaffe sowie die Entwicklung der deutschen Luftkriegstheorie* (Stuttgart: Deutsche Verlags Anstalt, 1967), pp. 198–201. Also Manfred Messerschmidt, "German Military Effectiveness between 1919 and 1939," in Allan R. Millet and Williamson Murray, eds., *Military Effectiveness,* vol. 3, *The Interwar Period* (Boston: Allen & Unwin, 1988), pp. 245–48.
[59] Baumbauch, *Broken Swastika,* p. 20, relates that the former army and navy officers that formed the new Luftwaffe were generally advocates of direct or indirect support of ground forces.
[60] Letter from Hauptmann Christ to an unnamed Oberstleutnant in the 1. Abteilung, 11 February 1938, RL 35/3, BA-MA.
[61] Williamson Murray, "The Luftwaffe Experience 1939–1941," in Benjamin Franklin Cooling, ed., *Case Studies in the Development of Close Air Support* (Washington, D.C.: Office of Air Force History, USAF, 1990), pp. 75–77; Samuel W. Mitcham, *Men of the Luftwaffe* (Novato, Calif.: Presidio Press, 1988), pp. 51–53; British Air Ministry, *Rise and Fall,* p. 17, notes the opposition Richtofen encountered in his advocacy of close air support.
[62] Maier, "Total War and German Air Doctrine," p. 215.
[63] Oberst Hans Heming Freiherr von Beust, Beitrag zur Studie 1, "Die deutsche Luftwaffe im spanischen Krieg," 18 August 1955, ZA 3/14, BA-MA. A memo issued by the

This evolution did *not* result in a Luftwaffe exclusively dedicated to direct support of the Army. Believers in strategic bombing remained, even believers in targeting civilian populations, including at times General Hans Jeschonnek, Chief of the Luftwaffe General Staff. But organizational momentum was headed away from the sort of Douhetian thinking found in the Royal Air Force. And those in Germany who trusted strategic bombing generally advocated a more limited version, focusing on shorter-range missions closer to an interdiction role such as targeting communications, force concentrations, and munitions depots in the rear of the battle lines, with occasional longer-range objectives on aircraft industry sites. These campaigns were also envisioned as relatively short term, usually as a prelude to or follow-up after a ground operation.[64] German planning and operations consistently listed the hierarchy of Luftwaffe's aims as (1) the destruction of enemy airpower, then (2) support of the Army and Navy, and finally (3) tasks that might be considered strategic bombing.[65] In the course of the war, strategic operations were rarely given priority over support of the ground forces.

The controversy over whether the Luftwaffe would be strategic or tactical was also played out in procurement. What capabilities would the Luftwaffe develop and produce? The central issue was whether a heavy bomber should be built. Those like Knauss who argued for a Douhetian strategic force favored a four-engine bomber capable of carrying heavier bomb loads greater distances. Dive-bombers, on the other hand, were generally smaller and faster and more capable of supporting land troops because of their accuracy in delivering munitions.

In the period 1933–35, when strategic bombing received a great deal of attention in the Luftwaffe, the heavy bomber had first priority in

General Staff in 1938 stated, "The emphasis in offensive bombardment has clearly shifted from area to pinpoint bombardment. For this reason, the development of a bombsight suitable for use in dive-bomber aircraft is more important than the development of any other aiming device." Suchenwirth, *Historical Turning Points*, p. 31.

[64] See, for example, the Felmy report of May 22, 1939, as cited in Maier, "Total War and German Air Doctrine," pp. 216–17. General D. Paul Deichmann, *German Air Force Operations in Support of the Army* (New York: Arno Press, 1968), pp. 54–55, 93, 121–23, 126; British Air Ministry, *Rise and Fall*, p. 42; Overy, "From 'Uralbomber' to 'Amerikabomber'," pp. 158–59; Boog, "Luftwaffe and Indiscriminate Bombing," pp. 373–90.

[65] See "Weisungen des Oberbefehlshabers der Luftwaffe für die Führung der Operationen in der ersten Zeit eines Krieges," 18 November 1935, as reprinted in Völker, *Dokumente and Dokumentarphotos*, pp. 445–49; "Aufmarsch-und Kampfanweisungen der Luftwaffe: Weisungen für den Einsatz gegen Osten," Mai 1939, RL 2 II/21, BA-MA; Führer War Directive no. 16 "Preparations for a Landing Operation against England," 16 July 1940.

the development program. Beginning in the middle of 1936, a series of decisions were made which downgraded the priority of the heavy-bomber program. Finally on 29 April 1937, Göring ordered the two prototypes for the heavy bombers to be scrapped. This happened despite information from abroad indicating that Germany's opponents considered the four-engine bomber the "air weapon of the future."[66]

There were a number of factors that weighed in this decision. The most authoritative study of the heavy bomber emphasizes economic and technological factors in explaining its setbacks. With across-the-board rearmament taking place, the Germans were facing budget constraints, raw-material shortages, and technical problems with engine developments.[67] Delaying development of the heavy bomber was natural. The program demanded a great deal of "input" with little faith in its "output." The dive-bomber, on the other hand, was already developed and did not waste resources through inaccurate bombing. And finally, as Göring related: "The Führer does not ask how big my bombers are, but how many there are."[68]

But what is overlooked in these important arguments is the bias against the heavy bomber, which affected its priority in a budget squeeze and consequently, the makeup and missions of the Luftwaffe. Richard Overy points out that when Göring and Colonel General Ernst Udet, Director General of Air Armament, emphasized the shortage of raw materials to justify postponing development of the heavy bomber, no one mentioned that even though such a plane required two and a half times the resources of a medium bomber, it could carry four to five times the bomb load twice as far.[69]

In contrast, there was a tendency to favor the dive-bomber. Richard Suchenwirth describes this bias: "Luftwaffe leaders clung to the dive-bomber concept with a stubbornness explainable only on the basis of sheer blindness. Horizontal bombing was completely out of the picture as far as they were concerned."[70] The precedent of battlefield support

[66] General Paul Deichmann, cited in Nielson, *The German Air Force General Staff*, p. 156. General Christian, among others, claimed in 1945 that Göring, Udet, and Jeschonnek were responsible for the decision to forgo building the heavy bomber. RL 2 IV/146, BA-MA. Wever himself, however, seems to have reached a decision on 6 May 1936 to produce mainly fast medium bombers for the time being. See Boog, *Die deutsche Luftwaffenführung*, pp. 165–66. Edward L. Homze, "The Luftwaffe's Failure to Develop a Heavy Bomber before WWII," *Aerospace Historian* 24 (spring 1977): 21–22.

[67] See Homze, *Arming the Luftwaffe*, or the summary of the argument in Homze, "Luftwaffe's Failure,"

[68] Irving, *Rise and Fall of the Luftwaffe*, p. 54.

[69] Overy, "From 'Uralbomber' to 'Amerikabomber'," pp. 171–72.

[70] Suchenwirth, *Historical Turning Points*, p. 38.

of the Army had been developed in World War I and its legacy would last through World War II. It is no accident that the heavy bombers that were developed such as the HE-177, were required by the Air General Staff to be able to dive-bomb also, which severely limited their operational capabilities as heavy bombers.[71] Hitler claimed ignorance of this crucial development. When the air manufacturer Ernst Heinkel told the Führer that the heavy bombers he was requesting had been held up by the dive-bombing requirement of six years earlier, Hitler replied: "But that's madness! I've heard nothing of this until today. Is it possible there could be so many idiots?"[72]

Hitler, of course, was part of the problem. He was an ex-"Army man" from World War I and shared many of the ground-force biases of the German continental tradition. He had little knowledge of, and paid little attention to, theories of airpower. The Army and its equipment took most of his time. He paid less attention to bombing than he did to defensive measures against enemy bombing. Furthermore, he showed more interest in static air defenses—particularly the 88mm gun—than in fighter air defenses. Hitler never insisted the Luftwaffe develop strategic bombing before the war and appeared to have little belief in it. This contrasts sharply with his enthusiasm for Blitzkrieg concepts.[73]

The Luftwaffe made no plans or preparations for the type of large-scale strategic bombing campaign possible under unrestricted air warfare. The Luftwaffe, like the Army that fathered it, relied on furthering the land campaign and viewed the defeat of enemy forces, not the destruction of civilian morale, as the key to victory. As the war went on, airpower became increasingly subordinated to the Army's needs.[74]

In line with this doctrine, the Germans argue that they never violated the air restrictions.[75] Attacks made on Warsaw during the invasion of Poland, although causing civilian deaths, were allegedly aimed at military targets and were intended to break the tactical defense of the city.

---

[71] On World War I, see Deichmann, *German Air Force Operations*, pp. 121–22; Corum, *Roots of Blitzkrieg*, pp. 13–18. Overy, "From 'Uralbomber' to 'Amerikabomber'," pp. 168–69; Homze, *Arming the Luftwaffe*, pp. 63–68; Mitcham, *Men of the Luftwaffe*, p. 59.

[72] Overy, "From 'Uralbomber' to 'Amerikabomber'," pp. 173–74.

[73] See Overy, "Hitler and Air Strategy."

[74] Deichmann, *German Air Force Operations*, pp. 125–27.

[75] Kesselring stated, "I also pledge my honor that the war, as I saw it, was conducted by us Germans with chivalry—as far as this is possible in war—and with humanity." Kesselring, *Memoirs*, p. 48. This of course is debatable. For different views on this matter, Murray, *Luftwaffe*, pp. 31 and 32; Olaf Groehler, "The Strategic Air War and Its Impact on the German Civilian Population," in Boog, *Conduct of the Air War*, pp. 282–83; and Boog, "Luftwaffe and Indiscriminate Bombing," p. 386.

The attacks that eventually brought the fall of the city were conducted only after numerous warnings were given and civilians had been permitted to leave.[76] The British history of the Luftwaffe points out that in the 1940 campaign leading to the fall of France German bombers were used strategically only during one four-day period in June for attacks on French aircraft industry in Paris and fuel dumps in Marseilles.[77] Even the well-publicized bombing of Rotterdam was a case of excessive firepower aimed at defeating the city's tactical defenses.[78]

When Britain bombed industrial targets in the Ruhr following the Rotterdam raid, Hitler's Luftwaffe did not even respond. It continued its support of the invasion rolling across Western Europe. Hitler himself seems to have dismissed the raids as inadvertent. He assumed that the bombing of German territory was the result of someone losing their head due to the pressure of the Battle of France or that the RAF had acted on its own. He saw no need to retaliate in kind.[79]

But the power of culture on German actions also had limits. Germany would not refrain from city-bombing indefinitely in the absence of British restraint. For reasons largely outside organizational culture—the engagement of national morale, the desire to retaliate against the British in kind, an urge to try a new strategy in the Battle of Britain—escalation overwhelmed the tendency for restraint. Finally, when the British struck at Berlin, Germany turned to unrestricted attacks on England.[80]

Conclusion: Custom, Calculation, Restraint

History indicates that a number of factors played a part in German restraint, including personalities, economics, and accidents. Nonethe-

---

[76] See the testimonies of Jodl in *IMT*, 15: 335 and Kesselring and Göring in *IMT*, 9: 25, 53, 131 (see Chap. 2, n. 22). The French Air attaché in Warsaw, General Armergaud reported, "I must emphasize that operations by the German Air Force have been in conformity with the rules of warfare." *IMT*, 9: 359–60. Nonetheless, as Boog, "Luftwaffe and Indiscriminate Bombing," p. 386, notes, the character of these attacks was akin to terror raids because of the means employed. Some of the attacks were carried out by shoveling incendiaries out the side of a transport plane. Butler, *Grand Strategy*, 2: 567 (see Chap. 2, n. 91), also notes that the bombing of Warsaw on 24 and 25 September was not limited to military objectives. The issue is whether these can be regarded as necessary attacks to weaken a "defended" city.

[77] British Air Ministry, *Rise and Fall*, p. 72.

[78] See William A. Swint, "The German Air-Attack on Rotterdam Revisited," *Aerospace Historian* 21 (March 1974): 14–22; Boog, "Luftwaffe and Indiscriminate Bombing," pp. 386–87.

[79] As reported by General Warlimont to Walter Ansel, *Hitler Confronts England* (Durham: Duke University Press, 1960), p. 113.

[80] Hitler on 4 September claimed, "For months I have not responded in the hope they will stop this nuisance. Herr Churchill has seen this as a sign of weakness. You will

less, one central theme emerges. Neither Hitler nor the Luftwaffe ever felt that unrestricted strategic bombing—in terms of attacking the civilian population of cities to break the fighting will of the country—could win the war. Restraint, therefore, never appeared illogical.

This policy was reaffirmed by several considerations related to institutionalist and realist theories. First, Hitler hoped for peace with Britain so he could turn his armies against Russia.[81] Due to the norms against bombing civilians, unrestricted bombing would have sent the wrong message. Yet even in July 1940, after it was clear that no accommodation could be reached, the Third Reich maintained restraint. Second, Hitler probably wanted to avoid provoking the bombing of German cities, especially when the benefits of unrestricted bombing were uncertain. Thus realism seems relevant. What a relative advantage cannot explain, however, is why the Nazis maintained limitations even when they realized that they could hurt much more than they would be hurt in a strategic air exchange.

To understand restraint, we must look to the source of doubt about bombing targeted against civilian morale. This resided primarily in Germany's strategic culture, of which, the Luftwaffe was a part. Germany was a Continental power heavily influenced by a traditional army outlook. Germany's air force evolved in a fashion different from that envisioned by Douhet and realized in Britain. It was certainly an independent service in the sense that it was organizationally separate from the Army and Navy and not subservient to their orders. Nonetheless, cultures often run deeper than formal structures and the Luftwaffe—affected by a number of factors, including Wever's death, the war in Spain, and constraints of time, resources and technology—evolved within Germany's orientation to surface combat. Hitler himself was an "Army man" and prone to a ground-forces mentality. In the short period the Nazi air organization had to develop in the prewar period it successively shifted closer to an Army support role and away from city bombing. This was hardly an outcome preordained by geography, as evident in the existence of different schools of airpower thought in Germany. Some saw morale bombing as just as likely a means to vic-

---

understand that we now give our reply night for night, and in increasing measure." Frederick M. Sallagar, *The Road to Total War* (New York: Van Nostrand Reinhold, 1969), p. 57, speculatively argues that Hitler bombed London to cover his embarrassment over his inability to invade Britain.

[81] Yet Hitler allowed unrestricted submarine attacks on British merchants and passenger liners, despite the negative impact this would have on the possibility of accommodation.

tory as interdiction or close air support.[82] A strategic bombing subculture certainly remained a part of the Luftwaffe, but it did not take root and dominate the organization like in Britain.

The Luftwaffe's orientation had several consequences for decisions on restricted aerial warfare. First, it shaped how the costs and benefits of strategic bombing were calculated. Restraint seemed a better decision when no bureaucratic authority was cohesively arguing that the war could be won by breaking Britain's morale directly through bombing. Second, no plans were ever developed for an unrestricted campaign, so such a campaign was not easily feasible when the opportunity presented itself. Finally, and perhaps most important, the turn of the Luftwaffe away from the strategic offensive meant the necessary capabilities for successful city bombing were never acquired. Given these effects of the Luftwaffe's organizational development, Germany's incentives to escalate were significantly circumscribed, if not determined: restraint was, therefore, the favored choice.

BRITAIN'S PROMISCUOUS BOMBING[83]

In the interwar period, Britain perceived that unrestricted bombing was not in its interests, particularly when Germany appeared as the main challenger. The United Kingdom's population, industry, and trade were more densely located in cities than was the case in the Third Reich. London was regarded as one of the most exposed of all cities in Europe to air attack. In 1934 Churchill called the British capital "a tremendous fat cow, a valuable fat cow tied up to attract the beasts of prey."[84] This perception of asymmetrical vulnerability was a key determinant of the British attitude toward the regulation of aerial war-

---

[82] Lacking a strong organizational history, individuals were apt to play a larger role in this case. One wonders whether having a strong strategic bombing enthusiast such as Knauss in charge of the Luftwaffe would have led to greater efforts to overcome technical barriers and the constraining influence of the broader German martial culture.

[83] The British referred to indiscriminate bombing in World War I as "promiscuous." See Best, *Humanity in Warfare*, p. 269.

[84] Spaight, *Air Power and War Rights*, p. 31. The British were particularly concerned about the threat that would result from the German occupation of the Low Countries. CID COS Sub-committee, "The Potential Air Menace to This Country from Germany," 12 June 1934, CAB 53/24, PRO (all documents cited as CAB can be found in the Cabinet Papers located at the Public Record Office); COS 786, 24 October 1938, as cited in *The R.A.F. in the Bomber Offensive against Germany, vol. 1, Pre-War Evolution of Bomber Command* (Air History Branch, Air Ministry), p. 256, AIR 41/39 (all documents cited as AIR are found in the Air Ministry Papers located at the PRO).

fare. By the outset of war, British strategic bombing policy was one of strict limitation.

In May 1940, however, Britain's worst fears were realized: Germany was overrunning the Low Countries and France. Soon Hitler would have not only numerically greater forces, but also a superior land base to strike at Britain. Nonetheless, it was the RAF, not the Luftwaffe, that took the lead in breaking the "no homelands" barrier when it attacked the Ruhr on 15–16 May 1940. Britain escalated the air war even though few outside the RAF believed that such a move would have any significant effect on Germany's blitzkrieg. Later that summer, with Germany in control of most of Western Europe and planning an imminent crossing of the Channel, Britain contributed further to the final collapse of the air regime by bombing Berlin. Given its concerns and policy, why was the United Kingdom so willing to escalate the air war?

The weak institutionalization of the air regime would suggest the likelihood of escalation in this case and that is indeed what happened—eventually. But even though Britain believed that Germany had violated the pledge to honor restrictions—allowing action in kind—the RAF still showed restraint for the first eight months of the war. And what is surprising is that Britain, the country that seemed most dedicated to restraint, initiated widespread escalation. Realism, on the other hand, would predict restraint, given Britain's disadvantages in bombing capabilities at the time, but cannot account for the escalation that occurred within a year of the beginning of the war despite Britain's continuing relative vulnerability. Some argue that Britain's escalation was actually a realistic adaptation to circumstances: it did the most it could with what it had, using the strategy it believed was most effective. This position has merit, but it glosses over why Britain had capabilities and beliefs that were ill-suited to its aims and circumstances. Organizational culture provides a more convincing answer by showing how the RAF's beliefs and customs decisively narrowed planning, capabilities, and thinking to one option— strategic bombing—so that when war came, escalation was virtually unavoidable.

An Advocate for Restraint

The interest of the British government in limiting air warfare was apparent from the end of the First World War. This desire was largely driven by a perception of asymmetric vulnerability. Some leaders regarded the rules of air warfare as a strategic tool that might be used to cover defensive needs. A look at the evolution of Britain's attitudes toward the limitation of aerial warfare from World War I to World War II reflects the interaction between its concerns about security and its interest in developing norms.

Britain's policy on the control of airpower in the interwar period can be divided into three phases. The first extended from the end of World War I to 1932. After the elimination of the German air force at Versailles, the initial effort at tackling the problem of bombing took place at the Hague in 1922–23. The British draft proposal at this conference advocated a prohibition on bombing anything other than military targets, which was a compromise between the RAF's desire for a free hand and the Government's wish to ban attacks on cities (especially London). In general, British policy in this period was to advocate limitations in air power wherever possible, while at the same time vowing to match the size of any air force within striking distance of England.[85]

The second phase of British interwar aerial policy lasted from 1932 to 1936. At the major international arms control forum of this period, the Geneva Disarmament Conference, Britain strongly advocated measures to control airpower. Both the British government and populace were very concerned over the danger of air attack, and diplomatic action on this issue was perceived as a political, if not a security, necessity by most officials. Britain forwarded a number of proposals, including such features as the prohibition of bombing among major powers, qualitative and quantitative limits on bomber forces, and controls on civilian aviation (to prevent its conversion to military purposes).[86] Government officials, however, disagreed on the total abolition of military aircraft or the total prohibition of bombing, despite momentum in the Cabinet and Disarmament Committee toward such a position.[87] Finding a way to control civilian airpower to prevent its conversion to military use was nearly impossible. And as the RAF was quick to point out, it was much cheaper to "police" the British empire (in places like Iraq, Somalia, and so on) with airpower than with land forces.[88]

The other armed services, the Navy and Army, were of a different mind and favored abolition. They disdained the RAF's strategy, which

---

[85] Bialer, *Shadow of the Bomber*; Quester, *Deterrence before Hiroshima*, pp. 77–78; Rolland A. Chaput, *Disarmament in British Foreign Policy* (London: George Allen & Unwin, 1935), pp. 333–36.

[86] Bialer, *Shadow of the Bomber*, pp. 8–9, 12, 44–55; Spaight, *Air Power and War Rights*, pp. 246–47.

[87] Bialer, *Shadow of the Bomber*, p. 25.

[88] The costs of controlling Iraq were allegedly cut in half in a year's time through the use of bombing. Chaput, *Disarmament in British Foreign Policy*, pp. 328–29.

was seen as divorced from their aims (not to mention a drain on military funding that could be used for land and sea forces). The Admiralty claimed in 1932 that "air bombing is aggressive and in no way defensive. . . . only the Air Ministry wants to retain these weapons for use against towns, a method of warfare which is revolting and un-English."[89] But the Air Ministry argued that strategic bombing was hardly more immoral than either naval blockades causing indiscriminate starvation or the mass murder of the World War I battlefield. Of course, the RAF was also aware of the implications of abolition for its future and fought tenaciously to block it.[90]

The third phase of British disarmament efforts in air warfare policy lasted from 1936 to the start of the war. The main focus during this period shifted to developing rules of air warfare, and away from the earlier emphasis on outlawing bombing from the air altogether. Once again, the Army and Navy zealously pushed the idea, even though the Cabinet was hesitant because it hoped for a more significant agreement. The Admiralty, however, was quite persuasive in arguing that air rules were more in the interests of Britain than of any of its likely European adversaries and therefore should be pursued.[91] Progress was blocked, however, by other states' lack of interest in the idea.

By the time of the crisis in Czechoslovakia in 1938, Britain was especially interested in a convention that might inhibit a German air attack on vulnerable English cities.[92] Britain hoped to break the impasse by promoting a bilateral agreement on bombing restrictions with Germany that others (such as the Soviet Union) might join later. The "Malkin Committee" headed by Sir William Malkin, legal adviser to the foreign office, was established in the summer of 1938 to determine what changes should be made to the Hague rules to make them to

[89] Bialer, *Shadow of the Bomber*, p. 24.

[90] Webster and Frankland, *Strategic Air Offensive*, p. 51. Ironically, the British agreed to abolition when the Americans presented the proposal—out of sensitivity to public opinion—but thought it impractical and would not agree to the abolition of air policing. See Bialer, *Shadow of the Bomber*, 1: 33.

[91] Some RAF officials were skeptical. The future "Bomber" Harris, then deputy director of plans, argued that the result of any rules would be that Britain would heed them but others would not. He further accused the Admiralty of trying to use the air conventions to undermine the RAF and air strategy. "Minute from D.D. Plans to Chief of the Air Staff (C.A.S.) and Deputy C.A.S.," 18 June 1936, AIR 8/155; Uri Bialer, "'Humanization' of Air Warfare in British Foreign Policy on the Eve of the Second World War," *Journal of Contemporary History* 13 (1978): 81–82.

[92] For example, in the period leading up to the crisis, see memorandum, Secretary of State of Air to CID, "The Restriction of Air Warfare," 1 March 1938, AIR 8/155. Recognizing Britain's vulnerability, especially in light of the inadequacies of Bomber Command, the Air Ministry dropped its resistance to the conventions.

Britain's advantage. It was expected that Germany would probably demand in return the prohibition of a Royal Navy sea blockade that would cause suffering among the Reich's civilian population. That this measure received serious consideration indicates Britain's concern about air attack. The blockade had been one of Britain's most effective tools in past conflicts. Support among the special committee considering the deal was surprisingly strong. In the end, the trade-off was rejected because officials recognized that it would sacrifice all benefits of naval superiority in exchange for an air restriction that could be easily violated. Ultimately, the idea of pushing a convention was abandoned because of the imminence of war. Britain decided in early 1939 that a proposal at that time would be mistaken for a sign of weakness.[93]

Without making Germany an official offer, the British had made their position on an air-warfare regime clear. On 21 June 1938, Chamberlain announced in Parliament that three principles of law were as applicable to air warfare as to land and sea combat:[94]

1. Bombing civilians is illegal.
2. Targets must be military objectives and capable of identification.
3. Reasonable care must be taken in bombing military objectives to avoid the surrounding population.

Given Britain's interest in the 1923 Hague rules, it is not surprising that it embraced Roosevelt's suggestion at the start of the war that all sides avoid bombing nonmilitary targets.

The principle of not bombing civilians, however, had a relatively modest impact on expectations, preparations, and decisions in war. In terms of expectations, none of the British leadership seemed to think that agreeing on rules could actually prevent escalation. Advocates hoped that it might inhibit immediate attacks on Britain. And any tool that could be used to fend off the feared "bolt-from-the-blue" was seen as positive. The RAF leaders realized in 1938 that it was not likely that the air limitations would last for long.[95] In May 1940, even after eight months of restraint, the CINC of Fighter Command, Air Chief Marshal Hugh Dowding, argued that Britain should not be afraid to attack the Ruhr for fear of the German retaliation because that was likely to hap-

---

[93] See files in "Humanization of Air Warfare," AIR 9/202; especially CID Limitation of Armaments Sub-Committee, 2nd Meeting, 18 July 1938. CID Limitation of Armaments Sub-Committee, 12 January 1939, AIR 9/84; also see CAB 21/738.

[94] Butler, *Grand Strategy*, 2: 567.

[95] Bialer, "'Humanization' of Air Warfare," pp. 79–84. Letter, Chief of the Air Staff (Newell) to CINC, Bomber Command, 28 September 1938, AIR 8/251.

pen in any event.[96] But when it came mattered tremendously for the preparations being made to defend Britain.

If we were to judge the impact of the air warfare institution simply by the RAF's attention to the rules, it would appear significant. The instructions on air bombing developed in August 1939—even before Roosevelt's appeal—were even stricter than the 1923 Hague code.[97] The air restrictions also seemed to influence the choice of strategy. Of the thirteen prewar plans, all were set aside by the time of war except the one that focused on attacks on the enemy navy because it was the only plan that probably would not cause civilian casualties.[98] Even when restraints had lifted somewhat in the summer of 1940 and Britain had begun night bombing of Germany, Bomber Command was warned by the Air Staff that its campaign should not "be allowed to degenerate into mere indiscriminate action, which is contrary to the policy of His Majesty's Government."[99]

The question, however, is why this restraint? Was it maintained in deference to nascent norms of air warfare or was it caused by other factors independent of such rules? As is evident, and as I will discuss further, much of Britain's interest and adherence to norms stemmed from its concern with relative vulnerability. Britain hoped that the rules might delay air attacks on its cities. This suggests that in Britain, the norms were simply a product of realpolitik calculation.

But Britain did take institutionalized restraint seriously because of its potential to affect the balance of power. Britain realized that initiating strategic bombing might cost it the political favor of neutral countries. When Sir Edgar Ludlow-Hewitt, CINC of Bomber Command, asked the Air Ministry in 1938 if attacks on German aircraft industry would be permitted in the event of war, the Deputy Director of Plans pointed out that it might be desirable to avoid targets, even if they were military, in order to avoid hitting civilians and alienating neutral countries. An inter-service committee, again headed by Sir William Malkin, that oversaw the formulation of bombing instructions noted in August 1939 that citizens must not be attacked or the support of neutrals, particularly

[96] Minutes of the War Cabinet (hereafter W. M.), (40) 115, Conclusions, Minute 6, 8 May 1940, CAB 65/13; Terraine, *Right of the Line*, p. 138.

[97] They permitted air action against strictly military objectives where no civilian casualties would be incurred. See "Instructions Governing Naval and Air Bombardment," 22 August 1939, AIR 14/249.

[98] Webster and Frankland, *Strategic Air Offensive*, 1: 92–105; Charles Messenger, *"Bomber" Harris and the Strategic Bombing Offensive, 1939–1945* (London: Arms & Armour Press, 1984), p. 27.

[99] Air Vice Marshal W. S. Douglas (deputy chief of the Air Staff) to Air Marshal Portal, 4 June 1940, in Webster and Frankland, *Strategic Air Offensive*, 4: 145.

the United States, could be lost.[100] When Britain was considering bombing the Ruhr in May of 1940 both Chamberlain and Churchill were concerned with the impact on U.S. opinion, since civilian deaths would likely result.[101] Ultimately, however, Churchill approved the attack.

At times, the norms on bombing were considered by some as a means of advantage. On Christmas Eve 1940, Sir Alexander Cadogan, the permanent under-secretary of the Foreign Office, noted in his diary, "We're not bombing tonight or tomorrow. Wonder whether the Germans will fall into the trap! . . . If they bomb and we don't, we can score on it."[102] In this instance, the norms of restraint shaped the calculations of states on how power might be accrued. By adhering to restrictions on air warfare, Britain hoped to attract, or at least not lose, the support of other countries. Had the norms been different or absent, Britain's actions might have been different.

Nonetheless, that the rules were a lesser force on British restraint is seen in the cynical attitude of some officials that any no-first-use agreement could be easily circumvented. Bombing, the Sub-Committee on Coast Defence concluded in 1932, "could always be resorted to as an act of reprisal against some real or imagined breach of the laws of war."[103] A British plan sent to France in October 1939 stated that if German actions in the West appeared decisive, the British should launch a bomber offensive against the Ruhr, which would likely cause heavy civilian casualties. The paper noted that such a mission would have to be "justified" by some previous German behavior such as the unrestricted bombing of France or England, or casualties caused in an invasion of Belgium.[104] It is apparent, though, that this would be more a pretext for than a cause of escalation. Indeed, although public behavior had to conform to the previously supported norms, actual attitudes, plans, and policy often deviated from them.

---

[100] J. M. Spaight, "International Law of the Air, 1939–1945: Confidential Supplement to *Air Power and War Rights*" (Air Historical Branch, Air Ministry, 1945), AIR 41/5; Messenger, *"Bomber" Harris*, p. 26, R.A.F. in the Bomber Offensive, 1: 260, AIR 41/39.

[101] W. M. (40) 123, Conclusions, Minute 2, 15 May 1940, CAB 65/13; Harvey B. Tress, *British Strategic Bombing Policy through 1940: Politics, Attitudes, and the Formation of a Lasting Pattern* (Lewiston, N.Y.: Edwin Mellen Press, 1988), pp. 164–67.

[102] David Dilks, ed., *The Diaries of Sir Alexander Cadogan, 1938–1945* (New York: G. P. Putnam's Sons, 1972), p. 344.

[103] This appears to refer to Britain's as well as the enemy's actions. CID Sub-Committee on Coast Defence, "Inquiry into Air Disarmament Policy," May 1932, AIR 8/139.

[104] War Cabinet, "Air Policy. Annex," 13–14 October 1939, AIR 8/227; War Cabinet, "Air Policy: Memorandum for Communication to the French High Command," 21 October 1939, AIR 14/194.

All of this, of course, is not to label the British criminals or immoral. As Noble Frankland has argued, "The great immorality open to us in 1940 and 1941 was to lose the war against Hitler's Germany. To have abandoned the only means of direct attack which we had at our disposal would have been a long step in that direction."[105] The point is that rules of air warfare and the Hague norms did not define Britain's interests or morality. Instead, the type of thinking on restraint so evident above is more fundamentally linked to the realist paradigm.

Escalation despite Relative Weakness

As realism would predict, Britain's appreciation for its relative weakness was central to how it viewed the world and its security in the years following the First World War and leading into the Second. One of the main areas of concern was the threat from the skies. How did this concern develop and what was its impact on air warfare policy?

In World War I, the English were shocked by German air raids on their country, especially the "second" German strategic air offensive of the war carried out by the Gotha bombers (the first wave in 1915 consisted of zeppelins). Violating the British populace's traditional exemption from direct exposure to continental conflict, these attacks caused panics, dissatisfaction toward the Government, and a drop in industrial output. In the interwar years marked by economic depression, national leaders were especially concerned about whether the working classes would be willing to support their government under the expected stresses of bombing. Right up to World War II, it was feared that people would become so panicked in the event of an air attack that if special measures were not taken, a collapse of the country might result.[106]

Airpower became an even greater concern with the rise of the Nazi threat in 1933–34.[107] When Germany left the Geneva Disarmament Conference, it was clear a new challenger was emerging. Britain judged

---

[105] Quoted in Terraine, *Right of the Line*, p. 507.

[106] Spaight, *Air Power and War Rights*, pp. 8–9; Quester, *Deterrence before Hiroshima*, pp. 28, 32, 36. Overy, "Air Power," p. 86; Malcolm Smith, "The Air Threat and British Foreign and Domestic Policy: The Background to the Strategic Air Offensive," in Boog, *Conduct of the Air War*, p. 622; Webster and Frankland, *Strategic Air Offensive*, 1: 45.

[107] The first big increase in airpower came with the scare of a French air threat in 1922. When an article in the *Times* announced that the French air force was some six times the size of the postwar RAF, the Government was jolted into action. A force of fifty-two squadrons was approved. See Barry D. Powers, *Strategy without Slide-Rule: British Air Strategy 1914–1939* (London: Croom Helm, 1976), pp. 183–87; Terraine, *Right of the Line*, pp. 10–11.

German airpower as the greatest threat, and priority in funding was given to the RAF. The prime minister, Stanley Baldwin, announced in the House of Commons the new "One Power" policy that "in air strength and in air power this country shall no longer be in a position inferior to any country within striking distance of our shores."[108] Thus began a period where the RAF's bomber force would be based on estimates of numbers of the main opponent—the Luftwaffe.

As Barry Posen has argued, an abrupt change in air policy—forced by international circumstance and implemented by civilian intervention—took place in 1937.[109] Thomas Inskip, as minister for defense coordination, ended any arms race in bomber production by introducing a strategic scheme that gave priority to air defense and fighter production. Inskip argued that the parity principle had not deterred the German air buildup and Britain could not afford such an arms race. Furthermore, Britain became sensitive to an air-defense gap: Germany was believed to be better prepared defensively and hence had a relative advantage in an all-out strategic campaign.[110] If Germany opted for war any time soon, the RAF bomber force would not be able to halt a German knockout blow.[111] Thus it would appear that Britain adapted to external circumstances by changing doctrine to favor a defensive policy. As we will see, however, this shift was more a modification than a fundamental displacement of organizational ethos.

The crisis in Czechoslovakia in the spring of 1938 forced British leaders to reassess their expected wartime strategy for bombing. More specifically, the German desire for hegemony over the Sudetenland raised the prospect that war could come much sooner than originally expected. The balance of power in the air was seen as being decidedly in favor of Germany. Given that the Third Reich might not attack immediately, Britain resolved not to provoke the Nazis by carrying out the Bomber Command's planned strategic air offensive. The prime minister had already announced in the House of Commons on 21 June 1938

---

[108] Webster and Frankland, *Strategic Air Offensive*, 1: 65–67.

[109] This is the argument found in Posen, *Sources of Military Doctrine*, pp. 171–78. (See Chap. 1, n. 4). Stephen Rosen points out that the RAF itself had supported development of active air defense. But this does not refute the premise that the idea of strategic bombing dominated the RAF and its evolution. See Rosen, "New Ways of War," pp. 143–46; Stephen Rosen, *Winning the Next War: Innovation in the Modern Military* (Ithaca: Cornell University Press, 1991), pp. 13–18.

[110] Wesley K. Wark, "The Air Defence Gap: British Air Doctrine and Intelligence Warnings in the 1930s," in Boog, *Conduct of the Air War*, pp. 511–26.

[111] "Aide Memoire by Sir Thomas Inskip, Minister for Coordination of Defence, for the Secretary of State for Air, 9 December 1937," in Webster and Frankland, *Strategic Air Offensive*, 4: 96–98.

that in the event of war, Britain would bomb only military targets, avoiding any civilian casualties.[112]

No one was more aware of the weakness of Britain's offensive bombers than Sir Edgar Ludlow-Hewitt. Since taking charge of Bomber Command in September of 1937, Ludlow-Hewitt had been critically evaluating the RAF's ability to carry out its doctrine. He concluded that Bomber Command's lack of readiness was disturbing. The RAF not only lacked aircraft, but also the necessary navigational equipment and trained pilots and crews. In the spring of 1939, Ludlow-Hewitt wrote of "an acute sense of the inadequacy of the Force, as it exists today for the purpose for which it was intended."[113] Plans were revised accordingly, at least for the time being, to avoid the possibility of civilian casualties in bombing operations.[114]

In the early stages of World War II, Britain's policy of restraint was reaffirmed by the Cabinet. Bomber Command's orders were to avoid at all cost attacks on targets that might incite a massive German retaliation and/or waste airplanes. Its main mission was to drop pamphlets on Germany, the effect of which, a RAF leader noted, was to supply the Third Reich with five years' worth of toilet paper. As long as the RAF was weaker than the Luftwaffe, Britain would not be the first to "take the gloves off."[115] The thinking behind this conclusion was clear. Bomber Command needed time to preserve and stockpile its resources until they could be employed effectively. Restraint bought that time. John Slessor, director of RAF Plans in 1939, wrote in his memoirs that conserving the bomber force had become a determining theme of policy. He further noted that had the RAF had sufficient forces it would not have restricted its bomber operations.[116]

The ability of realist theory to explain British restraint more satisfactorily than institutionalism is evident in the events surrounding the German invasion of Poland. The RAF concluded in October that the

[112] Webster and Frankland, *Strategic Air Offensive*, 1: 99–100.

[113] Terraine, *Right of the Line*, pp. 84–85. Also see the files in AIR 14/298.

[114] Neville Jones, *The Beginnings of Strategic Air Power: A History of the British Bomber Force, 1923–1939* (London: Frank Cass, 1987), pp. 140–42.

[115] War Cabinet, "Air Policy: Memorandum for Communication to the French High Command," 21 October 1939, AIR 14/194, lists factors governing air policy beginning with "the Allied inferiority *vis-à-vis* Germany in existing air strengths. From this it follows that for the present the initiative is with Germany; our nation must be conditioned by her action." Terraine, *Right of the Line*, p. 107.

[116] Director of Plans (DoP—at that time Slessor), "Note on Relaxing the Bombardment Instructions and Initiating Extended Air Action," 7 September 1939, AIR 14/194; John Slessor, *The Central Blue* (New York: Praeger, 1957), pp. 206, 212. War Cabinet, COS, "Air Policy," 11 September 1939, CAB 80/1.

German bombing in Poland transgressed the air rules and justified the removal of restrictions. Had Britain been restrained simply (or primarily) by the air regime, it could have claimed legal retaliation.[117] But because the unfavorable balance of forces was the source of British policy, restraint prevailed. The Chiefs of Staff explained their behavior in a November 1939 report: "The only reason that we refrained at the time from taking similar action against comparable German objectives was that of military expediency."[118] On 8 May 1940, Churchill referred to the problem of Britain's air inferiority, which would continue to impose difficult conditions—"until more favorable conditions can be established" in the air balance.[119]

Realism, however, cannot explain why Britain decided to escalate the air war in the spring and summer of 1940. Air Marshal Sir Charles Portal, CINC of Bomber Command, advocated attacking the Ruhr, a campaign which would inevitably involve civilian casualties. The vice chief of the Air Staff argued against such a move, noting that Germany possessed four times the bombing capacity of the RAF and it was questionable whether the alleged durability of the British could endure such a disparity: "Could it be said that our people would be four times as steady as Germans?"[120] Churchill, three days before he became prime minister, backed this opinion in a Cabinet meeting noting that "it would be very dangerous and undesirable to take the initiative in opening unrestricted air warfare at a time when we possessed only a quarter of the striking power of the German Air Force . . . [this] might result in the wholesale indiscriminate bombing of this country."[121] Given this perception of the balance of forces, it is on the surface surprising from a realist viewpoint that only four days later the first raids on the German homeland were ordered by Churchill himself.

Why was England so willing to escalate the air war given its emphasis on avoiding unrestricted bombing and the acknowledged asymmetry in forces favoring Germany? With the German invasion of the Low Countries and France, England faced the possibility of the collapse of its most important ally and the destruction of the British Army forces

[117] W.P. (39) 118, report by COS, "Air Policy," 11 November 1939, CAB 66/3. Secret Cipher, Chief of the Air Staff, to Air Marshal Barrat, 16 October 1939, AIR 9/131, notes "owing to German action in Poland, we are no longer bound by restrictions under the instructions governing naval and air bombardment."

[118] W.P. (39) 118, report by COS, "Air Policy," 11 November 1939, CAB 66/3.

[119] Spaight, *Air Power and War Rights*, p. 266.

[120] "Final Record of a Conference Held in CAS's Room, Air Ministry, 28 April 1940," AIR 14/194.

[121] W.M. (40) 114, Conclusions, Minute 1, 7 May 1940, CAB 65/13.

on the continent. Therefore, the RAF was permitted to do what civilians had overseen and approved in the prewar period—the strategic bombing of industrial targets—even though it was recognized such operations would incur civilian casualties and thus violate restraint. Those who would want to rescue realist logic in this situation would argue that Britain was in fact merely reacting to a change in circumstances—Germany's invasion of France—that led to a change in preferences from restraint to escalation. But this argument ignores the facts that (1) the RAF's strategy developed largely untested against external circumstances until late in the interwar period; (2) Britain's leaders *did not believe* RAF strategic bombing was "optimal" for fighting Germany; and (3) they critically misinterpreted the external situation by misinterpreting German strategy. To fully understand these deviations from strategic rationality that were so central to Britain's preferences, we must look to the logic of organizational culture.

Bent on Strategic Bombing

British decisions on air policy are closely related to the organizational culture of the RAF. This culture was shaped and propagated by a leader of the air force in its infancy. Because it was believed that he would most effectively preserve the integrity of the infant service, Sir Hugh Trenchard was named chief of the Air Staff in February of 1919 and remained the official head for the next ten years.[122] The ideas that shaped culture under his reign, however, were to influence British airpower policy through World War II.

Although he was champion of tactical support in World War I, as chief of the Air Staff Trenchard built on the views of his predecessor Major-General Sir Frederick Sykes to establish a new doctrine for the young RAF. This doctrine was to serve as the basis of RAF creed for the next twenty years. Essentially, it was a theory of airpower shaped around reasons well articulated by traditional organization theory: a desire to preserve the independence and autonomy of the RAF. The central theme was that a strategic bombing offensive was the key to both the defense of Britain and victory in the next war. Several ideas were part of this theory. First, it relied on the faith that the bomber "would always get through"—that there was no effective defense against air raids and therefore it did not make sense to spend money

---

[122] Powers, *Strategy without Slide-Rule*, p. 161. Trenchard was also named head of the RAF at its founding in 1917 but resigned shortly thereafter. Major General Frederick Sykes filled the interim period.

on air defense. Security would be provided by the threat of a large counterattack. In the event of war, the aim of the counteroffensive would be twofold: (1) to deprive the enemy of the physical means to wage war, and (2) to break the opponent's morale to continue to fight. Trenchard had no doubt about which was more important: "The moral effect of bombing stands undoubtedly to the material effect in a proportion of 20 to 1."[123] The implication of his argument was that it was primarily through the independent operations of the RAF that enemy willpower could be undermined. In the RAF mindset tactical support of land forces was considered a waste of resources. Trenchard claimed his pilots would be misused if they were to serve merely as "tactical chauffeurs" for the other services.[124]

The philosophy of the bomber offensive was promoted in a number of ways. One was the leader's personal mark. Trenchard was the dominant power of the service in its formative years, and his views became orthodoxy. His influence on subordinates was significant. Nearly all of the subsequent chiefs of the Air Staff were protégés. He was known to have kept on only those officers who agreed with him.[125] One former assistant chief of the Air Staff wrote that "anyone who pressed, as I did, the claims of fighters could not escape the charge of heresy."[126]

Trenchard is also responsible for establishing the basic institutions that would mold Britain's future airpower leaders and theorists. Instead of spending the service's funds immediately on planes, he founded an air force staff college, a cadet college, technical training schools, and other facilities. Along with these physical structures, a less tangible, but very real and separate air force culture blossomed, which had its own ranks, language, and attitude.[127] All of these vessels bore the imprimatur of Trenchard's thinking.

This creed of strategic bombing molded several different areas of the peacetime RAF which would subsequently affect wartime decisions on restraint. Most important was the development of capabilities. As Nev-

---

[123] Webster and Frankland, *Strategic Air Offensive,* 1: 46, 55; N. Jones, *Beginnings of Strategic Air Power,* p. 31–34. The Army and Navy saw the fledgling air arm as an unwanted competitor in a time of scarce resources, and they argued that its planes should be incorporated into their own forces.

[124] He denied, however, the RAF's ability to cause victory by itself. Webster and Frankland, *Strategic Air Offensive,* 1: 64. Powers, *Strategy without Slide-Rule,* p. 167.

[125] See H. R. Allen, *The Legacy of Lord Trenchard* (London: Cassell, 1972), pp. 32, 68. Robin Higham, *The Military Intellectuals in Britain, 1918–1939* (New Brunswick: Rutgers University Press, 1966), p. 200.

[126] Tress, *British Strategic Bombing Policy,* p. 49.

[127] Powers, *Strategy without Slide-Rule,* p. 165. Terraine, *Right of the Line,* pp. 3–5.

ille Jones points out, the emphasis on morale bombing gave few incentives for developing the necessary equipment and skills for accuracy.[128] If "material damage" targets were not hit, something else, such as citizens, would be, and morale would suffer. Already believing that the bomber would always get through, the Air Staff assumed that attacking urban areas would present few problems. Thus when the war came and the RAF was called on to carry out restricted bombing it was not capable of the precision necessary to avoid civilian casualties.[129] Much of the story of Britain's escalation is based on similar operational constraints and determinants related to RAF culture.

The RAF's commitment to the strategic air offensive was also illustrated in its pursuit of a heavy bomber. In 1937, when Inskip successfully reoriented policy toward fighter defense, he also wanted to end heavy bomber development in favor of less expensive light and medium bombers in much the same way that Germany had done in 1936.[130] But the difference between the fate of the heavy bomber in the two countries is striking. The Air Staff contended that the country that could drop the most bombs would win and heavy bombers could shoulder a large load. Unlike Germany, Britain explicitly made the calculation that a heavy bomber could carry up to four times the weight of bombs that a medium bomber could and do so over a longer distance. This was the reason the larger plane was adopted.[131]

How the creed of the bomber offensive inspired the RAF's learning is particularly interesting. First, this culture was not affected by the experience of the First World War, the lessons of which emphasized air superiority by fighter aircraft. Furthermore, the RAF uncritically interpreted the events of local wars in the interwar years as confirming the utility of strategic bombing, despite contrary or ambiguous evidence. For example, the experience the British gained using bombers to police Iraq in the early 1920s was taken as proof that the bomber offensive would work, even though the RAF's opponents in that conflict lacked the air and ground offenses that would be central to continental combat. Even after the German display of the effectiveness of tactical support of ground forces in the Spanish civil war, the Air Staff

---

[128] N. Jones, *Beginnings of Strategic Air Power*, pp. xx–xxi.

[129] This is in sharp contrast to the U.S. air arm, which emphasized accuracy and developed the means to achieve it. See Schaffer, *Wings of Judgment* (see Chap. 1, n. 89).

[130] Webster and Frankland, *Strategic Air Offensive*, 1: 74–77.

[131] "Brief to Secretary of State for Ministerial Discussion," C.P. 218 (1938), AIR 8/247.

refused to recognize the validity of the close air support mission.[132] The peacetime exercises that were intended as objective measures of effectiveness did not correct the situation, but were often biased to support the validity of the strategic offensive mentality.

In 1930, for instance, Blue Force used a policy of direct attack on the enemy capital while Red Force concentrated on a counter-force campaign. The umpires calculated Blue to have lost 150 bombers, having begun with only 138! A Blue staff officer admitted that their effort would have collapsed on the fourth day of the Exercise, had the umpires not ruled that the Blue raids on Red cities would have caused a moral collapse on the third night.[133]

Maneuvers that indicated the "relative impotence rather than power of bombing" were given short shrift. Strategic bombing plans remained the touchstone of RAF thinking. Little attention was paid to tactical support. After a 1939 exercise, one air officer noted that pilots were incapable of carrying out a mission supporting ground forces. The lessons apparent in Germany's use of close air support in the invasion of Poland did not disturb the RAF bias.[134]

Another area affected by the strategic offensive concept was the RAF's structure and basing policy. A separate Bomber Command, the physical embodiment of the air offensive, was established in 1936. Britain also decided to move its air bases from primarily in the south to the eastern part of the country. Even though this would make the airfields more vulnerable to enemy attacks, it would also allow the air campaign easier access to the Continent.[135]

The strategic bombing culture also prejudiced analysis of the threat. The RAF tended to attribute to Germany the same doctrine of the bomber offensive that it had and then use that view in support of its

---

[132] Murray, "Influence of Pre-War Anglo-American Doctrine," pp. 237–38. Webster and Frankland, *Strategic Air Offensive*, 1: 60. Hallion, *Strike from the Sky*, p. 110, Williamson Murray, "British and German Air Doctrine between the Wars," *Air University Review* 31 (March–April 1980): 48.

[133] Malcolm Smith, *British Air Strategy between the Wars* (Oxford: Clarendon Press, 1984), p. 72. See also Webster and Frankland, *Strategic Air Offensive*, 1: 117.

[134] This refers to trials in 1938–39. See *R.A.F. in the Bomber Offensive*, 1: 34, AIR 41/39. CINC Bomber Command, "Readiness for War Report," 10 March 1939, AIR 14/298, suggests WA.5. (which would include attacks on the Ruhr, which exceeded Britain's notion of restraint) was the central scheme for planning. This was General Wavell. See Murray, "British and German Air Doctrine," p. 48. Murray, "Influence of Pre-War Anglo-American Doctrine," pp. 242–43.

[135] J. M. Spaight, "International Law of the Air, *1939–45:* Confidential Supplement to *Air Power and War Rights*" (Air Historical Branch, Air Ministry, 1945), p. 32, AIR 14/5.

own doctrine. This, of course, led to false notions about Luftwaffe strategy. Those individuals who had different views of the threat were discouraged from voicing them.[136] Of course, German doctrine and British doctrine were actually quite different. Britain's planners did not believe, for example, that the enemy's air forces had to be defeated before strategic operations could begin. Most important, the RAF viewed its independent operations as the greatest contribution to victory. Reversing the priority seen in Germany, cooperation with the Navy and Army was seen as an additional, not the primary, mission.[137]

Despite this evidence, two events falsely suggest that the influence of the culture of the bomber offensive was not all that powerful in the interwar period. The first was the dramatic revision of airpower policy in 1937–38 away from the bomber offensive in favor of fighters and homeland defense. This change, however, did not mean the end of the bomber offensive, but instead its postponement because of the blatant inadequacies of the bomber force. Both national and RAF strategy envisioned a defensive phase in a future conflict that would provide time to build the necessary forces and skills for the bomber offensive. The RAF pursued the heavy bomber and its offensive, despite intense economic and interservice pressure to abandon it, and despite its knowledge that its foremost competitor, Germany, was giving up the development of its own heavy bomber. Likewise, the unfavorable changes in technology such as the appearance of radar, which favored air defense, never affected the RAF's preconceptions about the viability of the bomber offensive, only the details of its operational implementation.[138] Thus despite the new attention given to air defense, the bomber culture was hardly finished. Resources (albeit reduced by the growth of Fighter Command) continued to flow to strategic bombing, and

---

[136] Jones, *Beginnings of Strategic Air Power*, p. 78; Wesley Wark, *The Ultimate Enemy: British Intelligence and Nazi Germany, 1933–1939* (Ithaca: Cornell University Press, 1985), esp. pp. 35–72. Robert Jervis, 'Deterrence and Perception," *International Security* (winter 1982/83): 15–16, argues that this was a result of motivated bias, not simple error. Admitting the Luftwaffe's main mission was ground support would have brought up the issue of why the RAF did not have a similar emphasis. F. H. Hinsley, *British Intelligence in the Second World War: Its Influence on Strategy and Operations* (New York: Cambridge University Press, 1979), 1: 78–79.

[137] "The Aim of the RAF," 1937, AIR 2/675.

[138] One RAF official called the emphasis on fighters like "putting all our players in goal." Wark, *Ultimate Enemy*, p. 62. This is reminiscent of the synergism between minimum capabilities and the viability of culture seen above in the case of U.S. submarine warfare policy. Wark, *Ultimate Enemy*, p. 70. Malcolm Smith, "'A Matter of Faith': British Strategic Air Doctrine in the Thirties," *Journal of Contemporary History* 15 (1980): 438–40.

it remained the dominant strategic mindset in the RAF throughout the war.

A second development that seems to indicate the limited influence of the Trenchard creed involves a shift in Air Staff thinking toward precision—as opposed to indiscriminate—bombing in the late 1930s and the first year and a half of war.[139] This change is relevant because it suggests that organizational creed did not in fact favor area bombing and therefore cannot be seen as a source of escalation. There is, of course, evidence that precision attack was a part of air policy, but like the turn to air defense under Inskip's influence, it was not central to culture.

Several factors account for the visibility of precision bombing. One reason why morale bombing was not prominently mentioned (in written records) was that it was impolitic to do so at a time when the government was attempting to negotiate humane limits. A second was that the RAF did not have the resources to carry out its long-favored strategic air offensive. It appears that Air Chief Marshal Sir Cyril Newall, chief of the Air Staff, tried to rationalize Bomber Command's ambitious plans with its limited capabilities by touting precision attack.[140] Accuracy in bombing would mean that fewer planes would have greater effect. This did not mean the RAF was wedded to precision bombing under any circumstances, particularly if it had a more capable force.

The problem was that the RAF's culture had not encouraged the development of highly accurate bombing capabilities. Ludlow-Hewitt recognized that Bomber Command would not be able to conduct precision bombing. In fact, exercises in 1937 indicated serious problems in accuracy, particularly in night operations.[141] But, nonetheless, the RAF's desire to use strategic bombing encouraged false—and probably cynical—optimism that it could effectively do so within restrictions. Although few said so explicitly, the conversations in the fall of 1939 indicated that area bombing would be the probable outcome of the RAF's so called "precision" attempts.[142]

[139] This shift is noted in Tress, *British Strategic Bombing Policy,* pp. 66–67.

[140] Max Hastings, *Bomber Command* (New York: Dial, 1979), pp. 46–49; Best, *Humanity in Warfare,* p. 273. Allen, *Legacy of Lord Trenchard,* pp. 79–80; Webster and Frankland, *Strategic Air Offensive,* 1: 79–80.

[141] Memorandum, HQ 3d Bomber Group to HQ, Bomber Command, "Sector and Combined Training Exercises, 1937," 1 September 1937, AIR 9/64.

[142] Quester, *Deterrence before Hiroshima,* p. 112. DoP, "The Question of Relaxing the Bombardment Instructions and Initiating Extended Air Action," 7 September 1939, AIR 14/194. For example, it was recognized that the so-called precision attacks on the Ruhr industry would involve significant civilian casualties. The Ruhr plan (WA.5) was a

The influence of culture is particularly evident in the first of two major steps to unrestricted bombing in 1940. This was the decision to initiate the targeting of the German homeland, specifically the industrial region of the Ruhr after eight months of showing restraint. The opening of this strategic bombing campaign on the Ruhr came in the wake of the air attack on Rotterdam on 15 May.[143] The official British histories of the air campaign suggest that retaliation was the motive for this unrestricted attack. But this justification appears to be more of a fig leaf than an explanation.

In fact, Britain's leaders considered attacking the Ruhr before Germany's invasion of Holland and the assault on Rotterdam even took place. The expected offensive would include attacks on oil targets, which it was recognized would incur civilian casualties.[144] It had been decided by 12 May that neutrals would not be offended, thus this factor was not the main concern. Presumably to set the stage for the first hundred-bomber raid against the Ruhr and preempt charges of illegality, Churchill directed the minister of information (that is, propaganda) that "discreet reference should be made in the press to the killing of civilians in France and the Low Countries" by the Germans.[145]

More important for the course of events was the RAF's culture, oriented as it was toward the bomber offensive. This influence manifested itself in a number of ways. First, RAF officials directly lobbied for strategic as opposed to tactical missions. The Air Staff recommended a strike at the Ruhr during the invasion, arguing that strategic bombing would contribute most to the campaign. British leaders, however, were not convinced, not only because they wish to avoid retaliation in kind, but also because many believed—including the British army, the French,

---

"gloves off" scheme. Plans, "Note on the Course of Action to Be Adopted from the Point of View of the Air War as soon as 'Gloves Off' Policy Is Approved by Government," 10 September 1939, AIR 9/96. Also see Anthony Verrier, *The Bomber Offensive* (New York: Macmillan, 1968), pp. 130–32.

[143] Actually the first raid on the German mainland appears to have been on the night of 11 May against Mönchen-Gladbach. Four people were killed, including an Englishwoman. This mission is little discussed in the literature, and it is not clear if it was sanctioned or accidental. See Martin Middlebrook and Chris Everitt, *The Bomber Command War Diaries: An Operational Reference Book 1939–1945* (New York: Viking, 1985), p. 42. That the raid took place is clear in W.M. (40) 123, Conclusions, Minute 2, 15 May 1940, CAB 65/13. H. W. Koch, "The Strategic Air Offensive against Germany: The Early Phase, May–September 1940," *Historical Journal* 34 (1991): 127, speculates that Bomber Command acted on its own authority.

[144] Letter, DoP to Air Ministry, 13 April 1940, AIR 14/774; memorandum CINC Bomber Command to Air Ministry, 4 May 1940, AIR 14/774; W.M. (40) 119C, Conclusions, Minute 4, 12 May 1940, CAB 65/113.

[145] Terraine, *Right of the Line*, p. 143.

and Churchill himself—that direct support of the armies in the field was the needed strategy and that strategic bombing would have little effect on the situation.[146] But in general there was an inbred resistance to tactical support of the Army on the battlefield. In sharp contrast to Germany, dive-bombing was not approved of by the RAF. In fact, the British never developed an adequate close-air-support bomber.[147] At the start of the war, Bomber Command was not prepared to carry out its strategic offensive, but it was also not willing to engage in tactical support. Its limited tactical support efforts resulted in large losses. General Edmund Ironside (Army) complained in his journal in the fall of 1939, "The Air Ministry are now hypnotized by action against morale and will hear of nothing else." Even when ordered to carry out tactical missions, the airmen tended to shortchange them in favor of strategic raids.[148]

Some British leaders further reasoned that there was no use in holding back, because Germany was expected to escalate in the air war anyway and strategic attacks might relieve the pressure on the battlefield by provoking assaults on Britain. Both of these claims, however, were largely based on the assumption that the Luftwaffe had a doctrine of strategic bombing similar to that of the RAF.[149] This intelligence assessment, of course, was not true, but as noted above was itself a product of culture.[150] Intelligence was also skewed during the Battle of France to suggest that the bombing campaign's morale-breaking aspect was working well when it was not.[151]

[146] Ibid., p. 137. For earlier indications of RAF desires, see W.M. (40) 90, Conclusions, Minute 2, 12 April 1940, CAB 65/13. Also see Webster and Frankland, *Strategic Air Offensive*, 1: 145. W.M. (40) 114, Conclusions, Minute 1, 7 May 1940, CAB 65/13; Tress, *British Strategic Bombing Policy*, pp. 69–70, 164.

[147] One squadron leader protested that the Air Ministry thought dive-bombing was a thing of the past. See minute, Squadron Leader Trgl. to W./ Commander Op., 20 October 1938, AIR 14/181. Terraine, *Right of the Line*, p. 144.

[148] Tress, *British Strategic Bombing Policy*, pp. 11, 124–26, 130, 178, 181, 191. Tress argues that the RAF's morale argument was actually an attempt to avoid coming under army control.

[149] Terraine, *Right of the Line*, pp. 141 and 145.

[150] In fact, Germany did not respond to the British actions by ordering direct attacks on cities for over three months. Germany's air doctrine was firmly linked to its ground forces, and it had no plans or capabilities for the type of strategic air offensive that Britain expected.

[151] Webster and Frankland, *Strategic Air Offensive*, 1: 145. It is not clear whether the bias was that of pilots and crews or one of higher-level analysis. Cf. Webster and Frankland, *Strategic Air Offensive*, 1: 219–220; Verrier, *Bomber Offensive*, pp. 132–34. On the general issue of the organizational bias of RAF intelligence, see Harold Wilensky, *Organizational Intelligence: Knowledge and Policy in Government and Industry* (New York: Basic Books, 1967), pp. 24–28.

Faced with a battlefield crisis, Britain gave the RAF the go-ahead for strategic operations, including attacks on oil targets on German territory that were recognized as likely to incur civilian casualties.[152] General Ironside wrote in his journal, "I never saw anything so light up the faces of the RAF when they heard that they were to be allowed to bomb the oil refineries in the Ruhr. It did one good to see it. They have built their big bombers for this work and they have been keyed up for the work ever since the war began. Now they have got their chance."[153] Of course, both civilians and the military made the decision to escalate. But given the advice and capabilities of the RAF, escalation was likely, if not inevitable.

The second step to unrestricted bombing occurred in late summer of 1940. Despite the strategic air raids in the spring of 1940, which did involve civilian casualties, a "no-capital-cities" restraint remained in effect into the summer: Berlin and London were spared. But on the night of 24–25 August, German bombers accidentally dropped their loads on London. The next day Churchill called for retaliation and some one-hundred bombers were dispatched against Berlin. Charles Webster and Noble Frankland's *Strategic Bombing Offensive* explains that escalation was motivated by the prime minister's desire that "the Germans get as good as they were giving."[154] The difference between this British response and that of Germany earlier to RAF air attacks that transgressed boundaries is striking. In the case of the RAF attacks on the Ruhr, Hitler assumed that they were inadvertent when they were not. In contrast, Churchill seemed to conclude the German raid on London of 24 August was intentional when it was an accident. As it turned out, both leaders erred on the side their air force cultures favored.

There is evidence that suggests, however, that Churchill was aware this was an accident and was looking for an excuse to start city bombing. Britain may have known from intercepted messages that Hitler had forbidden the Luftwaffe to bomb London.[155] Yet even without such intelligence, there was good reason to believe the raid was accidental.

---

[152] Letter, DoP to Air Ministry, 13 April 1940, AIR 14/774; memorandum, CINC Bomber Command to Air Ministry, 4 May 1940, AIR 14/774; W.M. (40) 119C, Conclusions, Minute 4, 12 May 1940, CAB 65/13.

[153] Quoted in Terraine, *Right of the Line*, p. 143.

[154] Webster and Frankland, *Strategic Air Offensive*, 1: 152.

[155] David Irving, *Churchill's War: The Struggle for Power* (Australia: Veritas, 1987), p. 365, especially note 30. This information is based on an interview with R. V. Jones and cannot be corroborated. However, it is not unthinkable that such knowledge was gleaned from intercepts of the signals traffic of the Luftwaffe. See Hinsley, *British Intelligence*, 1: 179–182.

The unintended foray only involved twelve planes. It caused light damage and only four fatalities, hardly the type of decisive operation to be expected from the purposeful violation of this important limitation.[156] Churchill himself had earlier played down the gravity of the German raids, noting that very few people were affected by any one attack.[157] Finally, Churchill had already shown an interest in bombing Berlin in July—well before the German assault. At that time he expressed interest in being able to respond to German attacks on London. But he also gave a planning date of 1 September, which suggests that he might have proceeded with city bombing without a pretext from the Germans.[158]

Why then did Churchill decide to escalate on 25 August? This is a question of considerable historical controversy and one not easily answered with the evidence available. Squaring most easily with realism is an explanation put forward by George Questar. At the time, Fighter Command was under severe pressure, and its ranks were rapidly thinning due to Luftwaffe attacks. Churchill recognized that command of the air was the key to Britain's defense: if Fighter Command failed, Britain was lost. Thus to buy Fighter Command breathing room, Churchill purposely attacked Berlin in order to draw the Luftwaffe away from RAF fighter bases.[159] Although that is in fact what happened, there are some difficulties with Quester's account. This is not the type of decision that Churchill would have made without high-level discussion, but there are very few records of such discussions. And as Frederick Sallagar has noted, the decision for escalation was

---

[156] Tress, *British Strategic Bombing Policy.*

[157] Martin Gilbert, *Winston S. Churchill* (London: Heinemann, 1983), 6: 602–63.

[158] Minute, Prime Minister to Secretary of State for Air and Chief of the Air Staff, 20 July 1940, AIR 19/458; minute, Director Home Office and Chief of the Air Staff, 21 July 1940, AIR 19/458. Churchill also noted the desirability of waiting, in case of the need to target Berlin, for longer nights and the arrival of the new Stirling bombers. Gilbert, *Winston S. Churchill,* 6: 673. Churchill invited Portal, CINC Bomber Command, out to his country home to discuss the idea on July 20 and August 17. See Irving, *Churchill's War,* pp. 371, 403.

[159] Quester, *Deterrence before Hiroshima,* pp. 117–18. As Captain David MacIsaac, "The Strategic Bombing Offensive: New Perspectives," *Air University Review* 18 (July–August 1967): 85, points out, others have hinted at the same dynamic. See, for example, Denis Richards, *The Royal Air Force, 1939–1945* (London: HMSO, 1953), 1: 122; Air Marshal Sir Robert Saundby, *Air Bombardment* (New York: Harper, 1951), p. 96; and Hanson Baldwin, *Battles Lost and Won* (New York: Harper, 1966), pp. 402–43. A more recent defense of this thesis is given by Harvey B. Tress, "Churchill, the First Berlin Raids, and the Blitz: A New Interpretation," *Militaergeschichtliche Mitteilungen* 32 (1982): 65–78.

made at a time on 24 August, *before* Fighter Command had taken its heaviest losses, which were suffered two weeks later.[160]

Here perhaps Churchill's personality deserves attention. He was a defiant scrapper, set on leading the British and defeating the Nazis. His individual fury may have overwhelmed other considerations. Churchill wrote after the war, "The War Cabinet were much in the mood to hit back, to raise the stakes, and to defy the enemy. I was sure they were right, and believed that nothing impressed or disturbed Hitler so much as his realisation of British wrath and will-power."[161] From this viewpoint, Churchill, always primed to seize the initiative, seized the only weapon left—the RAF and the strategic air offensive. Nonetheless, even if Churchill's personality played a role, we must also consider the origin of his views on strategic bombing and why he had the options he did.

There is evidence that the RAF culture swayed Churchill's evaluation of the worth and expected success of the strategic air offensive. Churchill had a history of opposition to, and lack of faith in, the independent strategic air offensive aimed at morale. What is clear is that with his assumption of the command of the war in May 1940, Churchill's views evolved.[162] Air force officials had been directly lobbying for escalation since the invasion of France, arguing that the battle had to be taken to the German homeland. RAF Intelligence boldly asserted that large "moral effects" were resulting from its bombing operations— a conclusion that seems to have been driven more by wishful thinking than objective evidence.[163] Influenced by these arguments, the Chiefs of Staff concluded on 25 May 1940 that Germany might be beaten by economic coercion, the bombing of economic and psychological targets, and the instigation of popular revolt in German-occupied territo-

---

[160] Sallagar, *Road to Total War*, pp. 181–82.

[161] Winston Churchill, *Their Finest Hour* (Boston: Houghton Mifflin, 1949), p. 342.

[162] At the end of World War I, Churchill doubted that victory could be had by terrorizing civilians. Webster and Frankland, *Strategic Air Offensive* 1: 47. In the 1930s, Churchill advocated air defenses as a means of mitigating air attacks. He did not believe the "bomber would always get through." See Churchill, *Gathering Storm*, pp. 147–52 (see Chap. 2, n. 103). Also see Tress, *British Strategic Bombing Policy*, pp. 69–70. In September 1939, citing the results of the Spanish civil war, Churchill doubted that "the essential elements of war" would be changed by the air arm. On 7 May 1940, Churchill had opposed unrestricted bombing because of Britain's perceived inferiority to Germany in airpower. See W.M. (40) 114, Conclusions, Minute 1, 7 May 1940, CAB 65/13. Churchill never fully accepted that air power, without a land invasion, could win the war on its own. Webster and Frankland, *Strategic Air Offensive*, 1: 184.

[163] Webster and Frankland, *Strategic Air Offensive*, 1: 145.

ries.[164] By late June Churchill had picked up on this thinking, arguing that airpower would cause Hitler "possibly decisive difficulties" in Germany and other areas he had to feed and defend.[165] On 8 July he asserted: "But there is one thing that will bring him [Hitler] back and bring him down and that is an absolutely devastating, exterminating attack by very heavy bombers from this country upon the Nazi homeland. We must be able to overwhelm them by this means, without which I do not see a way through."[166]

Churchill's evolution from skeptic to supporter is at least partially a product of culture in that the RAF's thinking influenced the advice he received from his military staff. Equally important, the RAF mindset ensured that Churchill had the tools needed to implement his plan. In fact, strategic bombing aimed at morale was one of the few developed options he had at his disposal. In the absence of the RAF's bomber culture, Churchill may well have shared Hitler's disposition against unrestricted air operations or lacked the capabilities to carry them out.[167] A difference in the compatibility of organizational culture with strategic bombing helps to explain why Britain and Germany responded so differently to incidents that violated restrictions on the use of airpower.

From this point on, the transition to a policy of indiscriminate or "area" bombing was a fairly short one. The debate between the Bomber Command and the Air Staff over whether the aim of British attacks should be "military" targets or civilian morale lasted from July to September of 1940. The issue of the debate was not whether it would be right to attack civilians from the air, but whether direct assaults on civilians would most rapidly produce the collapse of the German war machine. Of course, the distinction between military and civilian tar-

---

[164] Webster and Frankland, *Strategic Air Offensive*, 1: 146.

[165] Gilbert, *Winston S. Churchill*, 6: 603.

[166] Ibid., pp. 655–56. At about the same time (July 17), Portal personally advocated unleashing the bomber offensive: "In the Bomber Command we have one directly offensive weapon in the whole of our armoury, the one means by which we can undermine the morale of a large part of the enemy people, shake their faith in the Nazi regime, and at the same time and with the very same bombs, dislocate the major part of their heavy industry, much of their chemical industry and a good part of their oil production." *R.A.F. in the Bomber Offensive*, 2: 117, AIR 41/40.

[167] From the perspective of Britain's main security concern in the summer of 1940, an invasion by Germany, the decision to focus on strategic bombing may have made little sense. Destruction of the German naval and amphibious force gathering across the Channel was more important than a strategic bombing campaign. Yet during July and August less than 13 percent of Bomber Command's tonnage was dropped on the potential invasion vessels. The attacks on Berlin would further cut into the resources of these counterforce tactical raids. See Tress, *British Strategic Bombing Policy*, pp. 215–220.

gets should not be overstated since Britain had no precision ability and its bombing of material targets inevitably involved civilian casualties. By 30 October 1940, RAF internal memos indicated that "the fiction that the bombers were attacking 'military objectives' in the towns was officially abandoned." The first British raid that deliberately targeted the center of a city was the attack on Mannheim on 16 December 1940.[168]

Perhaps there is no more fitting accolade to Trenchard's legacy than an incident that occurred in June 1941. Long since retired, the former Chief of the Air Staff wrote to Churchill requesting that Germany be hit harder from the air, that not enough was being done in this respect. To resolve the matter, Trenchard was invited to a conference at the Air Ministry where it was explained that Britain's current air campaign differed little from his ideas.[169]

Conclusion: Beliefs, Options, and Choices

The evolution of British policy on strategic bombing was one of initial restraint that after eight months of war eroded into an unrestricted strategic bombing offensive against Germany. Why did Britain restrict its air campaign? First and foremost, it wanted to avoid an unlimited strategic bombing exchange because it perceived that the Third Reich had the advantage in both offensive capability and defensive position. Restraint protected the British populace and gained time for the RAF. Thus realism largely accounts for British air policy in the first stage of war.

A second factor in Britain's restraint, albeit of lesser importance, relates to institutional theory. In a few instances, British leaders expressed the need to limit RAF operations in order to avoid offending neutrals, especially the United States, by killing civilians. Despite the absence of a well-developed air-warfare regime, there was a stigma attached to bombing noncombatants. Britain feared that violating this norm could lead to the loss of critical third party support. This consideration, however, appears less significant than the realistic concerns over relative advantage. Even when Britain decided that Germany had violated the rules of air warfare in Poland, thus nullifying any conventions, it continued to restrict its operations. The British limited their efforts because they did not want to start a battle in which they would get worse than they could give.

---

[168] Webster and Frankland, *Strategic Air Offensive*, 1: 157, 215.
[169] Letter, Prime Minister to CINC Bomber Command, 4 June 1941, AIR 14/1926.

Why then did Britain escalate? Here realism is not so helpful. Britain initiated attacks on Germany that would bring retaliation at a time when it perceived itself at a disadvantage in airpower and relatively vulnerable to strategic bombing, particularly in May of 1940. Britain's attack on Berlin in August 1940 seems to fit better with realism (at least in hindsight) as a rational response to the travails of Fighter Command. But this was a gamble, one that was taken with little or no discussion of its relative merits and before Fighter Command was actually near collapse. Here Churchill's aggressive risk-taking personality played some role, but it can hardly be considered the decisive factor. Churchill, after all, also advanced risky schemes in submarine and chemical warfare, but in these areas, his ideas were thwarted, primarily because of their clash with prevailing military thinking.

To understand Britain's air escalation we must look to the Royal Air Force's organizational culture. Shaped by Trenchard's philosophy of victory through independent air operations intended to break the enemy's willpower, the RAF culture was suited to an unrestricted air war. In effect, the RAF's approach to warfare determined what Britain would do by its effect on plans, capabilities, structure, and training. Given what the RAF wanted to do and what it could do, Britain's turn to unrestricted bombing was highly probable, even inevitable. This dynamic was evident in the options available and the choices made in May and August of 1940.

Yet if organizational culture is so influential, we must also wonder why air warfare planning shifted away from the RAF's favored bomber offense to a fighter-oriented defense in 1937–38 and why the RAF supported bombing restrictions at the beginning of the war. Did external factors (such as the threat from Germany) overshadow organizational influence? As Posen has illustrated, certainly from 1937 to 1939 the German threat did intrude on organizational preferences. But these forces, despite their magnitude, did not fundamentally alter either peacetime culture or its ensuing impact on decisions in war. Organizational culture only changed ephemerally, despite overwhelming circumstances. The shift to emphasizing fighter production and restraint was regarded as a transitory phase that would allow Bomber Command to build its offensive power. In fact, what did *not* happen, is again, just as telling as what did. There was little serious discussion of altering Bomber Command's role to supporting the Army or Navy. The RAF did *not* shift to an overall fighter-dominated scheme that extended the massive air-defense umbrella, used to defend Britain, across the channel to protect the British Expeditionary Force and France on the Continental battlefield. Nor did the RAF assume a close air support role as the Luftwaffe had. Instead, attention, resources, and training continued to pour into the bomber offensive. RAF culture remained largely intact. It is certainly no coincidence that by the fall of 1940, British bombers were implementing the strategic offensive that had been formulated some twenty years earlier.

[4]

Chemical Warfare

One of the most intriguing questions in the history of warfare is why chemical weapons were not used in the Second World War. Poison gas was employed on a massive scale in the First World War, especially in its latter stages. In the 1920s and 1930s, nations expected, and went to considerable efforts preparing for, chemical warfare in a future conflict. Yet in the midst of the "total war" conditions of World War II, even states facing imminent political extinction did not take advantage of all the defenses available to them. The major combatants never purposefully employed chemical weapons.[1] To understand this anomaly we must first review the use of poison gas in World War I, the interwar history of efforts to control chemical means of warfare, and the perceived military value of poison gas.

On 22 April 1915, near Ypres, France, Germany initiated modern chemical warfare by releasing 150 tons of chlorine gas, which drifted over the French lines causing them to collapse. But the Germans, skeptical at first, were not prepared to follow up on this opportunity.[2] From this point on, gas was a standard tool of violence in World War I. As new types of agents and means of delivery were developed, chemical warfare became increasingly effective. There were, of course, bumps in this road. From 1915 to 1917 the use of gas expanded, but then dropped off as countermeasures were developed. The second surge came with the introduction of mustard gas, which dramatically in-

[1] The Japanese, however, did use chemical weapons against the Chinese, who had no comparable capabilities. Yuri Tanaka, "Poison Gas: The Story Japan Would Like to Forget," *Bulletin of the Atomic Scientists* 44 (October 1988): 10–19.

[2] Ludwig F. Haber, *The Poisonous Cloud: Chemical Warfare in the First World War* (Oxford: Clarendon Press, 1986), pp. 34–35.

creased the number of casualties. Mustard gas attacked not only the lungs but also the skin through the clothing, causing burns that were very difficult to treat. Mustard gas was "persistent," which meant that it contaminated objects for days or sometimes weeks. No effective protective measure against mustard gas was discovered before the war's end.[3]

The scale of gas use in World War I was considerable. It has been calculated that some 125,000 tons of battle gas were employed.[4] Casualty estimates range from 530,000 to some 1,300,000.[5] It is likely, however, that the total was higher rather than lower, because of problems with official statistics.[6] One of the most notable aspects in the scale of chemical use was its dramatic increase in the last year of the war. Over the conflict as a whole, 4 percent of Britain's shells were filled with gas, yet in 1918, that number was 8.4 percent. Sixty percent of Germany's total chemical shell use was in the last year. Had the war continued, the belligerents planned to increase the intensity of gas warfare. The United States and Britain intended to raise the percentage of toxic shells to some 25–30 percent of the total. The Allies also seriously considered bombing Berlin with gas.[7]

Chemical weapons were used in military tasks involving both positional and mobile warfare. The Germans, hoping to break the deadlock of trench warfare, had initiated gas attacks as an experiment. The chlorine clouds were intended to overcome the enemy's forward positions to permit a German advance. As protective equipment became effective, however, defenders were able to continue to fire machine guns

[3] Frederic J. Brown, *Chemical Warfare: A Study in Restraints* (Princeton: Princeton University Press, 1968), pp. 10–12. Stockholm International Peace Research Institute (SIPRI), *The Problem of Chemical and Biological Warfare* (New York: Humanities Press, 1971), 1:41–50, 58. The bulk of casualty-causing agents employed in 1915–1917 endangered the respiratory system when inhaled. These were countered when effective gas masks were developed.

[4] A. M. Prentiss, *Chemicals in War* (New York: McGraw-Hill, 1937), p. 661.

[5] The lower figure comes from Haber, *Poisonous Cloud*, p. 243, who does not include Russian casualties and likely underestimates other figures because they are based on official numbers, which are problematic for the reasons listed in the text. The high end is from Prentiss's 1937 study, *Chemicals in War*, pp. 653–54.

[6] For example, the British did not count important categories of gas victims, such as those attacked in 1915, those captured by the Germans, those missing, those who died on the battlefield, those who died after being evacuated to Britain, those who were able to quickly rejoin their units, and those who died of illnesses brought on by gas. See Robert Harris and Jeremy Paxman, *A Higher Form of Killing: The Secret Story of Chemical and Biological Warfare:* (New York: Hill & Wang, 1982), p. 34.

[7] Haber, *Poisonous Cloud*, pp. 260–61. Sir Henry F. Thuillier, *Gas in the Next War* (London: Geoffrey Bles, 1939), p. 74; Brown, *Chemical Warfare*, pp. 32, 46; Quester, *Deterrence before Hiroshima*, pp. 44–45 (see Chap. 3, n. 4).

and the assaults were halted. Gas then became a tool for inflicting casualties and harassing the enemy. With the introduction of mustard gas, chemical warfare was once again suitable for mobile combat. The Germans would bombard the sectors of Allied lines they planned on attacking with nonpersistent agents and Allied flanks and troop-staging areas with mustard gas.[8] This system allowed Germany to drive back British troops some forty miles over a fifty-mile front on the Somme. Mustard gas could have also been used to lay a defensive barrier by contaminating the areas in front of defensive lines. This, however, never occurred because when the Allies were on the defensive, they had little mustard gas, and later, when Germany was retreating, it did not use mustard gas because its stocks were nearly exhausted.

Gas had a prominent role in disarmament negotiations even before World War I. At the Hague Conference of 1899, the contracting powers agreed not to employ "projectiles the sole object of which is the diffusion of asphyxiating or deleterious gases." At the Second Hague Peace Conference of 1907, the delegates again pledged not to use "poison or poisoned weapons."[9] When the Germans released the chlorine cloud in 1915, there was an outcry that they had violated the Hague conventions. The Kaiser's government claimed that gas was not inhumane. In any case, it denied any violation on the grounds that Germany had not used *projectiles*, but had released the gas from cylinders. Germany also accused France of having already set the precedent by using bullets and shells containing chemical agents. Soon toxic agents were being used by both sides, in "retaliation." Although Britain was allowed the moral high ground by Germany's first massive use, it also took questionable actions from the viewpoint of international treaties. For example, the British employed gas first against the Turks in World War I even though there had been restraint for some two years of fighting between the two countries.[10]

The interwar period was marked by the efforts of statesmen to achieve peace through disarmament. Chemical warfare was one of their focal points. Limitations on the use or manufacture of gas were

[8] Over time, the Allies figured out the system and could anticipate where the attacks would come. SIPRI, *Chemical and Biological Warfare*, 1:135–40.

[9] The history of prohibitions on poison and chemicals is reviewed in John Ellis van Courtland Moon, "Controlling Chemical and Biological Weapons through World War II," in Burns, *Encyclopedia of Arms Control and Disarmament*, 2:657–59 (see Chap. 2, n. 11), and Richard M. Price, "A Genealogy of the Chemical Weapons Taboo" (Ph.D. diss., Cornell University, 1994).

[10] Haber, *Poisonous Cloud*, pp. 19 and 290–91; George Macmunn and Cyril Falls, *Military Operations Egypt and Palestine: From the Outbreak of War with Germany to June 1917* (London: HMSO, 1928), pp. 336–50; Harris and Paxman, *Higher Form of Killing*, p. 5.

discussed in some four disarmament forums in the 1920s and 1930s. The issue of limits on chemical warfare first came up at the Paris Peace Conference in 1919, which prohibited Germany from using, manufacturing, or importing poisonous gases, along with the related raw materials and equipment.[11]

Chemical warfare received considerable attention at the Washington Conference of 1921–22. A subcommittee of experts concluded that neither research nor manufacture of chemicals could realistically be controlled, that a total prohibition on use was unrealistic because high explosives produced small amounts of deadly gases, that the surprise use of gas could provide crucial advantage against an unprepared nation, and that the only possible restraint was to prohibit the use of gas against noncombatants. Nonetheless, the United States pushed through a provision based on the Versailles treaty which prohibited the use of poison gases in war. The resolution would become part of international law, but as delegates noted, the absence of any enforcement measures meant that national readiness was the only safety mechanism.[12] The treaty was signed by the five attending powers, the United States, Britain, France, Japan, and Italy, but never came into force because France objected to the provisions on the submarine.

The 1925 Geneva Conference for the Supervision of the International Trade in Arms and Ammunition and in Implements of War provided another forum where chemical warfare was discussed. After proposals to prohibit the export of poisonous gases and related materials were rejected, it was decided to resurrect the chemical warfare provisions of the Washington Conference. This became known as the Geneva Protocol and was the only agreement on chemical warfare concluded during the interwar period (see the Appendix).[13] Again there was no explicit enforcement mechanism, although the contracting parties promised "to exert every effort to induce other states to accede to the

---

[11] What was not included was a British proposal that would have required the Germans to turn over their technology to the Allies, effectively erasing Germany's leadership in the industry. President Wilson successfully opposed this resolution, despite British claims of military necessity, because he believed the aim was commercial advantage disguised as national security. Brown, *Chemical Warfare*, pp. 52–56.

[12] SIPRI, *Problem of Chemical and Biological Warfare: CB Disarmament Negotiations, 1920–1970*, 4:47. Brown, *Chemical Warfare*, p. 68.

[13] From 1926 to 33, a preparatory commission and then representatives of sixty-four nations met at the Geneva Conference for the Reduction and Limitation of Armaments to discuss various aspects of disarmament, including studies on chemical warfare. No consensus, however, was achieved on such suggestions as prohibiting production or committing states to implement sanctions against the violations of the Protocol. See SIPRI, *Chemical and Biological Warfare*, 4:72–174; Boggs, "Attempts to Define and Limit," pp. 57–60 (see Chap. 3, n. 11).

present Protocol." France ratified in 1926, the USSR in 1928, Germany in 1929, and Britain in 1930. But the United States and Japan did not approve it until the 1970s. France, Britain, and the USSR signed with the stipulation that it would bind them only vis-à-vis other signatories and their allies that also did not use chemical warfare.[14] It was in effect a no-first-use agreement applicable only to those that ratified it.

Even before the Second World War, the Geneva Protocol was put to the test. A 1934 border dispute between Italian Somaliland and Ethiopia (Abyssinia) led to an invasion by Italy and a war in 1935–36. Both nations had signed the Geneva Protocol, Italy in 1928, and Ethiopia in 1935 (when it discovered that Italy was stockpiling chemical weapons). Nonetheless, in 1935–36, Italy used gas in combat, mainly through attacks from the air with bombs and spraying. Mustard gas was the primary agent, and it was used to protect the flanks of advancing salients against ambush, to attack communication centers, and to inflict casualties and chaos on retreating troops. According to J. F. C. Fuller, who was in Ethiopia during the war, the results were impressive. "It is no exaggeration to say that mustard gas, sprinkled from aeroplanes, was the decisive tactical factor in the war."[15]

Ethiopia complained to the League of Nations, and in 1935 the Coordination Committee of the League imposed an arms embargo on Italy for its unprovoked aggression. Trade was not cut off, but financial assistance and a list of munitions and equipment related to chemical warfare were prohibited.[16] Clearly the use of gas by a fascist government was of concern to the other major powers. The British prime minister lamented in Parliament that "if a great European nation, in spite of having given its signature to the Geneva Protocol against the use of such gases, employs them in Africa, what guarantee have we that they may not be used in Europe?"[17] The emperor of Ethiopia reinforced this fear in June 1936 at the Assembly of the League of Nations: "In tens of thousands the victims of the Italian mustard gas fell . . . I . . . come . . . to give Europe warning of the doom that awaits

---

[14] This meant that it was legitimate to use chemical warfare against an opposing state that had either not ratified the treaty or had an ally that had used a chemical weapon. See SIPRI, *Chemical and Biological Warfare*, 4:58–71 and Appendix 5, pp. 341–46.

[15] Quoted in Colonel Stanley D. Fair, "Mussolini's Chemical War," *Army*, January 1985, p. 52. The defenders, however, had little or no protective capabilities. Also see SIPRI, *Chemical and Biological Warfare*, 1:145–46.

[16] Fair, "Mussolini's Chemical War," p. 45. Italy attempted to justify its actions by claiming that its use of gas was in reprisal for Ethiopian atrocities. SIPRI, *Chemical and Biological Warfare*, 4:180.

[17] Harris and Paxman, *Higher Form of Killing*, p. 50.

it."[18] Yet despite these concerns, the economic sanctions were not fully implemented, and no military sanctions were ever adopted. In 1938 the League was informed that Japan had used gas against China, but no action was taken in that instance either.[19]

At the very beginning of World War II one last diplomatic effort was made to contain the chemical threat. The British ambassador to Switzerland delivered a message to the Swiss foreign ministry which was to be passed on to German officials. The note pledged not to use poison gas as long as the Third Reich would do the same. Germany signaled its agreement to the bargain.[20]

How then can the institution of restraint in chemical warfare be characterized? The three criteria of specificity, concordance, and durability provide a useful meter. In terms of the first standard, the Geneva Protocol was simple but specific. Signatory nations would not use poison gas first if the other side was a signatory and also showed restraint. There were a few gray areas in this agreement. High explosives released small amounts of poisonous chemicals—was this a violation? Did the Protocol pertain to the use of nonlethal gas (that is, tear gas)? Some countries, such as the United States, wanted the freedom to use such gases for domestic crowd control.[21] Concordance was more of a problem; not all nations had ratified the Protocol by the start of the war, the most important holdouts being the United States and Japan. Furthermore, influential nations (such as France and Britain) only agreed to apply the norm in conflicts with other signatories whose allies also adhered to the agreement. Thus concordance was, at best, in doubt. Finally, the Protocol's conventions showed mixed durability. On the one hand, the norm against the use of poison agents had existed for centuries. Constraints on chemical use had been a part of international law from the turn of the century. On the other, it had been violated egregiously in World War I. And even after the no-first-use principle was reaffirmed at Geneva in 1925, the Italians violated the agreement a decade later—just two years before the war—and paid little for doing so. Overall, the institution against chemical warfare was more developed than that attached to strategic bombing but less than that against unrestricted submarine warfare.

The experience of World War I seemed to indicate that gas had a

[18] Fair, "Mussolini's Chemical War," p. 48.
[19] SIPRI, *Chemical and Biological Warfare*, 4: 189–90.
[20] Harris and Paxman, *Higher Form of Killing*, p. 107; Brown, *Chemical Warfare*, pp. 230–31.
[21] SIPRI, *Chemical and Biological Warfare*, 4:102–4; Moon, "Controlling Chemical and Biological Weapons," pp. 664–66.

role to play in modern warfare, even if it was a more limited role than originally anticipated. To be sure, chemical warfare had significant drawbacks. It complicated an already complex battlefield. Gas supplies and protective equipment were a burdensome strain on supply lines. Large amounts were needed to cover relatively small areas. Moreover, waging chemical warfare demanded high discipline and extensive training. Especially troubling in the beginning of the war, gas "cloud" attacks were dependent on the weather—wind, precipitation, and temperature. Weather diminished in importance as new agents and delivery means (such as chemical-filled artillery shells) were developed, but remained a limiting concern.[22]

One of the barriers to effective chemical warfare was human. Military men did not like chemical warfare and used it only half-heartedly. First, there was the question of honor. Gas killed indiscriminately and impersonally, both warrior and civilian alike. It was seen as unchivalrous by users and victims. More important, it dramatically affected how soldiers were used to doing business. As Major General J. F. C. Fuller noted, "A man in a gas mask is only half a soldier."[23] Fighting men were hesitant to attack under conditions of chemical use, a cardinal sin in an era when armies were weaned on the importance of the offensive. "Every change in sensation transmitted by smell and taste troubles the mind with fresh anxieties of unknown effects and further strains the soldier's power of endurance at the very moment when his entire mental energy is required for battle."[24] Soldiers were known to suffer from "Gas Fright" where all the symptoms of chemical poisoning would appear after an alarm even when no toxic substances were present. The British played mind games on the enemy by mixing smoke and gas discharges that were difficult to distinguish. The final affront to the military was that it did not even have jurisdiction over this weapon. Chemical warfare was controlled by civilians, and because of its technical nature, chemists especially had a large say in its employment. It should be no surprise that the soldiers and scientists

---

[22] Haber, *Poisonous Cloud*, pp. 200–201. In Britain, General Foulkes, the head of the Chemical Troops, remained more attached to cylinders and the "gas cloud." See Donald Richter, *Chemical Soldiers: British Gas Warfare in World War I* (Lawrence: University Press of Kansas, 1992), pp. 169–71, 193–94.

[23] Major General J. F. C. Fuller, *Armored Warfare: Lectures on Field Service Regulation III* (Harrisburg, Pa.: Military Service, 1943), p. 28. The troops also hated the extra work chemical warfare entailed. Richter, *Chemical Soldiers*, pp. 221–22.

[24] Fritz Haber, quoted in Haber, *Poisonous Cloud*, p. 277.

did not get along very well. The result was that gas was not well incorporated into existing strategy and tactics.[25]

Gas was not a decisive weapon, but it did have its advantages. Major General H. T. Thuillier, head of British chemical warfare in the Great War, argued in 1939 that gas was especially useful for causing casualties and demoralizing the enemy. The wearing of masks inhibited soldiers both physically and psychologically. Chemical weapons also came in a variety of types—persistent, nonpersistent, harassing, and lethal—which could be applied in a number of different circumstances. Economically, gas munitions were attractive because they required relatively little labor and raw material to produce.[26]

The leverage gas afforded did, of course, depend on the situation. In World War I many came to realize that mustard gas was particularly useful in the defensive where it could be used to slow the enemy's advance.[27] The use of artillery shells significantly increased the effectiveness of chemical warfare by improving the accuracy of fire and decreasing dependence on weather. Advocates of gas warfare maintained that it was actually cost effective in terms of casualties produced. Based on the experiences of World War I, A. M. Prentiss calculated that the same tonnage of gas would produce two times as many casualties as high explosives.[28] Yet it was also true that conventional and chemical munitions were not necessarily alternatives but rather complements: High explosives provided immediate casualties, whereas gas was persistently harassing and harmful.[29]

In the 1920s and 1930s, operational thinking about gas was largely based on the results of World War I. Official military histories shunned the topic, but individual analysts and journals did discuss it. Toxic substances were seen as useful in the defense for holding ground and on the offense for achieving surprise and blocking flanks. The strategic use of gas to attack cities directly was also discussed. The purpose was to demoralize the enemy's populace (and the will to fight) by subjecting it to chemical warfare conditions over a long period of time. Some experts, however, believed that defensive preparations would be sufficient to pre-

---

[25] On the friction between the military and chemical warfare, see J. B. S. Haldane, *Callinicus: A Defence of Chemical Warfare* (New York: Dutton, 1925), pp. 28–38; Thuillier, *Gas in the Next War*, p. 124; SIPRI, *Chemical and Biological Warfare*, 1:234–35; Brown, *Chemical Warfare*, pp. 36, 40–42; Richter, *Chemical Soldiers*, p. 220–24; and Haber, *Poisonous Cloud* pp. 266–67, 272–73.

[26] Thuillier, *Gas in the Next War*, pp. 69–74. Brown, *Chemical Warfare*, p. 33. Haber *Poisonous Cloud*, p. 277.

[27] Thuiller, *Gas in the Next War*, p. 71; Haber, *Poisonous Cloud*, pp. 265, 447.

[28] Prentiss, *Chemicals in War*, as cited in SIPRI, *Chemical and Biological Warfare*, 1:128.

[29] Haber, *Poisonous Cloud*, pp. 264–65.

vent such an outcome. But it was also recognized that even without the psychological effect, combinations of high explosives and gas might be very damaging simply in terms of casualties and contamination.[30]

In short, chemical weapons, however disagreeable, were accepted as having military utility. They were not a decisive factor in the First World War, but then again, neither were the tank or the airplane. Hitler predicted in a May 1939 speech that "a weapon will only be of decisive importance in winning battles if the enemy does not possess it. This applies to gas, U-boats, and the Air Force."[31] Fredric J. Brown has also noted that gas, "if used unilaterally was effective, but when both sides used it, little gain was had."[32] Of course, the same was true of other, more conventional weapons, which were used without a second thought. The advantages of chemical warfare varied with how and when it was employed. Yet in the Second World War, chemical warfare was not used at all. To understand this, we must examine the deliberations of the combatants themselves.

THE BRITISH WAY OF CHEMICAL WARFARE

Britain, by most accounts, was one of the countries where pacifist sentiment was strongest in the 1920s and 1930s. It is alleged that among the English no weapon was more reviled than poison gas. Britain affirmed that it would only use chemical weapons in retaliation, a policy which held up throughout the war. Ironically, however, of all the European powers involved in World War II, this one came closest to initiating chemical warfare. On two occasions Britain was poised to use gas. The first was in planning the defense against the expected invasion of England by the Nazis in 1940. British leaders developed and, apparently, approved the use of gas to defend the integrity of the realm. In this instance, Britain made a contingent decision for escalation. The second was in 1944. Germany had begun the V-rocket assault on London. Britain's leaders debated using gas either to retaliate or to shorten the war. Yet despite Churchill's vigorous advocacy of escalation

[30] Ibid., pp. 279 and 299. DuPuy and Eliot, *If War Comes*, pp. 205 (see Chap. 3, n. 21). Douhet noted that attacks against cities with high-explosive, incendiary, and gas bombs could have more impact on the war by undermining morale than by material damage. Douhet, *Command of the Air*, pp. 57–58 (see Chap. 3, n. 20). Thuillier, *Gas in the Next War*, pp. 78–79.
[31] Hinsley, *Hitler's Strategy*, p. 22 (see Chap. 2, n. 15). Edward M. Spiers, *Chemical Weaponry: A Continuing Challenge* (New York: St. Martins, 1989), pp. 80–81.
[32] Brown, *Chemical Warfare*, p. 37.

and Britain's relative immunity to retaliation in kind, restraint pre-vailed.[33] The official histories on chemical warfare are perplexing in that they ignore the "dog that didn't bark." One states that there was never any question of the British using gas first.[34] This was clearly not the case. A second simply omits the topic because gas was never used,[35] thus failing to ask why chemical weapons were not employed.

Institutionalism, realism, and organizational culture all provide some insight into this mystery, yet as distinct explanations, they are not equally convincing. At a macrolevel, institutionalism might expect some degree of restraint based on the medium robustness of conventions against first use. Yet given the shortcomings of the norm in terms of international acceptance, this restraint should also have been challenged and violated in the intense environment of World War II. It was not. Furthermore, when we examine Britain's actual decision making, there is little evidence that the prevailing norm was the central factor in the choice for restraint. Realism would anticipate that Britain would have opted for use when chemical warfare was to its advantage and for restraint when it was relatively vulnerable. This, however, is almost the exact opposite of what occurred. Nonetheless, when the political survival of the United Kingdom was challenged, Britain did appear ready to pick up the chemical sword, as realism would predict. Finally, the organizational-culture perspective predicts British escalation as un-likely. Given the ill-fit of chemical warfare with the prevailing "way of war" of the British army, restraint is not surprising. Chemical warfare was pushed to the side before the war, and during the war was generally ignored or resisted. Organizational culture, both in process and result, best accounts for Britain's restraint.

Norms and Threats

Britain's policy on limiting chemical warfare in the interwar period was, for a time, a prisoner of the popular revulsion against such weapons. This political pressure led Britain not only to accept the Geneva Protocol, but also to conceal its chemical-weapons program. In the

[33] Britain's advantage derived primarily from its air superiority coupled with its expanded chemical warfare stocks. It still lagged in technology in that only Germany had nerve gas.

[34] Butler, *Grand Strategy*, 2:552 (see Chap. 2, n. 91).

[35] "Chemical warfare equipment is not discussed in this book. Although it absorbed a great deal of energy and many notable developments occurred, the fact that gas warfare did not take place makes its omission less serious." See M. M. Postan, D. Hay, and J. D. Scott, *Design and Development of Weapons* (London: HMSO, 1964), p. 253, n. 1.

1930s, however, popular sentiment was reversed by the perception of external threat. Later, in World War II, the popular opposition to poison gas was muted. Both in peace and war, the norm against chemical warfare was relevant, but not decisive.

The English learned to despise chemical weapons during World War I when the British government exploited Germany's first use of gas for anti-German propaganda. After the war, Britain was swept by a wave of pacifist feeling in reaction against its massive losses. The poison cloud came to symbolize the horrors of that war and was referred to simply as "frightfulness."[36] One author, W. Irwin, claimed in 1921 that a dozen bombs could destroy the population of an entire city. In Parliament a speaker declared that chemical bombs threaten "the wiping out of our entire civilization."[37] Noel Baker, a disarmament advocate, announced on the radio in 1927 that all gas experts agree that it would be impossible to devise means to protect the civilian population from chemical attack.[38] Major General J. F. C. Fuller described how a mustard gas attack on London would turn the city for several days into "one vast raving Bedlam, the hospitals will be stormed, traffic will cease, the homeless will shriek for help, the city will be pandemonium . . . the government will be swept away by an avalanche of terror."[39]

The influence of popular sentiment in the first half of the interwar period on preparations and negotiations was significant. The limited chemical warfare programs of the 1920s had to be kept secret. The public was war-weary, and there was little support for rearmament. The Government decided in the early 1920s not to speak out on the value of chemical defense because it did not want to accept the political risk of appearing to advocate chemical warfare. Thus many of the exaggerations of the threat of gas attacks went unanswered, whereas public education efforts that would have increased support for chemical warfare research were ignored.[40] The stigma against chemical warfare was such that those in charge of its development worried about the

[36] Harris and Paxman, *Higher Form of Killing,* pp. 5, 20.

[37] SIPRI, *Chemical and Biological Warfare,* 1:101–2.

[38] Terrence H. O'Brien, *Civil Defence* (London: HMSO, 1955), pp. 31–32.

[39] Quoted in Moon, "Controlling Chemical and Biological Weapons" p. 668, and Lord Michael Carver, *Twentieth-Century Warriors* (New York: Weidenfeld & Nicolson, 1988), p. 27.

[40] Harris and Paxman, *Higher Form of Killing,* p. 34. CID, "Chemical Warfare Policy," November 1924, WO 188/144 (all documents cited as WO are found in the War Office files located at the PRO); "A Summary of Important Notes and Papers in Connection with the Policy of Gas Warfare in order of dates from 1899," 1927, WO 188/212; O'Brien, *Civil Defence,* pp. 31–32.

lack of inspiration among their employees.[41] The Hon. W. E. Guinness, undersecretary of state for war, even had to answer questions in Parliament on the number of animals being used and killed in chemical warfare research. After the undersecretary provided figures, his interrogator was quick to inject, "Can the honourable and gallant Gentleman say how many ex-ministers were among them?"[42]

Britain signed the Washington Conference Treaty and ratified the Geneva Protocol, but this was due more to the political implications (both domestic and international) of not signing rather than belief in the efficacy of the agreements. The British support of the interwar chemical warfare regime was tepid at best. Chemical warfare was not seen as being in the British interest because British industrial and population centers were extremely vulnerable to gas attack. Britain, however, was opposed to comprehensive efforts on the issue because of a lack of verification and sanction mechanisms. Officials calculated that it was impossible to restrict or prohibit the manufacture of chemicals in peacetime, and in wartime such capacity could be quickly adapted for chemical warfare. When restraints on chemical warfare were incorporated into the Washington Conference Treaty, Britain was initially opposed, but felt that in light of U.S. (and other) support, public opposition would be difficult.[43] The significant influence of popular sentiment in this outcome is evident when compared with the military's advice, which was not to support the treaty.[44]

The formal institutionalization of popular antigas sentiment in Britain's acceptance of the Protocol seemed to add slightly to constraints on the development of chemical weapons. Terms were changed to avoid any reference to offensive chemical warfare so that Britain's actions would be more acceptable. Sensitivity to public opinion also influenced some material decisions. The General Staff decided in 1930 not to circulate a manual that had been prepared on chemical offense because it felt that secrecy was more important, especially given the political situation. All official statements up to 1936 emphasized that experimental work had been restricted to defensive studies. Using gas in a surprise attack was discussed in Britain in 1925, but in accordance

---

[41] "Review of Present System of Direction and Control of Chemical Warfare Research," 1922, WO 188/144.

[42] "Parliamentary Questions on Chemical Warfare," 14 May 1923, WO 188/177.

[43] The British were afraid that they would be charged with supporting only those measures that were clearly in their interests as opposed to the overall disarmament program. See CID, "Chemical Warfare Policy," November 1924, WO 188/144.

[44] CID, "Chemical Warfare Policy," memorandum, Secretary of State for War, 29 July 1926, CAB 4/15.

[155]

with the Geneva Protocol, the official policy was fixed at retaliation only. The armed services up to 1936 were apparently not given any training in the offensive use of gas. And even the public development of civil-defense measures against gas were deferred in 1929 as being ill-timed in light of Britain's ratification of the Protocol. Finally, the chemical warfare regime of the interwar period acted as a constraint on policy and behavior. The Foreign Office considered the Protocol a binding commitment. When this was challenged in the mid 1920s by proposals to use gas on the Indian North-West Frontier, the Foreign Office was adamantly opposed. It did not see how Britain could do such a quick policy reversal. Austen Chamberlain, the foreign secretary, argued that Germany had been vilified for its use, and Britain had to wait longer for its advocacy of gas until "our charges against Germany were less present in the minds of the public."[45]

Yet even before the mid-1930s, one must be careful not to overstate the influence of the antigas norm and the treaties that embodied and reinforced it. Britain's chemical weapons program was pushed underground but it was not suspended. After Britain signed the Geneva Protocol, the work previously done in the Offensive Munitions Department was simply conducted under the heading of "chemical weapons against which defense is required." A variety of research and development for offensive weaponry was conducted under this disguise.[46]

By the late 1930s, any restraint that public opinion or international agreement may have had on preparations for chemical warfare vanished in the face of the rising threat of war with Germany. For example, in 1937, the War Office and the Air Staff recommended that the stock of gas for retaliation be increased and production upped to 512 tons a week. The Treasury argued that this was excessive and that the services were preparing for extensive gas attacks on civilian populations. Treasury officials further contended that increased chemical preparation was against the government's retaliation-only policy and it needed to be justified on political grounds. The armed services responded that the British masses were no longer so squeamish about gas readiness

---

[45] Edward M. Spiers, *Chemical Warfare* (Urbana: University of Illinois Press, 1986), pp. 47–49. On the impact of antigas sentiment, see Harris and Paxman, *Higher Form of Killing*, pp. 46–47; "Lecture to Staff College, Camberly," 10 April 1931, WO 188/390; "Preparation of Training Manuals on Chemical Warfare," 30 September 1930, WO 188/446; SIPRI, *Chemical and Biological Warfare*, 1:269, 300; Haber, *Poisonous Cloud*, p. 300.

[46] Harris and Paxman, *Higher Form of Killing*, pp. 42 and 47.

and would not disapprove of preparations. The Cabinet accepted these arguments and approved the production of 300 tons per week.[47]

In terms of impact on decisions during the war, the norm against first use was influential but not decisive. The main concern was that in using gas first, Britain might alienate U.S. opinion and support. When General Sir John Dill, chief of the Imperial General Staff, first proposed the use of gas to defend Britain in 1940, he noted that one of the drawbacks might be a weakening of U.S. support, but he considered the risks worthwhile. Churchill too worried about endangering U.S. support by employing gas to defend Britain, but he was assured by a British officer working with the Americans that the United States would accept such use despite the Geneva Protocol.[48] Others suggested that Britain's domestic and fighting morale would be damaged by using a weapon that imperiled England's sense of its purpose. Major-General Henderson, assistant chief to Dill, concluded that "some of us would begin to wonder whether it really mattered which side won."[49] Ultimately, however, such feelings did not carry the day. The majority of military planners (based on the Joint Planning Committee's views) did not consider the prohibitions of the Geneva Protocol binding and did not believe there would be significant negative reaction among neutrals if Britain were to use gas.[50]

When Britain again considered initiating chemical warfare in 1944, Churchill asked his military men not to consider the political implications for the Alliance, though he realized he would have to "square Uncle Joe and the President." In fact, Churchill specifically urged that the norms against gas use be discounted:

It is absurd to consider morality on this topic when everybody used it in the last war without a word of complaint from the moralists or the Church. On the other hand, in the last war the bombing of open cities was regarded as forbidden. Now everybody does it as a matter of course. It is simply a question of fashion changing as she does between long skirts and short skirts for women. . . . One really must not be bound

---

[47] The Air Ministry readily yielded to the lower amount based on priorities: Britain did not wish to be forced to spend less in other areas just to develop a weapon that it did not want to use anyway. See Paul Harris, "British Preparations for Offensive Chemical Warfare, 1935–1939," *Royal United Services Institute Journal* 125 (June 1980): 60–61.

[48] Harris and Paxman, *Higher Form of Killing*, p. 115; memorandum, Chief of the Imperial General Staff (CIGS), "The Use of Gas in Home Defence," 15 June 1940, WO 193/732. In fact, the United States had supplied Britain with gas in 1940.

[49] Minute, ACIGS(c) to CIGS, 16 June 1940, WO 193/732.

[50] Minute, DoP to the Chief of the Air Staff, 18 June 1940, AIR 2/5117.

within silly conventions of the mind whether they be those that ruled in the last war or those in reverse which rule in this.[51]

That such a discussion even took place attests to the impact of norms on decisions. Yet in the end, the political implications of using gas first was not the primary cause of restraint. In 1940 the choice was escalation. In 1944, the choice was restraint, but not because of the costs of breaking a norm but because of the professional military bias against chemical weapons.

Realist Asymmetry and Advantage

Realist considerations had much to do with the development of Britain's chemical warfare policy in the interwar period. Even Britain's interest in, and acceptance of, the Geneva Protocol was related to relative advantage. But realism cannot easily explain British chemical warfare policies during World War II. Before turning to these matters, however, I need first to dispose of the simplest of realist explanations for Britain's restraint, namely, that chemical weapons were not used because they had no military value.

Official views in Britain from just after World War I and just before World War II contradict the "no value" argument. In 1919, the Committee on Chemical Warfare (also called the Holland Committee) was formed to decide Britain's future gas policy. The committee agreed "with no shadow of a doubt" that gas was a legitimate weapon and that it was a "foregone conclusion" that gas would be used in future wars. After all, no weapon that had worked had "ever been abandoned by Nations fighting for their existence."[52] Lectures on chemical warfare at the Army's staff college emphasized the value of gas.[53]

Jumping to the other end of the interwar period, in the summer of 1939, the worth of chemical warfare was again confirmed. A review of gas requirements concluded that "with added and improved weapons chemical troops will be used in future war more than they were in the last."[54] A new weapon was not long in coming. Trials conducted in

---

[51] Churchill to Ismay (for the COS), 6 July 1944, PREM 3/89. (all documents cited as PREM are found in the Prime Minister's Papers located at the PRO).

[52] Haber, *Poisonous Cloud*, p. 293.

[53] Chemical Warfare Committee (CWC), "Memorandum on the Protection of the Civil Population against Gas Attack," WO 188/144. "Lecture on Chemical Warfare to Be Delivered at the Staff College on February 26th at 10:45 am," 1926, WO 188/48; "Lecture to the Staff College, Camberly, 10 April 1931," WO 188/390.

[54] See "Gases for Use in the Field and the Quantity of Each Required," prepared by the Director of Military Training and Director of Staff Studies by request of the Intra-

Southern Algeria in the latter half of December 1939 indicated that the high-altitude spraying of gas from bombers was successful.[55] Just before Germany's blitzkrieg through its western neighbors in the spring of 1940, Sir John Dill, chief of the Imperial General Staff, noted that gas was particularly effective in hampering the forward movement of an Army.[56] These views indicate that the notion that gas had no military value does not match expert opinion at that time.

Realism does capture important aspects of Britain's interwar policy on chemical warfare, which like security policy as a whole, was directly tied to the international environment. In overall defense planning, Britain's need to conserve resources became the primary constraint. To attain this economy, Britain adopted the "Ten-Year Rule," which "assumed for framing revised estimates that the British Empire will not be engaged in any great war during the next ten years, and that no Expeditionary Force is required for this purpose."[57] The rule guaranteed that British security efforts would be directly tied to those of its competitors. If there was no threat of war in terms of a challenge from a outside power, little attention would be devoted to military capabilities. If there was, estimates would be revised. This rule dominated defense planning until 1932. It also helped to limit the development of chemical weapons. Only a few days after the armistice in 1918, British gas manufacturing shut down, and for the most part, remained out of action until the end of the 1930s.[58]

Not everyone in Britain was ready to let chemical capabilities disappear. The Holland Committee contended that gas was a legitimate weapon and would be used in a future war. Backed by the General Staff and the Admiralty, the committee stressed the danger of falling behind other countries. From the mid-1920s through the early 1930s the main argument used in favor of chemical warfare preparations was

---

service Committee on Anglo-French Chemical Warfare Conversations, 7 July 1939, 193/740.

[55] "We have at our disposal a potential weapon of great value and which (so far as is known) the Germans are unaware," in "Chemical Warfare—High Spray Trials," MO1 to DDMO, 30 January 1940, WO 193/726.

[56] Dill was one of the few soldiers who were interested in chemical warfare, "Chemical Warfare Policy," COS Meeting, 6 May 1940, WO 193/713.

[57] War Cabinet 'A' Minutes, 616A, 15 August 1919, as cited in N. H. Gibbs, *Grand Strategy*, vol 1, *Rearmament Policy* (London: HMSO, 1976), p. 3. For a thorough account of this topic, see John Ferris, *Men, Money, and Diplomacy: The Evolution of British Strategic Policy, 1919–1926* (Ithaca: Cornel University Press, 1989).

[58] Brian Bond, *British Military Policy between the Two World Wars* (Oxford: Clarendon Press, 1980), pp. 22–23.

that Britain had to keep pace with its potential competitors.[59] The logic behind such preparations was explicitly realist: "If we are known to be in a state of readiness equal or nearly equal, to that of the enemy, it is very possible that he will be restrained from gas attack on our towns by the knowledge of retribution which he will therefore bring on his own."[60] In 1925 Britain again demonstrated that its policy was significantly shaped by external sources. Britain decided to emulate France's policy, which was no initiation of chemical warfare with all-out use should an adversary employ gas. With this policy the British Government could justify both defensive and offensive research and development.[61]

Spurred largely by international events, the sea change in chemical warfare preparations came in the mid-1930s. As early as 1933 Britain discarded its Ten-Year Rule in order to meet the growing threat from Hitler's Germany. In 1932, British Intelligence was well aware of Germany's chemical readiness, for it had acquired a 1928 German army manual on the offensive use of war gases. Britain also knew that Germany was a huge producer of chemicals and that the government was subsidizing chemical research. It was around the same time that the decision was taken to loosen secrecy around gas "defence" preparations.[62]

It took the shock of actual gas use in the Ethiopian war to spur Britain to implement its preparations for chemical warfare. Britain's Prime Minister Stanley Baldwin declared on 16 April 1936 that Italy's use of chemicals was a peril to the world. As Italy had signed the Geneva Protocol, Baldwin openly wondered what would stop similar chemical use in a war in Europe. The United Kingdom stepped up its readiness schedule. The British Army Council had already authorized a development program for both offensive and defensive chemical warfare. A further expansion of production facilities was discussed and approved. In November 1936, officials announced that everyone would

[59] CWC, "Memorandum on the Protection of the Civil Population against Gas Attack," n.d. (probably 1922), pp. 3–4, WO 188/144. CID Meeting, 3 April 1924, WO 188/389; "Chronological Summary of Decisions Affecting British Policy with Regard to Chemical Warfare since December 1927," 23 January 1931, WO 188/389.

[60] CWC, "Memorandum on the Protection of the Civil Population Against Gas Attack," n.d. (probably 1922), WO 188/144. Also see First Lord of the Admiralty, "Necessity for Holding a Stock of Gas," 18 December 1924, WO 188/144.

[61] CID Meeting, 3 April 1924, WO 188/389.

[62] Brief on Chemical Warfare, 1932, WO 190/142. O'Brien, *Civil Defence*, pp. 39, 68.

be issued a gas mask. The first British air-raid precautions booklet was published, and it dealt solely with antigas measures.[63]

Yet another international shock speeded preparations further. The crisis in Czechoslovakia in 1938 raised fears of a "knock-out blow" from German airpower which would devastate England. Intelligence was presenting Germany as a country preparing to use chemical weapons. The Nazis were forming gas units, holding offensive exercises with comparatively large numbers of men, and developing land and air weapons. The British anticipated that the Third Reich's decision to initiate chemical warfare would depend on a number of factors, including political expediency, resistance encountered, and the scale of attack required. Thirty million gas masks were issued. In November, the Cabinet approved a further increase in chemical industrial production capacity.[64] Britain's acquisition of retaliatory capability had begun.

By the onset of war in September 1939, Britain's gas defenses surpassed those of any other nation, including Germany. For psychological reasons, personal protection received the most attention. Every adult had a mask and baby equipment. Upgraded masks and protective clothing were being issued. Plans for gas-proofing rooms were distributed, and decontamination schemes were developed. Yet on the offensive side, capabilities were limited. Britain had only five hundred tons of mustard gas on hand when Germany invaded Poland. The War Office had stocks of equipment for four chemical warfare companies and gas-filled shells for the artillery; however, there was only one chemical warfare company in existence. Industrial output was fifty tons of mustard gas per week for the Army. The Air Ministry had gas bombs, sprayers, and a gas supply, but lacked planes to reach Germany.[65]

From a realist perspective, Britain's meager offensive capacity is inexplicable. Britain, after all, believed that Germany had a considerable, and growing, chemical warfare potential. The Government's policy, in line with the Geneva Protocol, was enforcement of no-first-use by the threat to retaliate in kind. Preparation for such a capacity was legiti-

---

[63] Harris, "British Preparations for Offensive CW," pp. 57–58. Harris and Paxman, *Higher Form of Killing*, pp. 49–50. SIPRI, *Chemical and Biological Warfare*, 1:260.

[64] "Probable Scale and Method of Gas Attack to Be Adopted by Germany When Directing Her Main Effort against France and Field Force in Western Europe," Summer 1937, WO 190/547. Harris and Paxman, *Higher Form of Killing*, p. 50. Harris, "British Preparations," p. 61.

[65] On these preparations, see Harris, "British Preparations," pp. 61–62; O'Brien, *Civil Defence*, pp. 286, 329; SIPRI, *Chemical and Biological Warfare*, 1:272.

mate within, if not encouraged by, the Geneva Protocol. In effect, that agreement was an international institution sanctioning a national policy of deterrence.[66] Yet in September 1939, Britain had limited offensive capability, a situation little different when the use of chemicals to defend against a German invasion was first considered the following spring.

In contrast to the influence of international circumstance in peacetime preparations, realism played less of a role in wartime decisions. Given its limited capabilities, Britain was quite relieved to exchange no-first-use pledges with the Third Reich in September 1939. It feared both gas attacks on its cities and the battlefield use of gas. The Army General Staff anticipated that when the British Expeditionary Force went to France at the beginning of the war, the Germans would use up to 160 bombers to deliver 18,000 gallons of mustard gas a day contaminating up to one third of the entire British force.[67] On 13 September 1939, the Cabinet once again ordered an increase in chemical production capacity. Britain clearly perceived itself as vulnerable. In 1940 and 1941, Churchill was constrained from making public announcements that Britain would retaliate against any German use of chemical weapons for fear that Germans would assume Britain was planning a preemptive chemical strike. He directed the Chiefs of Staff to ensure that chemical weapons would not be mentioned in the British media lest Germany be alarmed.[68]

What appears less consistent with a relative-advantage argument is that Britain first considered using chemical warfare when it saw itself as vastly inferior to Germany. The British recognized that their chemical potential and airpower delivery capacity lagged behind Germany's by a factor of at least four.[69] Indeed, that was not Britain's only disadvantage. In the summer of 1940, Britain's cities were within easy strik-

[66] Britain would only sign the agreement after Germany. In addition, Britain refused to recognize the Protocol in conflicts with countries that had not signed it. SIPRI, *Chemical and Biological Warfare*, 4:345, n. 2, 1:269.

[67] Harris and Paxman, *Higher Form of Killing*, p. 108. Another estimate predicted 27 percent losses in one corps if it were the target of concentrated aerial spray attacks. Contamination from other sources would be 4 percent. Such intense attacks were not expected to last more than a fortnight. Over a year a chemical war would cause 2 percent *daily* contamination to British forces on the Continent. See "Chemical Warfare: Scale of Gas Attack to Which BEF May Be Subjected," n.d. (probably 1939), WO 193/717.

[68] Minute, Churchill to Ismay (for COS), 28 September 1940, PREM 3/88/3. SIPRI, *Chemical and Biological Warfare*, 1:314.

[69] See memorandum, Ismay to Churchill, 2 July 1940, PREM 3/88/3, in which Ismay notes that the CIGS (Dill) stresses "the general use of gas would be to our disadvantage owing to the fact that the Germans at present have much greater resources than we have." The Inspector of Chemical Warfare also underscores British inferiority in "Memo-

ing distance of German aircraft, but the reverse was not true. In addition, London was especially vulnerable to chemical attack because its frequent fog would retain gas.[70]

Despite this imbalance, Britain made a contingent decision in 1940 to use chemical weapons. With the fall of France in the spring of 1940, Britain was confronted with the possibility of a German invasion of the British Isles. One of the means of defense suggested by the chief of the Imperial General Staff, Sir John Dill, was to spray the invading army on the beachhead with mustard gas. He concluded that gas would be very useful. Even though objections were raised based on the possible reaction of international opinion and German retaliation, Dill believed initiating chemical warfare still made sense.[71]

Dill's proposal met resistance in the military establishment, most immediately from his own staff and the Director of Home Defence, not because of military utility, but instead because of the expected negative impact on the nation's morale. Dill withdrew the idea. Winston Churchill heard about it, however, and the plan was revived in full force. The prime minister felt that mustard gas would be very effective against German beachheads—and that Britain should initiate chemical operations. General Hastings Ismay, Churchill's chief of staff, passing on Dill's advice, responded that Britain's (small) supply of gas would be ready to attack from the air by 5 July 1940.[72] Britain's willingness to initiate chemical warfare was evident in a January 1941 anti-invasion exercise where the War Cabinet sanctioned the use of gas.[73]

---

randum on the Use of Gas in the Defence of the United Kingdom," 21 June 1940, WO 193/732. On airpower, see the chapter on British strategic bombing.

[70] "Chemical Warfare Position: Following the German Occupation of NorthWest Europe and Italy's Entry into the War," 9 May 1940, WO 188/446.

[71] Memorandum, CIGS (Dill), "The Use of Gas in Home Defence," 15 June 1940, WO 193/732.

[72] Minute, ACIGS(c)(Henderson) to CIGS, 16 June 1940, WO 193/732; Minute, Major, G. S., to M.O.1, 8 July 1940, WO 193/732. Churchill to Ismay, 30 June 1940, WO 193/732. Chemical warfare on land would not be ready for a year. It was estimated that existing stocks could contaminate a strip sixty yards wide and 4,000 miles long if delivered by aerial spray. Annex to Minute from Ismay to Churchill, 2 July 1940, PREM 3/88/3; CIGS (Dill) to Ismay with Appendix on Gas Resources, 2 July 1940, WO 193/732.

[73] "Chemical Warfare: Policy—Use in Home Defence 1940–1941," CIGS to COS, 28 April 1941, WO 193/732. Although this was a retaliation scenario, the meaning of "retaliatory use" often appears to include British first use when German employment of gas is anticipated. Whether this actually would have transpired is certainly arguable. Some British military leaders did appreciate the vulnerability of civilians in such a situation. See Minute, DoP., 18 June 1940, AIR 2/5117; Minute, ACIGS (c) (Henderson) to CIGS, 16 June 1940, WO 193/732.

In addition, equipment was readied expressly for chemical operations against an invasion force.[74]

Why did Britain choose escalation when it was so behind in capabilities? In this instance, the absolute priority of political survival as stressed in realist thought seems to have overwhelmed all other considerations. British territory was at stake, including the possibility of imminent political subjugation. As early as 1919, the Holland Committee had noted that countries could be expected to use all their means when facing defeat. In 1940 Dill argued, "At a time when our National existence is at stake, when we are threatened by an implacable enemy who himself recognizes no rules save those of expediency, we should not hesitate to adopt whatever means appear to offer the best chance of success."[75] The deputy chief of the Air Staff, Air Vice-Marshal W. S. Douglas, seconded the view, noting that "it is better to break our word than to lose the British Empire."[76]

Would Britain have actually initiated chemical warfare? This is a difficult question. On the basis of existing evidence, Britain appeared willing to unleash its poisonous gases in defense of the realm. Yet Germany would have only invaded if it had air superiority. This would have meant that had Britain initiated, its civilians and troops would have been highly vulnerable to retaliatory gas attacks. As the decision for first use neared, other factors inhibiting escalation would have come more into play, as we will see occurred in Germany, the Soviet Union, and even Britain itself.

Britain considered using chemical weapons again in 1944. On 13 June 1944, six days after the Normandy invasion, Germany's first "V-rockets" landed in England. Over the next two weeks some two thousand were launched. The Home Secretary, Herbert Morrison, warned of a possible serious deterioration in morale. Some 50 percent of the British air effort was diverted to destroying targets tied to the rocket attacks.[77]

On 4 July, the military weighed the use of gas. Within twenty-four

[74] For example, wheeled containers that could spray chemical agents. These "chemical lorries" would be pulled behind vehicles and used to contaminate areas where the enemy had landed to inhibit his movement inland. Major I. J. Toler, "War Gases in the Second World War," *British Army Review* 95 (August 1990): 70.

[75] Memorandum, CIGS (Dill), "The Use of Gas in Home Defence," 15 June 1940, WO 193/732.

[76] Minute, Deputy Chief of the Air Staff to the Chief of the Air Staff, 16 June 1940, AIR 2/5117.

[77] Harris and Paxman, *Higher Form of Killing*, p. 125. Minute, Colonel L. C. Hollis, secretary to the COS, to Churchill, 5 July 1944, PREM 3/89.

hours the Chiefs of Staff rejected the idea. Based on a study by the their Joint Planning Staff, the Chiefs feared such use would have only a harassing effect on the actual rocket launches, but could cause the outbreak of chemical warfare throughout Europe, which would impede the forward advance of Allied forces. But once again Churchill had other ideas. On 6 July, he called for a "cold-blooded calculation . . . by sensible people and not by that particular set of psalm-singing uniformed defeatists."[78] Ethical and political considerations were to be set aside and military factors highlighted. Churchill wanted to know—as soon as possible—if gas would be useful for shortening the war or avoiding the kind of stalemate that characterized World War I. By 25 July, he had still not received an answer; he put his foot down and demanded a reply within three days.[79]

On 27 July, the Joint Planning Staff gave the Chiefs of Staff a fourteen-page report laying out the costs and benefits of employing toxic munitions. If gas was to be used, they recommended a massive blow with a combination of phosgene and high explosive at 1,000 tactical targets or twenty German cities, or the use of mustard gas against 1500 tactical targets or sixty cities. The aim of the city attacks would be to contribute to the collapse of civilian morale. The downside of attacking German cities was that the Third Reich would retaliate against Britain, which might unsettle English morale. Furthermore, it would involve substituting an untried form of attack for the perceived success of the high-explosive and incendiary bombing already underway. On the battlefield, the advantage of using gas was that it could cause a large-scale breakthrough, but since Allied operations after Normandy were already moving forward fluidly, this was not a high-priority mission. Chemical weapons were seen as useful in achieving a breakthrough, but generally worked in favor of the defense. The expected drawbacks of using gas in the land war included the hampering of operations (by causing massive civilian casualties) and antagonizing the French population. There was also concern over retaliation

---

[78] Minute, Hollis to Churchill, 5 July 1944, PREM 3/89. War Cabinet. Joint Planning Staff. "Chemical Warfare in Connection with CROSSBOW," 5 July 1944, PREM 3/89. Churchill is known to have pushed off-beat ideas at various times in a somewhat whimsical fashion. (See, for example, Gilbert, *Winston S. Churchill*, 3:470 (see Chap. 3, n. 157), for Lord Fisher's comment that Churchill is "very brilliant, but too changeable; he has a different scheme every day." Yet as discussed below, Churchill had a long-term, serious interest in chemical warfare that cannot be dismissed as peripheral. Minute, Churchill to General Ismay (for COS Committee), 6 July 1944, PREM 3/89.

[79] Minute, Churchill to Ismay (for COS) 25 July 1944, PREM 3/89.

against Allied prisoners. Overall, the Joint Planning Staff recommended against use.[80]

The Chiefs of Staff agreed and passed the report on to Churchill, emphasizing a few key points. The Chiefs explicitly recognized that Britain was superior in chemical warfare, and all other things being equal, that it was in Britain's interest to use gas. But they concluded that all other things were not equal. Because of the difference between Britain's and Germany's political systems they believed that Nazi authorities would find it easier to "hold down the cowed German population" under conditions of chemical warfare.[81] Churchill responded to this assessment on 29 July: "I am not at all convinced by this negative report. But clearly I cannot make head against the parsons and the warriors at the same time. This matter should be kept under review and brought up again when things get worse."[82]

This argument for restraint seems to conform to the principle of relative advantage that the realist perspective would predict. The Chiefs of Staff anticipated a disadvantage and advised restraint. The problem with this conclusion is that an asymmetry between two sides in a given situation can always be found (both by decision makers and historians). In this case it was the relative strength of popular support for the war. The issue then becomes one of why certain asymmetries are highlighted and whether they correspond to the actual circumstances. Which advantages and disadvantages are valued in a realist calculation? Do they correspond to the actual situation? Who decides, and what assumptions do they make?

In this instance, the Chiefs' judgment was key. They, and their Joint Planning Staff, made some important points. But their effort to block escalation is striking (particularly when contrasted with the untested assumptions offered in support of strategic bombing which they favored). Churchill certainly found their argument against chemical warfare a bit stretched. Their main emphasis on British disadvantage seems odd in two respects. First, their assessment seems more of a political analysis rather than a military one, although they were, after all, primarily a military body. Second, the appraisal was faulty. Relative to Germany, British morale was high. The Allies were on the Continent

---

[80] Joint Planning Staff, "Military Considerations Affecting the Initiation of Chemical and Other Special Forms of Warfare," 27 July 1944, PREM 3/89.

[81] The Chiefs explicitly recognized that Britain was superior in chemical warfare. Memo, Ismay (for the OCS) to Churchill, 28 July 1944, PREM 3/89.

[82] Minute, Churchill to Ismay (for the COS), 29 July 1944, PREM 3/89.

and headed toward Germany.[83] It was the Nazis that faced difficult times ahead. The military's claim regarding the relative strength of morale in England and Germany was also odd because when lobbying for strategic bombing it had been arguing *exactly the opposite* since 1940.[84] The RAF's strategic bomber offensive was promoted on the assumption that German morale was more fragile than that of the English.

They also made the unfounded, and rather odd, assumption that if Britain showed restraint in this area, Germany would too. This premise contradicts the general view that Hitler would do anything in his power to stave off defeat and gain victory, as evinced by the V-rocket attacks. The Chiefs of Staff were more than willing to believe that Hitler would inevitably escalate strategic bombing, but not that he would escalate in chemical warfare. Why? Indeed, the 1944 British decision not to use chemical weapons is interesting not because a relative advantage calculation was made, but because "advantage" was so peculiarly interpreted given the relative situations of Britain and Germany. To explain such dynamics we must look to the influence of military culture.

Tradition and Restraint

The military's organizational culture helped to shape British chemical warfare policy, both in peacetime and in World War II. The legacy of chemical warfare in World War I was not a favorable one for conventional military officers. Little attention was given to chemical warfare in the interwar British Army, which was an institution governed by rigid social mores and a slavish obedience to tradition. Gas use was more compatible with RAF thinking, yet research and development was in the hands of the Army and was therefore relatively ignored in the Air Ministry. In the Second World War, the military's prejudice against chemical warfare played a key role in turning aside Churchill's desire to use it.

Even in World War I, the British military was skeptical of gas. It was

---

[83] Hinsley, *British Intelligence*, vol 3, part 2, pp. 893–966 (see Chap. 3, n. 136). The official in charge of monitoring morale, Brendan Bracken, minister of information, at no time felt the need in June–July 1944 to warn the Cabinet about morale problems. See Ian McLaine, *Ministry of Morale: Home Front Morale and the Ministry of Information in WWII* (London: George Allen & Unwin, 1979), pp. 274–75 and jacket copy. For anecdotal reports on morale, see Mollie Painter-Downes, *London War Notes, 1939–1945*, ed. William Shawn (New York: Farrar, Straus & Giroux, 1971), pp. 325–40.

[84] Memorandum, Senior Air Staff Officer to CINC Bomber Command, 24 September 1940, AIR 14/194. Terraine, *Right of Line* 263–66. (see Chap. 3, n. 5).

not that they saw it is as particularly unethical. There was little difference to the combat soldier between gas, a sniper's bullet, and a "belly
ripping hunk of shell." If anything the war as a whole was considered
an outrage. The Army was slow to introduce mustard gas because its
developers could not convince the soldiers that it would be of any use.
Germany's successful use of the weapon was required for that. Briga-
dier General Wigram, staff officer Personnel at GHQ, noted in 1918,
"Armies do not like gas cloud work and there has been objection and
obstruction to it all along."[85] Chemists and soldiers had to work together and, as in Germany, they did not get along well.[86]

The way chemical operations were organized in the Great War only
provoked resentment among regular soldiers. Britain's offensive chemical warfare was waged by an elite department of the Army called Special Companies (later Special Brigades). All its members received extra
pay, and were at least corporals; and most were new recruits or had
science backgrounds. Unlike other soldiers they were allowed to carry
revolvers instead of rifles and were often excused from the discipline
of the parade ground. This last alone was probably enough to draw
the contempt of the line soldiers.[87]

Given this background, it is interesting to find that in the few years
immediately following the war there is some evidence to indicate that
the Army resisted agreements prohibiting the use of chemical weapons.[88] The Army apparently believed that the restraints being discussed would not hold up in a future war, but, in democratic Britain,
would hinder the development of defenses against such use. Gas had
established itself in World War I as a very dangerous weapon, and
British soldiers were wary of being caught unprepared by less scrupu-
lous states that would build and use chemical weapons despite international agreements.[89]

What is clear is that the Army's dislike of chemical weapons contin-

[85] As quoted in Haber, *Poisonous Cloud*, p. 269. Richter, *Chemical Soldiers*, pp. 216–17.
SIPRI, *Chemical and Biological Warfare* 1:49.

[86] Haber, *Poisonous Cloud*, p. 273.

[87] The story of the Special Companies is told in Richter, *Chemical Soldiers*.

[88] See CID, "Chemical Warfare Policy," November 1924, p. 3, WO 188/144; CID, "Gas
Warfare," memorandum by the Secretary of State for War, 3 May 1930, CAB 24/105; CID,
"Chemical Warfare Policy," memorandum by the Secretary of State for War, 29 July 1926,
CAB 4/15; "A Summary of Important Notes and Papers in Connection with the Policy
of Gas Warfare in Order of Dates from 1899," 1927, WO 188/212.

[89] CID, "Chemical Warfare Policy," memorandum by the Secretary of State of War, 29
July 1926, CAB 4/15. Another reason for military interest in chemical warfare in the early
1920s may related to the desire to use gas in policing colonial areas (see Spiers, *Chemical
Weaponry*, pp. 82–84).

ued into the interwar period. The bias against gas has been noted by several observers. The military neglected chemical warfare despite their own requests for freedom of action and Cabinet approval to work on gas weapons and training.[90] This lack of interest in gas is particularly apparent in the late 1930s when the rise of the Nazi threat removed the political constraints on development, yet efforts lagged.

The culture of the Army in the interwar years did not favor the development of chemical weapons. Two aspects of Army culture were particularly hostile to chemical warfare. First, the Army's main unifying theme was tradition. One analyst has noted that the Army was not an army at all but a collection of regiments that more closely resembled sports and social clubs than fighting units. Many saw the regimental system as a refuge from social and technological change. Within this system, the technical or mechanical officer was looked down on, and gas is a technical weapon. The Director of Artillery was left in charge of chemical warfare, yet his artillerymen seemed more concerned with their horses than their technical equipment.[91]

The second trait hostile to chemical warfare involved strategic posture. To be more specific, the Army lacked a central task or enemy to confront. Instead, it had many missions ranging from colonial defense, to internal policing, to sending out expeditionary forces to provide security wherever it was needed. This last category included sending an army to Europe, a mission ranked last in priority for most of the interwar period. There were no agreed-upon war scenarios. "Weapons development proceeded in a doctrinal vacuum."[92] This mattered because the provision of equipment, especially for chemical warfare, was directly tied to the conditions of the war to be fought. The Army was also lower on the priority list for funding than the other services. The needs of the Navy that protected Britain's shores and commerce could not be denied. Likewise, the widespread fear of strategic bombing en-

[90] Richter, *Chemical Soldiers*, pp. 139, 220–21; Haber, *Poisonous Cloud*, p. 273; Haldane, *Callinicus*, pp. 34 and 37. Haldane notes the end of antigas instruction in Britain in 1922 (p. 34), and Staff Academy lectures mention the dearth of offensive chemical warfare effort. See "Lecture on Chemical Warfare: Part II—Tactics," 27 February 1926, WO 188/48; "Gas Tactics (Offensive)," Lecture Delivered to Staff College in Autumn 1923, WO 188/48.

[91] Bond, *British Military Policy*, chap. 2, pp. 35–71, 132; Shelford Bidwell and Dominick Graham, *Firepower: British Army Weapons and Theories of War 1904–1945* (London: George Allen & Unwin, 1982), chap. 9; Postan, Hay, and Scott, *Design and Development*, pp. 240, 253.

[92] To the extent chemical weapons might be useful in policing, political constraints were an inhibiting factor. Spiers, *Chemical Warfare*, pp. 47–48. Bidwell and Graham, *Firepower*, pp. 180, 185–89.

sured funding for the Air Force. This left the Army a distant third in terms of budget priority. This affected Britain's chemical warfare policy because the War Office—the administrative home of the Army—was the center of chemical warfare development. The result was that the General Staff listlessly pursued chemical warfare.[93]

The slighting of the role of chemical weapons was not simply a product of clear-cut strategic reasoning. Chemical weapons had important advocates outside the military. Some experts felt that gas should be promoted as both an efficient and humane means of war. Two of the leaders of this camp were the prominent strategists J. F. C. Fuller and B. H. Liddell Hart.[94] Liddell Hart, who like Hitler was gassed in World War I, advocated the future use of chemical weapons because they produced fewer deaths per casualty than conventional munitions. With the flair of an advertising executive, Liddell Hart proclaimed that "gas promises to do for warfare what chloroform has done for surgery." He further believed that nations would use gas because it was in their self interest: fewer deaths and less destruction would result. Limiting damage was important because "to destroy is to sow the seeds of revenge and future insecurity," and "the enemy of today is the customer of tomorrow."[95] Fuller, likewise, saw chemical warfare as advantageous in that it was nonlethal, did not destroy property, was cheap and secret, and helped industry in peacetime.[96] Gas could be used to incapacitate enemy forces, which could then be rounded up. In official circles, however, this thinking made little headway.

In short, the Army ignored chemical warfare. What is ironic is that the Air Force did too. After all, the Air Force's mission was much more compatible with the use of gas. Indeed, the RAF under Trenchard developed the single-minded goal of defeating the enemy through demoralization by strategic bombing. Gas was recognized first and fore-

---

[93] Postan, Hay and Scott, *Design and Development*, p. 238. CID, "Chemical Warfare Policy," November 1924, p. 15, WO 188/144. Robin Higham, *Armed Forces in Peacetime: Britain, 1918–1940, A Case Study* (London: G. T. Foulis, 1962), p. 80; Bond, *British Military Policy*, p. 33. Harris, "British Preparations for Offensive CW," pp. 57–58. The Commandant of the Staff College in 1940 wrote how he had "vainly" attempted to get the Army interested in blister gas spray in 1930 with no luck. He noted that preparations to spray gas were even less developed ten years later. See letter, Jack Collins to John Dill (CIGS), 27 June 1940, WO 193/732.

[94] Much of their thinking was based on avoiding the destructive battles of attrition of World War I and achieving victory through rapid advances of armor, the disruption of supply lines and command centers, and the demoralization of the enemy.

[95] B. H. Liddell Hart, *The Remaking of Modern Armies* (Boston: Little, Brown, 1928), pp. 25, 82, 85.

[96] Robin Higham, *The Military Intellectuals in Britain: 1918–1939* (New Brunswick: Rutgers University Press, 1966), p. 69.

most as a weapon suited for demoralization. The Air Ministry acknowledged in 1937 that gas could add to the destructive and harassing effect of high explosives and incendiaries. Gas sprayers were developed by 1936, but, for the sake of secrecy, were not to be used for training until they went into production. It was estimated that from 15,000 feet, thirty-seven gallons of mustard gas could contaminate 3,000 square yards.[97] Gas bombs could also be used against a variety of targets, including the civilian population, troops in landing area, barracks, docks, and so on. Most of the poison agents that were scheduled for production in the late 1930s were to go to the Air Force.[98]

Despite the potential for chemical warfare in RAF doctrine, it was never given the attention or favor that conventional munitions received, either in peacetime or in war. When the possibility of Britain using gas first came up in the spring of 1940, a check was done on the Air Staff's files concerning the offensive use of gas. Little was found: "Few people have given the subject much attention."[99] The Air Staff made a bid for increased chemical capabilities in the late interwar budget battles. But when it appeared that the request might cut into its own funding, the Air Force was willing to give up the chemical capabilities, which might never be employed, in favor of other "more important directions."[100]

Why the RAF ignored chemical weapons in the interwar period is puzzling, but seems to be the result of several factors. First, during the early development of gas the RAF appears to have had little say on the subject—only General Staff and Admiralty opinions appear in the record. By the later 1930s when the Air Force became an important participant, the Air Staff shifted its official orientation toward physical destruction (as the best way to break morale) through strategic bombing. As was later noted, gas was considered less effective than conventional munitions for physical destruction. This tendency, in addition

[97] Harris, "British Preparations," p. 61. Also see CID, "The Manufacture of Toxic Gas for Use in War," memorandum by the War Office and Air Staff, 26 July 1938, CAB 4/28. "Minutes of the Second Meeting of the Bombing Committee's Sub-Committee on Gas Questions," 26 October 1936, WO 188/645. The production goal for mustard gas in 1941 was 900 tons a week. COS Committee Meeting (41) 646, 23 October 1941, WO 193/711.
[98] "Minutes of the Second Meeting of the Bombing Committee's Sub-Committee on Gas Questions," 26 October 1936, WO 188/645. Also see CID, "The Manufacture of Toxic Gas for Use in War," memorandum by the War Office and Air Staff, 26 July 1938, CAB 4/28.
[99] Minute, Plans Staff member to Deputy Director of Plans, 19 April 1940, AIR 2/5117.
[100] Also see CID, "The Manufacture of Toxic Gas for Use in War," memorandum by the War Office and Air Staff, 26 July 1938, CAB 4/28. Harris, "British Preparations for Offensive CW," p. 61.

to a declared reluctance to spend resources on a weapon that might not be used, lowered the priority of chemical weapons development. Even when the threat that the Germans might use gas was high during the war, chemical munitions received little attention relative to high explosives.[101]

As in the Army, airmen also were not schooled to think in terms of its use when preparing for the upcoming war. The individuals who did advocate chemical warfare were censored by higher authorities. In 1942, Air Chief Marshal Hugh Dowding, CINC of Fighter Command, wrote in a draft of an article that gas should be used against Germany. But this view was not approved by the Chiefs of Staff, and he had to suppress it.[102]

During the war, chemical use was often seen as a threat to the RAF's preferred style of strategic bombing. In June 1940 the chief of the Air Staff pointed out that gas operations would cut into bombing operations.[103] In April 1940 when talk of chemical use was circulating, the CINC of Bomber Command complained about lack of direction in chemical warfare. Neither the RAF manual nor any of the official war plans mentioned gas use. The only plan where chemical warfare seemed compatible was one involving the RAF's support of land forces (Plan W.A. 4b), a role the RAF shunned.[104] In November 1940, the chief of the Air Staff successfully argued against the full Army and Air requirements for chemical warfare because the effect "may be to impair not only our general war effort, but also to restrict the development of our aircraft output."[105] In 1944 when Britain once again considered the first use of gas, the Joint Planning Staff maintained that "by adopting gas bombing we should be substituting an untried form of attack for the present incendiary and high explosive bombing which is well tried and is known to be achieving a very grave effect upon German war production."[106] Of course, the strategic bombing campaign was

[101] "Notes on Agenda for RAF CW Committee Meeting, 14 September 1940," AIR 2/5200. Spraying gas, however, was seen as effective. Harris, "British Preparations." "Chemical Warfare Position: Following the German Occupation of NorthWest Europe and Italy's Entry into the War," 5 September 1940, WO 188/446.

[102] This anecdote was found in a letter from Dowding to Liddell Hart. See B. H. Reid, "Gas Warfare: The Perils of Prediction," in David Carlton and Carlo Schaerf, eds., *Reassessing Arms Control* (London: Macmillan, 1984), p. 153.

[103] COS Meeting, "Chemical Warfare Policy," 6 May 1940, WO 193/713.

[104] Minute, CINC Bomber Command to the Air Staff, 3 April 1940, AIR 2/5117.

[105] Minute, Chief of the Air Staff to the COS, "Chemical Warfare," 14 November 1941, WO 193/711.

[106] Joint Planning Staff, "Military Considerations Affecting the Initiation of Chemical and Other Forms of Warfare," 27 July 1944, PREM 3/89.

not working as planned, but the RAF's culture blinded it to this conclusion.[107]

The military's foot-dragging on chemical warfare is especially stark in light of Churchill's own efforts to promote it. From the summer of 1940 on, the prime minister began to pay close attention to chemical warfare. He felt that not enough was being done. On 28 September 1940, he erupted in anger, wanting to know why supplies had not matched plans. Had not the Cabinet ordered increased capacity in October 1939? Where were the goods? An inquiry was ordered, the results of which blamed no individual. Gas preparations had been pushed to the end of the queue in the rush to rearm. Thereafter Churchill had weekly reports on gas production delivered to him personally, and he pressed hard to increase production. He also demanded that "the possibility of our having to retaliate on the German civil population must be studied and on the largest scale possible."[108] By the end of 1941 Churchill's advocacy had changed the situation. Britain could take offensive action on five-hour's notice. Four Blenheim and three Wellington Squadrons were trained in the use of aerial spraying. Fifteen percent of the bomber force could be used in chemical warfare.[109] By the spring of 1942 Britain had almost 20,000 tons of gas.[110]

In the two British wartime decisions on use, organizational neglect of chemical warfare was apparently a key factor only in 1944, when the military's opposition played a key role in the decision for restraint. Churchill asked for a "cold blooded calculation" based on military factors on whether or not to use chemical warfare and was told that the battle was going well with the plans already accepted and no change was necessary. This analysis may have made sense in the context of tactical use on the battlefields of France, but it did not make sense in the context of strategic bombing. The attempt to break German morale through conventional bombing was not working, despite Bomber Command's assertions to the contrary.[111] In rejecting gas use, the Chiefs of Staff emphasized the perceived vulnerability of British morale

[107] See Wilensky, *Organizational Intelligence* (see Chap. 3, n. 151).

[108] Minute, Churchill to Ismay (for COS), 28 September 1940, PREM 3/88/3. For a chronology, see memorandum by the Prime Minister and Minister of Defence (Churchill), "Chemical Warfare," 25 September 1941, WO 193/711.

[109] Extract from COS Meeting Minutes, 28 December 1941, WO 193/711.

[110] Despite preparations, according to 1942 COS statements, British policy was not to initiate chemical warfare with one important exception—an invasion of the homeland. See Harris and Paxman, *Higher Form of Killing*, pp. 114–15.

[111] See Hinsley, *British Intelligence*, vol. 3, part 1, pp. 298–307 (see Chap. 3, n. 136). Wilensky, *Organizational Intelligence*, pp. 24–28.

and seemed to assume that Germany would continue to show restraint. It is telling that the RAF used the opposite argument—that British morale was stronger and that Germany would inevitably escalate—to advocate escalation in strategic bombing, a means of warfare suited to its culture.

Why Churchill agreed not to use gas is unclear. Assessing morale was a political judgment, not a military one, and one would think that Churchill was at least equally capable of making the call.[112] More important, there was little evidence to support the military's conclusion that British spirits were weak, especially in light of Allied successes and Hitler's own problems with domestic support. But in the end Churchill was not willing to buck the experts. The military had never accepted chemical warfare—despite the recognized military utility of strategic gas bombing—and it was not inclined to do so in the midst of conflict.

The influence of organizational culture is also evinced by what did not happen—there was no inadvertent escalation in British chemical warfare. There were a few incidents involving chemical weapons, yet unlike those in submarine warfare and strategic bombing, they never resulted in escalation. Traditional escalation perspectives would all predict a spiral of use for restricted weapons—even if by accident. Important sources of friction—intense conflict, complex operations, and great uncertainty—characterized many of the accidental uses of gas, but escalation did not. All of the military organizations involved also had plans, troops, and weapons for chemical warfare, but contrary to traditional organization theory, their routines did not also generate escalation. According to the security-dilemma argument both sides should have felt insecure because of the advantages to using gas in a surprise attack; they should have been poised to strike back to minimize disadvantage and been leery of any type of trust in enemy restraint. Indeed, it was widely acknowledged that gas was most effectively used in a surprise attack.[113] For example, General Herman

---

[112] Perhaps it was because the initial stimulus to use gas came from concern about a drop in morale from the V-rocket attacks. Thus the last thing Churchill wanted was to risk another blow at morale.

[113] Still, gas could be used for both offense and defense. Generally, it was seen as benefiting those interested in inhibiting fast-moving operations—*after* it had been introduced to the battlefield. Initial use could facilitate an offensive by opening wide gaps in enemy lines—as occurred with Germany's first use in World War I. British planners, for example, argued that gas might be used to break through enemy lines if the offensive toward Germany were stalled in Italy or France. See Joint Planning Staff memorandum, "Military Considerations Affecting the Initiation of Chemical and Other Special Forms of Warfare," 27 July 1944, PREM 3/89.

Ochsner, the head of German chemical operations in World War II, argued that the attacker has the advantage because of ability to complete preparations, achieve surprise, and choose time, place, and scale of attack. The defender would be hard-pressed to keep defenses ready and would have to fight under the most unfavorable conditions.[114] Inadvertent escalation would seem likely in these circumstances; however, the history of incidents involving British chemical warfare in World War II challenges this notion. An important part of the explanation for this result was the military's efforts (driven by cultural disposition) to avoid an inadvertent spiral in chemical warfare. Events that could have led to escalation were ignored or purposefully suppressed.

The first was in late 1940 when the War Office received reports from the Middle East that Italy was preparing to use gas in Ethiopia. The CINC of Middle East Forces suggested that a threat of retaliation in kind be made to deter it. The War Office squashed the suggestion, fearing that giving attention to cases of possible use without actually retaliating (there was doubt Britain could or would), might indicate to Germany that Britain feared a gas war, thus providing incentives for Nazi use. It was decided that should the Italians employ gas, the whole matter would be swept under the rug: "Publicity should not (repeat not) be given to the fact."[115]

In 1942 reports were received from the Far East that left little doubt that Japan was using gas in China. The Army thought that it was best to ignore this use since any British retaliation might lead to unrestricted Japanese chemical attacks in India, an area that was considered vulnerable to gas attacks.[116] This was a strategic calculation, but one that was defined by a culture hostile to the use of poison gas. For even when strategic circumstances changed, when India was not at risk in 1944, the Chiefs of Staff still refused to accept the evidence that the Japanese had used gas.[117] They apparently had significant interest in not opening the Pandora's box of chemical warfare.

In the winter of 1942 the Soviets became worried that the Germans were readying to unleash a gas war. Stalin asked Churchill for help, and Churchill pledged that if the Germans used gas against the Russians, the Allies would use gas against the Germans. This idea threw

[114] Lieutenant General Herman Ochsner, *History of German Chemical Warfare in World War II*, part 1, *The Military Aspect* P-004a (Historical Office of the Chief of the Chemical Corps, 1949), p. 4, NA.

[115] Telegram, War Office to the CINC Middle East, 16 December 1940, WO 193/721; "Chemical Warfare: Use of Gas by Italians and Policy for Retaliation," WO 193/725.

[116] "Japanese Gas Warfare in China," 14 July 1942, WO 193/723.

[117] Ismay (for COS) to PM, 28 June 1944, PREM 3/89.

the British military into frenzy. The Chiefs of Staff felt the promise might lead to immediate chemical warfare. Many were especially upset because the United Kingdom had no means to verify Soviet claims that the Germans had actually used gas.[118]

A final incident occurred during the German bombing of Bari Harbor in Italy in December 1943. One of the Luftwaffe bombs hit a U.S. supply ship the S.S. *John Harvey*, which was carrying two thousand hundred-pound mustard bombs to be used in the event of chemical warfare. The gas was released into the harbor killing many sailors. Clouds of the toxic agent drifted over the town. Some one thousand civilians, not to mention soldiers, were killed in Bari, many from the contaminated water and air. In contrast to Britain's reaction to the accidental bombing of London, the Allies did not propagandize the event or use it as an excuse for retaliation, but instead covered it up. Medical reports of wounds were only allowed to describe chemical weapon injuries in general terms, and strict censorship was instituted at all military bases. When it was clear that the accident could not be kept secret, the Combined Chiefs of Staff prepared a statement to the effect that "Allied policy is not (repeat not) to use gas unless or until the enemy does so first but that we are fully prepared to retaliate and do not deny the accident, which was a calculated risk."[119] In the realm of inadvertence, culture subtly influenced what did not happen, as well as what did. To permit strategic bombing, Britain had declared Germany's accidental bombing of London intentional, yet to prevent chemical warfare, incidents involving the use of gas were hushed up and restraint was maintained.

Conclusion: Britain Restrained

Although none of the theories examined comprehensively accounts for British chemical policy, a few conclusions on relative influence are possible. The power of institutionalism should have been evident in British chemical warfare policy. British public opinion and British interwar diplomacy had been clearly and consistently against chemical weapons. We cannot prove that these norms did not turn the military away from the poison cloud any more than it would have on its own. Nonetheless, in both peacetime and wartime decisions, the effects of

[118] Defence Committee, 17 April 1942, WO 193/711.

[119] Both the Allies and Germany moved stocks of gas munitions to keep large supplies ready in case of escalation. This was kept secret to avoid giving the enemy a pretext for use. Harris and Paxman, *Higher Form of Killing*, pp. 119–23.

antigas institutions were overtaken by other considerations. In the first case, resistance to rearmament shifted with the international environment. In the second, escalation was chosen, contingent on a German invasion, despite the implicit violation of the Geneva Protocol.

Realism offers a good account of important aspects of interwar chemical policy. Most important, we see that the British public sentiment that constrained British preparations changed with the nature of the external challenge—namely, the rise of the Nazi threat. What realism cannot explain is why offensive capabilities were ignored when such preparations would be both allowed by the Protocol and required by deterrent plans. In war, the shadow decision for use in 1940 is compatible with realism's survival dictum. Whether this decision would have been implemented is an open question. The 1944 decision not to use gas was the result of a calculation of relative advantage that was based on odd assumptions. It seems that the British military favored restraint in chemical warfare more for reasons of internal inclination than of external circumstance.

To be more specific, I contend that organizational culture had much to do with Britain's restraint in World War II, both in 1944 and throughout the war. The military neglected gas in peacetime because it was not compatible with the Army's culture, particularly at a time when resources were thin. The RAF, which played a minor role in the development of chemical weapons, was not generous to its chemical capabilities either. It did not want to take away resources from its bombers and their high-explosive bombs. By 1944 chemical weapons were seen as almost a hostile competitor for the resources needed to wage war as Britain's armed services had expected war to be waged. That is why neither intentional decision nor unexpected incidents were allowed to spiral into the undesired chemical escalation long expected but never realized.

A TYPICALLY GERMAN WEAPON

Hitler is widely believed to have been a psychotic leader so driven by a lust for territorial expansion that he was beyond being deterred by more powerful opponents. After all, how could he have hoped to take on and defeat both Great Britain and the USSR at the same time? Yet when we turn to the topic of chemical warfare, it is often maintained that Germany showed restraint because it was (rationally) deterred by Allied capabilities.[120] This is supposedly true from the first period of the war when Germany had superior chemical might through the end of the conflict when the Third Reich faced political extinction.

Yet from the standpoint of relative advantage, what may have been irrational was Germany's restraint. During the 1930s, the German chemical industry was the leader of its field.[121] Moreover, the country had the appropriate raw materials for making poison agents. At the beginning of the war, Germany's chemical warfare stocks exceeded those of its adversaries several times over.[122] The Third Reich also discovered two new powerful nerve agents, Tabun and Sarin, against which Allied protective masks and clothing did not work. Germany did have some shortcomings in defensive preparations, but none that could not have been overcome with a concerted effort. During the war, there appear to have been several situations where the use of chemical weapons would have significantly benefited Germany. Some analysts have even contended that if Germany had developed and used its advanced nerve gases, the course and perhaps outcome of the war would have been different.[123] Why did the Third Reich show restraint?

Institutionalism would not have predicted restraint, given the middling strength of the no-first-use convention. Germany's outlaw character casts further doubt on this possibility. Realism would have also predicted that Germany would exploit its superiority in chemical warfare. But instead, it pursued gas with a listlessness that left it ill-prepared to seize the initiative. Particularly as the Third Reich faced political extinction, its failure to use its chemical warfare capabilities is puzzling. The organizational-culture approach, however, directs our attention to the conflict between chemical warfare and the dominant thinking that emerged within the Wehrmacht on how to gain military victory. From this perspective, restraint is less surprising. First, however, I must clarify Hitler's role as the "all-powerful" dictator.

[120] For example, see Overy, "Air Power," 93–94 (see Chap. 3, n. 6); Stephen L. McFarland, "Preparing for What Never Came," *Defense Analysis* 2, no. 2 (1986): 117; John Ellis van Courtland Moon, "Chemical Weapons and Deterrence: The World War II Experience," *International Security* (spring 1984): 25–28. Moon's wise article offers more than a simple deterrence account.

[121] Hence the title to this section. This description is from Rolf-Dieter Mueller, "World Power Status through the Use of Poison Gas? German Preparations for Chemical Warfare, 1919–1945," in Diest, *German Military*, p. 172 (see Chap. 3, n. 55).

[122] Mueller, "German Preparations for Chemical Warfare," p. 172. Germany had some 10,000 tons, whereas Britain had under 1000 tons. See Chart 5.1, in SIPRI, *Chemical and Biological Warfare*, 1: 304.

[123] Harris and Paxman, *Higher Form of Killing*, p. 64.

German restraint is often explained by Hitler's personal aversion to chemical warfare from his experience in World War I.[124] In *Mein Kampf*, Hitler claims to have been overcome by mustard gas on 13 October 1918 near Ypres. "I stumbled back with burning eyes taking with me my last report of the war. A few hours later, my eyes had turned into burning coals, it had grown dark around me."[125] It appears that Hitler associated this attack with Germany's defeat. His eyesight had slowly recovered that fall until he heard of the "Fatherland's" surrender. Then everything went black again, and the future Führer threw himself on his bunk, buried his head in his pillow, and cried for the first time since his mother's death. Apparently, Hitler connected some very unhappy times in his life with chemical warfare. Perhaps this explains why the chemical warfare development area at Raubkammer was the only military testing grounds he never visited in the interwar period.[126]

But to conclude that Hitler's aversion to gas explains German restraint is to push the point too far even given his influence on military decision making. After all, he explicitly considered the use of chemical weapons and turned them down, not because of personal distaste, but because Germany was unprepared.[127] Brown contends that Hitler actually ordered chemical use (although there is no clear evidence he did) at the end of the war because of his psychological makeup: "To an unbalanced mind, the very horror of poison gas became a compelling reason to order its use."[128] But, of course, Germany did not employ chemicals so that even if Brown has described Hitler's personal tendencies and choices accurately, he has still not accounted for national behavior. Furthermore, if Hitler's personal aversions were central, why did his fear of drowning not stop him from allowing his U-boats to torpedo unarmed merchant ships in the same way his dislike of gas prevented chemical use? This was a man who was so concerned about drowning that he would awake early when staying in his Berlin bunker out of concern that a bomb would hit at the exact angle that would allow the groundwater around the structure to rush in and suffocate

---

[124] For example, see Ochsner, *History of German Chemical Warfare*, 13; Brown, *Chemical Warfare*, pp. 235–37; Richter, *Chemical Soldiers*, p. 230. As of August 1940, the German military's use of gas had to have the direct approval of Hitler. Mueller, "German Preparations for Chemical Warfare," p. 191.

[125] Adolph Hitler, *Mein Kampf* (Boston: Houghton Mifflin, 1943), p. 202.

[126] Ibid., p. 204. Spiers, *Chemical Warfare*, p. 78.

[127] Reports received by U.S. intelligence in 1939 suggested that Hitler was advocating the use of gas but was firmly opposed by the military. See Brown, *Chemical Warfare*, p. 238 n. 120.

[128] Brown, *Chemical Warfare*, p. 237 and note 121. It should be noted that Brown uses other factors and levels of analysis in his rich study of chemical warfare in World War II.

him.[129] There would seem to be more to the story of German restraint than Hitler's personality.

My explanation is that organizational preferences shaped allocation priorities in peacetime, allocation priorities shaped readiness, and readiness determined national policy options in war. More specifically, in the situations where German leaders considered the use of chemical weapons, they often ruled against doing so because of perceived inadequate readiness. Germany was unprepared to use gas largely due to a military culture that favored mobile operations with which gas was seen as incompatible. Culture shaped preparations, intelligence, and operations, all of which emphasized the costs and overlooked the capabilities of chemical weapons. Restraint was the result.

Nazis and the Norms of Chemical Warfare

The international norms and rules on chemical warfare do not appear to have been important to the German decision for restraint. Several international accords should have inhibited German chemical warfare efforts, yet there is no evidence that these understandings had any significant impact on preparations, expectations, or decisions.

Even before the Geneva Protocol, the Versailles treaty, which formally ended the First World War, strictly forbade the use, manufacture, and import of poisonous materials by Germany. Nonetheless, by 1923, Germany was already negotiating with the Soviet Union over covert cooperation between the two states in the development of chemical warfare capabilities. Joint German-Soviet efforts were to continue until 1933 when Hitler ended them. This cooperation included a chemical research and development program, a joint-stock company to manufacture poison gases, and field testing and exercises, most of which took place in the USSR. Tests on the use of poison gas were made with airplanes, artillery, and a variety of motorized vehicles. Major-General Werner von Blomberg, the head of the Truppenamt, visited the exercise area at Trotsk on the lower Volga in 1928. His report noted that the gassing of ground troops from airplanes, along with the effort of other chemical warfare troops, played an important and successful part in the maneuvers. The German military remained interested in continuing cooperation with the Red Army on chemical weapons even when the program was being shut down.[130]

---

[129] Peter Hoffman, *Hitler's Personal Security* (London: Macmillan, 1979), p. 261.

[130] See Gustav Hilger and Alfred G. Meyer, *The Incompatible Allies: A Memoir History of German-Soviet Relations, 1918–1941* (New York: Macmillan, 1953), pp. 188–89; Carsten, *Reichswehr and Politics* (see Chap. 3, no. 30); F. L. Carsten, "Reports by Two German

In the 1920s, Germany expected that poison gas would be used in a future war. Military publications anticipated massive chemical battles that would have a significant impact on the outcome of a conflict. In the early postwar period, the disrepair of Germany's military capabilities permitted only defensive war plans. These were based on a buffer zone between the Weser and Oder rivers. In this area, the Reichswehr anticipated using mustard gas as a terrain barrier or as a tool of guerrilla warfare.[131] This plan, however, was confined to the blackboard by Germany's miniscule reserves of chemical weapons and limited production capacity.

Concern over its limited capabilities may have been why Germany ratified the Geneva Protocol in 1929.[132] Ochsner claimed that his country joined the regime with honest intentions and with relief.[133] Did Germany hope that the Geneva Protocol would provide added security? Such a belief would seem to reflect the power of the antigas norm. Yet if institutionalism is correct, Germany's acceptance of the Protocol should have marked a turning point in its own chemical warfare policy. Two areas seem particularly important: expectations and military planning.

The Geneva Protocol had little effect on expectations. Although Germany had accepted the Protocol in 1929, in 1931 military cadets were being taught that despite the slander against it, poison gas would be used "just as firearms were accepted despite the protests of knights."[134] In 1933, the General Military Bureau concluded that chemical weapons would be exploited at least on the scale of World War I.[135] Ochsner argued in 1939 that based on World War I and the 1937 Ethiopian War, chemical weapons would play an even larger role in a future war.[136]

Officers on the Red Army," *Slavonic and East European Review* (December 1962): 217–44; Mueller, "German Preparations for Chemical Warfare," pp. 177, 180–81; and SIPRI, *Chemical and Biological Warfare*, 1:42.

[131] Mueller "German Preparations for Chemical Warfare," p. 175.

[132] Günther W. Gellerman, *Der Krieg, der nicht stattfand: Möglichkeiten, Überlegungen und Entscheidungen der deutschen Obersten Führung zur Verwendung chemischer Kampfstoffe im Zweiten Weltkrieg* (Koblenz: Bernard & Graef, 1986), p. 208.

[133] Ochsner, *History of German Chemical Warfare*, p. 13.

[134] Hauptmann Ochsner, "Chemische Kampfmittel und Nebelstoffe in neuzeitliche Heeren," vor Waffenlehren, 23 November 1931, RH 12–9/v. 21. BA-MA.

[135] Inspektion 4 an Wehramt, "Gasschutzdienst," 7 September 1933, RH 12–9/v. 28, BA-MA. Inspektion 4 was the Artillery Division which oversaw chemical warfare up to 1934.

[136] Oberst Ochsner, "Grundsätzliche Gedanken über den Einsatz von Kampfstoffen im Krieg," für die 1. Abteilung des Generalstabs des Heeres vom 28. Juni 1939. RH 12–9/v. 25, BA-MA.

Expectations that chemical weapons would be used continued into the war.[137]

The seeming legitimacy of a prohibition on chemical weapons should have also affected how the German military prepared for the coming war. Germany and the Soviet Union, however, continued to develop and expand their joint efforts on chemical warfare. The Protocol might have actually provoked the development of gas in Germany, for its provisions could not be enforced unless the signatories had their own retaliatory capabilities. Advocates of chemical warfare used the Protocol to demand that Germany develop offensive capabilities. In March 1935, the chief of the General Staff, General Ludwig von Beck, attended a conference on chemical warfare that decided that Germany's acceptance of the Geneva Protocol "compelled gas defense and the theoretical employment of poison chemical means."[138] Ochsner explicitly contended in 1936 that Germany must be fully ready for chemical warfare since the Geneva Protocol provided no steps against a violation of its provisions. He pointed to the futile British efforts to sanction Italy over its use of chemicals in Ethiopia as proof of the need to prepare.[139]

But German efforts went beyond simple retaliation. A new interest in the offensive use of poison gas is evident in military thought in the early 1930s in line with the emergence of an offense-oriented general doctrine. Some theorists hoped that gas could be used to capture industrial areas in Poland and Czechoslovakia with a minimum of damage. In 1933, a secret memorandum forecast large-scale surprise use of both high explosives and gas bombs at the beginning of a future conflict.[140] In 1935, one prognosis was that chemical agents used in

---

[137] Even after two years of war, Germany still believed chemical weapons would be employed. Although the Soviet Union had signed the Protocol, Germany anticipated the USSR would use chemical weapons during the Nazi invasion. Colonel-General Halder, chief of the Army General Staff, thought there would be chemical spraying and location contamination. Hitler was apparently relieved that Stalin did not use gas against the onslaught of Barbarossa. Aus einer Besprechung von Generaloberst Halder, Chef des Generalstabs des Heeres, mit den Oberfehlshabern der Ost-Armeen am 5. Juni 1941, as found in Hans Günter Branch and Rolf Dieter Müller, *Chemische Kriegführung, Chemische Abrüstung: Dokumente und Kommentare* (Berlin: Arno Spitz, 1985), p. 174; Mueller, "German Preparations for Chemical Warfare," p. 192.

[138] Olaf Groehler, *Der lautlose Tod* (Berlin: Verlag der Nation, 1978), pp. 119–20.

[139] Inspektion 9, "Vortragsnotizen," 15 Mai 1936, RH 12–9/v. 23, BA-MA.

[140] Groehler, *Der lautlose Tod*, pp. 95 and 109; Mueller, "German Preparations for Chemical Warfare," pp. 178–79. This is the Knauss memo discussed above in the German air warfare case. See Bernard Heiman and Joachim Schunke, "Eine geheime Denkschrift zur Luftkriegskonzeption Hitler-Deutschlands vom Mai 1933," *Zeitschrift für Militärgeschichte* 3 (1964): 72–86.

large quantities would have an effect that could only be equaled by days and weeks of operations by stronger artillery and airpower.[141]

Like in Britain, the main effect of the chemical regime during the interwar period was to drive the Third Reich's chemical warfare program underground.[142] On 25 October 1935, General Werner von Fritsch, CINC of the German army, declared that Germany must avoid giving the impression it was preparing for chemical warfare. Already in August the Army High Command had classified as secret the possible use of gas while Germany was officially bound by the Geneva Protocol. That the Protocol was used to justify offensive preparations was made explicit in a December 1935 memorandum. The artillery inspectorate stated that development of chemical warfare would be masked with the pretext "that we must be able to pay back in kind an enemy who violates the Geneva Protocol of 1925. We support the use of this argument that we have to be able to retaliate because the training frees us from all limitations."[143]

Ochsner, the head of the chemical warfare troops, thought that the Protocol should neither limit development nor be allowed to stand in the way of first use. He believed that a "determined political leadership" could always find grounds to justify initiation that would take care of any problems with world opinion. Like Dönitz's suggestion for declaring zones in which submarines could ignore restrictions, Ochsner proposed creating "operational areas" that would "legally" circumvent the Protocol and allow the unrestricted use of chemical weapons.[144]

At the very beginning of war in September 1939, the British ambassador to Switzerland delivered a message to the Swiss foreign ministry, which was to be passed on to German officials. The note pledged not to use poison gas as long as the Third Reich did not. Germany signaled its agreement to the bargain.[145] Despite this assurance, however, there is little evidence that a convention of no-first-use had any significant

[141] WaffenAmt an A.H.A. mit 1 Nebensusf. für In 4 usw., "Gasangriff," 15 November 1935, RH 12–9/v. 28, BA – MA.
[142] Of course, unlike Britain, Germany was more concerned with international rather than domestic opinion. This was not a "cost-free" effect. Soldiers complained that the secrecy inhibited readiness. See, for example, 2. Abteilung, Generalstabs des Heeres, "Aufbau der chemischen Waffen" 6 Januar 1936, RH 2/1141, BA-MA.
[143] Groehler, *Der lautlose Tod*, p. 123. Der Inspekteur der Artillerie an A.H.A. (mit der Bitte um Weiterleitung an der Generalstab), "Vorbereitung für den chemischen Krieg," 16 Dezember 1935, RH 12–9/v. 28, BA-MA; Mueller, "German Preparations for Warfare," p. 183.
[144] Ochsner, "Grundsätzliche Gedanken."
[145] Harris and Paxman, *Higher Form of Killing*, p. 107; Brown, *Chemical Warfare*, p. 210.

effect on German expectations, preparations, or decision making during the war. Only near the end of the conflict was international law discussed explicitly. Albert Speer reports that the Geneva Protocol came up in 1945 when Goebbels, in advocating first use, recommended German withdrawal from the regime. But it appears that Hitler had already brushed aside the legal proprieties and ordered the use of all available means.[146]

There is scant evidence that the regime against first use was an important source of German restraint. It did not diminish expectations of use nor inhibit preparations for war. In fact, in some instances, the Geneva Protocol was used to argue for the development of offensive capabilities. To be sure, the informal pledge offered by Britain at the beginning of the war undoubtedly reassured Germany that its opponent would not be quick to use chemical weapons, yet one finds little evidence that the Protocol had much effect on Germany's decision making.

Readiness and Realism

The most common explanations for German restraint are based on realism. The Nazis allegedly did not use chemical weapons because they were unprepared or perceived themselves to be inferior in that form of warfare. To the extent this was true, we must ask (1) why Germany was not prepared for a form of warfare that it felt was effective and likely and (2) why Germany misperceived (at least in the first part of the war) that it was at a disadvantage in chemical warfare.

The answer to these questions begins at the end of World War I. German interest in chemical weapons was evident even as the armistice for the Great War was signed in 1919. The German army retained a significant cache of gas projectiles, which it intended to use if conflict renewed. The Army leadership even speculated about using the poison gas in a "war of liberation" against the victors of World War I.[147]

In the interwar years the justification for chemical warfare preparations was stated in terms of the need to keep up with foreign powers. Germany, after all, had been banned by the Versailles treaty from developing chemical weapons. By 1929, the military was already demanding parity in chemical weapons with its adversaries. In 1934 the chemical warfare arm of the Armaments office concluded that foreign countries were rapidly increasing their chemical arms despite the Ge-

---

[146] See IMT, 16:526 (see Chap. 2, n. 22).
[147] Mueller, "German Preparations for Chemical Warfare," p. 173.

neva Protocol and Germany needed to keep pace. In 1936, the Truppenamt stated bluntly that the preparations of foreign countries were "forcing" Germany to pursue chemical weapons. In 1937, it announced that it considered supplies dangerously low.[148]

In short, Germany felt that it had fallen behind its potential adversaries in chemical weapons production. Under the Versailles treaty Germany was forbidden to manufacture or import chemical weapons. The factories producing such arms were closed in the interwar period, and through 1924 this part of Germany's industry was monitored by the Inter-Allied Control Commission. But even under Hitler, production facilities for chemical weapons were not significantly developed. By 1936, Germany had only 1,300 tons of mustard and tear gas, which is significantly less than the 7,038 tons of mustard gas Germany produced in 1918. This low level was due in part to the dislocations in industry resulting from the Versailles treaty, but also to the general inhibition against rearming prior to Hitler's ascent to power. The actual supply of shells and bombs was also purposely kept low in order to avoid large stocks of obsolete matériel in the event that new types of gases and delivery vehicles were discovered.[149]

The irony of Germany's insecurity is that relative to its adversaries, the Third Reich was in a superior position to wage chemical warfare. Even with a limited economy, Germany had the largest supply of chemical agents on hand at the beginning of the war by far with some 12,000 tons, 80 percent of which was mustard gas. Through most of the war, Germany had a production advantage. In total, the Third Reich produced some 65,000 tones of poison substances, most of which (approximately 70 percent) was in shells and bombs.[150]

---

[148] These arguments can be found in "Anweisung des Truppenamtes zum Schutz der deutschen Interessen auf dem Gaskriegsgebiet bei den Genfer Abrüstungsverhandlungen vom 28. November 1929," II H 474, BA-MA, as reprinted in Brauch and Müller, *Chemische Kriegführung,* p. 118. Inspektion 4 an Wehramt, "Gasschutzdienst," 7 September 1933, RH 12–9/v. 28, BA-MA. Oberkommando des Heeres, "Ausbildung in Gasabwehrdienst,"15 September 1936, RH 53–7/v. 67, BA-MA. Generalstab des Heeres an Generalstab der Luftwaffe—6.Abteilung, "Kampf-and Nebelstoffe," 11 Dezember 1937, RH2/3008, BA-MA.

[149] SIPRI, *Chemical and Biological Warfare,* 1:278–79. Mueller, "German Preparations for Chemical Warfare," pp. 182 and 190.

[150] SIPRI, *Chemical and Biological Warfare,* 1:297. Moon, "Chemical Weapons and Deterrence," p. 27. Groehler, *Der lautlose Tod,* p. 301; Mueller, "German Preparations for Chemical Warfare," p. 201; SIPRI, *Chemical and Biological Warfare,* 1:304. One British interrogation indicated that the Luftwaffe had a half million bombs and a capability to spray troops with a 50 percent casualty rate. This was supposedly true even in situations where the enemy expected an attack. See Harris and Paxman, *Higher Form of Killing,* p. 59. Of course, such interrogations are not always reliable.

Germany was also the economic and technological leader in chemical warfare. The Third Reich had the premier chemical industry in Europe. Military leaders hoped for a new gas that would quickly kill unprotected persons and even be effective against those wearing masks. Ironically, I. G. Farben, the large German industrial concern, had developed just such a substance—the nerve gas Tabun—in 1936. But it was difficult to produce and like the rest of Germany's chemical potential, given low priority when the Third Reich rearmed.[151] The postwar Allied assessment of German chemical warfare capabilities concluded that stocks were greater than expected, of higher quality, and included weapons of "outstanding merit."[152] Nonetheless, this war-making potential was never employed. This, of course, is not to say that German leaders correctly perceived their advantage. In fact, they may not have. Before and during the conflict the military leadership seemed to believe that its opponents were ahead in chemical weaponry. As Brown has noted, the Third Reich was "predisposed to regard any foreign chemical warfare product as a sign of superiority."[153]

To the extent Germany's leaders were biased, it is analytically useful to understand why they were biased. Was this perceived inferiority a simple error or a typical psychological distortion? The organizational-culture approach explains this bias as a systematic product of a belief hierarchy that provided mental constraints and material incentives to view the world in a certain way. Brown argues that Germany's faulty evaluations were the result of a crisis of confidence caused by restrictions on rearmament. Enemy countries that had no constraints were simply assumed to have superior means.[154]

Yet not all in Germany or the military were overwhelmed by the potential of other states, which suggests that a general bias was not the single determining factor. Instead, it appears that organizational affiliation shaped how different individuals viewed the situation. Those connected with the chemical warfare effort believed in Germany's advantage, those who were not saw only disadvantage.[155] For example, the Army Armaments Bureau concluded in 1931 that other countries had not made progress in chemical warfare and that the

[151] Harris and Paxman, *Higher Form of Killing*, pp. 53–56; Mueller, "German Preparations for Chemical Warfare," pp. 183 and 190.

[152] Hinsley, *British Intelligence*, vol. 3, part 2, pp. 929–30.

[153] Brown, *Chemical Warfare*, p. 234.

[154] Ibid., pp. 231–35. His conclusions are based on interrogations done after the war.

[155] This cultural effect was also evident in Britain's belief in asdic and the ability of the bomber to get through, and in German faith in submarine attack and dive-bombing.

German effort in this area could produce maximum effect with little effort. In 1938, I. G. Farben representatives claimed that chemical weapons could be decisive in war when used against the civilian population in a way that conventional munitions could not. This they argued gave Germany the advantage because German citizens were "morally strong, highly disciplined, and technically equipped," and would therefore do relatively well under chemical warfare conditions. In 1939, Ochsner, head of the chemical troops in the Army, pointed out that the German chemical industry was at the forefront of all nations. He recommended the development and even the first use of gas. Ochsner described how a large-scale attack against enemy rear areas could significantly damage enemy morale. Moreover, he suggested focusing air attacks on the enemy's chemical defense industry. When soldiers discovered that no more masks were coming to the front, they would fold. Carl Krauch, a director of I. G. Farben whom Göring had named "plenipotentiary for questions of chemical production," argued in 1939 that since Germany could not match the lead of its adversaries in high explosive munitions, it should focus on chemical weapons, where a greater effect could be had for the labor and raw materials required. As late as 1942, Ochsner promoted the advantages of chemical warfare, arguing that gas could be a decisive weapon against the Russians.[156] Yet even though chemical warfare, like unrestricted submarine warfare, provided Germany with a relative advantage, Ochsner and Krauch's argument never took root for reasons connected to culture.

To evaluate the realist explanation, we should examine four phases of the war more closely: (1) the period after the defeat of France, (2) the German campaign in the East, (3) the defense at Normandy, and (4) the end of the war. The events of these phases indicated that realism can only partially account for Germany's restraint.[157]

After the fall of France, when Britain refused to accept a peace settlement, up through the Battle of Britain, it seemed very likely that Germany would use gas. Germany was much less vulnerable to the RAF than Britain was to the Luftwaffe. In addition, Germany had a better supply of chemical weapons and had improved its readiness since the

---

[156] Groehler, *Der lautlose Tod*, p. 84. Mueller, "German Preparations for Chemical Warfare," pp 185–86, 189. Ochsner, "Grundsätzliche Gedanken." Der General der Nebeltruppe an den Herrn Chef des Generalstabes des Heeres, "Verwendung von Kampfstoffen," 22 Mai 1942, RH2/429, BA-MA. Ochsner also noted the inadequacies in chemical readiness at that time.

[157] Other situations entailed a lesser relative advantage. I consider these later.

beginning of the war.[158] Retaliation in kind against German troops was not a realistic threat, as it did not seem likely that Britain would strike with gas against conquered France.[159] Rolf-Dieter Mueller speculates that some German leaders feared that even small-scale gas attacks on German civilians would have a devastating effect on the public's ability to withstand the trials of war and that this fear was an important factor in the decision to forego use. The security police compiled reports on public morale that indicated some anxiety that Britain would resort to gas in desperation.[160] This consideration, however, does not seem as compelling as others, particularly at this point in the war. Certainly German citizens might have been concerned about such attacks, but the very fact that they were thought of as desperation raids is more important. Germany had just conquered the European continent with no significant losses. Public support was relatively high in those heady days of the Third Reich.[161]

Considerations linked to supplies and war plans probably had more to do with why Germany chose restraint. In 1939, Ochsner suggested that a chemical offensive with large-scale attacks against enemy armies and civilian populations would break the will of the enemy government. London was singled out as an especially inviting target.[162] The period 1940–1941 seemed like the opportune time to implement such a plan.[163] But, even though Germany had relative superiority in chemical supplies, it may not have had the capacity needed for such an ambitious undertaking. Furthermore, as discussed below, Germany lacked comprehensive protection for its civilians. Also, Hitler and his generals may have feared that the use of gas in the West would be mimicked

---

[158] Following an inadvertent use of mustard gas by Poland, which injured several German soldiers, it was decided that gas preparedness had to be improved. Der Befehlshaber des Ersatzheeres, "Schutz gegen Kampfstoffverwendung," 3 Oktober 1939, RH 53–7/v. 206, BA-MA; Ochsner, *History of German Chemical Warfare*, p. 9.

[159] See William Moore, *Gas Attack! Chemical Warfare 1915–1918 and Afterwards* (London: Leo Cooper, 1987), p. 223.

[160] There was even a rumor that the RAF had dropped pamphlets reading, "There are eight of us and we come every night. If you come with Stukas, we'll come with gas!" Mueller, "German Preparations for Chemical Warfare," p. 192.

[161] Heinz Boberach, *Meldungen aus dem Reich* (Neuwied: Herman Luchterhard, 1965), pp. 79–97; Martin Broszat, "The Third Reich and the German People," in Hedley Bull, ed., *The Challenge of the Third Reich* (Oxford: Clarendon Press, 1986), p. 87; Lukacs, *The Duel*, pp. 173–74 (see Chap. 3, n. 48).

[162] Ochsner, "Grundsätzliche Gedanken."

[163] Once Germany realized air superiority and successful invasion were not possible, there should have been consideration of the relative merits of high explosive and gas, however, there is no evidence of this.

by the Russians in the East, which would hinder the planned invasion of the USSR. Göring was allegedly confident that high explosives alone could finish off Britain.[164]

The German campaign against the Soviet Union involved several decisions on chemical warfare suggesting the power of realist considerations. When the German invasion stalled, the idea of using gas against the Russians surfaced a number of times. At the end of 1941 when success in the East was in doubt, the Armaments Bureau concluded that the enemy did not have the types of harmful gases that Germany had, and that Germany was superior in gas warfare. At the same time Colonel Ochsner pressed General Franz Halder, the chief of the Army General Staff, to initiate chemical warfare against the Russians. Nonetheless, by March 1942 the Armaments Bureau declared that there was not enough available production capacity for starting a gas war. The idea of using gas in the summer operations of 1942 was dropped.[165]

After the disaster at Stalingrad, efforts were made by some of Hitler's top aides, including Goebbels, Bormann, and Robert Ley, to convince him to use gas. In the spring of 1943, Hitler asked several times about the progress on chemical weapons. The Führer called a conference with Speer and Otto Ambros, a director of I. G. Farben. Ambros told Hitler that the Allies could produce more mustard gas than Germany because of a better supply of the necessary raw materials. More important, the Farben director informed the Führer that contrary to previous information, Germany might not have a monopoloy in nerve gases. Hitler ordered that the production of Tabun be doubled and Sarin quintupled, but immediate use was rejected, apparently out of fear that the opponent could retaliate in kind. Hitler appointed his former personal physician, Professor Karl Brandt, to oversee distribution of gas masks to all Germans.[166] What is interesting in this incident is not only that Germany was apparently deterred from use, but that it had not developed the nerve gases that it had an advantage in, and that it

---

[164] Moore, *Gas Attack!* p. 223. Moore also notes, "the Luftwaffe could have inflicted critical wounds on Britain's defences. Had airfields and radar stations been attacked with bombs containing a vesicant, the cratering of runways would have posed extra problems and heavy strain on the men required to repair them."

[165] WaffenAmt. "Vortragsnotiz für den Fuhrer und Obersten Befehlshaber der Wehrmacht," 2 Dezember 1941, RH 2/929, BA-MA. Groehler, *Der lautlose Tod*, p. 226.

[166] Official Transcript of the U.S. Military Court (at Nurnberg), Case VI, 28 Februay 48-M-ATD-11-3-Primeu (Int. Lea) Court 6, Case 6, pp. 8002–3, International Law Library, Harvard University. Mueller, "German Preparations for Chemical Warfare," pp. 196–97.

perceived foreign countries to have equal capabilities.[167] As we will see below, culture was central to these calculations.

In the summer of 1944, Hitler's cronies, this time Goebbels and Ley, were again pressing Hitler to permit use of the chemical "secret weapon"—at least on the Eastern front. In his conversation with Speer, Ley, the chief of the German Labor Front, agitatedly cried, "You know we have this new poison gas—I've heard about it. The Führer must do it. He must use it. Now he has to do it! This is the last moment. You too must make him realize that it's time." Ley lobbied Hitler and Goebbels, but the idea was abandoned when the military would not back it. Hitler was especially interested in how gas might stop the Soviet advance. He speculated that the Allies might tolerate such use since they too wanted the Soviets stopped. This time Speer alleges that he put off Hitler and his military chief Wilhelm Keitel by arguing that technical problems and raw material shortages (and indirectly enemy capabilities) necessitated a reduction in chemical weapons production if not the cessation of the chemical program.[168]

Perhaps the most puzzling occurrence of German restraint in chemical warfare in World War II was the invasion of Normandy. Arguably the most important Allied military operation of the war, the amphibious assaults on Omaha and Utah beaches were ideal targets for chemical counterattack. As General Ochsner explained after the war, contaminating those beaches would have hindered the tempo of the attack, deflated morale, and forced the allies to burden their supply lines with special decontamination troops and equipment. "In short: from all angles the idea seemed to hold out good prospects of success, and no technical difficulties were expected."[169]

Allied military leaders echoed this judgment. Rear Admiral Sir Anthony Buzzard, a British member of the joint planning committee on Allied chemical use, wrote in 1968 that the use of gas against the assault at Normandy might have been decisive in that battle.[170] General Omar Bradley, one of the key Allied invasion planners, was "vastly relieved" when D-Day ended without chemical weapons being used, "for even

---

[167] Brown, *Chemical Warfare*, p. 234, n. 112, relates how the Germans believed the Allies had nerve gas because of their interest in hydrocyanic acid and because public mention of insecticide development (because of the promise of the newly discovered DDT) had vanished from the U.S. press.

[168] The latter was rejected. Albert Speer, *Inside the Third Reich* (New York: Macmillan, 1970), pp. 413–14.

[169] Ochsner, *History of German Chemical Warfare*, p. 23. For the reasons listed below, Ochsner concludes, "Nevertheless, the idea had to be abandoned."

[170] SIPRI, *Chemical and Biological Warfare*, 1:312.

a light sprinkling of persistent gas on Omaha Beach could have cost our footing there."[171] Major General Alden Waitt, head of the U.S. Chemical Warfare Service, noted in 1946 that if the Germans had used chemical weapons, the invasion might have been delayed by six months or moved to new landing points. True, Waitt conceded, the Allies could have retaliated massively, but even in light of this threat, he believes it would have made sense for Germany to use its chemical arsenal.[172]

Two related factors seem to deserve equal weight in the German decision for restraint at Normandy. The first is insufficient preparation. By 1944, Germany's supply of chemical weapons in standing stocks would last six months. The number of chemical shells and bombs was even less because of the demand for conventional munitions. Nonetheless, the Luftwaffe is reported to have had a half-million gas bombs and aircraft spray tanks. The Germans were also worried about being able to sustain production. The day before the invasion of Normandy, Ambros mentioned in a report the difficulties and shortages being encountered in gas production.[173]

Perhaps more important was a sense of relative vulnerability. Germany may have perceived itself as defensively ill prepared both on the battlefield and in civil defense. Hitler told Rumania's Marshal Antonescu in March 1944 that it was only Germany's lack of protective equipment that prevented its use of new poison gases, which would be used if the situation could be improved.[174] By the end of 1942, 28 million gas masks had been distributed and the antigas civil-defense program was relatively well planned. But by 1945, 25 million Germans still lacked masks, despite the production of 1,760,000 masks in December 1944.[175] Whether *every* citizen needed a mask to maintain an effective civil defense, however, is questionable.

Germany had also become strategically vulnerable to retaliation. By 1944, Allied airpower dominated the skies, and strategic bombing was devastating Germany. If the Third Reich had used chemical weapons, it would have suffered retaliatory strikes. Given German concerns over its defense preparedness, this was a powerful deterrent. As Ochsner

[171] Omar N. Bradley, *A Soldier's Story* (New York: Henry Holt, 1951), p. 279.

[172] SIPRI, *Chemical and Biological Warfare*, 1:297.

[173] Ibid., p. 325, n. 17; Harris and Paxman, *Higher Form of Killing*, p. 59; Mueller, "German Preparations for Chemical Warfare," p. 198.

[174] Andreas Hillgruber, ed., *Staatsmaenner und Diplomaten bei Hitler*, part 2, *Vertrauliche Aufzeichnugen ueber Unturredungen mit Vertreten des Auslandes 1942–1944* (Frankfurt: Bernard & Graefe, 1970), p. 403.

[175] Brown, *Chemical Warfare*, pp. 242–43.

notes, "We would but have furnished our enemies . . . with a good excuse also to use gas against our armies on all fronts, and perhaps even against our homeland. In such an event we would not have been able to retaliate as enemy air power was growing perceptibly. These sober deliberations not only justified the decision of our Supreme command under no circumstances to use gas, but in fact, made the decision obligatory."[176]

What would have happened if Germany had used its gases at Normandy will never by known. Robert Harris and Jeremy Paxman speculatively hazard that it could have changed the outcome of the war. They argue that the British forces under Montgomery did not even carry antigas equipment. Omaha Beach was taken by the skin of the Allies' teeth, a result chemical weapons could have reversed. A successful defense would have damaged Allied willpower and given Germany time to consolidate its position. The delay of the second front, they contend, might have ultimately led to a separate peace with Hitler.[177] Such claims are exaggerated. The atomic bomb would have broken any such deadlock. Nonetheless, it is clear that chemical warfare would have altered the nature of the war as we know it.

As the defeat of Germany became increasingly likely, Hitler gave the appearance that he would take any available measure to avoid or delay its realization. He announced a slogan of "Victory or Destruction" and ordered a scorched-earth strategy, "If the war is to be lost, the nation, too, will be lost. . . . There is no need to consider the basic requirements that a people need in order to continue to live a primitive life. On the contrary, it is better ourselves to destroy such things, for this nation will have proved itself the weaker, and the future will belong exclusively to the stronger eastern nation. Those who remain alive after the battles are over are in any case inferior persons, since the best have fallen."[178] The Allies also believed that the fall of Germany might bring the initiation of chemical warfare. As Western forces reached the German border respirators were reissued to forward troops. If Joseph Goebbels had had his way, this action would have been justified. After the Allied air raid on Dresden, Goebbels pressed Hitler to use nerve gas in retaliation. It is not clear whether Hitler finally approved the use of gas. Albert Speer, Minister for War Production, testified that the Führer did give such an order. Brandt has main-

---

[176] Ochsner, *History of German Chemical Warfare*, p. 23.

[177] Harris and Paxman, *Higher Form of Killing*, pp. 63–64.

[178] This statement was made in March 1945. Matthew Cooper, *The German Army, 1933–1945: Its Political and Military Failure* (New York: Stein & Day, 1978), p. 543.

tained that he, Speer, and General Kennes, assistant chief of the General Staff, had an agreement to undermine any order to start a gas war by holding up supplies.[179] Again at the end of war, a lack of readiness inhibited use.

Despite a superficial applicability to these wartime decisions, the realist explanation of German chemical warfare policy has several key shortcomings. Germany had chemical superiority for the first part of World War II in terms of output, stocks on hand, and possibly even effectiveness of defensive measures. And no other country had the advanced level of chemical technology symbolized by Germany's monopoly in the lethal nerve gases Tabun and Sarin. As Mueller has noted, gas was a typically German weapon yet inexplicably from a relative advantage perspective, Germany maintained restraint. Realism does seem to account for many of the German decisions made in the last part of the war: restraint made sense as long as Germany believed it had other weapons to do the job which did not have the disadvantages of chemical warfare. Nonetheless, restraint at Normandy is puzzling. And realism cannot explain why restraint endured in the face of certain defeat.

All in all, however, to say the Third Reich was restrained by the costs of escalation does not tell us enough about the sources of German restraint because German calculations do not seem to have matched Germany's circumstances. Why did Germany persist in seeing itself as inferior when it was not? Why was the Reich never ready to employ its chemical capability when favorable opportunities to do so presented themselves?

The Blitzkrieg Culture and Gas

The German military played a significant role in Nazi restraint in chemical warfare. In light of the degree to which Hitler dominated even military decisions, this assertion may seem surprising. The point is not that military men made the actual decisions. They did not. Nor is it the case that one particular general was able to determine the situation by acting "behind the scenes." The influence of the military derived from its bureaucratic power and its accompanying culture that gave that power purpose.[180] The German army favored a particular strategic outlook that clashed with employing chemical weapons. All

---

[179] SIPRI, *Chemical and Biological Warfare*, 1:298. *IMT*, 16:526 (see Chap. 2, n. 22). Brown, *Chemical Warfare*, p. 237 n. 121. Harris and Paxman, *Higher Form of Killing*, p. 63.

[180] This is also not to deny that Hitler affected the Wehrmacht's culture.

aspects of chemical warfare subsequently suffered benign neglect, and this neglect was at the root of German restraint.

German strategic culture and the lessons of World War I are central to understanding the Third Reich's choices on poison gas in World War II. Dating back to Graf von Moltke, Germany's military thought had focused on fast, decisive maneuver and encirclement to reach victory. The irony of World War I, of course, is that this strategy was thwarted. Mired in trench warfare and short of ammunition, the military accepted chemical weapons, which were advocated by civilians and reservists. Gas was sold to the military as a way out of the trenches.[181]

The poison cloud did not end trench warfare as the Germans had hoped. The military of World War I disdained the weapon, despite agreeing to employ it. In fact it may have been the antipathy of the armed forces that produced Germany's half-hearted commitment to, and inefficient use of, gas in the Great War. Soldiers did not like it for a number of reasons. It was difficult to use, especially in offensive operations, and it made the military less aggressive as an attacking force. It generally did not fit well into Army operations, but it went least badly with artillery and this became its institutional home. Yet even artillerymen were not keen on chemical weapons. They resented the civilian interference that was part and parcel of gas warfare. Chemists were as important to the use of gas as soldiers were, and the military disliked this loss of operational autonomy. The point is especially important when we recall that most of the Third Reich's High Command came from the artillery; the officer's corps of the German infantry was largely decimated in World War I.[182]

Ironically, the Versailles treaty helped to turn the German army even more toward a doctrine of speed and maneuver. It prohibited Germany from keeping a large standing army, therefore, it had to do the most it could with numerically fewer troops. Although there were certainly elements of stationary defense in interwar German strategic thought (such as the "West Wall" concept), it was dominated by a focus on mobile operations. The roots of "blitzkrieg" can be found in Germany's preexisting strategic culture, the lessons of World War I, and the in-

---

[181] Robert M. Citino, *The Evolution of Blitzkrieg Tactics: Germany Defends Itself against Poland, 1918–1933* (Westport, Conn.: Greenwood Press, 1987), p. 81; Brown, *Chemical Warfare*, p. 5.

[182] As with the British reaction to chemical warfare, some of the reasons for the German aversion to it can be found in traditional organization theory, for example, the preference for offense and autonomy. Haber, *Poisonous Cloud*, pp. 269, 273, 277; Cooper, *German Army*, p. 151.

terwar determination to defeat foes with larger forces (such as Poland and France).[183]

Larry H. Addington describes German doctrine on the eve of war as follows: fast-moving and long-ranged armored and motorized units were to spearhead the attack, break through the enemy's front, and penetrate quickly and deeply into the rear—counter moves to block encirclement or escape—and sever communications. Infantry divisions would then move in to annihilate the enemy from the front. Chemical weapons, which were unwieldy and slowed the tempo of advance and maneuver, could play only a limited role in such a strategy. Chemical equipment and munitions jammed supply lines. Chemical casualties did not die easily and demanded intensive care.[184]

It was largely this incompatibility with the German creed of offensive mobility that explains why the chemical troops never really took hold in the German army. The military, of course, acknowledged a role for gas. Tactical studies after World War I indicated the effectiveness of chemical weapons on the battlefield. This was evident in Germany's cooperative efforts with the Soviet Union from 1926 to 1933. The Wehramt's *Inspektion 4* (after April 1934 the *Allgemeine Heeresamt*) concluded on 7 September 1933 that in the coming war chemicals would be used at least on the scale that occurred at the end of World War I. In 1935, General Werner von Fritsch, the CINC of the Army, declared after a gas demonstration that chemical weapons were ready for combat and could be introduced on a significant scale.[185]

In addition, a formal organization for chemical warfare took shape between 1934 and 1936. In 1934 a special unit for testing chemical weapons was installed within an artillery division at Koenigsbrueck. On 1 October 1935, the first gas division came into being with one battery stationed at Koenigsbrueck, and the other at Bremen. A special

---

[183] A 1937 conference considered the use of gas as a means of defending the border with France. Besprechung bei Gen St d H 1. Abt., "Verwendung von chemischen Kampfstoffen in Kampf um Festungen," 13 March 1937, RN 12–9/v. 28, BA-MA. For a discussion of the different schools of thought in the German military in the 1920s, see Corum, *Roots of Blitzkrieg*, chap. 3 (see Chap. 3, no. 56). Citino, *Evolution of Blitzkrieg Tactics*, emphasizes the role of planning to fight Poland.

[184] Larry H. Addington, *The Blitzkrieg Era and the German General Staff, 1865–1941* (New Brunswick: Rutgers University Press, 1971), p. 42. It does appear that at least a brief inquiry into the use of gas in mobile warfare was made in 1923. "Vortrag beim Chef der H. L. am 20 November 1923," 27 November 1923, RN 2/2207, BA-MA. Ochsner, *History of German Chemical Warfare*, p. 5.

[185] Corum, *Roots of Blitzkrieg*, p. 106. Groehler, *Der lautlose Tod*, p. 105. Der Inspekteur der Artillerie an A.H.A. (mit der Bitte um Weiterleitung an der Generalstab), "Vorbereitung für den chemischen Krieg," 16 Demcember 1935, RH 12–9/v. 28, BA-MA.

department (Waffen Pruefung 9) for the development of chemical warfare was established in the Armaments Bureau. Chemical and gas defense schools were located near Hannover. To oversee the entire effort, a department was created in the General Army Office and was headed by Ochsner. In 1935, the Army development plan called for a gas regiment for every corps. By the first year of war some twenty-one battalions had been created that were responsible for both smoke screening and gas duties. At the Wehrmacht Academy, chemical warfare was integrated into the curriculum. Although the Army was the center of chemical warfare development, both the Air Force and the Navy had their own chemical programs and training facilities.[186]

But any substantial programs for chemical production and armament proposed were repeatedly scaled back. The reason for this phenomenon was also fairly constant. The economy of the Third Reich simply could not meet all the demands of the rapid 1930s rearmament, and then later, those of war. Germany could not develop and build all the weapons it needed at once. Priorities had to be set, and chemical weapons rarely ranked high. In 1936, the Army was planning on filling 15 percent of its shells with chemicals, surpassing the 6.4 percent level of all German shells used in World War I. In 1937, however, due to production problems, this was cut to 10 percent for smoke and gas combined. The steel and iron needed to construct chemical production and storage facilities went to tank and plane manufacturing; concrete was diverted to the construction of the West Wall. During the war, even though such ventures as the mass production of the new nerve gas Tabun were seen as important, production was slowed as resources were shifted to other projects supporting more traditional weapons, such as the development of synthetic fuels and conventional artillery shells. The Tabun plant was not turning out gas until September 1942, and even then, at only one-tenth capacity. By that time, raw materials shortages in the German economy prohibited sharp increases in production.[187]

The main advocate for development of gas capability was an alliance of industrial representatives and those offices within the military (such as Waffen Pruefung 9) specially responsible for chemical warfare. The

[186] Joachim Emde, *Die Nebelwerfer: Entwicklung und Einsatz der Werfertruppen im Zweten Weltkrieg* (Friedburg: Podzun-Pallas-Verlag, 1979), pp. 9–10. SIPRI, *Chemical and Biological Warfare*, 1:280–81. There would also be gas and decontamination units. Mueller, "German Preparations for Chemical Warfare," p. 183. Wehrmachtakademie, "Vortrag and der Wehrmachtakademie im Januar/Februar 1938," 8 Dezember 1937, RH 12–9/v. 22, BA-MA.
[187] See Groehler, *Der lautlose Tod*, chap. 5, also pp. 140–41; Mueller "German Preparations for Chemical Warfare," pp. 188, 194–95; Brown, *Chemical Warfare*, p. 239 n. 128.

former undoubtedly hoped for contracts, and the latter foresaw a powerful role for their weapon. Both believed that the role of poison gas was not receiving its just recognition. Like Dönitz in submarine policy and Trenchard in the RAF's bombing offensive, the German chemical corps's top officer, Hermann Ochsner, energetically lobbied for chemical weapons. But in this case the outcome was quite different.

In Germany, the advocates of chemical warfare were swimming against too strong an organizational current. Some attempted to achieve outside legitimation. One bureau claimed, "If the Führer wants to use gas," it must be ready.[188] Ochsner's department argued in June of 1936 that because the chemical arm was the youngest "child" of the Army, it needed special attention to become viable.[189] But the chemical troops simply never got that attention. One civilian connected with the German chemical warfare program noted, "The German General Staff and the German general officers, with few exceptions, were not interested in chemical warfare. The lack of interest was not based on a lack of faith or disbelief of its promises of success; the reason was simply that, first, chemical warfare was not understood, nor did the majority of generals try to understand it."[190] The Luftwaffe does not seem to have been much better. It was also unwilling to divert attention and material away from favored systems. Göring was fixated on airplanes, especially bombers, and this is where the Luftwaffe's efforts were concentrated.[191]

The organizational origins of the disregard for chemical warfare were recognized by Carl Krauch. In 1938, he advocated the formation of a chemical officer corps so that "leaders will develop who will ensure that the value and use of chemical weapons are appreciated at the highest command levels. In the course of the next few years a military organization will be created which will only be possible in Germany and which will guarantee that the superior German chemical weapons will also be used appropriately."[192] The implication here, of course, was that up to that time, the weapons had not been appreciated. But no such corps was established. Maneuvers were held that were discouraging for gas enthusiasts. Commanding officers did not understand the chemical weapon and were hesitant to call in the gas troops in

---

[188] Inspektion 4, "Vorbereitung für Kampfstoff-Verwendung," 19 June 1934, RH 12–9/v. 28, BA-MA.

[189] Groehler, *Der lautlose Tod*, p. 126.

[190] J. H. Rothschild, *Tomorrow's Weapons: Chemical and Biological* (New York: McGraw-Hill, 1964), as cited in SIPRI, *Chemical and Biological Warfare*, 1:317.

[191] Gellerman, *Der Krieg, der nicht stattfand*, pp. 209–11.

[192] Cited in Mueller, "German Preparations for Chemical Warfare," pp. 186–87.

exercises. Many soldiers simply ignored the gas simulation by not wearing their masks.[193]

In war, the effect of culture on chemical weapons policy was that Germany did not use gas either because it saw itself at a disadvantage, or because it was not ready to do so when it had the advantage. I contend that both of these tendencies were products of organizational beliefs hostile to the employment of chemical weapons. Several other wartime situations also reflected the organizational bias against, and neglect of, the chemical weapon. These occurred during the Phony War and the invasion of the Soviet Union.

From before the war to the "Phony War" following Germany's defeat of Poland, some consideration was given to using gas against France. Germany had weighed the benefits of using chemicals both defensively and offensively in the interwar period. Defensively, large amounts of mustard gas could be spread in front of the West Wall to fend off a French attack. Offensively, gas could be used to break through the Maginot line. After the quick victory in Poland, however, thoughts of using poison agents to annihilate French forces were abandoned as blitzkrieg concepts came to center stage.[194]

A second instance of the partnership of culture and restraint was the planning of the invasion of the Soviet Union. The Germans did not dwell over whether to use gas or not. Barbarossa was to be a blitzkrieg, and chemical weapons would slow its tempo in several ways. Gas used in one area would complicate operations in others because preparations and precautions would be demanded everywhere. Persistent gases from earlier actions would slow subsequent ones. The necessary logistical hassles of wearing masks, carting chemical supplies, and decontaminating equipment would also slow the advance. Gas would also put new demands on logistical lines of communication and could be employed only at the expense of a reduction in other types of munitions. German use would likely provide enemy retaliation in kind, further impeding operations. This was especially significant for Barbarossa because the Germans initially believed Soviet troops were well equipped and prepared. Finally, gas might have been used even in the offensive for securing the flanks of the main salients, but this would have demanded centralized coordination in-

---

[193] Groehler, *Der lautlose Tod,* pp. 143–44.

[194] Besprechung bei Gen St d H. 1. Abt., "Verwendung von chemischen Kampfstoffen in Kampf um Festungen," 13 März 1937, RH 12–9/v. 28, BA-MA. Groehler, *Der lautlose Tod,* pp. 141, 194–95.

consistent with Germany's decentralized command and control system.[195]

A final area of wartime activity related to culture is inadvertent escalation. As with Britain's chemical warfare policy, the puzzle is why unintended escalation did not occur, given the complexity, first-strike incentives, and organizational routines that would suggest the likelihood of accidents leading to the use of chemical weapons. But they did not, and the reason for this absence appears to be organizational culture. In those cases in which incidents might have led to widespread use, military organizations seemed to go out of their way to maintain restraint. This behavior is quite distinct from that found in those means that organizational ethos deemed desirable for use.

During Germany's invasion of Poland, the Poles used mustard gas to defend the Jaslo bridge. Instead of responding in kind, however, the Third Reich's military assumed that the Polish Supreme Command had not ordered the use of gas. They were right, but their conclusion seemed more a product of wishful thinking than shrewd analysis.[196] The benign assumption the Germans made in this situation—that the gas use was not intentional—contrasts sharply with what Britain concluded about the Luftwaffe raid on London and Lemp's judgment on the status of the *Athenia*. When the German foreign ministry wanted to use the incident for propaganda, General Halder was quick to quash the idea. It appears that he, like his British counterparts, was afraid it might lead to the initiation of chemical warfare.[197]

A second incident in July 1941 testifies to the unusual efforts some states made to avoid escalation in chemical warfare. The Soviet Union claimed that Germany was getting ready to use chemical weapons. This accusation was based on the capture of a German manual on the offensive use of gas. In response, Germany was quick to announce through its official news agency that the manual was merely a training guide—as allowed by the Geneva Protocol—and not a plan.[198] That same summer, German military leaders had received five reports from the field that the Soviets had used chemical weapons. One involved a

---

[195] Ochsner, *History of German Chemical Warfare*, pp. 18, 21. See SIPRI, *Chemical and Biological Warfare*, 1:307–8.

[196] Ochsner states that this finding was "a great relief to us." Ochsner, *History of German Chemical Warfare*, p. 16.

[197] "Pressepropaganda Gelbkreuzgasverwendung durch die polnischen Truppen," 23 September 1939, RW 5/v. 346, BA-MA.

[198] But, "if the Soviets use the discovery of German instructions about gas as an excuse to begin gas warfare, Germany will answer appropriately." "Abschrift. Anszug aus der Times vom 26 July 1941," RW 5/v. 346, BA-MA.

bomber, two were artillery attacks, and two were armored-vehicle assaults. The Germans decided that not enough "objective" evidence existed that the attacks had occurred. But since they had twelve soldiers with mustard gas wounds it was conceded that perhaps a single gas bomb had been dropped. Otherwise, the incident was ignored.[199]

Another provocative accident occurred during the Allied invasion of Italy at Anzio in 1943. A German shell struck an Allied weapons depot that contained chemical munitions. The explosion released a cloud of gas, which drifted toward the German lines. The Allied commander was quick to notify his German counterpart that this release of gas was strictly inadvertent. The German officer accepted the explanation, despite the disadvantage he might have been at, had the Allied officer been lying.[200]

Even at the end of the war, when the Germans faced imminent political extinction and the Allies feared desperation escalation, there was no last resort to chemical weapons in the frenzied disintegration of the Third Reich. In fact, Germany became particularly cautious about unauthorized use. Supplies were ordered moved, not destroyed, to avoid any event that might give the enemy a pretext to use gas.[201] Chemical stocks and factories were given top priority when scarce transport space was allocated. Despite precautions, on 18 April 1945, an accident at a chemical depot in central Germany led to the contamination of the surrounding twenty kilometers. The Wehrmacht anticipated the enemy might use such an incident as an excuse to initiate the deliberate use of chemical weapons and recommended halting the risky transfer of chemical stocks and giving the Allies the location of the sites. Hitler vetoed this order.[202] Nonetheless, the Third Reich

[199] See Armeeoberkommando 11 an Oberkommando des Heeres, 1 Juli 1941, RW 5/v. 346, BA-MA, for a list and description of the injured soldiers. For the analysis of the incidents, see "Mitteilungen über Gaskriegsvorbereitungen im Ausland Nr. 10," 12 August 1941, RH 11 IV/v. 17, BA-MA.

[200] This incident is told by Lord Ritchie-Calder who was director of political warfare in the Foreign Office during the Second World War. See Steven Rose, ed., *CBW: Chemical and Biological Warfare* (Boston: Beacon Press, 1968), p. 14.

[201] Oberkommando der Wehrmacht, "Gaskriegsvorbereitungen," 4 Februar 1945, RW 4/v. 720, BA-MA.

[202] Mueller, "German Preparations for Chemical Warfare," pp. 200–201; Stephen L. McFarland, "Preparing for What Never Came," p. 114; Hinsley, *British Intelligence*, vol. 3, part 2, pp. 577 and 929–30. Brown, *Chemical Warfare*, p. 237, suggests that Hitler may have ordered gas attacks at the end of the war but was not obeyed.

accepted its political "death" without using means that might have, at a minimum, prolonged its life.

Conclusion: Culture, Then Realism

Why did the Third Reich show restraint in chemical warfare? Of the three theories, institutionalism is the weakest in this case. The norm did contribute to a tendency toward secret preparations, but there is only limited evidence that it affected expectations, preparations and decisions.

Realism provides the main prima facie explanation for restraint. Germany considered its ability to wage chemical warfare inferior to that of other powers in general or inadequate in specific situations. These decisions have all the characteristics of realism—concern with relative advantage, estimates of means ands ends, and assessments of the adversary. Yet in a very important way this explanation falls short. For before the realist calculation was made, culture had structured its outcome by giving context to what was valued and providing a lens for the interpretation—however skewed—of events and "reality." To discover the sources of restraint we must ask two further questions of the reality the Germans knew. Was their perception of inferiority correct? And why was the Third Reich not prepared?

In exploring these issues, the powerful role of organizational culture is revealed. First, Germany's perception of inferiority was *incorrect* for a good part of the interwar period and most of the war. The source of this misperception was a culture that essentially downgraded chemical efforts relative to others. The lack of interest led to the exaggeration of enemy capabilities and depreciation of Germany's own. These depressed estimates of strength and readiness in an area of warfare that was shunned by professional soldiers contrasts neatly with the inflated estimates of strength and readiness in means that they embraced. For example, in German submarine warfare, expected operational results were repeatedly exaggerated and off-setting enemy potential was denigrated. Bomber Command skewed its projections the same way to promote Britain's strategic bombing effort. To the extent we find misguided calculations of relative advantage in German decisions on chemical warfare, it seems they were significantly affected by organizationally biased perception. It is noteworthy that those connected with the chemical warfare mission were the main voice against the bias.

The lack of preparation for chemical warfare in Germany also has organizational origins. Chemical weapons were generally not ready for

use in the situations where decision makers considered their employment. As seen above, suitable offensive stocks or adequate defensive
equipment were lacking (or perceived to be) when the question "might
we use gas?" arose. The Army recognized the utility of chemical weapons, yet between the financial crunch of the Third Reich's rearmament
period and wartime scarcity, chemical equipment was cut back. This
occurred despite the consensus in the interwar period that Germany
lagged behind its adversaries in chemical might. Realism cannot explain this lack of attention when chemical weapons offered significant
relative advantage. Chemical weapons were discontinued because gas
warfare was not compatible with the mobile war, integral to German
military thought, that worked so well in Poland and on which Germany would again rely in the invasions of France and the Soviet Union.
Therefore, resources were shifted to favor such means of warfare as
tanks and planes that were compatible with the creed of mobility. As
Brown has aptly summarized, "Chemical warfare readiness starved
from lack of priority."[203]

Finally, the inadvertent incidents involving chemical weapons never
led to escalation because the German military had no interest in chemical warfare. They allowed chemical accidents to remain accidents. Germany simply was unwilling to take advantage of the opportunities for
escalation that these incidents provided.

THE SILENCE OF SOVIET CHEMICAL WARFARE

John F. Kennedy once remarked that no nation in the history of
battle has ever suffered more than the Soviet Union did during World
War II. At least twenty million lost their lives and many more their
homes. A third of the nation's territory was ravaged, and two-thirds
of its industrial base was destroyed.[204] The city of Leningrad was be-
sieged for "900 days" and lost ten times as many as the atomic bomb
killed in Hiroshima.[205] The Russian-German war has often been described as one of the bloodiest and most barbaric conflicts in history.
Stalin claimed the Germans had the morality of animals and should

[203] Brown, *Chemical Warfare*, p. 239.
[204] John F. Kennedy's speech at American University, 10 June 1963, as quoted in Alexander Werth, *Russia at War, 1941–1945* (New York: Carroll & Graf, 1964), p. xi.
[205] There were 78,000 fatalities at Hiroshima. See Harrison E. Salisbury, *The 900 Days:
The Siege of Leningrad* (New York: Harper & Row, 1969), p. 513.

be destroyed to the last man.[206] When the Germans invaded, they slaughtered soldiers and civilians alike and forced the Red Army back to the very outskirts of Moscow. Yet during that year and the entire course of the war, the Soviets never used readily available and potent chemical weapons. Why did they show restraint?

The analysis of Soviet chemical warfare policy must be set apart from the case studies above. For other countries there is documentary evidence available on both the underlying structural conditions and the actual path of preferences. Unfortunately, however, there are few primary materials on the calculations of the Soviet government on use and restraint. Without access to documents on foreign policy aims, military plans and exercises, and some of the details of particular decisions, it is difficult to distinguish in any definitive manner the influence of different variables in shaping choices.[207] Some of these documents may exist, but even with the political changes in the former Soviet Union they are surfacing slowly, if at all. Although what follows is necessarily speculative, the history that is available deserves attention because of the inherent curiousness of Soviet behavior in World War II.

The three schools offer different predictions. Institutionalism anticipates escalation, given the somewhat shallow development of the chemical warfare norm. Realism's forecast is somewhat divided. On the one hand, the expected defensive value of chemical warfare and the dire situation of the Soviet Union in 1941 would suggest that escalation should have occurred. On the other hand, there are reasons to believe that the Soviets were lacking in certain material and readiness categories, and that this (perceived) deficiency added to an existing sense of technological disadvantage causing restraint. But if the latter is true (and I believe that Soviet disadvantage was more a perception than a reality), then realism cannot account for why these deficiencies occurred in areas of defensive chemical warfare (such as, gas discipline and the supply of masks) that should and could have been remedied, given the external threat. Finally, organizational culture expects both a shortfall in readiness and a policy of restraint. The Red Army's prewar

---

[206] An examination of the cruelty of the war is Omer Bartov's *Eastern Front, 1941–1945: German Troops and the Barbarisation of Warfare* (London: Macmillan, 1985). Werth, *Russia at War*, p. 246.

[207] The lack of internal documents in this case means that to some degree I inferred, national preferences from behavior. I have, however, come across quite a bit of data on Soviet chemical warfare in British, German, and American archives. In addition, the first comprehensive study on Soviet chemical weapons in World War II has recently been published. See Joachim Krause and Charles K. Mallory, *Chemical Weapons in Soviet Military Doctrine: Military and Historical Experience, 1915–1991* (Boulder, Colo.: Westview Press, 1992).

doctrine was dominated by offensive thought, yet chemical weapons are more effective in defense. Thus from a cultural perspective, use was unlikely. The facts available indicate that organizational culture was a central impetus for restraint, although realist considerations were also important.

The Conscience of Comrades

Marshal Sergei Akhromeyev, former chief of the Soviet General Staff, national security advisor to President Gorbachev, and a veteran of World War II, claimed that the Soviet Union showed restraint because it was committed to upholding the Geneva Protocol.[208] Did the norms and constraints represented by this agreement inhibit a country from an action that otherwise appeared to be in its interests? There is little in the historical record that conclusively refutes this idea and there is even evidence that is compatible with it. Nonetheless, aspects of Soviet peacetime and wartime behavior cast doubt on an institutionalist explanation of restraint.

In the interwar period, the Soviet Union was a latecomer to negotiations attempting to develop prohibitions on chemical warfare.[209] It sent no representatives to either the Washington Conference or the Conference on the International Trade in Arms, which resulted in the Geneva Protocol of 1925. In the talks related to chemical arms that followed, the Soviet Union consistently advocated that preparation for chemical warfare be outlawed both in peace and war. On 15 April 1928, the Soviets acceded to the provisions of the Geneva Protocol, but with reservations: the Red Army would only show restraint if enemy countries had also ratified the Protocol and neither they *nor their allies* used chemical weapons.[210]

There is at least a superficial link between the institutionalization of the no-first-use norm in the Geneva Protocol and Soviet chemical warfare preparations. The Soviet Union did accede to the Protocol and did note in many publications that it would adhere to the agreement. For example, this order was incorporated in the authoritative *Provisional Field Service Regulations* issued at the end of 1936. In fact, as early as 1927, before the Soviet Union had signed the Protocol, the Red Army's

---

[208] Interview with Marshal Sergei Akhromeyev, March 1990.

[209] Russia and later the Soviet Union played an active role in developing an institution of restraint in chemical warfare. In 1898 Tsar Nicholas II sponsored a meeting that became known as the Hague Peace Conference.

[210] SIPRI, *Chemical and Biological Warfare*, 4:63, 91, 115, 345–47.

infantry manual declared that chemical weapons would only be used in retaliation.[211] In a 1938 speech K. E. Voroshilov, commissar for defense, stated that Soviet chemical units were only for defense and the USSR would vigorously adhere to the Geneva Protocol.[212]

The effect of Soviet participation in the chemical warfare regime can be examined relative to its expectations, preparations, and wartime decisions on use. Starting with impact on expectations, it appears that the Geneva Protocol did not alter forecasts. Soviet officials anticipated the use of chemical weapons in the next war, if not in any military operation.[213] Ia. M. Fishman, the head of the Military-Chemical Administration, asserted that chemical warfare was likely because of weak international constraints, military effectiveness, and ideology. In the first instance, the Geneva Protocol was seen as an inadequate constraint on use because it did not affect peacetime preparations. If the production of chemical weapons could not be controlled, he considered it unlikely that the use of chemical weapons could be restrained. This was especially true because the decision to use chemical weapons would be judged by their effectiveness, not whether they were humane or not. In the Soviet view, these weapons were indeed effective, particularly when used with the element of surprise—a quality that made no-first-use pledges especially fragile. And one certainly could not expect capitalist countries to act humanely toward their class enemies.[214]

Red Army preparations also cast doubt on the effect of the Protocol on policy.[215] Soviet interest in the potential of chemical weapons

[211] See the forward to *Vremennyi polevoi ustav RKKA 1936* (Moscow: Gosudarstvennoe Voennoe Izdatel'stvo Narkomata Oborony Soiuza SSR, 1936). Krause and Mallory, *Chemical Weapons in Soviet Military Doctrine*, pp. 82–83.

[212] Speech by the People's Commissar for Defense, Marshal of the Soviet Union, Comrade K. E. Voroshilov on the twentieth anniversary of the RKKA (The Workers' and Peasants' Red Army) and Navy, as printed in *Voennaia mysl'* 3 (1938): esp. 13.

[213] See, for example, *Vremennoe nastavlenie po protivo-khimicheskoi oborone* (Moscow: Otdel Izdat' Narodnogo Kommisariata Oborony SSSR, 1936), p. 5; V. Denisov, "Khimicheskoe oruzhie vo vtoroi imperialisticheskoi voine," *Voennaia mysl'* 4 (1939): 140, 147; S. Azar'ev and N. Balashov, *Voenno-khimicheskoe delo* (Moscow: Gosudarstvennoe Voennoe Izdatel'stvo Narkomata Oborony Soiuza SSR, 1939), p. 5.

[214] Ia. M. Fishman, *Voenno-khimicheskoe delo* (Moscow: Gosudarstvennoe Izdatel'stvo, 1929), pp. 44–46; Khimicheskoe upravlenie Krasnoi Armii, *Voenno-khimicheskoe delo*, (Moscow: Voenizdat, 1940), pp. 3–4. I am indebted to Eugene Rumer for leading me to several of these Soviet sources and, in general, to the Library of Congress as a repository of interwar Soviet military writings.

[215] It may be that Soviet practice in the interwar period did not conform to international standards. Chemical shells were employed to suppress an uprising in the Caucasus in the 1920s. In the 1930s, mustard gas was allegedly sprayed by aircraft in actions against the rebellious Basmachi tribesman in Central Asia. The Red Army did not, however, use gas in its skirmishes with Japan and its war with Finland in the late 1930s.

changed little after signing the Geneva Protocol. In fact, the USSR stepped up its collaboration with the Germans in preparation for chemical warfare in the three years following the ratification of that agreement. Of course the Protocol did not prohibit countries from developing chemical weapons. Nonetheless, the Soviet chemical warfare program went beyond defensive or deterrent aims: significant research was undertaken in offensive chemical operations that was kept strictly secret.[216]

From an institutionalist perspective, Soviet restraint during the war is curious because there were grounds for disregarding the Geneva Protocol. In a broad sense, the German campaign in the East was particularly inhumane. The German soldiers were indoctrinated on both ideological and racist grounds to treat the Soviet enemy barbarously. First, communism was a special target of Hitler's hate. Second, Nazi propaganda spread the notion that Slavs were subhuman, and German soldiers did not treat the Russian folk gently.[217] And finally, Germany's ally Japan was actually using gas in China. This, of course, allowed the Soviets to use it too, given the conditions under which they had signed the Protocol.

Although Akhromeyev's claim cannot be dismissed, from the evidence available, the Geneva Protocol does not appear to be the key factor in Soviet decisions. In terms of expectations, preparations, and actions taken (and not taken), there is little to indicate that the Soviet Union was decisively constrained by international prohibitions on the use of gas. There is more reason to think that Soviet support of the norm in the first place and its subsequent restraint are more a product of forces described by realism and organizational culture.

Vulnerabilities and Advantages

Realism anticipates key elements of Soviet policy, but also raises several questions that it cannot answer. In the 1920s and 1930s, the USSR

---

[216] As Voroshilov also noted in his 1938 speech, "Chemical units will keep in step with other parts of the armed forces and work much and well and if any aggressive enemy takes it into his head to sprinkle our forces with chemical means, he will get a terrible chemical on his own head" (see note 212). But secret preparations cannot deter, and the Soviet's preparations were secret. See the literature on Soviet-German cooperation cited elsewhere and Krause and Mallory, *Chemical Weapons in Soviet Military Doctrine*, chap. 2. The Germans captured a secret Voroshilov Academy study that gave extensive attention to the offensive use of gas—a topic not emphasized in the open literature. Dozent Skorobogatin, *Die chemische Waffe in Kampf und Operation* (Moscow: Woroschilow-Akademie, 1941). See "Mitteilungen über Gaskriegsvorbereitungen im Ausland Nr. 13," from General der Nebeltruppe Ochsner to Oberkommando des Heeres, 6 November 1941, Series T-78, Roll 270, NA.

[217] See Bartov, *Eastern Front,* esp. chap. 3.

displayed a keen interest in chemical weapons. The likely source of this concern was the effectiveness of gas in World War I. More to the point, the Russians suffered significant losses from Germany's use of gas. The first attack on 31 May 1915 near Warsaw took the Russian Army completely by surprise—the result was some nine thousand casualties in thirty to forty minutes. Overall in World War I, a Soviet source indicates that the Russians suffered two to six times as many casualties as Germany, France, or Britain. The percentage of deaths per casualty was two to five times higher than in other armies. Russian forces had little gas protection equipment and chemical production capacity was underdeveloped and inadequate.[218] The experience of the Great War, along with exposure to Allied chemical weapons in the civil war, caused the Soviets to both appreciate, and fear chemical warfare. They considered poison gas a basic means of combat, but one in which they were at a technological disadvantage.[219]

The new Soviet Union did begin to pursue the development of chemical weapons more aggressively to compensate for its weakness. The mainstay of this effort was the covert military cooperation with Germany in the wake of the 1922 Treaty of Rapallo. Russia and Germany were the two outcasts of the post–World War I order and they formed a symbiotic alliance. The Soviets needed German military know-how, and Germany needed a place to secretly develop weapons forbidden by the Versailles treaty. From the beginning of this alliance, the USSR made the delivery of German chemical weapon technology the centerpiece of improved ties. The Germans and Soviets took up a range of collaborative activities in chemical warfare that lasted until 1933 when Hitler ordered his countrymen home. The Red Army continued on its own.[220]

[218] Leitenant Ostanenko, "Bol'she vnimanie khimicheskoi podgotovke," *Voennyi vestnik* 4 (April 1938). These figures roughly correspond to those in A. M. Prentiss, *Chemicals in War* (New York: McGraw-Hill, 1937). See Vladimir N. Ipatieff, *The Life of a Chemist* (Stanford: Stanford University Press, 1946), pp. 218–35. Denisov, "Khimicheskoe oruzhie," p. 139.

[219] Khimicheskoe upravlenie Krasnoi Armii, *Voenno-khimicheskoe delo*, p. 3, discusses the important role of technological innovations in the effectiveness of chemical weapons in World War I.

[220] The range of cooperation is detailed in Mueller, "German Preparations for Chemical Warfare," pp. 171–209. Cecil F. Melville, *The Russian Face of Germany: An Account of the Secret Military Relations between the German and Soviet-Russian Governments* (London: Wishart, 1932), pp. 110–13; Carsten, *Reichswehr and Politics* (Oxford: Clarendon, 1966). When the Germans began to pull out in 1931, the Red Army enlarged TOMKA for its own purposes. And even though Soviet-German relations were worsening dramatically, Marshal Mikhail Tuchachevskii, the chief of the Soviet General Staff, wanted to continue cooperation with the German Army on chemical warfare. John Erickson, *The Soviet High Command: A Military-Political History, 1918–1941* (London: St. Martin's, 1962), p. 344.

The Soviets also appreciated that chemical weapons presented a threat to unprepared citizens. To deal with this challenge, the civil-defense organization Dobrokhim was founded in 1924. Its purpose was to prepare the general populace for large-scale chemical warfare and also support development of the chemical industry. In 1927, Dobrokhim was incorporated into the larger Society for the Promotion of Aviation and Chemical Defense (Osoviakhim).[221] Osoviakhim's efforts were extensive. Soviet air-raid drills in the 1930s were some of the most comprehensive in the world. Osoviakhim was especially interested in having gas masks, a vast number of which had been distributed to city workers in the mid-thirties, accepted as a normal part of life.[222]

By the beginning of the war, outsiders considered the Soviet Union to have potent chemical warfare capabilities. Just before its invasion in 1941, Germany concluded that "theoretically gas could be the most meaningful of Russian means."[223] After the war, the German General Gunther Blumentritt, who took part in the invasion remarked that the Soviets were especially well prepared in chemical warfare, even though they did not use any of their chemical weapons.[224] Actual capabilities were probably less impressive than these comments would suggest, but they included both offensive and defensive capabilities for chemical warfare in winter and summer. Offensively, the Soviet Union had developed a variety of means for delivering gas.[225] Defensively, the Red

[221] This history is reviewed in William Odom, *The Soviet Volunteers: Modernization and Bureaucracy in Public Mass Organization* (Princeton: Princeton University Press, 1973), esp. chap. 4.

[222] Toward this end, many publicity events were staged. For example, in 1935, twenty men and women marched 745 miles in gas masks—from the Ukraine to Moscow. In 1939, the entire personnel of a machine tool plant worked an hour in masks. In 1940, doctors, nurses, and orderlies at one hospital wore gas masks for a part of each eight-hour shift for three days. Brochures were published describing games—including "tug-of-war" and "three-legged races"—to be played while wearing masks in order to encourage leisure activities and exercises in conditions of chemical warfare. See T. Komarevich and D. Gorbovskii, *Voenno-khimicheskie igryi* (Moscow: Izdanie TsS Soiuza OSOAVIAKHM SSSR, 1936); Ellsworth L. Raymond, "Soviet Preparation for Total War, 1925–1951" (Ph.D. diss., University of Michigan, 1951), pp. 252–53.

[223] This report also noted that actual employment would be problematic given the lack of organic gas troops. "Merkblatt über den Stand der Gaskriegsvorbereitungen in der UdSSR," 7 Juni 1941, RHD 30/5, BA-MA.

[224] B. H. Liddell Hart, *The Soviet Army* (London: Weiderfeld & Nicolson, 1956), p. 138.

[225] These were catalogued in great detail by a German chemical warfare specialist just after the war. See Col. Dr. Walter Hirsch, *Soviet BW and CW Preparations and Capabilities* (Plans, Training and Intelligence Division, U.S. Army Chemical Warfare Service, 1951), pp. 114–410. I am grateful to John Ellis van Courtland Moon for a copy of this document. For dispensing chemical agents, both toxic and nontoxic, there were bombs, high-altitude aerial sprayers, artillery and mortar shells, chemical tanks, and even automo-

Army equipment was well respected. At the beginning of the conflict, each soldier had a gas mask and cape, protective stockings, and a decontamination kit. Soldiers in chemical units had additional specialized equipment.[226] And although not a great deal is known about the Soviet supply and production of chemical agents, it seems clear that the USSR had *at least* matching capabilities.[227]

Given the above, the paradox (from a realist perspective) is, if the Soviet Union had such significant chemical warfare potential, why was it not used in the dark days of 1941? Although the surprise German invasion caught the Red Army asleep, the chemical troops were allegedly trained and ready at the time. In the first month of war, the units sent to the front had a full complement of chemical troops with all their supplies, but these were apparently kept in a central storehouse. Soviet leaders, however, opted for restraint and even prohibited the employment of smoke, fearing that the Germans might use it as a pretext to release gas.[228] In effect the Soviet leadership decreed that there would be no unwanted escalation in chemical warfare.

The paradox of the Red Army's restraint is further heightened by the existence of significant incentives to use gas. Employing persistent contaminating agents might have helped check the rapid German advance. After all, the Soviets had adopted a scorched-earth strategy

---

biles. Available were asphyxiating agents, such as phosgene and chlorpicrin; poisonous agents such as cyanogen chloride and hydrochloric acid; and various skin, eye, and nose irritants, including mustard gas. One type of air-delivered bomblet was thought to be able to produce a ground concentration of hydrogen cyanide dense enough to penetrate existing German respirators. Also see Colonel V. Pozdnyakov, "The Chemical Arm," in B. H. Liddell Hart, ed., *The Red Army* (New York: Harcourt, Brace, 1958), pp. 385–87.

[226] Hirsch, *Soviet BW and CW*, p. 510; SIPRI, *Chemical and Biological Warfare*, 1:287. There were of course problems with this equipment, as there was with the equipment of all countries. See Krause and Mallory, *Chemical Weapons in Soviet Military Doctrine*, pp. 62 and 90. Pozdnyakov, "Chemical Arm," p. 389.

[227] The Germans estimated that Soviet chemical agent output was at least 8,000 tons per month, which would have given the Soviet Union some of the largest stocks of any participant in the war. General Ochsner did not believe the Soviets lacked chemical weapons, even though the Germans captured very few. Like everything else, he concluded the Russians had either moved or destroyed them before retreating. Brown, *Chemical Warfare*, pp. 234–35. Hirsch, *Soviet BW and CW*, p. 17; Krause and Mallory, *Chemical Weapons in Soviet Military Doctrine*, pp. 37 ad 46; Ochsner, *History of German Chemical Warfare*, p. 20.

[228] Pozdnyakov, "Chemical Arm," p. 390. At least one commander on the ground asked for release of at least defensive means, but was turned down. See B. I. Petrov, "O strategicheskom razvertyvanii Krasnoi Armii nakanune voine," *Voenno-istoricheskii zhurnal* 12 (1991): 16. Lt. Gen. F. Manets, "Khimicheskaia slushba i khimicheskie voiska," *Voennyi vestnik* 48, no. 2 (1968). Pozdnyakov. "Chemical Arm," pp. 390–91. Krause and Mallory, *Chemical Weapons in Soviet Military Doctrine*, pp. 105 n. 75.

intended to deny any usable materials to the invading foe. Stalin declared, "In the occupied areas intolerable conditions must be created."[229] The Red Army certainly appreciated the impact of chemical weapons on mobil defensive operations. They were also well aware that the use of gas could inhibit a high-tempo offensive with stretched lines of communication. With the enemy driving through successive lines of defense toward the political nerve center of Moscow, the temptation to employ chemical weapons must have been great. General Ochsner, the head of the German Chemical Troops, reported after the war that the Germans were surprised that the Red Army had not resorted to the use of gas. Yet despite an improvised strategy of relying on a series of well-constructed defensive lines, the Soviets did not use gas even in dire situations such as the siege of Leningrad, the defense of the "Stalin Line," or during the large German offensive in the summer of 1942.[230]

Perhaps in the initial period of World War II, the apparent paradox of restraint can be resolved by realism itself. Colonel V. Pozdnyakov, who served in the Chemical Troops, recounted after the war that a calculus of relative (dis)advantage had indeed led to restraint. The Germans had overrun forward chemical supplies. More important, Red Army gas discipline was poor, particularly among the many fresh recruits that were hurried to the front. In the strategic retreats, troops discarded their gas masks and capes, drawing down supplies. And most important, German retaliatory action would have caused even more problems for the disorganized army. An intercepted Red Army order from 13 August 1941 directed a stepped-up effort to improve chemical readiness. It was primarily because of the Soviet problems with gas defense that the Germans did not expect any gas attacks from the USSR.[231]

---

[229] Werth, *Russia at War*, p. 164.

[230] *Vremennyi polevoi ustav*, pp. 141, 153–54; Ochsner, *History of German Chemical Warfare*, p. 20. A Soviet prisoner claimed that an order had been issued on 14 May 1942 that the Red Army should employ poison agents if the Germans made a breakthrough at Stalingrad and advanced 200 kilometers past the Volga. "Heerestechnische Auslandsmitteilungen: 10. Heft," 1 Oktober 1943, RH2/2540, BA-MA. Prisoner reports are notoriously unreliable, and there is no confirmation that such an order was actually given. It is also questionable whether it would have been carried out had the Germans successfully made the described advances.

[231] Pozdnyakov, "Chemical Arm," p. 391. This report is corroborated by German intelligence. See "Mitteilungen über Gaskriegsvorbereitungen im Ausland Nr. 10," from General der Nebeltruppe to Oberkommando des Heeres, 12 August 1941, RH11IV/v. 17, BA-MA. For example, see "Mitteilungen über Gaskriegsvorbereitungen im Ausland Nr. 9," from General der Nebeltruppe to Oberkommando des Heeres, 23 July 1941, Series T-

This explanation seems plausible for the first weeks of war, but it makes less sense later when the Red Army had regrouped, and the country had time to ready itself for chemical warfare.[232] The use of chemicals at that point would have complemented Soviet defense efforts. Furthermore, it seems unlikely that the Soviet military-political leadership was inhibited by the fear of civilian chemical casualties.[233] The Soviet populace had been prepared for chemical warfare and was known for tolerating difficult circumstances.

Soviet restraint in this case was undoubtedly shaped by a perceived inferiority in chemical weapons, the lack of chemical equipment, and poor discipline in the training of Soviet troops for chemical warfare. All of the drawbacks put the Soviet Union at a disadvantage and as realism would expect, restraint obtained. Still the questions remains, Why did these perceptions and conditions occur? Whether the Soviet Union was actually significantly inferior in chemical weapons, for example, is debatable.[234] And if the USSR was vulnerable, it should have made every effort to have defensive capabilities on hand and to train its soldiers adequately in their use. Where were the civilians that would intervene and correct the situation, as British leaders allegedly did in the case of Britain's air defense? But no one did, an outcome compatible with organizational culture but not realism.

The Monolithic Red Army

A prima facie case can be made that organizational culture should have mattered in Soviet decisions. Perhaps more than those of any other country, the armed forces of the USSR were developed around a centralized and official body of assumptions, ideas, and beliefs. This

---

78, Roll 270, NA; memorandum, General der Nebeltruppe to Oberkommando des Heeres, 10 November 1941, Series T-78, Roll 573, NA.

[232] Another factor that might have inhibited the Soviets from first use was the desire of Britain and the United States for restraint. The evidence, however, suggests that had Stalin wanted to claim German first use as an excuse for escalation, he could have done so with Churchill's support. See Hinsley, *British Intelligence in the Second World War*, 2:116–20.

[233] After all, in the interwar years, the Red Army had conducted gas exercises in areas where civilians were located! Mueller, "German Preparations for Chemical Warfare," pp. 177–178.

[234] For example, the Germans also had significant problems with their defensive equipment and weaknesses in the discipline of the troops in chemical warfare. And although Germany may have been more technically advanced, the Soviets had poison agents (phosgene oxime) and means of delivery (spraying from aircraft) that the Germans were not prepared to defend against. See Brown, *Chemical Warfare*, p. 235 n. 113; Krause and Mallory, *Chemical Weapons in Soviet Military Doctrine*, pp. 98–101.

unified doctrine played a key role in the development of Soviet chemical warfare capabilities in peacetime and in the decisions it made during the war.

In the early 1920s, following the consolidation of Soviet power in Russia, controversy broke out concerning the future development of the Red Army. A central point of debate was the desirability of a unified doctrine to guide the evolution of the military. On one side the revolutionary Leon Trotsky and the military theorist Alexander Svechin argued against any doctrinaire approach to military affairs. Such rigidity, they contended, would be harmful because situation not doctrine should dictate action, and the Army must be flexible enough to respond as needed. Trotsky cogently summarized his view: "The only doctrine for us should be to keep alert and keep our eyes open."[235]

At the head of the opposite camp was Mikhail Frunze, a Red Army general. He advocated a unified doctrine that would change the military into a monolithic entity, cemented by a dominant political outlook and a unity of views on military issues. Part of Frunze's belief concerned the forms of warfare that should be incorporated in doctrine. Based on his civil war experience, Frunze believed that mobile warfare, particularly the offensive, was the superior mode of combat and that positional defensive fighting should be thrown on the "dust-heap." The justification was not only military but also political. Maneuver better reflected the revolutionary spirit and energy.[236]

The victor in this debate was Frunze. Not only did a monolithic unified doctrine dominate Soviet national security thinking in the mid-1920s, but over the next decade, Frunze's ideas on maneuver and the offensive received even greater emphasis. One of the leaders in this evolution was Mikhail Tukhachevskii, the chief of the Red Army staff from 1926 to 1928 and one of the drafters of the *Field Service Regulations*, which represented a codification of Soviet views on warfare. Tukhachevskii was an unabashed promoter of mobile warfare and the offensive. Not only did he believe that the civil war had proved the offense militarily superior, but without it, the USSR could hardly hope for the overthrow of bourgeois nations. Preference for the offense became Red Army doctrine. The main aim of military operations was the annihilation of the enemy. This could only be achieved by a "decisive offensive on the main line of advance."[237] The Soviet air force, which had the

[235] D. Fedotoff White, *The Growth of the Red Army* (Princeton: Princeton University Press, 1944), pp. 160–63; Erickson, *Soviet High Command*, chap. 5.

[236] White, *Growth of the Red Army*, pp. 169–70; J. M. Mackintosh, "The Red Army, 1920–1936," in Liddell Hart, *Red Army*, pp. 52–53.

[237] Erickson, *Soviet High Command*, pp. 308–9. *Vremennyi polevoi ustav*, pp. 9–10.

main responsibility for offensive chemical warfare, was little more than an adjunct to the ground forces. Its chief mission was to support the offensive mobile land campaign.[238]

Not surprisingly, the emphasis on offense and maneuver led to developmental priorities on weapons and operations that supported these themes. The importance of defense, even positional defense, was acknowledged, but slighted.[239] As John Erickson notes (citing a Soviet general), the dogma of the offensive was widespread and inhibited defensive planning.[240] Capabilities and training in defense were also weak. This tendency in Red Army culture is relevant for chemical warfare because poison agents were largely associated with defensive operations. The USSR appears to have attempted to accommodate chemical warfare to its doctrine of mobility but did not effectively do so, despite the arguments of proponents.[241]

For example, the small community within the Army responsible for

[238] As in Germany, attention was given to long-range independent missions, but strategic bombing was eclipsed by an army support role as the central approach to air warfare. On Soviet thinking on air warfare, see Erickson, *Soviet High Command*, pp. 382–83; Raymond L. Garthoff, *Soviet Military Doctrine* (Glencoe, Ill.: Free Press, 1953), pp. 325–50; and Kenneth Whiting, *Soviet Air Power* (Boulder, Colo.: Westview Press, 1986), pp. 6–36. On the role of air power in chemical warfare, see Hirsch, *Soviet BW and CW*, p. 202; Ia. Zhigur, *Khimicheskoe oruzhie v sovremennoi voine* (Moscow: Gosudarstvennoe Voennoe Izdatel'stvo Narkomata Oborony SSSR, 1936), pp. 76–77.

[239] With the purge of Tukhachevskii and the experience of the Spanish civil war there was greater interest in defense and positional warfare in 1938 and 1939, but no significant changes were made in terms of developing defensives capabilities and skills. By 1940 attention had more openly returned to deep operations and the offensive. See, for example, G. S. Isserson's *Novye formy bor'by* (Moscow: Voennoe Izdatel'stvo Narodnogo Komissariata Oborony Soiuza SSR, 1940), pp. 64–75. In general, the Army in this period was in disarray because of Stalin's purges of the officer corps. For an overview, see Condoleeza Rice, "The Making of Soviet Strategy," in Peter Paret, ed., *Makers of Modern Strategy* (Princeton: Princeton University Press, 1986), pp. 668–72.

[240] Erickson, *Soviet High Command*, p. 582, also see p. 576. Of course, as Erickson, pp. 406 and 576, notes, defense was not altogether neglected. For example, work was initiated on the "Stalin Line"—a positional-defense scheme. In addition, there may have been some variations in attention given to offense and defense in the few years just before the war; however, offense remained dominant. See Beth M. Gerard, "Mistakes in Force Structure and Strategy on the Eve of the Great Patriotic War," *Journal of Soviet Military Studies* 4 (September 1991): 471–86.

[241] For example, the 1936 *Field Regulations* (*Vremennyi polevoi ustav*) discuss chemical warfare primarily within the context of defensive operations. Also see Krause and Mallory, *Chemical Weapons in Soviet Military Doctrine*, pp. 79–82. The Soviet air force was also poorly prepared. This is evident from planning documents on a series of chemical exercises held at the Klichev airfield in 1941. See "Prikaz voenno-vozdushnym silam zapadnogo osobogo voennogo okruga," iiunia 1941, from Komanduiuschii VVS ZAPOVO General-Major Aviatsii I. Konets and Zam. Nach. Shtaba VVS ZAPOVO Polkovnik Taranenko, found in RW5/v. 346, BA-MA.

chemical warfare was a particularly strong advocate of the poison cloud. Although history will not remember him like Dönitz or Trenchard, the Soviet chemical troops also had an enthusiastic, eager leader who promoted their cause. Ia. M. Fishman became the head of the Military Chemical Army Administration when it was formed in Moscow in 1924. General von Blomberg, head of the German Truppenamt, described him as having "burning energy and a head full of ideas" concerning how to build a chemical warfare arm in the Red Army.[242] Fishman wrote in the introduction of his book published in the late 1920s that even after exaggerations of chemical warfare potential had been discounted, "the real military significance of the chemical army is so great that . . . a very impressive field is left."[243] The chemical specialists of the Red Army envisioned different uses for their weapon, depending on the situation. For example, on the defensive, areas could be sprayed with toxic substances to delay and block the enemy's advance and inflict casualties. On the offensive, chemicals could be utilized for assaults on artillery positions, for breaking through the front edge of fortified positions, or for causing casualties and disorder among retreating troop. Chemical weapons were considered valuable because of their capacity to contaminate and inflict mass casualties over an extensive area suddenly, persistently, and cheaply.[244]

Despite these developments and despite Fishman's ardent advocacy, chemical weapons remained the preserve of a minor subculture within the Red Army's overall offense-dominated society. Organizationally, chemical units were kept separate from the main-line forces, and one of the reasons the Germans did not expect escalation from the Red Army was this lack of organic chemical troops.[245] As with Germany's blitzkrieg, chemical weapons presented special problems for the mobile offensive which the Soviets envisioned. In particular, they bogged down the supply lines, the efficiency of which are crucial to rapid advance. The incompatibility of chemical weapons with the dominant

[242] Erickson, *Soviet High Command*, p. 266; Pozdnyakov, "Chemical Arm," p. 384. Ipatieff described Fishman in unfavorable terms as a "miniature chemical Napoleon." Ipatieff, *Life of a Chemist*, p. 419.

[243] Fishman, *Voenno-khimicheskoe delo*, p. 10.

[244] Ibid., p. 51; *Vremennyi polevoi ustav*, 39–44, 85, 122, 192; Pozdnyakov, "Chemical Arm," pp. 387–89.

[245] By 1935 the Soviet Union had three independent chemical warfare regiments on the Western front and eleven independent battalions elsewhere. By 1939, the chemical troops were double what they had been five years earlier. Each chemical depot also had a complement of planes for chemical warfare by 1941–42 with each squadron being assigned three day-bombers suited for chemical attacks. Pozdnyakov, "Chemical Arm," p. 384; Erickson, *Soviet High Command*, pp. 389 and 510; Hirsch, *Soviet BW and CW*, p. 380.

offensive culture had the result of relegating the chemical troops to second-class status. With the offensive as the touchstone of the Soviet way of war, chemical warfare was slighted and readiness in that area was relatively neglected. The commissar for defense issued an order just a few months before Germany's invasion in June of 1941 that because the undervaluation and weak knowledge of chemical warfare in the Red Army, training in that area had to be improved. In August 1941, Stalin personally intervened in an attempt to correct the status of the chemical troops and improve the discipline related to chemical warfare in the Red Army. But these problems remained for at least several more years.[246]

Perhaps more puzzling than the lack of intentional escalation is the absence of an inadvertent spiral of chemical warfare. The Soviets, after all, believed that a surprise attack on a massive scale was the most effective way to wage chemical warfare. They also believed that early detection of enemy preparations and a response that would minimize such use was desirable. This, of course, suggested a preference for preemptive strikes if an enemy chemical attack was suspected.[247] At several points in the war the USSR believed Germany escalation was imminent.[248] Nonetheless, the Soviet and German accidents that did occur were not allowed to escalate. Despite the expectations of security dilemma, traditional organization theory, and friction logic, restraint

---

[246] This order was intercepted by the Germans. "Befehl des Volkskommissarsfür die Verteidigung der Sowjetunion, Nr. 024, 18 Januar 1941," von Der Stellvertr. d. Volkskommissars f.d. Marschall d. Sowjetunon S. Budennyi, RW5/v. 346, BA-MA. *Vremennyi polevoi ustav*, pp. 153–54; Krause and Mallory, *Chemical Weapons in Soviet Military Doctrine*, p. 79–80. A. Babushkin, "Sovershenstvovanie khimicheskoi sluzhby v gody voiny," *Voenno-istoricheskii zhurnal* 7 (1978): 88, 90. In the Soviet case, political factors may have contributed to organizational tendency in limiting chemical readiness. Stalin's purges decimated the Soviet officer ranks, and the leader of the chemical troops, Fishman, was apparently executed.

[247] Pointing to World War I and Ethiopia, the secret study captured by the Germans emphasized the effectiveness of the surprise use of gas on a massive scale. See "Mitteilungen über Gaskriegsvorbereitungen im Ausland Nr. 13," from General der Nebeltruppe Ochsner to Oberkommando des Heeres, 6 November 1941, Series T-78, Roll 270, NA. The importance of the massive concentrated use of chemical warfare is also evident in the open literature. See A. Vol'pe, "Venezapnost'" *Voennaia mysl'* 3 (1937): 20; Khimicheskoe upravlenie Krasnoi Armii, *Voenno-khimicheskoe delo*, p. 4. *Vremennyi polevoi ustav*, pp. 40–42.

[248] For example, before the battle of Kursk, a notice signed by Stalin and Vasilevskii (Red Army chief of staff) warned of increasing German chemical readiness. A. Babushkin, "Sovershenstvovanie khimicheskoi slushby," p. 91. Cipher telegram from Military Mission Moscow to the War Office, 25 February 1943, WO 193/723.

endured, probably because, as in other cases, military culture encouraged suppression of any escalatory tendencies.

Conclusion: Culture and Neglect

Why did the Soviet Union show restraint in the use of chemical weapons suited to its cause? Because of the paucity of our knowledge, we can only speculate. First, the institutionalist viewpoint does find some support in that the USSR backed the Protocol and repeated its adherence to the agreement in its internal procedures. But there are grounds to believe that it was not international prohibitions that led to restraint. The USSR had other reasons related to perceived inferiority and organizational bias to support the Protocol. Furthermore, it is clear that the antigas norm had little impact on Soviet expectations and preparations. The Soviets expected gas to be used and they sought ways to use it effectively. Red Army efforts to develop chemical weapons tapered off, however, when it became clear that chemical warfare would not fit the culturally dominant doctrine of the mobile offensive.

Realist factors play a central role. When the Germans invaded, the Red Army was caught unprepared for chemical warfare, both in terms of offense and defense. Given the shock to the armed forces and the country that the German invasion produced, Soviet leaders likely saw little leverage in initiating chemical use. The relative power logic of realism provides a convincing explanation for this initial restraint in the first weeks of war.

Realism does not explain why the Soviet Union was caught so badly prepared and why restraint was maintained once the situation had stabilized and the USSR was able to mount a defense. In the first instance we should have seen more effective efforts to reduce chemical vulnerability, especially in manageable areas such as antigas discipline. And when the shock of the German invasion had worn off and the Red Army established a series of defensive lines, chemical warfare would have given the Soviets the advantage by slowing the Wehrmacht offensive. But it is likely that the Red Army was neither psychologically nor perhaps physically prepared to turn to chemical warfare. The Soviet military was weaned on a doctrine of maneuver and offense. This dominant war-fighting outlook saw poison agents as primarily a defensive tool. Accordingly, like defensive operations as a whole, chemical warfare was overlooked and underdeveloped in preparations for war and the Red Army was simply not ready to risk employing chemical weapons despite the incentives to do so.

[5]

Explaining Cooperation

Restraint in the use of force in World War II was a form of collusion. In some areas it endured, in others it failed. In this chapter I attempt to account for this variation in cooperation "under fire." First, I summarize the empirical findings and relative explanatory value of the three perspectives. I argue that organizational culture provides the best explanation for the variation in cooperation in World War II, but also recognize the influence of realist and institutionalist factors. This discussion suggests the explanatory potential of a conceptual synthesis among the three schools, and I offer an outline of such an approach. Finally, I consider the implications of the argument for the study of international relations.

AN EXPLANATION

In a head-to-head test with realism and institutionalism, two of the dominant schools of thought in the field of international relations, organizational culture gives a superior account of international cooperation in the three specific means of warfare in World War II. The evidence for this judgment can be summarized in the tables displayed in Figure 1. Each table shows the prediction of each school (either "use" or "restraint") for each case on the horizontal axis and the outcome (use or restraint) on the vertical axis.

The placement of cases in the boxes follows from the propositions and outcomes. For realism, if a country's position indicated that relative advantage could be gained from escalation, it is in the "use" category. If the situation was one of disadvantage, the case is placed in the "restraint" category. The table for institutionalism is somewhat different from the other two in that the horizontal axis, "prediction," is not dichotomous. What varies here is not the fact but the *degree* of institutionalization. Those cases where institutions of nonuse were most developed (in terms of specificity, durability, concordance) are placed closer to "restraint" and those less-developed are near the "use" pole. For organizational culture, where the military's way of war did *not* favor the means under consideration, "restraint" is the chosen category. "Use" was picked if the opposite was true. Outcome for all three approaches refers to the preferences of the country in that means. If the preferred policy was escalation, the placement is under "use," otherwise it falls under "restraint." As noted in Chapter 1, with the exception of cases of reciprocity and sometimes inadvertence, the actions states took mirrored their preferences.[1]

To the extent a particular approach provides a good account of decisions, the cases will line up in boxes (1) and (3). This implies that where an approach would lead us to expect escalation, escalation occurs. And where it predicts restraint, restraint occurs. As even a quick glance at the tables indicates, organizational culture renders a strong account of restraint. Before examining this relationship, let us first review realism and institutionalism.

Realism

Realism does a poor job of explaining the events of the Second World War. As Figure 1 indicates, there is little congruence between prediction and outcome, which is supported by the details of the case studies. In general, where realism should work, it often does not.

For example, in many situations in which escalation promised relative advantage, states preferred restraint. Germany defeated France and could have launched a strategic bombing campaign at Britain's civilians, but did not. The United Kingdom recognized it had superiority in chemical weapons in 1944, but did not escalate. Concepts central to realism such as "military necessity" or "strategic rationality" fail to describe the criteria by which states often made decisions. Despite the apparent military logic of a situation, states sometimes acted in a contrary fashion because of the imprint of organizational culture. Britain had a valuable strategic opportunity to put its underused sub-

---

[1] Thus although Britain eventually used submarine warfare and Germany unrestricted bombing, they did not initiate that use and therefore those cases fall under "restraint." And unintentional incidents, such as Germany's sinking of the *Athenia* or its bombing of London, are not considered "use."

Figure 1. Predictions versus outcomes in World War II

Realism

		Prediction Use	Prediction Restraint
Outcome	Use	(1) USW	(2) BSB GSW
	Restraint	(4) GSB BCW GCW	(3) BSW SCW

Institutionalism

		Prediction Use	Prediction Restraint
Outcome	Use	(1) BSB	(2) USW GSW
	Restraint	(4) GSB BCW SCW GCW	(3) BSW

Organizational Culture

		Prediction Use	Prediction Restraint
Outcome	Use	(1) GSW BSB	(2) USW
	Restraint	(4)	(3) GCW BSW GSB SCW BCW

Cases: BSB = British Strategic Bombing; GSB = German Strategic Bombing; USW = U.S. Submarine Warfare; GSW = German Submarine Warfare; BSW = British Submarine Warfare; GCW = German Chemical Warfare; SCW = Soviet Chemical Warfare; BCW = British Chemical Warfare.

marine force to work in 1939–40. Unrestricted British submarine warfare could have impeded Germany's crucial iron-ore imports from Norway and Sweden, the Nazi invasion of Norway, and Italy's campaign in Africa. But British naval culture, driven by its battleship mentality, did not appreciate the contribution of the submarine, particularly in an antitrade role. Thus when calculations on the desirability of unrestricted submarine warfare were made, restraint was only belatedly challenged because the organizational culture of the Royal Navy did not value the submarine. Organizational culture in effect governed how strategic costs and benefits were estimated.

Indeed, realism notwithstanding, in many situations in which escalation threatened relative disadvantage, states opted for escalation anyway. This was the case in British strategic-bombing policy in 1940. Even before the beginning of the war, Britain had decided on a strict policy of limited bombing for reasons very dear to realist theory. The RAF was inferior in airpower to the Luftwaffe and Britain was more vulnerable to city bombing than Germany. Yet in the spring of 1940, Britain opted for escalation. In this situation, organizational culture virtually determined outcomes because it led to the serious development of *only one option*. Leaders were caught in an "option funnel" where their number of choices was narrowed to one plan. Thus, during the Battle of France, although most British leaders wanted the RAF to be used in close support of the Army (and had little faith that strategic bombing could stop the Blitzkrieg), the RAF was allowed to start strategic bombing anyway because it could do nothing else.

Perhaps most puzzling for realism, in some situations nations suffered defeat without ever breaking restraints. The Nazi state was vanquished without ever using its huge chemical arsenal. The Soviet Union faced a similar fate, yet resisted any temptation to turn to the poison cloud. Only Britain in 1940 appeared ready to resort to chemical weapons to avoid defeat, but whether the United Kingdom would have actually taken the first step is debatable.

What realism inaccurately describes in these cases is why certain considerations were emphasized over others. Realism is essentially about how state aims are influenced by international power conditions. When the calculations of nations do not match those conditions, some other variable is likely at work. And it is that factor (primarily organizational culture here)—not realism—that better explains the actual variance in outcomes. In World War II the preferences and choices of states did not correspond to or change with what realism would expect, given the situation. Perceptions, preparations, and actions often deviated from strategic rationality regardless of the adequacy of information and the nonprohibitive costs of adaptation.

The argument here, however, should not be taken as a repudiation of realism. In fact, the variables associated with realism do matter to the extent that actors cannot and do not ignore all aspects of relative power. Neither states nor organizations are blind to extreme material asymmetries. As I discuss later, organizational cultures can only ignore external circumstance within limits. Beyond those limits culture will most likely adapt. In terms of decisions on restraint, extreme asymmetries in power may also be crucial. For example, consider how events might have been different had one of the sides been unable to retaliate. Germany, for example, would surely have used poison gas if the Allies hadn't had chemical weapons of their own. Likewise, Churchill might not have been thwarted in his desire to initiate chemical warfare if Germany had not been able to respond.[2] Even though states were not particularly sensitive to balances of power when choosing restraint, a *minimum* retaliatory potential may be necessary to maintain limitations in wars where state survival is at stake.[3] In sum, external power considerations do matter, but they are not as powerful a determinant of state desires and choices—even in war—as is generally considered in international relations theory.

Institutionalism

Like realism, institutionalism does not provide a satisfying account of restraint in World War II. The main issue from this perspective is whether the degree of institutionalization affects actors' calculations and preferences. In those areas where institutions of nonuse are most developed, we should expect restraint (or the slowest escalation). Conversely, in those areas where institutions are thinly developed, escalation is more likely. As Figure 1 indicates, however, institutional effect on outcomes was not decisive, even if it is apparent at times in the course of state decision making. For example, in submarine warfare where the institution of restraint was most robust in terms of durability, concordance, and specificity, escalation occurred first. Yet in chemical warfare, where the institution was less developed, restraint obtained throughout the conflict.

---

[2] Even military authorities, regardless of cultural disposition, may be more likely to favor use if the other side cannot retaliate. This knowledge may help explain why "secret" weapons such as chemical warfare and aerial bombing in World War I and atomic bombs and missiles in World War II were used despite their "newness" or potential discord with organizational culture.

[3] In World War II, however, the survival of the state was threatened. When survival is clearly not threatened, this dynamic may be less influential and either norms or culture more determinant. For example, the United States did not use nuclear weapons against Viet Nam; Britain did not use them against Argentina in the Falklands.

The weaker influence of international institutions—relative to the variables associated with realism and organizational culture—is confirmed in the details of decision making of individual states. In most instances, the principles of the institutions played a relatively minor role in both the preparations for war and choices made in the heat of battle. The norms led to official, but superficial, changes in the internal procedures (specifically, the military regulations) of nations and had little or no effect on what military and political leaders expected regarding the possibility of restraint. In short, regardless of the norms, they generally anticipated that all weapons would be employed in a major conflict.

Although institutionalism cannot explain the variance in cooperation in World War II, there is evidence that norms of restraint did figure in the calculations of states. Most apparent, international principles affected the expectations of states regarding the reactions of other parties. The different rules of warfare set guidelines for what was considered acceptable behavior. And states did believe that unacceptable behavior could affect their position—either in terms of support from other countries or sometimes domestic patronage. Deviations from such norms could incur penalties. Leaders worried about what costs— such as the withdrawal of another country's assistance or the provocation of animosity—might have to be paid for transgressing principles of restraint. Germany, for example, fretted that its unrestricted submarine warfare would antagonize Britain or the United States. Britain pondered how unrestricted bombing or the use of chemical weapons would affect its support in America.

Ultimately, however, these concerns did not change the ordering of preferences, but they did sometimes lead to delays or confusion in policy implementation. Countries searched for pretexts and justifications to escalate. There was a perceived need to be seen responding to, instead of initiating, stigmatized types of force. Germany delayed the order for unrestricted submarine warfare for a few days to wait for a more diplomatically opportune time to violate the London Protocol. Britain worried that its unrestricted strategic bombing campaign would alienate neutral countries and devised schemes to blame escalation on the enemy in order to mitigate political damage. States transgressed international norms based on perceived self-interest, yet acknowledged the influence of institutions on their own and other states' calculations in the timing and implementation of their choices.

Perhaps most important, institutionalism directs our attention to the possibility that international norms are a necessary condition of limited warfare. After all, submarine warfare, strategic bombing, and chemical warfare were only considered as candidates for restraint because each was related to an institution of limitation. The innate inhumanity of a weapon has little to do with its restriction. States hardly blinked over blowing people to bits with high-explosive artillery shells or burning them to death with flamethrowers. And was it really less moral to bomb London than to starve Leningrad? The number of casualties suffered and the conditions endured in Leningrad suggests not. What set submarines, strategic bombing, and chemical weapons apart was not some objective measure of inhumanity but rather recognized norms that dictated boundaries of acceptable use.

Organizational Culture

The organizational-culture approach furnishes a strong explanation for differences in restraint in submarine warfare, strategic bombing, and chemical warfare. The distribution of cases primarily in boxes (1) and (3) in the Organizational-Culture table in Figure 1 indicates a powerfully counterintuitive proposition: subnational forces were largely able to determine state preferences, choices and international outcomes. When culture favored use, states tended to desire and pursue escalation. And when culture was biased against use, states tended to prefer and exercise restraint. The impact of culture is seen both in intentional national calculations and the unintentional realm of accidents and inadvertence.

Culture's causal force can be distinguished in the intentional calculations that states make in three areas: perception and learning, the development of plans, and the process of choice. First, how states interpreted new situations and learned from their experiences was a function of organizational beliefs and customs. Military services use peacetime maneuvers and the lessons of war to judge whether their plans are suited to the strategic challenges they face. But in the interwar period it is evident that these exercises and experiences were hardly fair tests or objective evaluations—they were, rather, the product of biases generated by culture. A difference in culture had much to do with why the Royal Navy exaggerated the effectiveness of asdic, but Dönitz dismissed it as impotent. The German and British air forces drew opposite conclusions—which matched their different philosophies of airpower—from the experience of the war in Spain.[4] And in

---

[4] Organizational culture here is largely seen as a domestic-level trait. Sometimes, of course, militaries learn from one another in the sense that they might emulate methods of another country. Such a process, however, is bounded by the conditions that inhibit and provoke cultural adaptation.

World War II, many problems were discovered with those modes of warfare inconsistent with a military's preferences (for example, chemical warfare and blitzkrieg), whereas those modes of warfare consistent with a military's preferences (such as strategic bombing and the RAF) were interpreted as effective, despite actual results. These distortions were not the product of a general human cognitive tendency to overestimate the enemy's capabilities. Rather, distortion followed culture, either exaggerating or underestimating the situation, depending on the fit with dominant organizational beliefs. Culture shaped the worldview of organizational actors, which led them to see events in a particular way—one that did not give equal weight to all the information that was readily available.

Second, culture also determined the repertoire of responses that states had to deal with their environments. The preparations militaries made in peacetime had a decisive impact on the choices states made in war. The weapons, plans, and skills developed often decided what national leaders would do even before they considered a situation. Better gas discipline would have made a chemical defense more attractive to the Red Army in 1941–42, but without it initiation seemed irrational. Germany simply did not have its forces ready in time to use gas against the D-day invasion, despite the effectiveness of chemical weapons in such situations. Finally, the United States was able to shift from a battleship to an antitrade submarine (and aircraft carrier) strategy, only with difficulty and only because the same underwater boat developed to fit the battleship culture also happened to be well-suited to attacking enemy merchant vessels.

Finally, organizational culture even affected policy choice. There is no doubt that in each of the countries examined, civilian leaders had the final say on the use of force. But in several instances—notably Hitler's desire for restraint in submarine warfare in 1939 and Churchill's push for escalation in chemical warfare in 1944—state policy conformed to the cultural preferences of military services and contradicted the desires of top political authorities.

Organizational culture, in effect, shaped national preferences. Where national preferences matched those of organizational culture, culture helped to reinforce those desires. Where organizational predilection conflicted with state aims, the influence of internal bureaucracies over time led to change in national preferences in accordance with military culture.

Organizational culture shapes accidents and inadvertence by determining which accidents are likely and whether such accidents lead to escalation or are contained. This influence defies prominent theories.

For example, traditional organization theory and Clausewitz's friction concept both predict that accidents will be equally likely across means of warfare. Yet in World War II, the military routines related to different means did not have equal effect on accidents and escalation Although many incidents were not predictable, some seemed less random than others. Is it an accident when a well-dressed person is mugged while walking through a high-crime area at night? Likewise, certain types of accidents are inherently more likely because of organizational beliefs.

The contrast between German and British submarine actions indicates the causal influence of culture on accidents. In Germany, where anticommerce submarine warfare was central to culture, the first German accident of the war was the sinking of an unarmed British passenger liner, the *Athenia*. In Britain, where submarines were seen as mere adjuncts to the war fleet that could be used in hunting U-boats, the first British underwater accident was the sinking by a Royal Navy submarine of one of its own boats. What did *not* happen may be as indicative as what did. When a British submarine found itself in a situation similar to that of the *Athenia* incident, instead of sinking the German liner *Bremen* (which was actually a legitimate target because it was carrying troops), it delayed to heed the London Protocol and was then chased off by a Luftwaffe plane.

Even more important, organizational culture often determined which accidents would lead to escalation. The security-dilemma concept, for example, implies that certain situations will produce fears of exploitation and unintended escalation spirals. Yet what we have seen is that the consequences of accidents are more a product of warfighting culture than the degree of anarchy or insecurity. Accidents in a mode of warfare favored by a military service tend to lead to a spiral of escalation with each side assuming the worst of the other and demanding retaliation. This was true, for example, of Britain's initiation of unrestricted city bombing in the wake of the inadvertent German raid on London. Yet accidents in those modes of warfare not favored, by militaries are played down, suppressed, or ignored. And even in chemical warfare, a type of warfare in which fear of vulnerability was high and surprise attack perceived as advantageous, restraint remained solid because of an established organizational culture aversion to use.[5] Neither Britain, the USSR, nor Germany attempted to seize on mishaps involving poison agents to justify its own employment of

[5] Germany accepted the release of mustard gas from the American side in Italy as inadvertent. Britain turned its back on reports of anticipated gas use attacks in Northern Africa and Japan's actual use of gas in China.

gas or some other type of escalation. What is apparent is that accidents may open escalation windows, but whether states jump through them is often decided by military culture.

An explanation of why organizational culture was influential requires answers to two questions. Why was the organizational culture of the military and not that of some other bureaucracy, or even the desires of politicians, so important? And why did internal cultural determinants and not the external determinants captured by realism and institutionalism dominate the preferences of states?

An answer to the first question, why the cultures of militaries mattered, is found in the organizational-salience model based on the variables of type, functional exclusivity, complexity, and time frame. First, all of the militaries involved were hierarchical, means-oriented organizations, which are fertile ground for the influence of culture. Second, these militaries also had functional exclusivity—that is, a monopoly— in the use of force. There was no alternative air force in Britain to turn to for close air support of ground forces on the Continent. There was no alternate navy in the United States training U.S. submariners in commerce raiding. There was no alternate army in the USSR preparing to wage defensive chemical warfare. When war came and the choices on the use of force were imminent, the exclusive authority of the military gave it an extraordinary degree of influence on national policy.

The complexity of war-making further enhanced the power of the military. It was difficult for nonprofessionals to fathom the technical and political implications of the operational use of force. How could British politicians have known that the Royal Navy's estimate of asdic was skewed and that submarines were far more effective than imagined? Recall Hitler's surprise when he discovered that one of the reasons he had no strategic bombers to strike at London was because all such planes had been required to have dive-bombing capabilities. Even when leaders such as Churchill and Hitler who were relatively knowledgeable about military affairs intervened, their wishes were often thwarted by specialist arguments.[6]

Still another trait affecting bureaucratic influence was the urgency of choice. Even when problems with existing options were recognized or new needs identified, the requirement for immediate action was overwhelming. The time needed for reformulating different choices was often prohibitive. As noted, Britain had one option in the air when

[6] For Hitler this occurred in submarine and chemical warfare. Churchill's desire to use the RAF to support the Allied ground forces and wage chemical warfare were also frustrated by his military.

Germany invaded France: strategic bombing. Britain grabbed it, not because it was thought to be optimal or even effective, but because time did not permit the development of other possibilities (such as ground support or air combat strategy).

Why, though, did organizational culture overwhelm the forces of realism and institutionalism? It would appear that the answer rests in the relative causal power of domestic structure, particularly the high degree of organizational salience in this case, vis-à-vis the international structure, which realism and institutionalism describe. Militaries were the locus of decision making on the use of force and they were governed by authoritative rules and norms based on the dominant philosophy of war-making. Although as organizations, the armed forces had the functional responsibility to adapt to the demands of the strategic setting, they often did not. Soldiers were socialized to adhere to the better-developed norms and mandates of internal culture, rather than those of the less certain, less immediate international arena. In short, internal structure more significantly shaped the psyches and calculations of warriors because it was more distinct and immediate than external structure defined by either norms or power.

Is organizational culture epiphenomenal? Organizational-culture theory as applied here also raises new questions and conceptual issues. Perhaps most obvious is the question of where culture comes from and how it changes. Although this is important, I have not, in general, set out to account for cultural birth and transformation. I have, however, tried to verify that organizational culture was not an artifact of the other two perspectives assessed, institutionalism and realism.

Institutionalists might argue that culture may have mattered, but that culture itself was a product of the norms of international society. In fact there is some evidence that norms acted as a constraint on the development of certain weapons. For example, chemical warfare in Britain in the 1920s was inhibited by popular opposition. Likewise, some officials in the United States in 1940–41 felt the need to adhere to the submarine protocol in official policy despite desires to do otherwise. And the Soviet Union had a feverish verbal allegiance to the Geneva Protocol.[7] Nonetheless, there is scant indication that international norms shaped organizational cultures. The strengthening of institutions by building international consensus rarely led to organizational change. Principles developed internationally were often

---

[7] There were propaganda incentives for this position, however, since the United States and Japan had never ratified the Protocol. Thus the "capitalist countries" could be charged with planning to wage heinous warfare.

accepted as official bureaucratic regulations, but rarely permitted to alter customs or attitudes. Despite international conventions, Germany continued to plan unrestricted submarine warfare, and Britain to plan a strategic bomber offensive biased toward morale attacks. Most often, the influence of international institutions was subsumed by organizational culture, not the reverse. Norms that were compatible with culture were promoted, and military adherence to them was rigorous; those not compatible with culture were circumvented or ignored.

The factors emphasized by realism had a stronger influence on shaping culture. For example, for Germany a change in external opponents from France and Russia to Britain helped push Germany toward a strategy of submarine commerce raiding. In Britain the rising threat of a war with Germany in the 1930s allowed Britain's chemical warfare preparations to come into the open and expand. Nonetheless, this influence was uneven at best. For example, international circumstance did not convince the United Kingdom or the United States to plan a commerce-raiding strategy against Japan for most of the interwar period, despite the clear advantages of such a strategy.[8] As is repeatedly illustrated in the cases, states learned to adapt in military policy, not according to the external balance of power, but instead in line with internal bureaucratic predilection.

One of the most telling instances of the influence of external conditions on culture I have discussed is the dramatic cultural change in U.S. submarine policy at the beginning of the war. The cause of this change was an influence central to realism: the *radical* transformation in the international environment in terms of expected enemies and the capabilities required to meet those foes.[9] This does not, however, make culture dependent on any alteration in the environment; the United States maintained a battleship strategy in the Pacific for twenty years despite almost overwhelming incentives and constraints favoring submarine warfare. Furthermore, even though the navy culture did adapt at the onset of World War II, it is not unthinkable that it might have

---

[8] See, for example, Stephen D. Krasner, "Are Bureaucracies Important?" p. 164 (see Chap. 1, n. 46), critiques the organizational viewpoint by arguing that SOPs are rational, given the costs of search procedures and the need for coordination. Yet throughout the interwar period, the United States pursued a battleship strategy against Japan when submarines were cheaper and more effective.

[9] Another source of change apparent in the logic of the organizational-culture approach concerns "cadre"—the individuals that fill out the personnel ranks. Culture perpetuates itself through the existing leadership that socializes new entrants. Those individuals who conform move up the ranks themselves and become the next guardians of the existing order. This dynamic implies the possibility that to the extent that entire generations change or are socialized in a new way, culture will also change.

endured under international circumstances that similarly pressed for change.[10] Had there been no European war, even after the losses at Pearl Harbor, the U.S. Navy might still have stuck with its battleship strategy despite its inefficiency compared to unrestricted submarine warfare.

The relationship between organizational culture and international cooperation also deserves attention. I have argued that the beliefs and ideas of subnational bureaucracies best account for the preference formation of states. In the two-step model of social choice, however, both preference formation and interaction are central to outcomes. Some might counter that the organization-culture approach does not account for the aggregation or interaction of preferences among states. This is true, with two exceptions: when both states have preferences that lead to dominant strategies of pure restraint or pure escalation.[11] But in this study, states rarely had such pure strategies. In almost every instance restraint was contingent on enemy behavior.[12] Neither nations nor organizations were entirely immune to reciprocity. This basic interactive component of restraint in World War II is not captured by the organizational-culture model. But this consideration was also constant across the three means of warfare. Thus preference formation is the linchpin of the variation in cooperation in World War II. And the argument here is that organizational culture was the most influential force in shaping preferences.

A Conceptual Synthesis

Implicit in these findings is a composite approach to international cooperation that captures the most persuasive elements of the three schools. In the broadest terms, this synthesis combines two strands of social science thought that have typically been considered antithetical: the rational and the cultural.[13] This approach is *generally* based on a

[10] Britain's emphasis on strategic bombing, for example, largely endured despite the evolution of effective air defenses.

[11] That is, regardless of what the other side does, a state will either escalate or maintain limitations.

[12] Coordination, even if sometimes tacit, is a necessary condition. In all three areas of warfare surveyed in this study, communication on restraint was largely explicit.

[13] See Brian Barry, *Sociologists, Economists, and Democracy* (London: Macmillan, 1970). Differences between the two are evident in the perspectives of two schools: the rational-choice approach of "positive political economy" (see Alt and Schepsle, *Perspectives on Positive Political Economy* [see Chap. 1, n. 65]) and the sociological emphasis of critical theory (see Yosef Lapid, "The Third Debate," *International Studies Quarterly* 33 [Septem-

view of states as rational actors. Leaders set goals, weigh alternative courses of action, and calculate whether benefits outweigh costs. In making choices, ends and means, as they are understood, are efficiently joined. What is at issue is what options are considered valid, how costs and benefits are defined, what means are available for implementing choices, and what standard is used in learning from past action or experience. On these crucial issues, states are as likely to take their cues from internal collective beliefs as they are from the objective conditions of the external environment.

A conceptual synthesis would accept—realistically—that states seek relative gains, at least in conflicts; that nations monitor and often respect what they see as the balance of capabilities; and that when the projected costs of use outweigh the projected benefits, restraint is likely. The actions of governments may reflect narrow self-interest. They sometimes do callously ignore or circumvent international norms when they conflict with instrumental goals. But this approach would not accept realism's assertion that states will formulate desires and actions to fit the prevailing international balance of power. Such a result is far from direct or likely.

A conceptual synthesis would also accept insights from institutionalism. It would recognize that the prevailing norms of the global community do constrain state action. Readily available strategies may be suppressed because of their normative prohibition. States that adopt such means can incur penalties by provoking new opponents. And if leaders are crafty, such norms can even be used to turn opinion against adversaries. Often the *balance of principles* helps define the balance of power.

Where both realism and institutionalism go astray, however, is in positing that states derive their preferences from the international system. In fact, a state's perceptions, desires, and actions are as likely to be determined by its *internal,* as by the external, world. This internal world is more than a second arena of objective conditions to which state actors must respond rationally. Leaders may be distracted from reacting optimally externally because they are maximizing utility in a different "game" such as the struggle for domestic political power.[14]

---

ber 1989]). Jon Elster explores the relationship between rational choice and social norms in *The Cement of Society: A Study of Social Order* (New York: Cambridge University Press, 1989); James Johnson explores the relationship between rational choice and critical theory in "Is Talk Really Cheap? Prompting Conversations between Critical Theory and Rational Choice," *American Political Science Review* 87 (March 1993): 74–86.

[14] This is the thrust of the popular two-level-game approach formulated by Putnam, "Diplomacy and Domestic Politics," pp. 427–59 (see Chap. 1, n. 9). Also see Peter B.

But a nation's internal arena can also be conceived differently as a cultural structure that shapes the goals states prefer and how they understand and manage the international system.

The domain of culture, however, also has limits. Reality can be socially constructed, but only with available materials and within the existing structures. Organizations will promote their views without respect for prevailing circumstances, however, when the contradiction between external conditions and cultural tendencies becomes too great, culture will likely adapt. Two considerations seem to mediate the impact of external environment on internal culture: the *magnitude* of the change in the strategic/international situation and its relationship to the *tenability* of organizational culture. As the case of U.S. submarine warfare suggests, when the dominant war-fighting culture faces an inescapable crisis of legitimacy, culture will evolve; but when organizational salience is high, culture tends to remain impervious to the demands of the international system. Thus, by ignoring culture, there is much that strategic/systemic-based perspectives cannot explain.

Finally, a conceptual synthesis would recognize that a rational-choice model cannot capture all the regularities of international relations, even when a cultural element serves as its foundation. The causal pattern between cultural predilection and unintended events cannot be explained by a rational-choice view of states. Nations do not instrumentally cause inadvertent escalation they do not want. Nor do political leaders knowingly uphold restraint when it does not serve their interests. But both of these dynamics occur, largely due to cultural effect that biases the weight of interpretation and action in directions that are neither part of nor compatible with a conscious calculus of costs and benefits by a unitary state.

THEORETICAL IMPLICATIONS

This study has clear import for international relations theory. Three topics are particularly relevant: international cooperation, the origins of preferences, and the role of culture in political analysis.

As was evident in World War II, understanding variations in international cooperation requires an appreciation for preference formation and change. To argue that preferences matter is hardly a controversial

---

Evans, Harold K. Jacobson, and Robert D. Putnam, eds., *Double-Edged Diplomacy: International Bargaining and Domestic Politics* (Berkeley: University of California Press, 1993).

statement. But to suggest the appropriateness of focusing on prefer-ences sets my argument apart from two major schools in the study of international relations. One is the predominant extant work on inter-national cooperation that concentrates on interaction. Such analyses have produced significant insights on why and when states collaborate, but most have bracketed the role of preferences. This is less a problem for formal models that aim simply to illuminate the logic of interaction. But it is troublesome when such logic is considered *the* road map for navigating the geography of international cooperation.

In this book I offer empirical weight for the relevance of studying preference formation to understand cooperation. On a topic that should be fertile ground for a strategic-interaction model, there is little evidence that factors of strategic interaction are the locus of variations in cooperation and restraint.[15] As the two-step model suggests, interac-tion was a necessary part of outcomes. But the central circumstances of interaction were roughly similar across the three types of warfare, and therefore cannot explain the different outcomes. Instead, prefer-ence formation—in some cases change, in others stability—is the key to understanding the variations in restraint and escalation that oc-curred in World War II.

My argument is also distinct from another school of scholars who suggest that we need to concentrate our efforts on the construction of the identities of states.[16] Certainly how states see themselves and their roles is fundamental to both their preferences and actions. Nonethe-less, the identities of states can remain constant for long periods of time. Thus a focus on preferences is useful for exploring why state desires in different issue areas change even as their basic identities remain relatively stable. In sum, the implication of restraint in World War II for the study of international cooperation is that interaction and identity dynamics must be supplemented by a better understanding of preference formation and change.

If changes in preferences matter, however, we must also account for the causes of those changes. Some will contend that factors internal to states are more consequential, whereas others will argue that systemic

---

[15] In the past, strategic interaction models have figured prominently in explanations of cooperation in war. For example, see Shelling, *Strategy of Conflict*, pp. 58–80 (see Chap. 1, n. 9), and Axelrod, *Evolution of Cooperation*, pp. 73–87 (also see Chap. 1, n. 9).

[16] See John G. Ruggie, "Territoriality and Beyond : Problematizing Modernity in Inter-national Relations," *International Organization* 47 (winter 1993): 139–74; William Bloom, *Personal Identity, National Identity, and International Relations* (Cambridge: Cambridge Uni-versity Press, 1990); Alexander Wendt, "Anarchy Is What States Make of It," (see Chap. 1, n. 13), and "Collective Identity Formation and the International State," *American Politi-cal Science Review* 88 (June 1994): 384–98; Peter Katzenstein, ed., *Norms, Identity, and Security*, manuscript, 1994.

circumstances dominate.[17] There is, however, a surprising degree of consensus among theorists that in matters involving the survival of states, systemic forces will determine state preferences. When a nation's security is at stake, domestic politics, class disputes, and interest-group politics are likely to be suspended as a country unites to protect its well-being. Deviations from the national interest produced by organizations will be corrected by the intervention of statesmen who pay more attention to security strategy in order to meet the external challenge.[18]

The organizational-culture approach reaches a different conclusion. Internal forces appear more important than external ones, even when the level of threat is highest—in wartime—when balance-of-power considerations should have dominated organizational dynamics. It is in the midst of conflict that military plans and capabilities are put into action, that soldiers assume an important role in decision making, and that time for developing alternative policies runs out. Civilian leaders often do intervene to alter organizational tendencies, but not infrequently they are thwarted or in the process change their own preferences to conform to that of the military culture.[19] This unexpected influence gives empirical backing to general calls that greater attention be directed to the national-level sources of collaboration and defection in world politics.

Organizational culture will not always determine national policy. The influence of the military services and their cultures depends on their organizational salience. Most important to this salience are a functional monopoly and a coherent organizational culture. Where these traits exist, organizational culture will influence if not set national policy.[20] Yet when organizational-culture salience is low, other domestic factors—such as politics, class differences, or formal structure—may become more critical. Or external factors such as the distribution of power, international norms, or strategic circumstances may shape out-

---

[17] Kenneth N. Waltz, *Man, the State, and War* (New York: Columbia University Press, 1959). Jervis, *Perception and Misperception*, pp. 15–31 (see Chap. 1, n. 50); Bruce Russett, "International Interactions and Processes: The Internal vs. External Debate Revisited," in Ada Finifter, ed., *Political Science: The State of the Discipline* (Washington, D.C.: American Political Science Association, 1983), pp. 541–68.

[18] This logic, part and parcel of realism, is admirably presented in Posen, *Sources of Military Doctrine*, pp. 59–79, 228–36 (see Chap. 1, n. 4). Also see Evangelista, "Issue-Area and Foreign Policy Revisited" (see Chap. 1, n. 4).

[19] This was Churchill's experience with chemical warfare; Hitler's, with German submarine policy.

[20] There is evidence of bureaucratic culture impact in other areas. In economic affairs, for example, see Bachman, *Bureaucracy, Economy, and Leadership in China* (see Chap. 1, n. 79). The influence of Japan's MITI may represent another case suited to an organizational-culture analysis. Chalmers Johnson, *MITI and the Japanese Miracle* (Stanford: Stanford

comes. Which of these is the case, however, seems to be affected by the potency of the national-level culture in its own right and the relationship between that culture and external forces.

Culture has often been a maligned variable in political analysis. It is commonly relegated to analytical backwaters as a "soft" variable or one that can only explain residual variance. Yet in the "hard" issue area of security affairs and armed conflict, we have seen that one form of culture was quite potent in shaping outcomes. The influence of culture in World War II suggests that it may be applicable to other areas of political (and social) science. To be more specific, theories relying on *formal* structure that ignore collective beliefs would benefit from greater attention to *informal* structure (such as culture) and to the relationship between the two.

First, formal structure involving the arrangement of different units in a collective entity, the distribution of material capabilities, or an official legal code often inadequately explains preferences and behavior. The informal structure represented by the hierarchy of collective beliefs and customs is also necessary.[21] This was most specifically illustrated by the shortcomings of traditional organization theory with its structural emphasis. Military organizations that were apparently quite similar or that adopted identical formal regulations (of restraint) exhibited different desires and behavior. Such differences cannot be accounted for by a generic tendency of "like" formal structures. Rather it is necessary to consider the beliefs and customs that dominated the collective thought of these entities.

More attention to beliefs and customs would contribute to approaches that consider only formal structure. Much of the work on democracies, for example, posits that they will have similar preferences and behavior due to common constitutional structures; an example of this view is the belief that democracies are less prone to fight each other. But this study would suggest the hierarchies of beliefs within democracies may differ with important implications for their conflict behavior.[22] Likewise, students of domestic political structure should be

---

University Press, 1982); also B. C. Koh, *Japan's Administrative Elite* (Berkeley: University of California Press, 1989), esp. pp. 205–18. In general, see Wilson, *Bureaucracy* (see Chap. 1, n. 60).

[21] I would not push the distinction between formal and informal structure too hard. The two at some point do overlap. For example, the norms of society are often expressed in formal legal codes. Yet the danger of conflating the two is apparent in the illegal, but widespread, practice of jaywalking.

[22] See Doyle, "Liberalism and World Politics" (see Chap. 1, n. 6). To the extent it is independent of formal constitutional structure, the so-called "normative" explanation for the democratic peace speaks to this point. Of course, if it is independent of the

wary of assuming that policies of states will be similar because they have a common regime type.[23] At the international level, it is generally assumed that similar power structures will lead to similar behavior. For example, hegemonic-stability theory posits that hegemons will seek open trading systems. The cultural analysis posited here, however, would expect different types of behavior depending on the beliefs and customs that differentiate hegemons.[24]

I am not saying that formal structure is irrelevant and the informal structure of culture clears up all puzzles. I contend, rather, that it is the combination of culture and organization that matters. Culture helps explain the shortcomings of formal-structure approaches by capturing the relevance of beliefs and customs. Nonetheless, formal organizational structure may be necessary to account for why some cultures are more uniform and influential than others. For example, in both democratic and autocratic states, the influence of military organizational culture was enhanced by the monopoly position in state structure and the hierarchical arrangement of military bureaucracies. Organizational monopoly means that with no competitors in expertise, military preferences played a large role in decisions on the use of force both directly in terms of advice and indirectly through the types of plans and strategies that were developed. The steep hierarchy in militaries favored the potent socialization of individual warriors that produce and reproduce dominant cultures. The lessons for soldiers were clear and immediate: conform or forget about career advancement. Thus the power of culture to endure and reproduce itself may to some degree depend on formal structural traits. This relationship—and other aspects of culture analysis—deserve more attention in the study of international relations.

---

formal structure of regime type, one might ask why it is the "democratic" peace. See Zeev Maoz and Bruce Russett, "Normative and Structural Causes of Democratic Peace, 1946–1986," *American Political Science Review* 87 (September 1993): 624–38; and Bruce Russett, *Grasping the Democratic Peace* (Princeton: Princeton University Press, 1993).

[23] For examples of how culture can differentiate structures, see Berger, "America's Reluctant Allies: The Genesis of the Political Military Cultures of Japan and West Germany" (see Chap. 1, n. 75); Peter Katzenstein, "Coping with Terrorism: Norms and Internal Security in Germany and Japan," in Goldstein and Keohane, eds., *Ideas and Foreign Policy* (see Chap. 1, n. 34); and Katzenstein, ed., *Norms, Identity, and Security*.

[24] This has been illustrated by John Gerard Ruggie, "International Regimes, Transactions, and Change: Embedded Liberalism in the Postwar Economic Order," *International Organization* 36 (spring 1982): 379–415. On the continuing viability of hegemonic stability theory, see Joanne Gowa, "Rational Hegemons, Excludable Goods, and Small Groups: An Epitaph for Hegemonic Stability Theory?" *World Politics* 41 (April 1992): 308–24.

Epilogue: The Future
of Restraint

Although some have argued that major-power war is obsolete, history's record of repetitive conflict suggests otherwise.[1] Restraint continues to demand attention. Some of the taboos discussed in the interwar period remain intact to varying degrees today. Chemical and biological warfare are still stigmatized. And given the general concern over civilian casualties in the Gulf War, so too is strategic bombing. The most striking distinction between World War II and the modern age is the appearance of the immensely destructive force of nuclear weapons. There is no doubt that the mere existence of nuclear arms has done much to suppress disputes by force, but the possibility of armed clashes remains. Particularly given the destructiveness of modern forms of "illegitimate" warfare—nuclear, chemical, and biological weapons and ecoterrorism—limitation is of central concern. How should states manage it? Modern tools of force do many things, but it is unlikely that they have neutralized the dynamics of the three perspectives surveyed here. In fact, realism, institutionalism, and organization theories have all figured prominently in research on the post-World War II nuclear age.[2] Thus a few brief remarks are in order on

[1] Compare John Mueller, *Retreat from Doomsday: The Obsolescence of Major War* (New York: Basic Books, 1989), and his article "The Essential Irrelevance of Nuclear Weapons: Stability in the Postwar World," *International Security* 13 (fall 1988): 55–79; Robert Jervis, "The Political Effects of Nuclear Weapons: A Comment," *International Security* 13 (fall 1988): 83–90, and *The Meaning of the Nuclear Revolution* (Ithaca: Cornell University Press, 1989).

[2] On realism, see John Mearsheimer, "Back to the Future: Instability in Europe after the Cold War," *International Security* 15 (summer 1990); for an institutionalist perspective, see Nye, "Nuclear Learning and U.S.-Soviet Security Regimes" (see Chap. 1, n. 32); on organization theory, see Posen, *Inadvertent Escalation*, pp. 16–19 (see Chap. 1, n. 45).

the policy relevance of my research. I focus on nuclear warfare, but the analysis is generally applicable to other forms of unthinkable warfare.[3]

Some believe that any serious armed clash between major-power antagonists would likely result in a nuclear exchange. Others assume that a nuclear accident, particularly during a war, would lead to nuclear escalation.[4] What the organizational-culture approach suggests, however, is that this need not be the case. In addition to the strong practical incentives for avoiding the use of nuclear weapons (such as the high costs of destruction), there can be powerful organizational incentives to avoid nuclear escalation.

This internal influence has generally not been recognized in the efforts of nations that are seeking restraint. Generally, states interested in limiting the use of force concentrate on realist considerations of relative power. They devote great energy to developing their own capabilities, be it battleships or intercontinental missiles, to deter the other side's use. These countries also rely on international institutions such as arms-control agreements and developing principles to govern the employment of military might. My results suggest, however, that such efforts are inadequate. States desiring limitation must look inward to manage the biases of their own strategy formulation as much as they look outward at the balance of forces and international rules and norms. My point is not that realist theory and institutionalism are irrelevant to limited war. In fact, I conclude quite the opposite. States interested in restraint must maintain at least a minimum retaliatory capability. Regardless of their culture of warfare, nations with their survival at risk are likely to brandish a tool of relative advantage if their opponent cannot respond in kind. Furthermore, to the extent nations desire restraint in a certain means of warfare, it behooves leaders to promote and cultivate international norms and rules of nonuse. Otherwise such means may never even be considered for restraint. But it is doubtful that decisions on restraint will be decided entirely by relative advantage or by a reliance on international principles and norms. The importance of organizational culture in World War II suggests the need to reconsider how states are organized to provide security in terms of the structure of civil-military relations.

---

[3] Of course, the subject of nuclear warfare is complex and the implications of my argument can only be treated in a cursory manner here.

[4] This is the predominant thrust of traditional organization theory and "friction" and "normal accident" theorists, along with most who study nuclear accidents. See Paul Bracken, "Accidental Nuclear War," in Graham T. Allison, Albert Carnesale, and Joseph S. Nye, Jr., eds., *Hawks, Doves, and Owls: An Agenda for Avoiding Nuclear War* (New York: Norton, 1985), pp. 37–49; and Sagan, *Limits of Safety*, pp. 250–51, 259–64 (see Chap. 1,

Inspired by Samuel P. Huntington's influential work, many consider the national interest best served by a civil-military structure that incorporates "objective" civilian political control with a "professional" military. Such an arrangement makes the civilian leadership the final arbiter of all questions of war and peace. But in questions concerning the actual development and employment of force, the military would be given operational autonomy.[5]

The problem with this model, as evident in this study, is that military autonomy does not always serve state interests. Organizational cultures can arise that distort strategic rationality and mold doctrines that do not match the demands of the external environment. Furthermore, culturally driven perceptions and plans may severely constrain and determine political decisions in ways that impede higher-level objectives.[6] This suggests that military autonomy, although desirable, should also be subject to checks. The boundary between Huntington's "objective civilian control" and "military professionalism" needs to be redrawn.

My findings indicate that one must understand bureaucratic culture to redraw this boundary. This is a different sort of enterprise than those suggested in other recent studies. It is not about the technical specifications and procedures of command and control systems.[7] Nor is it about the formal structural traits of organizations themselves.[8] Furthermore, the primary focus is not about the *explicit* nature of civil-military relations and the problem of getting soldiers to adhere to the orders and aims of the higher (often civilian) leadership, although that is certainly a concern.[9]

Rather, the central policy task is twofold. First, there is a need for the highest-level officials to understand the beliefs and customs of

---

n. 26). For an argument that rejects this thinking, see Mueller, *Retreat from Doomsday*, pp. 237–38.

[5] See Samuel P. Huntington's *Soldier and the State: The Theory and Politics of Civil-Military Relations* (Cambridge: Harvard University Press, 1957), and the insightful Peter D. Feaver, *Guarding the Guardians: Civilian Control of Nuclear Weapons in the United States* (Ithaca: Cornell University Press, 1992), pp. 7–12.

[6] Another example here is the contribution that rigid mobilization schedules made to the onset of World War I. See Barbara Tuchman, *The Guns of August* (New York: Dell, 1962), and the articles by Stephen Van Evera and Jack Snyder in Stephen Miller, ed., *Military Strategy and the Origins of the First World War* (Princeton: Princeton University Press, 1985).

[7] See, for example, Bruce G. Blair, *The Logic of Accidental Nuclear War* (Washington, D.C.: Brookings Institution, 1993).

[8] Although they acknowledge the role of culture, this is the focus of the "high-reliability" theorists discussed in Sagan, *Limits of Safety*, pp. 14–28.

[9] On control of U.S. nuclear weapons, see Feaver, *Guarding the Guardians.*

military services on war-fighting that permeate the plans, capabilities, and skills available to keep the peace. Second, national leaders must actively intervene in culture, if necessary, to ensure that it is compatible with national objectives. These tasks are far from simple. Professional military cultures arise apart from the societies they serve, and such organizations have no domestic competitors to ensure that the consumer (that is, the national interest) is getting good value. Even in the United States, where there is a tradition of civilian oversight and "independent" bodies to contribute to military thinking, outsiders (particularly ones who spend four years in Washington and then move on) sometimes have problems gaining even explicit obedience, let alone access to culture.[10] There are, of course, obvious problems—such as costs—with attempting to set up a national-level market in security production by establishing equal competitors to the existing services. Nonetheless, it is desirable that alternative parties—probably civilian experts authorized by the highest level of government—be organized to review operational plans and act as conceptual competitors to the military.[11]

This proposal is not about who has the final say in using force—that authority clearly belongs to the political leadership. Instead, the issue is how political choice is subtly, but powerfully, circumscribed by the preexisting organizational mindset—and its attendant capabilities, skills, and perceptions—which dominates operational thinking.[12] The assumptions and beliefs that undergird how militaries think about practical war-fighting must be examined relative to alternatives in terms of both their own efficacy and their political objectives. Modern leaders should not—and must not—be allowed to repeat Theobald von Bethmann-Hollweg's performance in approving Germany's invasion of Belgium, a key event in the escalation of World War I: "General von Moltke . . . declared that it was a case of absolute military necessity. I had to accommodate my view to his. . . . It would have been too heavy

---

[10] A range of anecdotes and analysis on this topic are found in Janne E. Nolan, *Guardians of the Arsenal: The Politics of Nuclear Strategy* (New York: Basic Books, 1989), pp. 5–6, 31–32, 248–85; and Feaver, *Guarding the Guardians*, pp. 227–29, 232–34, 242–44.

[11] Posen, *Inadvertent Escalation*, p. 217, offers some ideas along these lines.

[12] Despite the overwhelming alterations in the international arena in the past decade, the Pentagon's recent review of strategy reveals few changes in war-fighting thinking. This finding is inexplicable from a realist perspective but is fully anticipated by an organizational-culture viewpoint. See Michael Gordon, "Pentagon Seeking to Cut Military but Equip for Two Regional Wars," *New York Times*, 2 September 1993, p. A1; Paul Quinn-Juage, "Pentagon's Bottoms Up Review Builds on Bush Ideas," *Boston Globe*, 5 September 1993, p. 10; John Isaacs, "Bottoms Up," *Bulletin of Atomic Scientists* 49 (November 1993): 12–13.

a burden of responsibility for a civilian authority to have thwarted a military plan that had been elaborated in every detail and declared to be essential."[13]

The aim of "cultural oversight" would not be to politicize competent armed forces.[14] Nor would it be to blame soldiers for doing an inadequate job. Militaries cannot be considered the cause of war, nor can they be pictured as being an unwavering source of escalation.[15] The armed forces can act as a friend of restraint as well as foe (and either role might serve national purpose). Nonetheless, the pervasive influence of military culture on restraint and escalation indicates the need to better understand the beliefs and customs that characterize these organizations.[16] It is certainly in the national interest—and, I hope, to the benefit of international security—that war-fighting cultures be compatible with broader political strategy and goals.

Although one of the world's most destructive conflicts, the Second World War contained a hopeful kernel. A form of cooperation—restraint in war—survived despite overwhelming discord. If international accommodation can exist in such a hostile environment, it would seem more likely at times and in issue areas where the degree of competition between states is less. In seeking cooperation with other countries, leaders and scholars have tended to focus on *interaction*, on the relationship with the "other," on how to anticipate and react to their choices, on how to persuade them of the necessity of an agreement, on how to reach such an accord, and on how to ensure that it is faithfully executed. These considerations are certainly important. Nonetheless, there is another, equally crucial element of cooperation, and that is preference formation: why, and how intensely, states seek collaboration with others. Although policymakers have appreciated how international factors such as the balance of power or international

[13] Theobold von Bethmann-Hollweg, *Reflections on the World War* (London: Butterworth, 1920), p. 147.

[14] The dangers of doing so have been articulated in Huntington, *Soldier and the State.*

[15] Richard K. Betts, *Soldiers, Statesmen, and Cold War Crises* (Cambridge: Harvard University Press, 1977), pp. 4–5 and Appendix A, argues that in crises, the military does not necessarily push for escalation, that civilians are actually more aggressive. But Betts also notes, that once war begins, the military opposes restraints on the use of force.

[16] Furthermore, countries must consider the military cultures of their adversaries (and even the dynamics that will result from a clash of cultures in conflict). Toward a better understanding in this area, international conferences on military doctrine may be useful. Such forums, of course, are not a panacea to the problems of restraint and escalation, but they may enhance transparency and awareness. These goals remain important in the post–cold war era as states develop new security strategies to deal with the changing international environment.

conventions shape what states seek, like scholars, they have neglected how domestic cultural structures determine preferences, especially in security affairs. Just as in theory, statesmen too must pay more attention in practice to the sources of cooperative interests, particularly those found within their own polities.

Appendix: The Laws and Rules of Warfare

SUBMARINE WARFARE

The provisions from the Washington Treaty Relating to the Use of Submarines and Noxious Gases in Warfare, as reprinted in Leon Friedman, ed., *The Law of War: A Documentary History* (New York: Random House, 1982), 1:450–52, read as follows:

Article I

(1) A merchant vessel must be ordered to submit to visit and search to determine its character before it can be seized. A merchant vessel must not be attacked unless it refuses to submit to visit and search after warning, or to proceed as directed after seizure. A merchant vessel must not be destroyed unless the crew and passengers have been first placed in safety.

(2) Belligerent submarines are not under any circumstances exempt from universal rules above stated; and if a submarine can not capture a merchant vessel in conformity with these rules the existing law of nations requires it to desist from attack and from seizure and to permit the merchant vessel to proceed unmolested.

Article II

The signatory Powers invite all other civilized Powers to express their assent to the foregoing statement of established law so that there may be a clear public understanding throughout the world of the standards of conduct by which the public opinion of the world is to pass judgement upon future belligerents.

Article III

The Signatory Powers, desiring to insure the enforcement of the humane rules of existing law declared by them with respect to attacks upon and the seizure and destruction of merchants ships, further declare that any person in the service of any Power who shall violate any of these rules, whether or not such person is under orders of a government superior, shall be deemed to have violated the laws of war and shall be liable to trial and punishment as if for an act of piracy and may be brought to trial before the civil or military authorities of any power within the jurisdiction of which they may be found.

Article IV

The Signatory Powers recognize the practical impossibility of using submarines as commerce destroyers without violating, as they were violated in the recent war of 1914–1918, the requirements universally accepted by civilized nations for the protection of the lives of neutrals and noncombatants, and to the end that the prohibition of the use of submarines as commerce destroyers shall be universally accepted as a part of the law of nations they now accept that prohibition as henceforth binding as between themselves and they invite all other nations to adhere thereto.

AIR WARFARE

"Rules of Air Warfare Drafted by a Commission of Jurists at the Hague, December 1922–February 1923," as reprinted in J. M. Spaight, *Air Power and War Rights*, 3d ed. (London: Longmans, Green, 1947), pp. 500–501. The relevant provisions are as follows:

Article 22

Aerial bombardment for the purpose of terrorising the civilian population, of destroying or damaging private property not of military character, or of injuring non-combatants, is prohibited.

Article 24

1. Aerial bombardment is legitimate only when directed at a military objective, that is to say, an object of which the destruction or injury would constitute a distinct military advantage to the belligerent.

[243]

2. Such bombardment is legitimate only when directed exclusively at the following objectives: military forces; military works; military establishments or depots; factories constituting important and well-known centres engaged in the manufacture of arms, ammunition or distinctively military supplies; lines of communication or transportation used for military purposes.

3. The bombardment of cities, towns, villages, dwellings or buildings not in the immediate neighbourhood of the operations of land forces is prohibited. In cases where the objectives specified in paragraph 2 are so situated that they cannot be bombarded without the indiscriminate bombardment of the civilian population, the aircraft must abstain from bombardment.

4. In the immediate neighbourhood of the operations of land forces, the bombardment of cities, towns, villages, dwellings or buildings is legitimate provided that there exists a reasonable presumption that the military concentration is sufficiently important to justify such bombardment, having regard to the danger thus caused to the civilian population.

5. A belligerent State is liable to pay compensation for injuries to person or property caused by the violation by any of its officers or forces the provision of this article.

CHEMICAL WARFARE

The text of the 1925 Geneva Protocol, as found in SIPRI, *The Problem of Chemical and Biological Warfare, vol. 3, CBW and the Law of War* (Stockholm: Almqvist & Wiksell, 1973), pp. 155–56, is as follows:

Whereas the use in war of asphyxiating, poisonous or other gases, and of all analogous liquids, materials or devices, has been justly condemned by the general opinion of the civilised world; and

Whereas the prohibition of such use has been declared in Treaties to which the majority of Powers of the world are Parties; and

To the end that this prohibition shall be universally accepted as a part of International Law, binding alike the conscience and the practice of nations;

Declare:

That the High Contracting Parties, so far as they are not already Parties to Treaties prohibiting such use, accept this prohibition, agree to extend this prohibition to the use of bacteriological methods of warfare and agree to be bound as between themselves according to the terms of this declaration.

The High Contracting parties will exert every effort to induce other States to accede to the present Protocol. . . .

The present Protocol will come into force for each signatory Power as from the date of deposit of its ratification, and, from that moment, each Power will be bound as regards other Powers which have already deposited their ratifications.

Index

Accidents. *See* Inadvertence
Addington, Larry, 195
Aircraft carrier, 40, 85, 85n
Akhromeyev, Sergei, 204
Albrecht, Erich, 46n
Allen, H. R., 130n, 134n
Allison, Graham, 4n, 17, 19n
Alt, James, 23n, 229n
Ambros, Otto, 189
Andrade, Ernest, Jr., 80n, 86n
Anglo-German Naval Negotiations,
    44–45
Anti-Submarine Detection Investigation
    Committee (asdic): British faith in,
    67–68; German perceptions of, 50;
    origins of, 67n
Art, Robert, 19n, 25, 84
Assman, Kurt, 44n, 59n, 61, 61n
Athenia: compared with *Bremen* encoun-
    ter, 77; Germany tightens restric-
    tions after sinking of, 44; and *Lusita-
    nia*, 49; sinking of not coded as
    intentional escalation, 218n; and
    start of British convoying, 67; U-
    boat attack on, 57–58
Axelrod, Robert, ix, 5n, 6n, 232n

Bachman, David, 27n, 233n
Baldwin, Stanley, 126, 160
Barry, Brian, 229n
Bartov, Omer, 203n, 206n
Battleships, thinking on, 39–40; and Brit-
    ain, 73–74; and Germany, 53–55;
    and United States, 85–86, 89–91. *See
    also entries for specific countries and*

military organizations, e.g., *Luftwaffe;
    Red Army; Royal Air Force; etc.*
Baumbach, Werner, 109n, 119n
Beck, Ludwig von, 182
Bekker, Cajus, 56n, 102n, 108n
Bemis, Samuel, 39n, 82n, 84n, 90n, 91n
Berger, Thomas, 26, 235n
Bernstein, Barton, 32n
Best, Geoffrey, 96n, 118n, 134n
Bethmann-Hollweg, Theobold von,
    239–40
Betts, Richard, 4n, 18n, 240n
Bialer, Uri, 97n, 98n, 106n, 120n, 121n,
    122n
Blair, Bruce, 238n
Blair, Clay, 80n, 81n, 86n, 87n
Bloom, William, 232n
Boberach, Heinz, 108n, 188n
Boggs, Marion William, 98n, 147n
Bombing. *See* Heavy bombers; Strategic
    bombing
Bond, Brian, 159n, 169n, 170n
Boog, Horst, 104n, 106n, 108n, 110n,
    113n, 114n, 115n, 116n
Bracken, Brendan, 167n
Bracken, Paul, 237n
Bradley, Omar, 190–91
Britain:
    chemical warfare: capabilities for,
        153n, 159, 160–62, 164n; defenses,
        160–61; effectiveness of, 158–59,
        162–63, 165–66, 170–71; escalation
        of considered (1940), 152–53, 157,
        163–64, 171, 173n, 177; escalation of
        considered (1944), 157–58, 164–67,

[247]

Cornell Studies in Security Affairs

edited by Robert J. Art, Robert Jervis,
and Stephen M. Walt

Political Institutions and Military Change: Lessons from Peripheral Wars,
  by Deborah D. Avant
Strategic Nuclear Targeting, edited by Desmond Ball and Jeffrey Richelson
Japan Prepares for Total War: The Search for Economic Security, 1919–1941,
  by Michael A. Barnhart
The German Nuclear Dilemma, by Jeffrey Boutwell
Flying Blind: The Politics of the U.S. Strategic Bomber Program,
  by Michael L. Brown
Citizens and Soldiers: The Dilemmas of Military Service, by Eliot A. Cohen
Great Power Politics and the Struggle over Austria, 1945–1955,
  by Audrey Kurth Cronin
*Military Organizations, Complex Machines: Modernization in the U.S. Armed
  Services,* by Chris C. Demchak
*Nuclear Arguments: Understanding the Strategic Nuclear Arms and Arms Control
  Debate,* edited by Lynn Eden and Steven E. Miller
Public Opinion and National Security in Western Europe, by Richard C. Eichenberg
*Innovation and the Arms Race: How the United States and the Soviet Union Develop
  New Military Technologies,* by Matthew Evangelista
Israel's Nuclear Dilemma, by Yair Evron
Guarding the Guardians: Civilian Control of Nuclear Weapons in the United States,
  by Peter Douglas Feaver
*Men, Money, and Diplomacy: The Evolution of British Strategic Foreign Policy, 1919–
  1926,* by John Robert Ferris
A Substitute for Victory: The Politics of Peacekeeping at the Korean Armistice Talks,
  by Rosemary Foot
*The Wrong War: American Policy and the Dimensions of the Korean Conflict, 1950–
  1953,* by Rosemary Foot
*The Best Defense: Policy Alternatives for U.S. Nuclear Security from the 1950s to the
  1990s,* by David Goldfischer
House of Cards: Why Arms Control Must Fail, by Colin S. Gray
The Soviet Union and the Politics of Nuclear Weapons in Europe, 1969–1987,
  by Jonathan Haslam
The Soviet Union and the Failure of Collective Security, 1934–1938, by Jiri Hochman
The Warsaw Pact: Alliance in Transition? edited by David Holloway and
  Jane M. O. Sharp